Those without a Country

Critical American Studies Series

George Lipsitz, University of California–San Diego, Series Editor

Those without a Country

The Political Culture of
Italian American Syndicalists

Michael Miller Topp

Critical American Studies

University of Minnesota Press
Minneapolis
London

Portions of chapters 3 and 6 appeared in "The Transnationalism of the Italian American Left: The Lawrence Strike of 1912 and the Italian Chamber of Labor of New York City," *Journal of American Ethnic History* 17, no. 1 (Fall 1997). Reprinted with permission of *Journal of American Ethnic History*.

Published by the University of Minnesota Press
111 Third Avenue South, Suite 290
Minneapolis, MN 55401-2520
http://www.upress.umn.edu

Library of Congress Cataloging-in-Publication Data

Topp, Michael Miller.
    Those without a country : the political culture of Italian American syndicalists / Michael Miller Topp.
        p.   cm. — (Critical American studies)
    Includes index.
    ISBN 0-8166-3649-4 (HC : alk. paper) — ISBN 0-8166-3650-8 (PB : alk. paper)
        1. Syndicalism—United States—History—20th century. 2. Radicalism—United States—History—20th century. 3. Italian Americans—Political activity—History—20th century. 4. Italian Socialist Federation (U.S.)—History. I. Title. II. Series.
    HD6508 .T66   2001
    331.88'6—dc21   2001002413

Printed in the United States of America on acid-free paper

The University of Minnesota is an equal-opportunity educator and employer.

11 10 09 08 07 06 05 04 03 02 01   10 9 8 7 6 5 4 3 2 1

Contents

Acknowledgments

Anything that takes this long to complete means that there are many people to thank. I will start with my mentors and fellow graduate students at Brown University. Without the immense help and support that Paul and Mari Jo Buhle provided, I would never have begun this project, much less finished it. I was fortunate to be a part of a wonderful dissertation reading group that included Lyde Sizer, Jim Cullen, and Bruce Dorsey; I can only hope that I helped them a fraction as much as they helped me. Michael Staub, a long-lost friend, sustained this project, and me, in ways for which I remain grateful. Glen Wrigley helped me with translations and with his sincere enthusiasm for my subject.

Many of my colleagues at the University of Texas at El Paso have been more than willing to read portions of this manuscript and have given me invaluable advice. They have also become close friends. My thanks go out to Emma Pérez, Charles Ambler, and Ernesto Chávez.

I have been lucky enough to have as mentors, and as friends, Donna Gabaccia and Nunzio Pernicone. Each provided voluminous criticism and, even more important, support as I worked on this project. Without their help, I would not have been able to finish this book. Ferdinando Fasce, Fraser Ottanelli, Salvatore Salerno, and Elisabetta Vezzosi offered invaluable support and advice at critical junctures. I owe thanks to several people who offered useful criticism and advice on portions of this manuscript or on papers at conferences: Dirk Hoerder, Rudolph Vecoli, Terence Kissack, Kathy Peiss, Leon Fink, and Peter Rachleff.

I would also like to thank Joel Wurl and, again, Rudolph Vecoli, for their assistance at the Immigration History Research Center in Minneapolis,

Minnesota, and whose vast knowledge was absolutely critical. Verbena Pastore was unceasingly helpful at the Barre Public Library, as was Andrew Lee at Tamiment Library. My special thanks to the entire staff in the photocopying room at the Archivio Centrale dello State in Rome, who, not once but twice, rushed to complete my thousands of copies weeks before I was supposed to receive them.

I received funding support for this project from a number of sources: a doctoral dissertation grant from the Institute for International Studies at Brown University in 1991, an Agnelli Foundation grant for research at the Immigration History Research Center in 1991, and a university research grant from the University of Texas at El Paso, all of which enabled me to complete my research in Rome in 1994; and a summer stipend from the National Endowment for the Humanities in 1994.

George Lipsitz, the editor of the series in which this book appears, not only helped this book see the light of day, but showed me possibilities in my manuscript that I had missed. I am grateful.

My heartfelt thanks to my parents, Lee J. and Joan Topp, for their unwavering love and support. Finally, I'd like to dedicate this book to my wife, Valerie, and especially to my children, Adam and Esmé. Together, they fill my heart.

Abbreviations for Political Organizations

AALD   American Alliance of Labor and Democracy
ACWA   Amalgamated Clothing Workers of America
AFANA   Anti-Fascist Alliance of North America
AFL   American Federation of Labor
ANI   Associazione Nazionalista Italiana
ATWA   Amalgamated Textile Workers of America
CGL   Confederazione Generale del Lavoro
CGT   Confédération Général du Travail
CIO   Congress of Industrial Organizations
CNCS   Confederazione Nazionale delle Corporazioni Sindacali
CNSF   Confederazione Nazionale dei Sindicate Fascisti
FLNA   Fascist League of North America
FSI   Federazione Socialista Italiana
FSI/SPA Federazione Socialista Italiana of the Socialist Party of
        America
ILGWU   International Ladies Garment Workers' Union
IWW   Industrial Workers of the World
PSI   Partito Socialista Italiana
SLP   Socialist Labor Party
SPA   Socialist Party of America
UGWA   United Garment Workers of America
UIL   Unione Italiana del Lavoro
USI   Unione Sindacale Italiana
USM   Unione Sindacale Milanese
UTW   United Textile Workers

Introduction

In late 1911, just before he became a leader of the famous Lawrence, Massachusetts, textile workers' strike, Arturo Giovannitti's eyes were on Italy. His native country had invaded Tripoli earlier that year. Though he had been in the United States for almost eight years, he not only carefully followed events in the country of his birth, he still sought to play an active role there. He was a member of the Federazione Socialista Italiana (FSI), which had just become a syndicalist organization—advocating revolution achieved through increasingly confrontational strikes waged by militant unions. Its members' first act under the mantle of this ideology was opposition to Italy's war in Tripoli, which they argued could only harm the Italian working class. Giovannitti and other Federation members spoke at public meetings in New York, where the Federation was based, and visited Italian American communities throughout the Northeast and Midwest to protest the war.[1] Giovannitti and other members used the pages of *Il Proletario*, the weekly FSI newspaper he edited, to combat the war, as well.

Throughout their protest, Federation members sought out concrete connections to the land of their birth. A former FSI member who had returned to Italy served as war correspondent for *Il Proletario*. One Federation member called for fellow syndicalists to return to Italy en masse to reclaim the country they had been forced to leave. The same Federation member addressed the proponents of the war in pointedly gendered terms. In a letter to the queen of Italy, he explained that revolutionaries had what they called the "cult of the woman" and appealed to

1

her as "a woman, a mother, a sister and a daughter" to help end the war.[2] Italian American syndicalists confronted for the first time a nascent nationalist movement in Italy, whose members were among the staunchest defenders of the conflict. Within the FSI itself, members sought to balance their commitment to internationalism and their continuing attachment to Italy. Though they had little hope of stopping the war, FSI members continued to fight against it in Italian immigrant communities and, to the extent possible, in Italy until the war ended in late 1912.

Although FSI members' opposition to Italy's war seemingly spoke to their insularity in the United States, they did not confine their protests to their ethnic communities. They voiced their opposition to the war not only in Italian American—and, through their correspondent— Italian communities, but also in American leftist circles. For FSI members, Italy's war was not an issue relevant only to their own community. It spoke to the nature of capitalism and imperialism and to motivations for migration, issues they regarded as crucial to their potential American allies, as well.

The Lawrence strike began while Italy was still fighting in Tripoli, and Giovannitti and the FSI rushed to assist the strikers. Giovannitti arrived in Lawrence in January 1912 and assumed leadership of the strike with Industrial Workers of the World (IWW) member Joseph Ettor. The strike, which united workers from over twenty-five different nationality groups, was a shocking success. The strikers won despite the violent atmosphere in Lawrence and despite the fact that Giovannitti and Ettor followed most of the action from prison cells.[3] City officials, worried about the two capable and charismatic men and about their advocacy of syndicalism, had them arrested on false murder charges. The trial lasted for months after the strike ended. Facing violence unflinchingly, and contrasting their own courage with cowardly acts by Lawrence's mill owners and city officials, FSI members during the strike and trial sought to establish their organization as a virile and revolutionary organization. They continued to lead protests until Ettor and Giovannitti were acquitted.

In a seeming paradox, the strike and trial intensified certain FSI members' connections to both the United States and Italy. Despite his arrest on a false charge and the possible death sentence he faced at the hands of the American judicial system, Giovannitti's experience in Lawrence drew him closer to American culture rather than alienating him from it.

Buoyed by the sense of possibility the strike offered, he became a familiar figure in the bohemian, leftist world of Greenwich Village and renewed his dedication to labor struggles in the United States. The Lawrence strike and the trial that followed, however, were not fought on only one nation's soil. FSI regularly relayed news of the strike and the trial to radical allies in their home country. These fellow radicals set up defense funds and issued calls for general strikes throughout Italy, and did their best to garner support for the prisoners throughout Europe. After the strike and trial ended successfully, Italian syndicalists lauded the FSI's efforts to free Ettor and Giovannitti, and hailed the triumph in Lawrence as a victory and a model for syndicalists everywhere.

These vignettes of overlapping moments in the history of the Italian American syndicalist movement reveal a great deal not only about the history of this movement, but also about the history of immigration, labor, the Left, and gender in the United States. The obvious importance of the syndicalists' ethnic identity and their continued ties to Italy, as well as their assertions of masculinity, blur the sharp distinctions certain scholars have drawn in recent years between "old" and "new" social movements. Many "new" social movements in the 1960s and 1970s focused on racial, gender, or sexual identity—the Civil Rights and Black Nationalist movements, the Chicano movement, the feminist movement, and the Gay Liberation movement. In the aftermath of these movements, many New Left veterans and scholars now complain that these issues of identity have assumed too central a place in leftist activism. They characterize "old" social movements, conversely, as having exhibited an ideological class consciousness that unified their adherents, virtually erasing emphasis on other aspects of members' identities.[4]

The weaknesses of this argument about pre-1960s social movements are easily detected when seen through the lens of race or gender identity. As Robin Kelley has argued, "Identity politics . . . has always been central to working class movements."[5] He has been explicit in his critique of this characterization of working-class movements historically. He explains that "there are many serious scholars—I count myself among them—trying to understand how various forms of fellowship, racial solidarity, communion, the creation of sexual communities, and nationalisms shape class politics and cross-racial alliances."[6] There was no way that African American sharecroppers involved with the Communist Party in Alabama or Chicana cannery workers in California unions in the 1930s, for example, could participate in working-class movements or politics without their race and gender becoming factors in how they—and others—perceived of their potential. When seen through these lenses, any argument about the singularity of class identity in working-class movements is indefensible.

It might seem that the participation of southern and eastern European immigrant men in Progressive Era labor movements would be a better fit for this argument. They were challenged on the basis of their ethnic identity, but there was a larger space available for them in the United States to organize and to participate in the labor movement. They were defined in disparaging terms racially in relation to northern and western Europeans, but their place in the racial hierarchy above non-European racial groups was rarely questioned. Their opportunities were not constricted in the ways that those of African Americans, Asian Americans, and Latinos usually were (and continue to be). These were the immigrants, after all, whose capacity for assimilation was (and is) presented as a model for—and at times used as a bludgeon against—non-European racial groups. Relatively unburdened by their ethnic identity and unhindered by their gender, they would arguably be able to concentrate solely on class politics.

But as this study argues, this was not the case. Italian American syndicalists brought much more to their labor activism than their commitment to a working-class revolution. The members of the FSI who fought against the war in Tripoli and for the strikers in Lawrence did so as syndicalists, arguing the class implications of both events. But social class was not the only aspect of their identity they drew on in their struggles; their class consciousness was continually informed by, and informed, their ethnic and gender identities. Indeed, the imperatives of their masculinity, their advocacy for the working class, and their often bitter experiences as immigrants (though these must be understood in context) were each so formative that their commitment to syndicalism was only one possible configuration of the juxtaposition of their identities.

The complexity of their experiences, and their responses to it, require a reconsideration of their position not only in the labor movement, but also as immigrants in the United States. These immigrant syndicalists do not fit comfortably into familiar paradigms of European immigrant history. They defy simple categorization as immigrants in either their process of assimilating into American culture or their clinging to old-world institutions and values in defiance of pressures to assimilate. Nor can they be neatly categorized as "diaspora" migrants, exiled from their land of birth, scorned in their new place of settlement, and seeking to remake their homeland. Instead, they manifested all of these tendencies, acting, often at one and the same time, as assimilationists, cultural pluralists, and exiles.

The Italian American syndicalists who are the subject of this study were transnational radical migrants. In the words of anthropologists Nina Glick Schiller, Linda Basch, and Cristina Blanc-Szanton, "transmigrants take actions, make decisions, and feel concerns, and develop identities within social networks that connect them to two or more societies simultaneously."[7] One of the central defining elements of Italian American syndicalists' political culture was the movement and evolution of ideas—in the form of strategies, institutions, and ideologies—between the United States and Italy. They maintained their connections to their homelands and facilitated the movement and evolution of ideas on a number of different, often overlapping, levels. These levels included cultural retention; communication with unionists and other activists in Italy; their reactions to events in Italy; their physical movement back and forth between countries. Giovannitti and the FSI's efforts simultaneously to oppose a war waged by Italy and to help lead a strike in Massachusetts did not seem odd or disjunctive to them.

The transnationalism of these radicals meant that they were, in the words of one FSI member, *i senza patria*—those without a country. The syndicalist who coined the phrase while protesting the war in Tripoli meant that FSI members sought an international working-class revolution and disclaimed the relevance of any particular state.[8] It is true that they never expressed either an unambiguous embrace of their host culture or an unadulterated attachment to their homeland, and that virtually all of them remained true to their internationalist principles. But their perspective on the United States and Italy was far more complex than this ideological stance indicates. In actively seeking revolution in both countries, they were also, in a sense, laying claim to both countries. They were without a country because they wanted to shape the course of events in both Italy and the United States.

Italian American syndicalists sought to build an organization and a community that was transnational—one through which they could fight simultaneously against an Italian war and for strikers in the United States.

The FSI was built on aspects of its members' class and ethnic identities, and especially on the interplay between those aspects of their identity; it was at once a radical and an Italian immigrant community. It was a community, for example, in which dedication to working-class revolution and a cultural nationalism borne of lingering attachment to Italy coexisted, at times in mutually reinforcing ways, at times uneasily. It was also an explicitly virile community, sustained by repeated assertions of masculinity. This analysis of these syndicalist migrants as transnationals is fueled by an exploration of the multiple—and at times contradictory—positions they occupied simultaneously. It seeks to move past romanticized portrayals of participants in old social movements as singularly class conscious and past static notions of immigrant culture as an unchanging synthesis of host and native institutions and values and to argue the fluidity of immigrant cultural identity.[9]

This study will focus on how Italian American syndicalists drew on three aspects of their identity—their transnationalism, the relationship between their class and ethnic identities, and their masculinity—in their attempt to challenge established powers in Italy, in Italian American communities, and in the United States as a whole. This is the fourth theme of this work—the impact this small sect was able to have in its efforts to transform Italian politics and foreign policy, to shape the direction of the American labor movement, and to confront competing ideologies in their immigrant neighborhoods.

In recent years, the fear has grown in the United States that we are in danger of becoming a balkanized nation. The concern that we are becoming deeply divided, principally along ethnic, racial, and gender lines, has manifested itself in a number of different ways. Assaults on affirmative action, attacks on the multicultural emphasis of the National History Standards, and accusations of "political correctness" have all played on the perception that recognizing the United States as a multicultural society is a recent, and deleterious, phenomenon. Attacks on identity politics are premised on the same assumption—that we were once a unified nation, and that we are now witnessing the "disuniting of America."[10]

Among the most recent, and most disturbing, developments in this discourse are the ideas now being echoed by leftist scholars and New Left veterans who speak disparagingly of the emergence of "identity politics" in the post–Civil Rights era. They build their critique of recent progressive movements on the same assumption as more conservative critics: that there was a time when American society—or, in their argument, the American Left—was solidly united, unhampered by issues of identity other than social class. It is with rueful nostalgia that they contrast the "fragmentation" of the American Left at present with the social movements of the Progressive era and the 1930s, when leftists organized centrally, even exclusively, around the far more inclusive issue of social class. Sean Wilentz has argued that the moral passion that characterized Progressives has not been seen in this country for decades. His asserts that "liberals and leftists have adopted a more cramped attitude about changing the world . . . in part because of the fragmentation of reformist efforts into so many finely calibrated interests and identities."[11] Others draw the contrast between old and new social movements even more sharply.

To Todd Gitlin, for example, the shift in emphases in social movements has been disastrous. He writes, "The squandering of energy on identity politics, the hardening of boundaries between groups . . . is an American tragedy. . . . The oddity is that the Left, which once stood for universal values, seems to speak today for select identities. . . ."[12] While he acknowledges the enormous diversity of the early twentieth-century United States, he argues that those involved in the labor movement— or, more broadly, those in the working class—defined themselves solely in terms of their relationship to the means of production. "[T]he overwhelming majority of human beings were united by their participation in labor. That was their 'identity'. But unlike the race, gender, sexual, and other birthright identities of today, this membership was ecumenical, open to anyone who migrated, or fell, into the proletariat. . . ."[13] What Gitlin is arguing, in privileging class identity over other forms of identity, is that recent social movements have abandoned the universal (social class) for the particular (any other form of identity). His point is that any assertion of an identity other than that of social class is arbitrary and unnecessarily divisive.

Gitlin argues that what distinguishes immigrants at the turn of the century from their present-day counterparts is that their participation in the labor movement, and, seemingly, their mere presence in the United States, Americanized them. The immigrants he describes did not make their ethnic identities central issues in the labor movement. Nor did they assert with any force the importance of that identity in establishing a place for themselves in the United States. "The longer white ethnics lived in the United States," Gitlin insists, "the more 'American'—assimilated, acculturated—they became." This, he argues, is one of the most significant distinctions between these older immigrants and the Latinos, Asians, and Africans who have arrived in the United States in recent decades. "In some respects," Gitlin claims, "the new ethnicity of color resembled the traditional urban ethnicity of the white working class. . . . What was new was the belief in ethnic militancy, the attack on assimilation, the assertion of pride, the stripping away of deference to the majority."[14] Gitlin's lament is that social movements, and the United States as a whole, have lost their power to Americanize immigrants.

Even those who present a somewhat more complex picture of Progressive Era working-class movements—who recognize that all aspects of their adherents' identities did not disappear as they united as workers—argue that they defined themselves by, and were thus marginalized by, their insistence on clinging to alien ideologies. Michael Kazin, in an overview of the American Left, states that in the Progressive Era and the 1930s, "[a]spects of republicanism, feminism, and ethnic nationalism flavored the activism of many leftists. . . . But," he continues, "to be a committed Socialist or Communist (or Trotskyist) meant accepting the validity of a set of categories and concepts borrowed from Europe. And few activists allowed themselves to reflect on how poorly these tools fit the realities of American society."[15] "Socialists," he comments elsewhere, "tended to wrap themselves in an ideological cocoon from which the world seemed garbed in absolute categories: workers had no country, the triumph of the proletariat was inevitable. . . . In a national environment already inhospitable to Marxism, this dogma could only bind leftists into a subculture that felt more and more like an intellectual ghetto."[16]

These are the two central ways in which those who disparage the current manifestation of the Left read immigrant involvement in social movements historically. Either the labor movement Americanized immigrants, or those immigrants with ideological roots in their native country remained too alien to be of any consequence. Either way, any aspect of identity other than social class is rendered invisible.

Far too much is lost in this historical narrative of the Left. To borrow Alice Kessler-Harris's phrase, it "rides roughshod over the lived experiences of women and men."[17] Immigrants such as the Italian American syndicalists participated in the Left in meaningful ways without either abandoning any element of their identity other than social class or confining themselves to the distant margins of the movement. They came to the class struggle as whole human beings; their class politics were always informed by their ethnic identity, their gender identity, and their complicated relationships to the United States and to Italy. Indeed, syndicalism was only one response to their experiences as working-class advocates, men, and immigrants; the FSI was badly damaged when, for a few of its members, nationalism and, ultimately, fascism became other equally viable options. Disregarding anything other than their class identity does more than allow for this convenient, but inaccurate, narrative of lost unity and commonness of purpose on the Left, which its proponents use to define the parameters of the Left to this day. It also renders the choices the FSI syndicalists made—and their lives—incomprehensible.

The Italian American syndicalist movement, its members deeply committed to working-class revolution, was so profoundly affected by recurring issues of ethnic and national identity that only a transnational paradigm can do justice to its complexity. This is an argument that must be made carefully, because most of the leading proponents of the paradigm of transnationalism have argued that it is relevant only to recent, nonwhite migrants to the United States. The first anthropologists to define this paradigm presented it as an alternative to older paradigms of European immigrant historiography, necessary because more recent migrants have little or nothing in common with previous immigrant waves. They argued that the assimilationist or cultural pluralist paradigms produced by scholars of European immigration cannot do justice to populations that have arrived in an era of global capitalism, exploited nonindustrial nations, and a postindustrial United States. They argued further that these older models ignored, and thus are irrelevant to, populations whose racial identities distinguish them from their European antecedents. Migrants to the United States in the last few decades have been predominantly nonwhite, and the Asians, Latinos, and blacks who constitute much of this population have faced enduring racism in this country. Oppressed by racial identification as nonwhite, and insecure financially in a postindustrial United States, they have found it necessary to brace themselves against the reception they are given either by maintaining close contact with those they left behind or by remaining mobile themselves.[18]

The argument that European immigrant historiography has failed to take into account the significance of race is well established. Early efforts by European immigrant historians to equate the experiences of their subjects and African Americans, for example, collapsed under the weight of indignant responses from scholars of African American history and culture.[19] The best critique of these efforts is still found in Michael Omi and Howard Winant's *Racial Formation in the United States*. They note that

> theoretical challenges originated with the black and other racial
> minority movements [in the 1960s] which rejected two central aspects of
> the ethnicity approach: the European immigrant analogy which
> suggested that racial minorities could be incorporated into American life
> in the same way that white ethnic groups had been, and the assumption
> of a fundamental, underlying American commitment to equality and
> social justice for racial minorities.[20]

As Omi and Winant pointed out, European immigrant experience was not analogous to African American experience because the latter was "in many cases a qualitatively different experience."[21] The legacy of slavery and Jim Crow laws and other forms of segregation before, during, and after the peak years of immigration rendered any attempt to equate the experiences of these two groups problematic at best and ahistorical at worst.

Scholars of Chicano and Asian American history likewise rejected comparisons of their subjects to European immigrants that did not take into account the implications of racial identity in the United States. The foundations of Asian American and especially Chicano historiography are built on a rejection of the paradigms of European immigrant historiography. Scholars of Chicano and Asian American history argued that advocates of both the assimilationist and the cultural pluralist models, the dominant paradigms from the earliest years of European immigrant historiography, usually ignored Chicanos and Asian Americans altogether. When they did deal with these populations, they downplayed or ignored the impact of ongoing racial discrimination against them.[22]

The immigrant analogy does not hold, but this does not mean that the converse is true, that newer modes of analysis of recent migrants have nothing to offer students of European immigration. Theoretical innovations such as the paradigm of transnationalism, which emphasize multiple aspects of identity, can be read back into the histories of older immigrant groups to great effect. Though the experiences of older and more recent migrants are by no means identical, there are parallels. Like the Mexicans, Dominicans, Haitians, Southeast Asians, and other recent immigrants analyzed as transnational migrants, southern and eastern European immigrants mobilized in the face of (an earlier stage of) the globalization of capital, which produced enormous economic and political disruptions in the lands of their birth. By the turn of the twentieth century, innovations in sea travel made it possible not only for them to travel to the United States cheaply, but even to continue to travel back and forth between countries. Many of these immigrants, but especially southern Italians, took advantage of relatively inexpensive travel to leave the United States during its recurring economic down-turns. In other words, many second-wave immigrants—again, espe-cially Italians—would probably have considered themselves, even at the height of the industrial era, economically insecure in the United States and highly mobile.[23]

The transnational paradigm is particularly effective in analyzing Ital-ian immigrants because, like the recent immigrants for whom the model was devised, they were in their time a profoundly challenged popula-tion. If Italian immigrants had access to the rights of citizenship in the strictest sense of the term—access nonwhites were often denied alto-gether—they were routinely deprived the fruits of citizenship in the broadest sense of the term.[24] Italian American immigrants were accepted into the body politic in the United States, but on an extremely limited basis. They were seen as little more than a segment of the labor force, and a particularly troublesome segment, at that—quick to anger, quick to leave either the job or the country altogether, and, for labor union leaders, difficult to organize. It should be no surprise that the first chal-lenge to Oscar Handlin's assimilationist paradigm back in the 1960s came from Rudolph Vecoli, a scholar of Italian immigrant history.[25] As-similation was not impossible for these immigrants, but as Vecoli ar-gued, they had ample motivation to draw on the institutions, values, and other resources they brought with them from their native country.

The paradigm of transnationalism offers a better vantage point on these immigrants than any of the dominant models of European immi-grant historiography. European immigrant historians have by now moved beyond the disparate paradigms of assimilation and cultural pluralism their critics often target.[26] John Bodnar's *The Transplanted* presents what remains the core assertion in the field. Immigrants brought with them a root structure, a capacity to provide for themselves from their native country, and these roots, these resources, were replanted in and adapted to a new culture.[27] In other words, immigrant culture was a synthesis, crafted by immigrants themselves, of a wide range of institutional and ideological materials drawn from the cultures of both home and adopted countries. This "culture of everyday life" was the means by which immigrants confronted the imperatives of capitalism.[28]

Recently, there has been some very valuable and insightful work that has characterized the participants in large-scale migrations as "diaspora" populations. Broadening the usage of the term beyond its familiar association with Jews, scholars have conceptualized African, Mexican, and European proletarian diasporas. James Clifford has argued that these diasporas are characterized primarily by a forced removal from a homeland (for political or economic reasons); a lack of acceptance in the host countries; a sense of connection—either imagined or real—to a homeland; and a desire to maintain or restore, and ultimately to return to, that homeland.[29]

But even these more recent historiographical developments have limitations. Bodnar's paradigm, which conceived of immigrant culture as a synthesis of home and received cultures, is certainly an advance over single-minded acceptance of the paradigms of either assimilation or cultural pluralism. But it doesn't allow for an analysis of home and host countries' cultures as organic, or for an exploration of how migrants' responses to these cultures and their relationships with both constantly evolve, as well. Despite the value of the concept of an immigrant diaspora as an analytical tool, there is the danger that concentration on the diasporic elements of the migration experience, like exclusive emphasis on the assimilative aspects of a migrant culture, may hide as much as it reveals.[30] This may be especially true for European immigrant populations, whose access to American culture, though challenged, was not blockaded, as it was so often for migrant groups racially identified as nonwhite.[31]

The paradigm of transnationalism is effective for analyzing Italian immigrants, and specifically Italian radical migrants, because it provides better access to their complex and fluid identities than existing paradigms in European immigrant historiography. It incorporates conceptually not only migrants' efforts to maintain communication with their homeland, but also their attempts to carve a niche for themselves in the country to which they migrated. It provides an avenue for exploring the ongoing relationship between these efforts to assimilate and to preserve contact with and influence in their native country.

The transnational paradigm makes it starkly clear just how important their ethnic identity was to the Italian American syndicalists in this "old" social movement. Their ongoing connections with their homeland were major reasons that their ethnic and class identities would remain intricately interrelated in their lives—the second theme of this book. Their ethnic identity continually informed the ways in which they came to terms with class issues. As they struggled to find a place in the American Left and in the labor movement without losing their links to the Italian Left, they developed a unique version of syndicalism forged of their experiences in both countries. The inverse was also true: their class identity was centrally important to the ways in which they confronted ethnic issues. The version of ethnicity they constructed and presented to fellow Italian immigrants was defined by their syndicalist antistatism and class consciousness.

Unfortunately, immigrant radicals such as the Italian American syndicalists, in whose lives both ethnic and class identity are central, have fallen for too long between the cracks of immigrant and working-class historiography. Immigrant and working-class historians each touch on issues crucial to understanding the lives and choices of immigrant leftists, but too often they see them through the singular lens of either class or ethnicity.

Immigrant historians' recent research on return migration provides one example. This is important work. Movement back and forth between native and host country was a significant, and previously underemphasized, element of the experiences of immigrant leftists and of immigrants generally. Many FSI members made repeated trips between Italy and the United States; they shared this tendency with their fellow Italian immigrants. Although they are notoriously difficult to measure, it is estimated that return migration rates for Italians reached as high as 50 to 60 percent in some years.[32] Studies of return migration make it clear that Italian Americans were not unique among European immigrants in maintaining contact with the land of their birth. Despite the ongoing debate about how to evaluate return migration figures, scholars such as Ewa Morawska, Mark Wyman, and Dino Cinel have argued convincingly that a continual flow of people to and from the United States characterizes immigrant experience in this country far better than a linear model of one-way migration and settlement.[33]

What these studies often fail to acknowledge, however, is that not only people, but also ideologies traveled between nations. Most Italian American syndicalists brought their working-class politics with them, and worked to present their version of radical ethnicity to their community. Often they battled in their neighborhoods with advocates of other ideologies, from parliamentary socialism to entrepreneurial capitalism to nationalism and, eventually, fascism. Confrontations between these partisans more often than not were infused by a history of conflict that stretched back to their days in Italy.

Nor were these Italian American syndicalists' efforts unique. Radicals who had left their countries briefly, either on propaganda tours or as exiles, were common figures in immigrant communities. These sojourners helped keep homeland politics alive in immigrant communities, guaranteeing that any political activism in those communities would continue to be influenced by the population's ethnic roots. Visiting Italian radicals were familiar faces in Italian immigrant colonies in the late nineteenth and early twentieth centuries. Certain Irish socialists and nationalists, most prominently Eamon de Valera and James Connolly, spent years in the United States organizing fellow immigrants before returning to Ireland. Connections between ethnic and class identity were most explicit in Connolly's efforts. An industrial unionist whose voyage to the United States was sponsored by the Socialist Labor Party (SLP) he nonetheless continued to be a vocal advocate for Irish nationalism. After his return to Ireland, he was one of the leaders of the 1916 Easter Rebellion who was executed by the British.[34] Spanish anarchist Pedro Esteve arrived in the United States in the last years of the nineteenth century; by 1899, he was in the anarchist stronghold of Paterson, New Jersey, editing *La Questione Sociale* with friend and fellow anarchist Errico Malatesta, who had himself just arrived from Italy. Esteve eventually made his way to Tampa, Florida, where he founded a radical publishing house, a cultural center, and a school based on the radical pedagogy of Spaniard Francisco Ferrer.[35] Cuban revolutionary leader José Martí also spent a considerable amount of time in Tampa. Before his death in 1895, Martí lived for about five years among Cubans in Tampa, where he led strikes in local cigar factories and galvanized the immigrant community's support for the Cuban revolution.[36] Until February 1917, Leon Trotsky was editing the Russian Socialist Federation newspaper *Novyi Mir,* criticizing the American Socialist party, and (legend has it) washing dishes in Brooklyn. He left when news of the February 1917 revolution in Russia reached the United States.[37] There was, in short, an ideological component and a pervasive radical presence in this back-and-forth movement that characterized many immigrant groups. But these are rarely acknowledged, much less analyzed, in the works of immigrant historians. Thus these radicals have rarely been recognized as constitutive elements of their immigrant communities, or of the American Left.

There are, however, certain immigrant historians who have begun to examine immigrant radicals in terms of both ethnicity and class and to evaluate their roles in their ethnic communities and in working-class politics. Donna Gabaccia and Bruno Cartosio have argued, for example, that Italian migrant radicals established connections across an ocean that enabled them to have an impact on activist communities both in Italy and in the United States.[38] Ferdinando Fasce and Hartmut Keil have begun to take notice of how migrant radicals' connections between countries, and attachments to their home country, are maintained in numerous ways other than physical movement back and forth. They have written essays analyzing the ways in which Italian and German migrant radicals, respectively, kept in touch with, and were influenced by, allies in their home countries.[39]

As this work and the work of certain scholars on Asian immigrants and Chicanos makes clear, there is ample material available for examining the relationship between ethnic and political identities in the lives of immigrant and exiled radicals, and for exploring their implications for their communities and for social movements in the United States. The United States during the Progressive Era was a hotbed of immigrant and exile radicalism. There were pockets of radical activity in immigrant communities throughout the country in which mobile or exiled radicals proselytized. Migrant radicals from Europe, Asia, and Mexico established revolutionary organizations and newspapers in immigrant communities in the United States. Douglas Monroy, Emilio Zamora, and others, for example, have analyzed the activities of the Flores Magón brothers in California and in the southwestern United States at the turn of the century. The brothers were instrumental in pushing the Partido Liberal Mexicano, based in the United States, toward anarchism. They used the organization both to attempt to push the Mexican revolution in a more radical direction and to defend the rights of Mexican immigrants north of the border.[40]

Recently, Judy Yung's excellent work has detailed how transnational connections between political forces in China and Chinese immigrant communities informed political movements in the United States. In California, Chinatowns, usually depicted as "bachelor communities" cut off from China by the Chinese Exclusion Act, Yung discovered that "Chinese Americans remained attached to homeland politics and highly influenced by developments there—including women's emancipation—until the 1940s."[41] The first sexually integrated organization in San Francisco's Chinatown, for example, was a branch of Chinese revolutionary Sun Yat-sen's party. When Qiu Jin, a woman revolutionary, was executed in China, her death provoked outrage in American Chinatowns. Chinese women began to appear in the streets of San Francisco having cut their hair short, as Qiu Jin had done, as a visible manifestation of their support for the revolution.[42]

There has also been some excellent work produced in recent years by working-class historians specifically focusing on white ethnic radicals in the 1910s and Communists in the 1930s. Paul Buhle, Dirk Hoerder, David Montgomery, and many others have argued convincingly that working-class immigrants involved in the Progressive Era labor movement inevitably confronted issues of ethnic identity, patriotism, and nationalism in formulating their relationships to their homeland and to the United States.[43] Michael Denning has argued recently in *The Cultural Front* that the ethnic and racial identity of CIO workers, especially for sons and daughters of European immigrants, constituted a sense of shared experience that bound them together in a new working-class culture in the 1930s.[44]

Despite this recent attention to white ethnic radicals, however, this work has just begun, and a great deal more needs to be done. In the field of working-class history, as in the field of immigration history, too often the nuances of immigrant radical identity, and thus the significance of their contribution, are missed. As a result, they are still too rarely written into the narratives of American social movements in any sort of meaningful way. This is even true of histories of the IWW, although scholars have long recognized Wobbly leaders' efforts at inclusivity and the presence of immigrants in the union.

For this reason, the history of the FSI's involvement with the IWW, though it has received scant attention, offers a very new perspective on the Wobbly union. There are several reasons Italian American syndicalists' contribution to the IWW has been overlooked. First, the role of immigrants in the organization (as opposed to the IWW's efforts to organize immigrants) has gone almost entirely unexamined. This study is the first work to deal in depth with the impact of any foreign-language group on the IWW. Two other reasons merit attention. One is that there has been considerable debate about whether there were any discernable syndicalist influences in the Wobbly organization. The other is that when syndicalist—specifically, European syndicalist—influences receive attention, the discussions almost invariably focus solely on French syndicalism, despite the fact that the FSI's version of syndicalism had a much more profound impact on the IWW.

Most IWW scholars have recognized that Wobbly leaders were well aware of European—especially French—syndicalist theories and organizations.[45] Certain Wobblies borrowed at least the terminology, if not the tactics, of syndicalism. The general strike, sabotage, and direct action, all elements of syndicalist philosophy, were also advocated and employed by many Wobblies. Especially when scholars have defined syndicalism very broadly, or as simply a set of tactics, they have concluded that the IWW represented an American version of syndicalism.[46] But it is also generally acknowledged that IWW leaders often explicitly rejected the notion that theirs was a syndicalist organization. Most Wobblies preferred to refer to themselves as "industrial unionists."[47]

Salvatore Salerno has offered the most reasoned perspective on the impact of European syndicalism on IWW ideology and tactics. Indeed, he is the only scholar to date to deal in depth with broadly European syndicalist influences on the IWW. Seeking "to establish the pluralistic nature of the IWW's philosophy of revolutionary unionism and the diverse cultural context out of which it developed," Salerno pointed out that syndicalism was one of several ideologies that the IWW was able to encompass within its wide embrace.[48] Primarily through an examination of IWW cartoons, poetry and songs, he argued convincingly that both immigrant laborers and native-born worker-intellectuals introduced syndicalist principles into the IWW.

Though scholars other than Salerno have focused almost exclusively on French syndicalism in evaluating the impact of the ideology on the IWW, FSI members played a considerably larger role in introducing syndicalism in the organization. Despite scholars' almost exclusive focus on the Confédération Général du Travail (CGT) in analyzing European syndicalism, French syndicalism was not the only form of this ideology on the continent. Italian American syndicalists were products of, and maintained close contact with, the Italian syndicalist movement, which shared a great many more parallels with the IWW than the CGT did.[49] Syndicalists who migrated from Italy felt an immediate affinity for the IWW. They saw the IWW as a union with which they shared ideological connections, a similar temperament, and a like-minded approach to organizing workers and leading strikes. Unlike French syndicalists, FSI members were a physical presence in the IWW, and they worked enthusiastically to bring syndicalist ideas into the organization. Particularly during the Lawrence strike in 1912, in a struggle informed not only by their ethnic and class identities, but also by their assertions of masculine resolve, FSI members would have a formative influence on the tactics and ideology of the IWW.

The sense of masculine resolve FSI members brought to Lawrence reflected an aspect of Italian American syndicalists' cultural identity which, interwoven with their identity as transnational migrants and coupled with their dedication to syndicalism, was critically important to them. Despite the fact that, as Pierrette Hondagneu-Sotelo has wryly noted, "[y]oung single men are the heroes of the mainstream immigration literature," only recently have working-class and immigrant men been recognized as gendered subjects.[50] In exploring the ways in which their gender identity and the imperatives of masculinity constituted a crucial—and fluid—element of their identity, this study contributes to the emergent body of literature on the construction of masculinity in the late nineteenth- and early twentieth-century United States.

A number of scholars in women's and working-class history have begun work to expand gender studies beyond the study of women's historical experience, and of how gender identity shaped that experience, to include gender analyses of men.[51] The project many of these scholars share, especially those whose work is rooted in field of women's studies, is to "dislodge 'man' as the universal historical subject."[52] What is necessary, Ava Baron argues, is "to understand men in terms of their particularity—making 'man' historically specific."[53] In other words, masculinity and masculine behavior must be analyzed as historically and culturally specific rather than as essentialized and unchanging. Working-class historians exploring the implications of gender identity have proceeded from this premise in examining the ways in which, for both men and women, in Elizabeth Faue's words, "gender ideologies and practices historically have shaped the meaning, content, and experience of work, class, and collective action."[54]

Certain early works in the new labor history already recognized gender as an important element in the construction of working-class identity. Both David Montgomery and Nick Salvatore have analyzed the constitutive role of manliness and manly behavior in the American working class. Montgomery noted in *Workers' Control in America* that maintaining a "manly bearing" toward the employer was an essential aspect of the nineteenth-century skilled worker's moral code. A male worker's sense of manliness carried, in Montgomery's words, "connotations of dignity, respectability, defiant egalitarianism, and patriarchal male supremacy."[55] This was the world, and the work culture, in which Eugene Debs, the subject of Nick Salvatore's biography, came of age. As Salvatore describes his early career, Debs embraced the notion that one's manliness was synonymous with one's sense of dignity and self-respect. As a socialist, Debs maintained the centrality of manliness at the core of his political philosophy throughout his life. "No man can rightly claim to be a man unless he is free," he told an audience of workers during one of his presidential campaigns. "There is something godlike about manhood. Manhood doesn't admit of ownership."[56] Manliness was a defining element of the self-respecting working man and, by extension, of working-class solidarity.

Gender and gendered discourse continued to be crucial, if until recently largely unexplored, aspects of American working-class male identity into the twentieth century. As Gail Bederman has argued so convincingly, around the turn of the century the concept of "manliness," with its connotations of dignity, respectability, and even social harmony, was largely supplanted in popular discourse by assertions of "masculinity," which emphasized physical prowess and virility. This was the conception of gender articulated, for example, by the Latin workers organizing at the turn of the century in Tampa, Florida, and analyzed by Nancy Hewitt.[57] It was also the construction of gender identity Elizabeth Faue argues was exerted by striking truckers in Minneapolis in the 1930s. Faue argues compellingly that the deskilling of industrial production and the accompanying loss of worker control in the workplace and economic security in the first decades of the century led to increasingly vehement and violent displays of masculinity in the American working class in the 1930s. Male labor leaders in this decade "gendered solidarity" by constructing the ideal worker as massive and masculine and by romanticizing violence.[58]

Although Faue argues that this glorification of violence was unprecedented, her analysis provides insight into tendencies that were manifest in certain elements of the working class well before the 1930s. FSI members' adamant and often violent assertions of masculinity were constitutive elements of their organization, their ideology, and their organizing strategies. The Federation was an almost entirely male organization whose members saw revolutionary gusto and masculine courage—and even, at times, sexual capacity—as deeply intertwined.

Faue's working-class truckers constructed a violent form of masculinity in the 1930s with which to confront their vulnerability in the workplace and in an economically depressed country. Italian American syndicalists decades earlier faced challenges not only in terms of class, but also in terms of ethnicity. Pierrette Hondagneu-Sotelo, in analyzing machismo and bravado in the late twentieth-century Mexican American community, has argued that men's public "masculine gender displays" are indicative of "marginalized and subordinated masculinities."[59] In other words, the very visible manifestations of bravery and physical prowess produced by working-class Mexican Americans, and arguably by Italian American syndicalists eighty years before, reflected, and at the same time confronted, their ethnic and class oppression by other men in society. The syndicalists' ability to face their enemies without fear, evident for example at Lawrence, was a defining element of their political ideology and their ethnic and class identity.

The syndicalists' quest for a virile community bolstered their courage at protests and strikes such as the one in Lawrence, but it also had negative consequences. Faue, Salvatore, and other scholars of working-class masculinity have all recognized that an embrace of masculinity can easily lead to the gendering of working-class solidarity, and even of the working class itself, as male. Hondagneu-Sotelo, too, has warned that there is a danger inherent in viewing masculine gender displays only as a liberatory form of resistance without regard for their implications for men's relations to and perspectives on women.[60] Their masculinist ethos prevented FSI members, for example, from recognizing the central importance of the women involved in the textile strike. It had even more disastrous consequences when their common agreement on the standards of masculine behavior that merited inclusion in the virile community broke down during the debate on Italian intervention in World War I. This disagreement contributed to the decision certain disillusioned FSI members eventually made to join Mussolini and the fascist movement.

Seen in the light of their shortcomings, and the brevity of their successes, the Italian American syndicalists, like so many other small sectarian groups, might seem easy to dismiss. One might argue, as Michael Kazin did of the IWW in his *The Populist Persuasion,* that although they led a few big strikes, their message "was not much shared beyond a dedicated core of single male migrants who had little left to lose."[61] Or one might consider them compelling only in terms of their aberrations— those members who ended up in the fascist movement. But they should not be so easily discounted. Like other radical émigrés and small sectarian groups of radicals who were ubiquitous in immigrant neighborhoods, FSI syndicalists could, and often did, play critical roles in their communities. They broadened debate by providing radical interpretations of, and generating pressure for radical responses to, events of importance to them and to fellow nationals. In Lawrence and elsewhere, they led strikes and other actions, experimenting with tactics, evoking memories of past struggles, and drawing international attention to their causes. They worked to construct movement infrastructures that played critical roles in generating mass movements—as during the Lawrence strike and defense campaign and the struggle to save Sacco and Vanzetti. Repeatedly, they functioned as front-line troops in the class struggle, putting their own lives on the line and using the attention their arrests and imprisonment attracted to broaden their movement. To downplay or ignore the contributions of the FSI because it didn't have as many members as the American Federation of Labor (AFL) is to miss the impact it had—especially in cumulative terms—not only in its own immigrant communities, but also in evoking mass protest and in shaping the course of the American and Italian labor movements.

In sum, this study seeks to recapture some of the complexity of the labor movement in the Progressive Era by focusing on four issues cen-

tral to the Italian American syndicalists who participated in that movement. The first issue is the transnationalism of the Italian American
syndicalists—the ways in which they, both during and after their involvement with the FSI, worked continually to forge an identity and a
political ideology connected to and drawing from the cultures of both
the United States and Italy. The second issue is the continual interplay
between ethnic and class identities, and the fluidity of those identities,
in the lives of these migrant radicals. Sometimes to their benefit, sometimes to their detriment, but unavoidably, their ethnic identity informed
their class identity and vice versa. The third issue is the centrality of
masculinity and masculine identity in the political culture of the Italian
American syndicalist movement. Though at times a sense of masculine
resolve and a gendered vocabulary could enhance their solidarity, they
could also be limiting and even destructive to the movement. The fourth
theme of this work is the significance of small sectarian groups such as
these migrant syndicalists. The contributions of migrant leftists to the
labor movement, and even to their own immigrant communities, are all
too often overlooked. Italian American syndicalists have been all but
lost to history. There has been no full-length study of this movement in
any language; only Carlo Tresca has been the subject of a biography, a
work was based almost exclusively on English-language sources.[62]

Each of these issues speaks to the complexity of ideas and issues of
identity that characterized the diverse labor movement in the Progressive Era. Despite the claims made by those calling for a "return" to the
universalism of old social movements guided solely by class consciousness, in the first decades of the twentieth century the United States and
the labor movement were full of small pockets of migrant radicals such
as the Italian American syndicalists. Though they were indeed class conscious, deeply concerned with advancing the cause of revolution, this
was by no means the only aspect of their identities that informed their
lives or their political choices.

This work is divided into two parts. Part I, chapters 1 through 4, traces
the emergence of the FSI as a transnational community and the ways in
which its transnationalism produced the complex interplay between,
and the fluidity of, Italian American syndicalists' class, ethnic, and masculine identity. FSI members drew on these elements of their identity, for
better or worse, as they vied with other ideologies within their ethnic

community and within the organization itself. In the FSI they sought, achieved, and then lost leadership of their community and the capacity to influence profoundly the American and Italian labor movements.

Chapter 1 provides the context for and charts the emergence of the FSI as a transnational syndicalist movement. Presenting the context of the Italian and Italian American Left which produced the FSI, it also introduces the various Left ideologies with which Federation syndicalists would contend until World War I and the core elements on which they would draw in defining their identity.

The FSI's protest against Italy's war in Tripoli, the subject of chapter 2, and the Lawrence strike, the subject of chapter 3, occurred nearly simultaneously. Opposing Italy's war, FSI members confronted Italian nationalism for the first time, and at a potentially vulnerable moment. Their protest compelled them to confront the relationship between their faith in working-class internationalism and the lingering pull of their affection for Italy. During the Lawrence strike and the subsequent trial of its imprisoned leader, the FSI achieved its greatest influence; its members' class and ethnic identities reinforced each other as they led their fellow immigrants. But the strike also revealed the limitations of the movement—an emphasis on masculinity, the drawbacks of which vastly outweighed the benefits, and a lack of common agreement about its members' relationship to American culture.

Chapter 4 examines the disastrous effect on the FSI of the debate about whether Italy should enter World War I. Certain members' disillusionment with syndicalism, combined with a breakdown of previously shared conceptions of masculinity, all but destroyed the Federation. The wartime debate made it clear that the syndicalist revolutionist was only one possible configuration of the relationship between FSI members' class, ethnic, and gender identities. The nationalist impulse had long lingered as a possibility for certain FSI members whose desire for a virile community, attachment to Italy, and ethnic loyalty were particularly strong. Their dismay about the state of the syndicalist movement led some ex–FSI members, and some in the Italian Left, as well, to embrace Italian nationalism and, eventually, the fascist movement.

Part II argues that the FSI, but not the Italian American Left or Italian American syndicalism, was destroyed by the World War I debate. Italian American syndicalists remained engaged with the American labor movement, albeit in new ways, and retained transnational connections that only became more important as time went on. Chapter 5 analyzes how these syndicalists reconstituted themselves yet again. They began to rethink the gender politics they brought to labor organizing. They also reworked the relationship between their ethnic and class identities, putting aside the rancor and factionalism that had characterized their interaction with other Italian American leftists for years. This newfound unity was built on, and provided Italian American syndicalists with an opportunity for, a new stage of involvement in the American labor movement. It enabled them to convey their ideology into more mainstream unions and to have a profound effect on another strike in Lawrence in 1919.

Chapter 6 analyzes the continuing importance of transnational connections for Italian American syndicalists and leftists, in general. A unified Italian American Left was built not only on its involvement in the American labor movement, but also on its efforts to oppose a proto-fascist workers' mission from Italy on a tour of the United States. Its unity was given institutional form in the Italian Chamber of Labor, an organization that underscored the flexibility of Italian American leftists' identity. The purposes of the chamber changed several times in response to the rapidly evolving political atmosphere of the postwar era. Ultimately, it became the first organized opposition to Mussolini and fascism in the United States.

Although the unity of the Italian American Left ultimately broke down, it lasted long enough for an adamant, if unsuccessful, defense of Sacco and Vanzetti. The conclusion examines the last collective action of this generation of Italian American syndicalists and leftists. It was a fitting close for a generation of activists who, time and again, had found that the most effective way to galvanize support for the cause of social justice was to offer themselves up as potential martyrs.

Part I

The Federazione Socialista Italiana

CHAPTER ONE

An International Organization of Nationalists

The early history of the Italian American syndicalist movement is that of a transnational community in formation. In its first years, the FSI, like the Italian American Left in general, was an outpost of the Italian Left.[1] Even its intense factionalism was often rooted in conflicts between radicals in their homeland. Its members had contact with various American Leftists, but were wary of affiliating themselves with any of them. By the end of the first decade of the twentieth century, the FSI—and syndicalism—had become the dominant force on the Italian American Left. The Federation remained connected to Italian political culture, but it was also in the position for the first time to forge a strong relationship to the American Left. It was by then a transnational community in the strictest sense of the term: a community with an increasingly intense connection to, and desire to evoke change in, both Italy and the United States.

This evolution, and the genesis of the central issues confronting FSI members in ensuing years, are the subjects of this chapter. Not only the emergent transnationalism of the FSI, but also the inextricable connections between its members' class and ethnic identities and the first inklings of the central importance of masculinity in their lives were already evident in the first years of the twentieth century. The FSI, founded in 1903, accomplished little in its first years comparable to its leadership of the Lawrence strike or its efforts on behalf of Sacco and Vanzetti. But the Italian American Left as a whole began to present an alternative to the colonial elite in their communities and to face danger and potential imprisonment for their beliefs. Equally important, in its earliest years the FSI developed an infrastructure and an ideology that prepared it to play a central role in generating mass support during strikes and defense campaigns in coming years.

From the first, the FSI was closely tied to the Left and the labor movement in Italy. Events in Italy and ideological shifts of allies and adversaries there had a formative influence on early FSI members. Indeed, the FSI's ideological evolution paralleled that of the Partito Socialista Italiana (PSI) so closely, Rudolph Vecoli and Bruno Cartosio have argued, that the Federation in its first decade constituted little more than an outpost of Italian socialism.[2] The same could be said of the Italian anarchists and socialists who arrived in the United States before the FSI was established. Italy remained the principle point of reference for these radicals once they migrated, either temporarily or permanently. All of them had formulated their political principles in Italy; virtually all intended to return to Italy. These radicals, and the groups they established, constituted the context within which the FSI was created.

The first Italian radicals to have an impact on Italian American communities were anarchist sojourners. Virtually all the leading anarchists in Italy visited the United States, staying from a few days to several years. Each helped build small but devoted groups of anarchists throughout the United States. The first to arrive was Francesco Saverio Merlino, a scholar and lawyer from Naples. He came to New York City in 1892, and, fluent in both Italian and English, founded both *Il Grido degli Oppressi* and the English-language paper *Solidarity*. After a speaking tour of the United States, he returned to Italy in 1893. The powerfully charismatic Pietro Gori arrived next, landing in New York in 1895. Like Merlino, Gori was trained as a lawyer; he was also an extremely gifted speaker, playwright, and poet. He remained in the United States for a year, holding between two hundred and four hundred meetings (estimates vary widely) from Boston to San Francisco. He would entice crowds by playing the guitar and singing, and then exhort them to fight against the dual evils of the state and capitalism. Gori also founded *La Questione Sociale* in Paterson, New Jersey, in 1895. The paper quickly became one of the most influential and widely read anarchist papers in the country, and Paterson became a center of anarchist activity. As sojourners, of course, these anarchists brought news of political developments in Italy— in these years, news of uprisings and political repression.

Certain of these anarchists embarked on their travels directly as a result of these developments, chased from Italy because of their agitation there. A number of them came to the United States as a result of Prime Minister Francesco Crispi's fiercely repressive policies in the aftermath of the uprising of the *fasci Siciliani* in 1893 and 1894. By 1893, Italian radicals had organized agricultural workers on Sicily into numerous *fasci* with a total membership in the hundreds of thousands. International depression, national tariff policies that severely hurt Sicilian peasants, and general resentment over their impoverished existence produced agrarian strikes in the spring of 1893. By December, peasants across Sicily, urged on by radical leaders, attacked private and public property. In early January, Prime Minister Crispi declared martial law. In the next seven months, the *fasci* were destroyed, and all of the leading revolutionaries were arrested.[3]

A few years later, an uprising called the Fatti di Maggio and its aftermath caused another wave of radicals to leave Italy. The Fatti di Maggio were the culmination of a series of labor protests and rebellions in the Marches, Apulia, and Sicily in early 1898. After the government declared martial law, soldiers spent the following three days searching out and shooting demonstrators. In all, two policemen and eighty protesters were killed; over four hundred fifty people were wounded.[4]

The most renowned Italian anarchist to visit the United States after the Fatti di Maggio was Neapolitan Errico Malatesta. Malatesta had joined the anarchist movement at age eighteen in 1872, and would fight for his ideals until he died in 1932. Already by the time of his visit, he was revered by fellow anarchists in Italy. He arrived in 1899, began editing *La Questione Sociale,* and held numerous meetings in Spanish and Italian throughout the eastern United States. He stayed briefly, for only a few months.

Anarchist groups spread across the country during the 1880s and 1890s as the visiting Italian anarchists organized circles and founded newspapers.[5] Those who remained in the United States continued to rely on connections to their homeland for inspiration and guidance. When the first circle was founded in New York City in 1885, its members named it after an Italian anarchist—the Gruppo Socialista Anarchico Rivoluzionario Carlo Cafiero. Cafiero had helped lead anarchist-inspired uprisings in Italy in 1874 and 1877.[6]

The most prominent Italian anarchist who decided to stay in the United States was antiorganizationalist Luigi Galleani, who settled in the remote quarry town of Barre, Vermont, in 1903. Like the other visiting anarchists, he was well-educated, having been trained as a lawyer in Turin. He entered the United States in 1901, after spending five years in *domicilio coatto* (internal exile) on the island of Pantelleria.

Although not a sojourner like his fellow anarchists, Galleani's politically formative years in Italy defined his radical activities in the United States. As Nunzio Pernicone has argued, Galleani was a product of the era of Italian anarchism during which he came of age. In its earliest years, the Left in Italy had been dominated by anarchists. The Italian Federation of the International Workers Association, established in 1872, had aligned itself with Mikhail Bakunin rather than with Marx as the two battled for control over the international workers' movement.[7] The leaders of the anarchist movement established branches of their organization in Tuscany, Romagna, Naples, and Sicily. By 1874, the anarchist movement claimed about 30,000 total members. The anarchists' initial optimism, however, was drained by the failure of the uprisings led by Malatesta, Cafiero, and Andrea Costa in 1874 and 1877. The Italian anarchist movement of the 1880s and early 1890s reacted to government suppression with increasing insularity, introspection, and secretiveness. Many anarchists rejected any form of organization, and embraced ideological purity and individual covert acts of terrorism. This was the dominant anarchist mindset in Italy when Galleani joined the movement, and he took this ideological bent with him to the United States.[8]

Until his deportation in 1919, Galleani was the leading Italian anarchist in the United States; his presence guaranteed that the antiorganizationalists would dominate the Italian American anarchist movement. Throughout his stay in this country, his influence on the anarchist movement was felt worldwide. He founded the *Cronaca Sovversiva* in Barre in June 1903. While the newspaper's circulation rarely exceeded four or five thousand, it was distributed and read across the United States and Europe and in Northern Africa, South America, and Australia. In his paper, Galleani railed against all forms of government, against capitalism, even against virtually all labor unions, which he argued quickly became just as corrupt as the institutions they opposed. He believed that only the wholesale destruction of the existing system would provide humanity with a chance to live in a just world. He never hesitated to call for or defend violent acts if he felt they would enhance his revolutionary cause. He defended Leon Czolgoz, who assassinated William McKinley in 1901, and Gaetano Bresci, who traveled from Paterson, New Jersey, to Italy in the same year to kill King Umberto. He also printed instructions on how to assemble and detonate dynamite bombs in the *Cronaca Sovversiva* and in a pamphlet titled *Health Is Within You!* (La Salute è in voi!).[9]

Like the anarchists, early socialist circles, many of which would come together to form the FSI, defined themselves in terms of Italian radical politics. By the middle of the 1890s there were dozens of socialist circles and workers' organizations in the West, the Midwest, and especially the northeastern United States. For example, the Circolo Camillo Prampolini was composed of coal miners from the province of Reggio Emilia who had settled outside Pittsburgh, Pennsylvania. The organization's name paid homage to the revered socialist from their province. The leader of this circle, Alessandro Mazzoli, former editor of a newspaper titled *Muggino* in his hometown of Modena, reconstituted the circle as the Partito Socialista Italiana della Pennsylvania in 1893. By 1896, with Mazzoli as editor, these socialists began publishing the future FSI weekly *Il Proletario*.[10]

Italian immigrant socialists remained so closely tied to Italy, they were doing little more in these early years than transporting Italian leftist politics to the United States. Mazzoli, who had named his socialist circle after the Italian Socialist Party, left when he was called back to his native town in Italy in 1897 to take part in an election as a member of the PSI. The editors after Mazzoli's departure, Camillo Cianfarra and Giusto Calvi—the latter a veteran of the uprisings in Sicily—filled *Il Proletario* with reprints of articles from Italian socialist papers.[11]

The early history of *Il Proletario* and, after it was founded, the FSI paralleled—and often intersected with—the course of the Italian socialist movement. Virtually all of *Il Proletario*'s editors were recent arrivals and veterans of the movement in Italy. The four early editors most responsible for shaping the course of the FSI ideologically—Dino Rondani, Giacinto Menotti Serrati, Carlo Tresca, and Giuseppe Bertelli—had all certainly been sent for from Italy by Italian American socialists. According to Bruno Cartosio, they may even have been assigned editorship of the paper by the PSI. Whether or not they were sent by the PSI or chosen by the immigrant socialist community, their ideological leanings and the directions in which they took *Il Proletario*, and eventually the FSI, corresponded to developments in the PSI almost exactly.[12]

Dino Rondani, editor of the paper between 1899 and 1900, had been a socialist deputy in the Italian parliament before migrating. He had written articles for *Il Proletario* from Italy since 1898, and left his native country to become editor of the paper once martial law was declared after his participation in the Fatti di Maggio.[13]

Rondani's perspective and actions in the United States were guided by his experience as an activist in Italy, and especially by a bitter debate in which he had been involved between reformist and revolutionary socialists in the PSI. The PSI, founded in 1892, spent the last decade of the nineteenth century wavering between the reformist and revolutionary—in Italian socialists' terms, transigent and intransigent—tendencies of its various members.[14] Several of its most prominent leaders emphasized electoral politics and even cooperation with progressive bourgeois parties as routes to socialist revolution. Other PSI leaders, Enrico Ferri most prominent among them, by the turn of the century believed in the irreconcilable conflict between social classes. Though not entirely coherent or consistent ideologically—some participated in elections themselves—the intransigents were adamant about their opposition to the transigents.

The two groups vied for control of the PSI from the first. Though the intransigents dominated the PSI in its early years, the transigents continued to gain strength in the party before the beginning of the new century. The Florence congress in 1895 condemned parliamentary politics and collaboration with bourgeois parties. But the fierce repression after the Fatti di Maggio in 1898 produced an enormous outpouring of sympathy, which the transigents were able to use to their benefit. A petition with four hundred thousand signatures requested amnesty from the Italian parliament for those convicted, and PSI leader Filippo Turati and another socialist deputy were reelected to their seats from their prison cells. The transigents overturned the intransigents' condemnation of parliamentary politics and built on their electoral successes. Throughout the last years of the century, the number of socialist deputies grew, from eight in 1893 to thirty-three in 1900.

Nonetheless, the lasting strength of the intransigents was evident at the 1900 congress in Rome; both transigent and intransigent platforms were approved. The intransigents' platform was couched in familiar terms of inevitable class struggle; the transigents' program called for a series of immediate reforms, including universal suffrage for men and women, state neutrality in labor disputes, social and workplace legislation, and the nationalization of transportation and mining. Though PSI members sought to ameliorate the two factions by adopting both platforms, the tension between the two tendencies would not disappear. It continued to affect both the Italian and the Italian American Left in the coming years.[15]

Rondani's activities in the United States were shaped by the debates in the socialist movement in Italy. He arrived at the turn of the century a transigent socialist, but chose to accommodate the largely intransigent Italian American movement at roughly the same time that PSI leaders were acting to reconcile the factions in the party—in other words, Rondani was confronting the same issue within the Italian American Left. Rondani also strongly supported the campaign in Italy against *domicilio coatto*. Especially under Crispi's governments in the 1890s, socialists and other political opponents of his were often sentenced to imprisonment on islands off the coast of Italy. Rondani had been sentenced to *domicilio coatto* himself for his involvement in the Fatti di Maggio.[16]

Like the earlier anarchist leaders who visited the United States, and like many of *Il Proletario*'s early editors, Rondani was a sojourner who had no intention of remaining in the country. When requested in 1900 to return to his native Biella to run for a parliamentary seat, he quickly agreed. He invited Giacinto Menotti Serrati, the man who would found the FSI, to replace him.

In Serrati, Italian American socialists again had an established Italian socialist serving as editor of *Il Proletario*. Though barely thirty years old when he arrived in the United States in March 1902, Serrati already had a lengthy history of socialist activity. The son of a former mayor of Oneglia, in Liguria, he had been a founding member of a socialist league in his hometown and had been present at the 1892 congress in Genoa at which the Italian Socialist Party was established. He had worked as an editor of *L'Italia del Popolo* in Milan and returned to Oneglia to help get another newspaper, *La Lima*, started. Arrested several times in Italy on charges ranging from "inciting class hatred" to slander, he was also chased out of France and Switzerland before migrating to the United States.[17]

The close attention that Serrati earned from authorities in Italy and elsewhere in Europe underlined his substantial abilities as an editor and organizer.

Serrati was an intransigent socialist; once again the political views of the editor of *Il Proletario* reflected the ideological trends of the PSI during this period of intransigent resurgence. Nonetheless, he sought to steer the Italian American socialist movement clear of the factional disputes that characterized both the Italian and the American Left. The founding of the Socialist Party of America (SPA) in 1901, led by Eugene Debs and ex-SLP member Morris Hillquit, introduced a new set of options for Italian immigrant socialists. Serrati moved quickly to head off a clash between advocates of the respective parties. He charted a third course: isolation from both parties and their squabbles.[18]

Arguing that it was far more important for Italian immigrant socialists to concentrate on issues internal to their community than to embroil themselves in American Left politics, Serrati founded the FSI two months into his stay in the United States. In May 1902, three or four *Il Proletario* sections met in New York City, adopted Serrati's proposed bylaws, and gave birth to the organization. It grew quickly. By the first FSI Congress in 1903, there were forty-five sections with at least one hundred members.[19]

Serrati stayed in the United States for only a short time—he returned to Italy early in 1904—but his legacy was a vital one. His decision to create the FSI shaped the course of Italian American radicalism for years to come: it extricated Italian American radicals from the two major American Left parties; it focused their attention even more closely on issues in the Italian American community and in Italy; and it ensured that, even as the FSI strengthened its links to the American Left, ethnic identity would remain central to its members.

A year of infighting and economic scandal followed Serrati's departure, and to resuscitate the new FSI, Federation members again turned to an experienced Italian comrade. Carlo Tresca, from Sulmona in the province of Abruzzi, arrived via Switzerland in October 1904 and assumed editorship of *Il Proletario*. Tresca, just twenty-five when he left Italy, had long been a radical presence in his native town. Attracted to the socialist movement by railroad union leaders exiled to Sulmona, he had edited his town's socialist paper, *Il Germe*. He had already faced charges leveled by local priests and *prominenti;* his conviction for libel despite an able defense by PSI lawyers had compelled his departure from Italy.[20]

Under Tresca's leadership, again developments in the Italian American socialist movement paralleled those in the PSI and the Italian labor movement. One of the first things he proposed was that the FSI establish a chamber of labor, based on those in Italy. The first chamber of labor in Italy had been established in 1891 in Milan; others quickly followed. By 1894, there were sixteen chambers with two hundred sections and around forty thousand members. Arranged along territorial lines in Italy, the chambers served numerous functions: settling disputes during strikes and between workers and their unions; organizing and propagandizing among workers; providing job placement and educational, medical, and legal advice and services. They also functioned as social centers for workers. By 1900, every major center in Italy, even in southern Italy, had a chamber of labor.[21] Tresca wanted the FSI to create a chamber of labor to coordinate Italian American strike activity and to circumvent the corrupt hiring practices of the *padrone.* As he eventually realized, however, the FSI was not yet prepared for this ambitious undertaking; an Italian chamber of labor would not be founded in the United States until after World War I. Tresca's greatest contribution to the FSI was, instead, the introduction of syndicalism.[22]

Despite the obvious opportunities this would create for the FSI to connect with the IWW, Tresca's enthusiasm for syndicalism came via the Italian rather than the American Left. Italian syndicalism began as a curative for what its advocates saw as fundamental flaws in the Left. Syndicalists were agitating in Italy by 1902, dissatisfied with increasing reformist strength in the PSI. The first meeting of syndicalists took place in Milan in late 1902. By December, Arturo Labriola, having just arrived from Naples, was publishing *Avanguardia Socialista* in the city. Other syndicalist journals soon followed, foremost among them *Il Divenire sociale,* edited by Enrico Leone and Paolo Mantica in Rome by 1905, and Angelo Olivetti's *Pagine libere,* published in Lugano, Switzerland, beginning in 1906. The syndicalists strove to present a coherent ideological alternative—rather than the ardent, but often disorganized, voice of the intransigents—to reformist socialism. Labriola, Leone, and the others called for the working class to foment revolution at the workplace through general strikes. They deemphasized, and eventually openly opposed, electoral politics. Often natives of southern Italy, even if many had re-located to northern cities, they also condemned transigent socialists for ignoring the plight of southern Italians. Southern Italy, after the *Risorgi-mento* which united the country in 1861, progressed far less quickly in industrial terms than northern Italy. The most industrially advanced regions of Italy were Piedmont, Lombardy, and Liguria—all in north-western Italy.[23] The syndicalists accused the PSI of focusing too exclu-sively on the northern proletariat and ignoring a far more exploited body of workers in the South.[24]

By the time Tresca began editing *Il Proletario* in 1904, syndicalists in Italy had launched a formidable bid for the leadership of the PSI. Within two years, the syndicalists enjoyed widespread support among Italian workers. Seamen and dockworkers, railroad workers, agricultural day laborers in Emilia and Romagna, and workers in the engineering indus-try in Lombardy all began to follow the syndicalists' lead between 1904 and 1906. The syndicalists also gained control of two of the most impor-tant chambers of labor in Italy—in Milan and Parma. A syndicalist-led general strike, the first in Italian history, paralyzed the country for four days in September 1904.[25]

Tresca arrived in Philadelphia an intransigent socialist, already with much in common with the Italian syndicalists.[26] He was a revolutionary industrial unionist, brought to socialism in his hometown under the tutelage of the same railroad unionists who were now part of the syndi-calist constituency. He got involved on the national level in Italy be-cause of the intransigent Enrico Ferri.[27] Though reputedly not the most clear-thinking of Italian socialists, Ferri did instill in Tresca an impa-tience with reformist socialism. He might even have urged Tresca to-ward syndicalism—Tresca reprinted an article in November 1904 in which Ferri described syndicalism as the corrective of the errors of the socialist movement.[28]

Tresca popularized the ideology in the FSI by tracking the activities of syndicalists in Italy. In the first *Il Proletario* issue he edited, he cov-ered the syndicalist-led general strike in Italy in 1904 on the front page.[29] Within a year, he was writing columns on Italian syndicalism regularly. For example, he devoted considerable space to Arturo Labriola's addresses explaining the principles of syndicalism in December 1905. The same month, he reprinted an article by Italian syndicalist Alfredo Polledro ex-plaining direct action.[30]

Despite the enormous impact he had on the organization, Tresca left the Federation in June 1906; both he and FSI members were weary of the constant fighting over his fierce independent streak. Though in later years he briefly rejoined the FSI, and would ally himself with it and the IWW during strikes, he never again placed his faith in a radical organization. He moved closer to the mining towns in western Pennsylvania, where there were contingents of Italian immigrant radicals. There he published his own newspapers—*La Plebe,* beginning in 1906, and *L'Avvenire,* beginning in 1909—before settling in New York to begin publishing *Il Martello* in 1917. Despite Tresca's efforts to introduce syndicalist ideas into the FSI, the organization, which still had a reformist minority, did not adopt syndicalism wholeheartedly for another six years. This was due at least in part to Tresca's departure and its aftermath.

Federation members were so weary of Tresca's temperament that they sent to Italy for a much more temperate man, a mathematician named Giuseppe Bertelli, to replace him.[31] Bertelli, like *Il Proletario* editors before him, had a well-established reputation in the Italian socialist movement. Born in Empoli, Tuscany, in 1870, he joined the PSI just after being released from military duty in October 1893. He taught mathematics in his native town until fired because of his political activities, after which he devoted himself entirely to socialism. By 1896 Bertelli was publishing a socialist newspaper in Empoli. Arrested several times for leading demonstrations, he briefly edited another socialist paper in Trieste before making his way to the United States.[32]

With the arrival of another veteran of the Italian socialist movement in the United States, once again the ripple effect of political battles in the PSI reached the Federation. When Bertelli left Italy, a new formulation of socialist strategy, integralism, had just been introduced in the socialist party there. Formulated by Enrico Ferri and Oddino Morgari, it was an attempt to reconcile the battling tendencies of reformist socialism and syndicalism within the party. The integralists sanctioned the syndicalist tactic of direct action, but only sparingly and as a last resort. They also condoned the support of bourgeois governments, but only in special circumstances.[33]

This compromise, however, proved unworkable. PSI socialists had been trying, increasingly effectively, to oust the syndicalists from the party and to isolate them in the labor movement since 1906. That year, PSI socialists helped found the Confederazione Generale del Lavoro

(CGL), a centralized coordinating body for national labor federations and regional and local chambers of labor. Though syndicalists still controlled certain key chambers, the socialists worked successfully to ensure that CGL leaders were sympathetic to them. The two factions' battle for control of the PSI came to a head during a general strike waged by the syndicalist chamber of labor in Parma in the summer of 1908. Chamber head Alceste de Ambris, who would play a central role in the FSI's debate on Italian intervention in World War I, led 33,000 agricultural workers in an eight-week strike. The effort collapsed only when the Italian army occupied the Parma chamber of labor to confiscate strike funds and documents. The syndicalists, furious that reformists had openly opposed the strike, broke from the PSI.[34]

Initially an integralist, Bertelli followed much the same course as the PSI itself when he arrived in the United States. He embraced reformist socialism and brought discord between syndicalist and reformist elements in the Federation to a boil. Bertelli and a vocal minority of reformist socialists tried briefly to reshape the FSI. But he was unable to sway the syndicalists through editorials or meetings—in fact, his editorial tendency to discard pieces he disagreed with elicited great antagonism toward him.[35] He and the other reformists who would leave the FSI realized how badly outnumbered they were at the 1906 congress. One of them, Arturo Culla, reflected later that not only the directors of *Il Proletario*, but most members and sections of the FSI were advocates of syndicalism, "causing the true socialists to leave the Boston convention." He lamented that the "movement was taken in by the ideas of Sorel the Syndicalist . . . and certainly aided the followers of Galleani's anti-electoral policies."[36] Culla's assertion about the assistance the FSI lent Galleani is certainly overstated; he and the FSI were, with rare exceptions, adversaries rather than allies. His larger point, however, was that the syndicalists' unwillingness to support electoral politics was a major reason he, Bertelli and the other transigents felt increasingly alienated in the Federation.

The fact that the four early editors of *Il Proletario* who had had the greatest impact on the evolution of the FSI all came directly from Italy to edit the newspaper underscores the centrality of Italian Left politics in the Federation during its first years. The editorial policy of *Il Proletario* and the trajectory of the FSI were determined by the state of the Italian Left at the time. Rondani, Serrati, Tresca, and Bertelli each brought the sense of urgency, the ideological innovations, and the factionalism that had defined their experiences in Italy.

Most FSI members, like these editors, not only had lengthy histories of radical activity in Italy, but also had agitated in countries across Europe and South America. Many, moreover, would remain mobile, transnational, advocates of revolution. Serrati was active in Italy and in socialist circles in Switzerland and France before arriving in the United States.[37] Giovanni Di Palma-Castiglione, who edited *Il Proletario* briefly after Serrati, had fought in Greece against a Turkish invasion as a young man in 1897. The volunteer Italian Legion he joined, along with future Italian syndicalist leader Arturo Labriola, was led by legendary Italian revolutionary Amilcare Cipriani.[38] Husband and wife Virgilio and Suprema Tedeschi, who edited the newspaper with Di Palma-Castiglione, left the United States in 1904 to join the sizable Italian migrant population in Buenos Aires.[39] Federation member Fortunato Vezzoli, shortly before arriving in the United States, spent time across the Italian border in Lugano, Switzerland, to evade arrest for resisting the draft. Arturo Giovannitti was not a typical FSI member. He had no history of radical activity in Italy before migrating; he had even studied for the ministry. Even he, however, had done his studies at a Protestant seminary in Canada.[40]

FSI member Edmondo Rossoni was particularly well-traveled when he landed in New York. In 1908 he left Italy, chased by impending charges for leading general strikes; he spent the next year organizing Italian immigrant workers in Switzerland and France. The following year he propagandized among the Italian immigrant population in Brazil. He also wrote for *Fanfulla*, a syndicalist newspaper edited by friend and fellow political exile Alceste De Ambris. Expelled from Brazil for leading a glass workers' strike, he stopped briefly in Paris before traveling to the United States.

Most places where these mobile Italian radicals spent time organizing fellow Italians or avoiding arrest in Italy—or both—were Italian immigrant population centers. This certainly characterized their choices of locale in the United States: New York City; Paterson, New Jersey; Tampa, Florida; and Chicago, to name just a few cities, were all popular destinations for migrating Italians. The same was true in Argentina and especially Brazil, where, proportional to the total population, the Italian migrant population was even larger than in the United States.[41]

The several cities throughout Europe that attracted these migrant radicals were often centers of radical activity as well as concentrations of Italian migrants. A temporary exile from Italy could always find compatriots and an opportunity for agitation in Paris or London, or in nearby Lausanne or Lugano in Switzerland. One of the most important Italian syndicalist newspapers, *Pagine libere,* was published in Lugano. In 1912, a future editor of *Il Proletario* would be arrested for organizing protests on behalf of the imprisoned leaders of the Lawrence strike. Migrant radicals from Italy might also find, as they so often did in the United States, partisan battles being fought out. In 1904, Carlo Tresca stopped in Lausanne, Switzerland, on his way to the United States. He met Benito Mussolini, then a fiery socialist temporarily exiled from Italy. The two spent the entire night arguing and, ironically, when they parted, Mussolini accused Tresca of not being fully committed to his principles. He told Tresca, "I am sure that in America you will become a true revolutionary comrade."[42] Tresca would look back on the conversation years later with bitter irony as he fought against Mussolini's fascist followers.

Italian migrant syndicalists like Tresca—despite Mussolini's dismissive comments—worked tirelessly to gain support for their ideology, traveling, organizing, and agitating not only in the United States, but also across Europe and the Americas. But there was a tension inherent in their efforts. Especially in the first decade of the twentieth century, these migrants usually concentrated their energies on fellow migrant Italians. The FSI was the consummate example of this tendency. Serrati had established the organization, after all, to avoid the fractious world of the American Left. FSI members could not avoid the American Left altogether—nor did all of them want to. But they interacted with American leftists and pushed for their internationalist ideals through a distinctly Italian organization. This meant that Federation members would spend their first decade in the organization, and the years ahead, focusing centrally on the complex relationship between their ethnic identity and their class ideals. They would have to constantly rework their relationships to Italy and the United States, and to the Italian and the American Left.

Ironically, it was an adversary of FSI syndicalists who posed most succinctly the question they confronted. Giuseppe Bertelli, after leaving the Federation, remained convinced that it was too insular an organization to succeed in the United States. The FSI, he asserted, "is undermined

by a vice of origin. It is a party that sustains proletarian internationalism while remaining secluded from the proletariat of all nations that
are not Italian. One could say, with a pun, that it is an international organization of nationalists."[43] The FSI was, in Bertelli's opinion, an organization defined by its unresolved contradictions.

His accusation was in many ways flawed. Bertelli later confessed that
he had never really understood the FSI, or the Italian American Left,
during his first years in the United States. Certainly, he overlooked the
fact that, despite Serrati's intentions, the FSI had never been completely
isolated in the United States. Serrati got only a handful of sections to
join the Federation at first because most circles chose to remain affiliated with the SLP. By 1903, the FSI claimed forty-five sections, but most
had already existed as SLP sections. FSI connections to the American
Left would only grow more intense.

Moreover, Bertelli's accusation that Federation members were "nationalists" was particularly troublesome. Enrico Corradini was at that
moment galvanizing support for his xenophobic and imperialist nationalist movement in Italy. Though Corradini would attempt to recruit
syndicalists to his movement, in these years he would find no followers
in the FSI. The distance at this time between the ethnic solidarity manifested by the exclusively Italian FSI and nationalism would become
starkly clear when certain Federation members embraced Italian nationalism during World War I and fascism in the postwar years.

Nonetheless, Bertelli put his finger on a crucial and complex issue.
FSI members consistently read their class identity through their ethnic
identity. The FSI was in many ways an organization with more intense
connections to the Italian Left and to Italy than to the American Left or
to the United States. It was an "international organization of nationalists" during these years in that, whether its members intended to remain
in the United States or not, they usually focused their organizing efforts
exclusively on Italian migrants. Serrati had ensured this by creating the
FSI; the fact that *Il Proletario* was written in Italian defined the principal
population to whom they would be communicating, as well.

Federation syndicalists, despite Bertelli's allegation, had ties to the
American Left; but they continually evaluated this relationship through
ethnic eyes and through the lens of Italian politics. This tendency predated the existence of the FSI. When Dino Rondani arrived in the United
States, a debate on Daniel De Leon's SLP had just erupted between re-

formist and revolutionary socialists in *Il Proletario.* Most sections of
Italian workers affiliated with the newspaper remained affiliated with
the SLP. By 1899, disgruntlement with De Leon's iron-handed leadership of the SLP and his increasingly doctrinaire tone and intolerance of
other radicals led to open rebellion in the party. Disagreements over the
viability of the AFL and the value of the SLP's alternative, the Socialist
Trades and Labor Alliance, pointed to larger disparities between revolutionary and reformist socialists. Eventually the two factions split, and
the reformist faction ended up in the SPA after its founding in 1901. The
SLP, under De Leon's control, dropped all immediatist demands from
its program.[44] Rondani's effort to reconcile the differences between reformists and revolutionaries, which had so closely paralleled actions
within the PSI, was in fact an attempt to placate the Italian American
sections connected to *Il Proletario* that remained attached to De Leon's
SLP. It was this conflict between the SLP and the SPA that Serrati was
trying to avoid when he founded the FSI.

Under Carlo Tresca, who followed Serrati as *Il Proletario* editor, the
FSI established a connection to the American Left that would last as
long as the Federation itself did. Tresca, remote but not totally discon-
nected from developments on the American Left, quickly saw the opportunity that the IWW provided. Soon after the founding convention
in 1905, Tresca, who had been enthusiastically covering the Italian syndicalist movement for over a year, formally declared himself a syndicalist. No one from the FSI attended the convention, and Tresca's English
was not good enough for him to comment extensively on the proceedings. But he was familiar with the IWW's principles, and he had already
met Bill Haywood. Tresca, his *paesano* Giovanni Di Silvestro (who had
edited *Il Proletario* briefly and had helped bring Tresca to the United
States), and Haywood had been arrested together in Philadelphia in October 1904 while holding street meetings.[45] Tresca embraced the new organization immediately and without reservation.

Tresca recognized that the IWW was an ideal organization for FSI
members. It came the closest of any American leftist organization to
paralleling the syndicalist movement in Italy. Like Italian syndicalists,
and like most Federation members, the IWW advocated revolutionary
industrial unionism and rejected the reformism of the Socialist Party
and the mainstream labor federation (the AFL in the United States).
Best of all, it allowed Federation members a potential entryway into

the American labor movement without having to choose between the SLP and the SPA.[46] Tresca was prescient in this regard—the FSI would achieve its greatest success working with the IWW in Lawrence, Massachusetts, in 1912.

Bertelli, of course, had pushed even harder to create and augment links between the FSI and the American Left. Although he had just arrived from Italy, Bertelli had been openly critical of what he regarded as the Federation's meager efforts to reach out to American leftists. He had called the FSI an "international organization of nationalists," because he considered it an organization caught between two worlds. He complained at the 1906 congress that it lacked a coherent philosophy because its members refused to sever their ties to Italy and create a place for themselves in the United States.[47] He called for the FSI to abandon its involvement with Italian politics, and advised Federation members to both join the IWW and ally themselves with the SLP.[48]

The issue of the FSI's connection to the American Left was what eventually drove Bertelli from the Federation. His advice was rejected soundly at the 1906 congress. Delegates voted enthusiastically for adherence to the IWW. But more importantly, from Bertelli's perspective, they voted to continue FSI neutrality toward the SLP and the SPA. Bertelli realized finally that he had no place in the FSI. He tendered his resignation weeks later, and eventually moved to Chicago to join a large settlement of fellow Tuscans.[49]

In Chicago Bertelli put together an organization that had the concrete links to the American Left he considered so vital. By 1908 he started his own newspaper, *La Parola dei Socialisti,* and organized his own federation, both based on the principles of reformist socialism. Though he had remained an SLP advocate while in the FSI, once he left he decided that De Leon's organization was too doctrinaire to succeed in the United States. By 1911 Bertelli affiliated his federation with the Socialist Party. Deeply embittered by his experience in his former organization, he took its name, calling his group the Federazione Socialista Italiana of the Socialist Party of America (FSI/SPA).

Bertelli's frustration belied the fact that the FSI had begun to forge much closer ties to the American Left and labor movement after he left the organization. In July 1909, Federation members decided it was necessary to find a new editor among comrades in the United States. All of the major editors of the paper since its founding, new arrivals from Italy, had been unable to speak English and were unfamiliar with the circumstances of Italian American workers. This had in many ways debilitated the movement.[50] The FSI chose Arturo Giovannitti as the new editor of the paper. For the first time, the editor of *Il Proletario* was someone who had been in the United States for several years and who spoke English.

During Giovannitti's tenure, the FSI would become a transnational organization in the strictest sense. Its members would strengthen their connections with the American Left, and hence their capacity to affect American political culture. They would nonetheless continue to view their class ideals through the prism of their ethnic identity, remaining closely in touch with, and deeply affected by, Italian political culture. This connection would continue to inform their ideology and their activism in the American labor movement.

This relationship between class and ethnic identities was not simply a matter of FSI members formulating their class politics in terms of their ethnicity. They also consistently read their ethnic identity in class terms. If they came to American Left and labor organizations, or decided not to do so, on the basis of their ethnic identity, the way in which they faced, and attempted to shape, their ethnic communities was equally informed by their class identity. The FSI presented a version, but certainly not the only version, of ethnic identity in vying for influence in Italian immigrant neighborhoods.

From the first, the FSI committed itself to the difficult task of battling against the colonial elite. Serrati briefly presented an alternative voice to the *prominenti* and the colonial newspapers that dominated New York's Italian American community. He focused particular attention on Carlo Barsotti, owner and editor of *Il Progresso Italo-Americano*, with whom he engaged in a running battle during his time in the United States. Serrati also called for efforts to organize and educate Italian immigrant workers and for concentrated efforts against "private and consular parasitism"—in other words, against exploitative government officials and *prominenti*.[51] He was even able to publish a daily edition of *Il Proletario* for a short time beginning on May 1, 1903. This was an enormous undertaking for the fledgling Federation—the start-up cost alone was eight thousand dollars, a staggering amount for an organization that often collected donations in fractions of dollars.[52]

Tresca continued Serrati's efforts with comparable energy. He fought the Italian immigrant elite, including the colonial press, the priests, and the *padroni,* the immigrant community's often corrupt labor agents. Tresca exposed their misdeeds in *Il Proletario* and proposed a chamber of labor to coordinate opposition to their leadership. He often undertook these efforts at considerable personal risk. He and *paesano* Giovanni Di Silvestro accused the Italian consul in Philadelphia, a man named Naselli, of having criminal associations. Naselli had the two men arrested for defamation of character. Tresca served three months in prison, and the lawsuits Naselli initiated would drag on for years.

The FSI battled the colonial elite through its first decade and beyond, at times successfully, and more often than not simply to sustain an alternative voice in the Italian American community. In 1910, for example, FSI members responded to a challenge posed by Giovanni Di Silvestro's call for a colonial congress drawing together Italian immigrant leaders in the northeastern United States. Despite his early friendship with Tresca, Di Silvestro by this point had abandoned his radical roots. The FSI was not invited to participate in the congress, but Edmondo Rossoni and Massimo Rocca traveled to Philadelphia to insist on a role in the congress. Rocca, who went by the name Libero Tancredi, was neither a syndicalist nor an FSI member—he was an anarchist who edited his own newspaper, *Il Novatore,* in New York. He and Rossoni were good friends, though, and would remain so for years. The two men addressed the congress only briefly; they were quickly expelled.[53] Nonetheless, the event was significant. First, the FSI was insisting that it had the right to be heard in the Italian American community. Second, the conflict at the congress foreshadowed not only the Italian American Left's eventual fight against fascism, but also the complexity and maleability of political identity in Italian American communities. By the time Italian American radicals battled against Mussolini and fascism, not only Di Silvestro, but Rossoni and Tancredi, as well, would be fascists.

Often to its detriment, the FSI spent at least as much time fighting for its particular version of ethnicity within the Italian American Left as it did battling against the colonial elite. Its first battles were against the anarchists. One series of events in particular that occurred early in the FSI's existence illustrates the wrath federation members and Italian migrant anarchists felt for each other. In 1902, a feud between Serrati and Luigi Galleani erupted during a silk dyers' strike in Paterson, New Jersey. Galleani, then editing the local anarchist paper *La Questione Sociale,* urged the strikers to violence to win their demands. Serrati disagreed with Galleani, feeling that caution and restraint were needed, and the two men argued bitterly.[54] Their animosity had ideological roots back in Italy. The two had fought with each other during the struggle between socialists and anarchists for control of the Italian Left in 1892.[55]

Their rivalry intensified during the strike, and continued to grow in its aftermath. During the strike, Galleani had been wounded in the face and charged with inciting to riot. He had fled north to Canada before settling in Barre, Vermont, home to a group of northern Italian marble workers, mostly Tuscans, who were dedicated anarchists. Barre was also home to a group of Serrati's followers, originally from Lombardy, who by 1903 had just built a socialist meeting hall.

Serrati accepted an invitation in October 1903 to deliver a lecture in Barre, knowing he would face an inevitable confrontation with the *Galleanisti*. Tensions between the two men had grown even worse since the Paterson strike. Serrati had—inadvertently, he insisted—revealed Galleani's whereabouts to New Jersey authorities in *Il Proletario*. Galleani, who had been publishing *Cronaca Sovversiva* under the name George Pimpino, had vowed that Serrati's betrayal would not go unpunished.

During Serrati's trip to Barre, the tension between the FSI and the anarchists erupted into violence. He was attacked by *Galleanisti* on his way to the meeting hall and missed the scheduled starting time for his lecture. At the hall, a fight broke out between socialists and anarchists, and a socialist who was stabbed in the neck shot and killed an anarchist named Elia Corti. Although Serrati hadn't even been at the hall, he was accused of complicity in the crime. Galleani followed Serrati's trial assiduously in his paper and wrote a series of articles titled "Giacinto Menotti Serrati: Spy and Assassin," which recounted his accusations of Serrati's betrayal of him to the New Jersey police and of his role in Corti's murder.[56] Although he was acquitted, Serrati was shaken by the experience. He had been contemplating a return to Italy, and the confrontation and trial hastened his decision. Shortly after his trial ended in early 1904, Serrati returned to Italy.[57]

The enmity between the *Galleanisti* and the FSI would last for as long as the radical factions themselves did. Though Galleani and his followers would do their best to lend the FSI support during the 1912 Lawrence strike and during the acrimonious debate over World War I, more often than not they were at odds with one another. Decades later, from their cells on death row, *Galleanisti* Nicola Sacco and Bartolomeo Vanzetti continued to criticize Italian American syndicalists even as these fellow radicals struggled to save their lives.

FSI members fought for their version of radical ethnicity not only against the anarchists, but against parliamentary socialists, as well. This battle, which began when Bertelli tried to change the direction of the FSI, escalated once he established his own organization. When Bertelli left the FSI, he took many capable socialists with him. Gioacchino Artoni, a founder of *Il Proletario* and director of a dramatic society that had funded the daily version of the paper during its brief life, followed Bertelli.[58] So did Arturo Caroti, who as an IWW organizer had once convinced almost an entire local to abandon the AFL for the revolutionary union in a single evening.[59] They were joined by Dr. Alberto Molinari, known in Chicago as *il medico del povero,* who eventually took over publishing *La Parola dei Socialisti.*[60] The reformist socialist FSI/SPA built bases of support not only in Chicago, but also in cities as distant as Tampa, Florida, and Buffalo, New York.[61]

For a decade and more, these parliamentary socialists would compete with FSI syndicalists for leadership of the Italian American labor movement. They sought to serve, in Elisabetta Vezzosi's apt phrase, as "radical ethnic brokers," organizing Italian immigrant workers and integrating them into mainstream AFL unions and American society at the same time.[62] They were instrumental in organizing certain Italians, especially in the garment industry. In Chicago, Bertelli and FSI/SPA member Emilio Grandinetti were vital contributors to the 1910 strike that led to the establishment of the Amalgamated Clothing Workers of America (ACWA) a few years later. Luigi Antonini, Anzuino Marimpietri, and Sicilian brothers Frank and Augusto Bellanca organized Italian garment workers in New York. They all would become officers in the ACWA or the International Ladies Garment Workers' Union (ILGWU) in later years.[63]

Despite their successes, though, Bertelli and the socialists never achieved the prominence the syndicalist FSI briefly enjoyed. By 1911, the FSI/SPA garnered enough members to merit a translator/secretary supplied by the Socialist Party, but Bertelli's federation never gained much attention or respect from the party hierarchy. He promoted socialist candidates in national and local elections, but—he had underestimated the logic of the syndicalists' disdain for electoral politics—most Italian immigrants were ineligible to vote. By 1910, only 25 percent of those eligible for citizenship had been naturalized.[64]

The emphasis FSI members put on battles waged within their communities not only indicates the ongoing importance of their ethnic identity, but also signals one of the ways in which their class identity was intertwined with their ethnic identity from the first. Leadership of their ethnic communities would always be a central priority for them; they confronted fellow Italian anarchists and socialists, as well as the colonial elite, in an effort to establish their syndicalist vision in their neighborhoods. In his accusations against the FSI, Bertelli had made an indisputable point: Federation members' ethnic identity was critically important to them. But he was incorrect to dismiss their class identity and their commitment to internationalism. The FSI had connections to the American Left that Bertelli downplayed or ignored, and its members were deeply committed to international revolution. In later years, their efforts to assert their syndicalist version of ethnic identity and the implications of their ethnic identity for their class identity and politics would become even more important. This was both because of their growing connections to the labor movement in the United States and because of the increasing allure of Italian nationalism and, eventually, fascism.

The identities of Italian American syndicalists as immigrants and as radicals produced not only a complex interplay between these two aspects of identity, but also an enormous emphasis on masculinity—at least in part to bolster their challenged positions in their immigrant communities and in American society as a whole. This aspect of their identity would have a formative influence on Italian American syndicalists' lives in ways foreshadowed in the first years of the FSI. Federation members' quest for a virile community emerged out of a political culture in which assertions about sexuality and virility constituted one of the ways they evaluated themselves and each other. They were part of the currency of their movement. Moreover, FSI members' violent assertions of masculinity, their "masculine gender displays" of bravado, which would be so much in evidence at Lawrence in 1912, had precedents in the infighting between Italian American (and Italian) leftists.[65] Finally, the FSI's unfortunate lack of concern for women in the workforce was also evident early on—in contrast to the efforts of its adversaries in the FSI/SPA.

Italian immigrant leftists regularly used assertions about their sexuality to bolster claims to ideological superiority during factional battles. When Bertelli split from the FSI, he engaged in a running verbal battle with the syndicalists. A syndicalist named Gian Carlo apparently accused him of sexual licentiousness—possibly of rape. Bertelli answered back, "However Gian Carlo flatters me, I have never raped a woman, no one has gone crazy for me and I do not believe I have robbed any hearts. . . . I could love women, but my little Celestina is most happy and tells all of her friends that I love her alone, and this means much to me."[66] He couched his counteraccusation in the rhetoric of sexual prowess and sexual conquest in its most base form. He demanded of Gian Carlo: "[A]re you still a priest? Or as thinks my friend Artoni, are you castrated?"[67] As happened so often in conflicts between Italian American Leftists, and even within the FSI, assertions about ideological issues— here, anticlericalism—were conflated with allegations about a foe's sexual capacity. This tendency would prove incredibly destructive when the debate on Italian intervention in World War I became an argument about standards of masculinity within the FSI.

Apparently, despite their rhetorical excess and their frequent references to sexual conquest, FSI members maintained standards about actual sexual conduct. One reason Tresca left the Federation was that he evidently violated these standards: He began an affair with someone from his neighborhood. Though the relationship was apparently consensual, she was only fifteen (she may have been the daughter of a fellow FSI member). Originally facing charges including statutory rape, rape, and assault, he pleaded guilty to adultery and spent nine months in jail. FSI members were upset by Tresca's indiscretion, which they felt—especially because he was married—violated, in FSI historian Mario de Ciampis's words, their sense of "socialist morality."[68]

But even constraints against sex with a minor could be wielded as a weapon within the FSI, when sexuality was the battlefield on which ideological issues were fought. When two editors of *Il Proletario* became embroiled in a nasty ideological dispute, one of them, Enrico Mombella, apparently manipulated the Federation's code of sexual conduct to force the other, Antonio de Bella, from the organization. De Bella was arrested in a public theater in New York in July 1908 for fornication with a minor. He protested that Mombello had set him up, sending the girl in to pick his pocket to get him to grab her. It is uncertain whether his explanation was accurate. The police dropped charges against him, and de Bella refused to cooperate with an FSI board of inquiry. Deeply shamed by the incident, he returned to Italy soon after.[69]

Despite the haziness of the outcome, it is clear that within the FSI sexuality provided a discourse through which ideological differences were aired and fought over. Within the Federation, and in the Italian American Left as a whole, sexual conquest, on both a rhetorical and a literal level, was at different times anticipated, manipulated, and mutually reinforced through comparison and competition. This was true well before the destructive World War I debate.

FSI members discussed violence and its use as a revolutionary tool from the first. The utility of violence was an issue at the core of the ideology of syndicalism. Georges Sorel, syndicalism's first and most important theoretician, defended its utility in *Reflections on Violence*.[70] Serrati, like future syndicalist FSI leaders, refused to endorse violence unquestioningly, or for its own sake. This is what caused the disagreement between him and Galleani during the 1902 strike, and it would continue to distinguish the syndicalists from *Galleanisti* in the years to come. Galleani endorsed any violence that would contribute to the destruction of capitalism and the state. FSI members were more deliberate, at least until World War I. Most had witnessed, or knew the history of, violence against the working class in moments such as the Fatti di Maggio. They were willing to meet this violence with violence of their own. For most of them, violence during strikes and protests was both an assertion of masculine pride and bravado and a viable strike strategy for a disempowered population.

But if FSI members were determined to wield violence thoughtfully in confronting bourgeois enemies, they were less prone to restrain themselves in factional disputes. Violent confrontations between Italian American leftists had a lengthy history that predated the FSI. Errico Malatesta, while in the United States, had fallen victim to the intense rivalry between Italian anarchists.[71] Malatesta's main opponent during his stay was Giuseppe Ciancabilla, an antiorganizational anarchist who had briefly edited *La Questione Sociale* before starting his own newspaper, *L'Aurora*, in West Hoboken, New Jersey. The rivalry between the two anarchist factions came to a head at a conference in West Hoboken, where an antiorganizational anarchist shot and badly wounded Malatesta. This incident convinced him to return to Italy.[72] The conflict between anarchists and socialists during Serrati's trip to Barre in 1903 had also turned violent. And FSI syndicalists and FSI/SPA socialists would battle each other physically for years, most famously after the Lawrence strike in 1912 and again in 1916 during an organizing drive in the garment industry.

Because of the pervasive masculinist ethos in the FSI, its members paid little attention to women's involvement in the labor movement, much less questioned patriarchal notions in the Italian immigrant community. For years, Federation members would virtually ignore the issues that women's increasing presence in the workplace raised.

This was one issue on which the FSI's reformist adversaries had something of an advantage in these years. Although the FSI/SPA too was almost entirely a male organization, certain reformist socialists devoted considerable energy to organizing women workers. In the early twentieth century, Italian immigrant women were reputedly difficult to organize. During the 1909 New York shirtwaist strike, faced with an impenetrable language barrier, the Women's Trade Union League turned to FSI/SPA member Arturo Caroti to convince Italian women to stay out on strike. Caroti soon learned that language was not the only barrier. He had a difficult time explaining to Italian fathers how their daughters, who sometimes earned more than they did, were being exploited at work. Caroti's solution hardly challenged the patriarchy of the Italian American household. He resorted to paying them to stay out on strike, a strategy viable only as long as his funds lasted.[73] Caroti and the FSI/SPA made an effort to organize women in extremely circumscribed ways; FSI members would not even do this much.

At times FSI masculinism—specifically, the sexualized rhetoric and capacity for violence—would bolster the organization. The rhetoric, however appalling, could unite Federation syndicalists, as could the shared willingness to meet violence with violence. But over time, the central importance of masculinity in the Federation and the ways in which it manifested itself would hinder and, ultimately, debilitate the movement. It would become harder to ignore the implications of women's presence in the workforce and on the picket lines. And agreement about the meaning of masculinity, and the distinction between revolutionary violence and violence for its own sake, would break down.

At this point, however, the best years of the FSI were ahead. The Federation would have its most profound impact on the labor movements and political cultures of the United States and Italy during the following decade. In its first years, the FSI had to struggle to survive, much less to foment a revolution. Years later, Carlo Tresca joked about the dire state of the Federation when he arrived in the United States. His first meeting with the executive committee of the FSI was held in a basement on Bleecker Street in Greenwich Village. "What a meeting! A big barrel with two lighted candles on it and four men seated around it, seriously... urging the necessity of marshaling the power of the Italian workers for the general, coming battle against capitalism."[74] As its own fortunes ebbed and flowed, the FSI could not provide much assistance to Italian migrant workers, or make its presence felt in the American labor movement. Indeed, the most significant act committed by the Italian American Left in these years did not come from the FSI, and it would have a far greater effect on Italy than the United States: the anarchist Bresci's assassination of the Italian king.

Though they were not a powerful presence as yet, Italian American syndicalists, and leftists in general, strove to galvanize their strength. Indisputably, they were ubiquitous in Italian American communities. The Italians, more so than other European immigrants, covered the entire spectrum of class-based radicalism. The anarchists organized radical circles as early as the 1880s. Socialists built their own organizations soon after, and the first syndicalists appeared early in the new century. By that time, there were pockets of Italian American radicals all across the country.[75] There were Italian American leftists organizing workers in coal mines in western Pennsylvania, Ohio, southern Colorado, and Utah; in iron ore mines in the Mesabi Range in Minnesota; in textile mills in Massachusetts; in garment factories in New York and Chicago; in marble quarries in Barre, Vermont; in silk factories in Paterson, New Jersey; and in cigar factories in Tampa, Florida.[76] In these cities, towns, and work camps, these migrant radicals—sometimes numbering a few dozen, sometimes in the thousands—battled against capitalism.

Italian American leftists faced a difficult task organizing their fellow immigrants. Especially before the immigrant strike wave that began in 1909, certain difficulties they faced were rooted in the characteristics of the Italian immigrant working-class population.[77] Southern Italians, the bulk of the over four million Italians who immigrated to the United States between 1880 and 1920, were often unskilled, disenfranchised, and illiterate. They were, like the leftists themselves, extremely mobile.

They were apt to move throughout the country in search of employment, and just as likely to return to Italy.[78] These Italian immigrants were subjected to the worst forms of exploitation, and were usually ignored by the exclusive, craft-oriented AFL.

Syndicalists and other Italian migrant leftists sought not only to organize immigrant workers, but also to present an alternative to the values of the colonial elite. When FSI members insisted on speaking at the 1910 colonial congress organized by former ally Di Silvestro, they were insisting on a voice in Italian colonies. The newspapers they edited and the literature they reproduced were efforts both to provide their own perspective on political and social events throughout the world and to argue for their own system of values. Anarchists, in particular, invested enormous energy in constructing alternatives to capitalist institutions and values that they abhorred. They established their own holidays and memorial days to replace nationalistic and religious holidays. Instead of celebrating Christmas or the Fourth of July, they would commemorate May Day and November 11, the day the Haymarket anarchists were executed. Continuing a tradition that had its roots in Italy, they acknowledged these days with special editions of their papers. Anarchists set up their own schools, many eventually named after Francisco Ferrer, a radical Spanish educator executed in Barcelona in 1909. Italian American anarchists and leftists also established cooperative stores to sell and purchase goods cheaply. Even their leisure activities frequently had political overtones. There were leftist amateur dramatic societies virtually anywhere there were anarchist circles. Leftist groups often used dances, festivals, and concert recitals both to enjoy themselves and to raise money for their papers or for a comrade in trouble.[79]

Even in these early years, Italian American syndicalists and other leftists risked their own personal safety in labor actions and confrontations with *prominenti*. Most FSI members had left Italy to avoid arrest for one militant action or another, or having already served a prison sentence. In the United States, they continued to face arrest and imprisonment to fight for their ideals. Tresca was arrested in 1904 with future IWW leader Bill Haywood for organizing street meetings. He spent time in prison for trying to expose the corruption of the Italian consul in Philadelphia. The first attempt on his life—fascists would try to kill him several times in later years—occurred in 1909 as a result of his attacks against the *prominenti* and the Black Hand (the precursor to the Mafia). He grew a beard to hide the scar on his cheek from a gash that had taken twenty-six stitches to close.[80] Luigi Galleani, who had escaped from *domicilio coatto,* was physically wounded during a strike in Paterson and forced to leave the city to avoid arrest.

As it struggled to assist fellow immigrants, to present an alternative to capitalism, and to battle its enemies in the streets, the most important thing the FSI did by the end of its first decade was develop an infrastructure and a sense of ideological coherence. Between 1909 and 1911, a new generation of leaders emerged in the FSI. Through the efforts of this generation of writers and activists, born between the late 1870s and late 1880s, the Federation would become a transnational vehicle of Italian American revolutionary syndicalism.

In a sense even the genesis of this new leadership in the FSI was connected to events in Italy. Giovannitti's appointment as editor of *Il Proletario* was the culmination of a process begun after Bertelli's departure and closely paralleled a similar, though earlier, development in the Italian syndicalist movement.

Zeev Sternhell has argued that a new generation of syndicalists arose in Italy after the syndicalist split with the PSI. The first syndicalists, Arturo Labriola, Enrico Leone, and Paolo Orano among them, were more often theoreticians than activists. As PSI members they had, moreover, tacitly condoned participation in electoral politics even as they strove to rechart the ideological direction of the party. Early in the century, certain syndicalists had even won seats in the Italian parliament. The new generation of syndicalists, led by Alceste de Ambris, Filippo Corridoni, and Michele Bianchi, emerged by 1904, and became a commanding presence in the movement by 1907 and 1908. They were activists rather than theoreticians, schooled in leading strikes as members of their local chambers of labor. According to Sternhell, this generation lent revolutionary syndicalism in Italy coherence as a "radical, class-centered and antiparty" ideology.[81]

The evolution of the FSI not only paralleled that of the syndicalist movement in Italy, but there were concrete links between the two movements, as well. Virtually all of the leading members of the Federation had a history of activism in Italy. The core of FSI leadership were not *paesani;* they came from provinces across Italy. But they were united, and linked to radicals in Italy, by a shared history of involvement in the syndicalist movement and/or antimilitarism before they arrived in the United States. Fortunato Vezzoli, for example, was born in Salò, near Brescia in Lombardy, in 1876. He moved to Milan with his family in 1890; by 1897, he had left for Lugano to avoid military service. He was in New York with his mother, his wife, and his two children by November 1905, and joined the FSI shortly thereafter.[82] Flavio Venanzi, born in Rome in 1882, was an active member of a socialist youth party there by 1906. A student of leading syndicalist theoretician Enrico Leone, Venanzi served as editor of *La Gioventù socialista*. He was arrested for leading an antimilitarist demonstration in Rome in December 1906. He migrated to Boston and joined the FSI in July 1908.[83]

Before arriving in the United States, Edmondo Rossoni was an active member of the new generation of the Italian syndicalists Sternhell has described. He was born in 1884 in Copparo, Emilia-Romagna, a stronghold of the syndicalist movement by the time he came of age politically. Rossoni became deeply involved in this movement when he was a young man. He participated in the general strike in 1904, leading strikers in Cresigallo until arrested and jailed. By early 1907 he was a member of the chamber of labor in Milan, and working on an antimilitarist newspaper edited by a socialist youth group. He was at the forefront of the syndicalist-led general strikes in Milan in 1907 and in Parma during the following year. He arrived in New York City in the spring of 1910, and within months the FSI appointed the experienced syndicalist as an organizer.[84]

Giovannitti was the exception among FSI leaders, having had no history of radical activism before migrating. Born in Ripabottoni, near Campobasso in Molise, in 1884, Giovannitti left Italy for North America at age seventeen. He was not, however, chased out of the country for antimilitarism or syndicalist exploits. He left of his own volition and, after studying briefly in a seminary, arrived in New York in 1904, apparently intending to become an evangelical minister. The reasons for his conversion to radicalism are not entirely certain. Nunzio Pernicone argues it was his exposure to the poverty of Italian immigrants, reading *Il Proletario*, and conversations with Carlo Tresca. Another historian has suggested he was urged to militant socialism by the son of the owner of his favorite restaurant.[85] In either case, his religious background followed him when he joined the adamantly anticlerical FSI in early 1907. He was questioned closely by Raimondo Fazio, secretary of the New York section he was attempting to join, about whether he was an atheist or a believer. Though he insisted that he was an agnostic, certain FSI members thought he had not completely liberated himself from his theological training.[86] Nonetheless, an extremely charismatic and intelligent man, he was soon able to gain the confidence of the majority of FSI members.

By the end of its first decade, the FSI was a solidly syndicalist organization led by a new generation of activists. All of them, including new editor Arturo Giovannitti, were adamantly opposed to militarism in any form, to reformist socialism, to electoral politics. All of them regarded direct action, and especially the general strike, as the most powerful weapons workers in any nation possessed. At their Third Congress in Utica, New York, in April 1911, FSI members formally voted to make the Federation a syndicalist organization.

Though FSI members would strive to maintain, and to build on, the connections to Italy and to the Italian Left that had so largely defined them, their relationship to their native country and to the United States would grow more complex. The imprint of the Italian Left on the FSI had been obvious in its first years. But this relationship between Italian and Italian American leftists increasingly flowed both ways. *Il Germe*, the newspaper Tresca edited in his hometown in Italy, had made it to the United States before he did—he had received donations from *paesani* living in Milford, Massachusetts; Brooklyn; and Philadelphia. When the early editors of *Il Proletario* and members of the FSI returned to Italy, moreover, they took something of their experience back with them. In later years they would often lead efforts on behalf of allies still in the United States when they were in trouble. Serrati and Arturo Caroti would organize support in Italy when Carlo Tresca was arrested in 1916, over a decade after the founder of the FSI had left the United States.[87]

The FSI by the end of its first decade was a transnational political community, not only shaped by, but also seeking to shape, the political cultures of both Italy and the United States. FSI members would strive to stay in close contact with Italian leftists, and would feel the impact when unable to. They would continue to travel back and forth between the two countries. Their first concerted action as a syndicalist organization would be to oppose Italy's imperialist war in Tripoli. At the same time, a new editor with experience living in the United States and a facility with English, and especially the prospect of joining their energies with the IWW, offered Federation members an unprecedented foothold in the United States. They would seek to use this foothold to shape their own immigrant communities and the American labor movement, as well.

CHAPTER TWO

A Transnational Syndicalist Identity

In October 1889, Italian Prime Minister Francesco Crispi was growing worried about the number of Italians migrating to other countries. Southern Italian immigration to the United States and South America was becoming a national problem. Crispi suggested in a speech that month in Palermo, the capital of his native Sicily, that Africa could be the solution to Italy's loss of population. He focused on Ethiopia, which he described as a country with "vast zones of cultiv[at]able land which will offer an outlet in the near future to that overflowing Italian fecundity which now goes to other civilized countries . . . [and] is lost to the mother country."[1] By the middle of the 1890s, the enormous poverty in southern Italy, which produced both large-scale emigration from the region and enormous unrest and violence in Sicily in 1893 and 1894, prompted Crispi to invade Ethiopia. The Italian army's efforts, however, ended in a humiliating defeat.[2] The defeat ended Italy's ambitions for colonizing the African nation. But Crispi and his successors never abandoned the idea of securing an African colony as an outlet for Italian emigration and as a safety valve for unrest in southern Italy; the prospect reemerged when Italy invaded the Libyan city of Tripoli in 1911.

Italy's war in Tripoli was opposed not only by most of the Italian Left, but also by the newly rejuvenated FSI, whose members had just voted to make their Federation a syndicalist organization.[3] The first concerted action by the newly unified organization would be to battle against the distant war. Though the FSI had little hope of stopping the war, the organization made its presence felt, not just in its New York stronghold, but in Italian American communities across the United States. Federation members on speaking tours and in their newspaper fostered, if not open rebellion against the conflict, often rancorous debate on its merits. This small but determined group of syndicalists ensured that Italian American support for the war would be neither unanimous nor uncritical.

FSI voices of dissent ensured debate in their immigrant community; their stance against the war was crucial to the ideological formation of the Federation. Members' efforts to fight against the war both highlighted and enhanced the complexity of their transnational connections to Italy and—perhaps surprisingly, given the object of their protest—to the United States. On one level, the FSI's opposition to Italy's imperialist venture in Tripoli drew on the continued connections of its members to their native country. Their critique of the war was firmly rooted in the core tenets of Italian syndicalism. They reaffirmed their convictions as antimilitarists and anticapitalists, rejecting any effort by capitalist and imperialist nations to fulfill their market-driven needs through force of arms. They rejected the war as staunch anticlericals, condemning the claims made by church leaders that Italy's presence in Tripoli constituted an effort to "civilize" the Muslim population there. They also reproduced Italian syndicalists' attitudes on southern Italy and southern Italians. Federation members insisted that Italian advocates of the war were fleeing from problems in southern Italy that they were unable or unwilling to solve. At the same time, FSI members shared with many Italian syndicalists disparaging attitudes about the population of southern Italy. This was a particularly potent issue for FSI members, who by the end of the war in Tripoli were leading a strike in Lawrence, Massachusetts, waged in large part by southern Italian immigrants—the very population about which they had such grave doubts. But despite its emphasis on issues central to Italian syndicalists, the FSI, even in opposing a war waged by Italy, was no longer simply an extension of the Italian movement in the United States.

By 1911 the FSI was a transnational community in the strictest sense of the term. It was not just a collection of migrants whose organization retained close contact with their home country—indeed, for the first time in its history, the Federation managed to avoid involvement in a factional crisis on the Italian Left. It was an association whose members were consciously and continuously constructing a political and cultural identity rooted in, and drawing from, both native and adopted communities. When FSI members critiqued the war in Tripoli, they did so not just as syndicalists, but as recent emigrants from Italy. When Italian statesmen presented Tripoli as an ideal outlet for impoverished southern Italians, FSI members were able to refute this claim from first-hand experience. Arturo Giovannitti, moreover, was the first editor of *Il Proletario* who had a command of English and who had spent a considerable amount of time in the United States before taking over the paper. Both he and FSI member Giovanni di Gregorio published articles in English on the war. The FSI was not only seeking a voice in its own ethnic community; for the first time, its members were also stretching beyond these boundaries to reach a larger audience with its protest. Further proof of the Federation's extended reach would come just months after the war began, when FSI members joined the textile strike in Lawrence, Massachusetts.

The history of this organization of white ethnics flies in the face of assertions made by scholars of both social movements in the United States and Italian American history about the nature of Progressive Era immigrants' identity and priorities. Historians of Italian Americans have long argued that in the years before World War I, Italian migrant radicals were, in the words of Carlo Tresca, "living and fighting in a world which was a slice of the mother country transplanted."[4] Arguments about the ethnic separatism of these radicals coexist awkwardly with claims made by Todd Gitlin and others that immigrant leftists in this era focused their energies almost exclusively on fighting for a class-based internationalism while ignoring ethnic issues.[5] John Diggins made the same assertion in a different context in his study of Italian American support for Mussolini. Leftists' obsession with social class, Diggins argued, created a vacuum in the community that Mussolini used to exploit feelings of ethnic inferiority and to build support for fascism among Italian immigrants in the 1920s.[6] Neither argument—for ethnic separatism or undiluted internationalism—tells the whole story. The FSI's enthusiastic, if unsuccessful, attempts to influence Italian foreign policy makes it clear that even as they argued for class-based revolution, Italian American syndicalists confronted issues central to their ethnic identity. In protesting the war in Tripoli, the FSI was no longer strictly an outpost of the Italian Left. On the other hand, nor would—or could—its members be oblivious to issues of ethnic identity.

This evolution of the FSI ensured that the political culture its members created would continue to be informed by both their ethnic and class identities. They had to reconcile feelings of *Italianità*—deep and unabated emotional attachments to Italy and to things Italian—with their loyalty to working-class internationalism. Their expressions of cultural nationalism, rooted in their experience as immigrants, were complicated by the emergence of a nationalist movement in Italy. Despite the best efforts of Nationalist leader Enrico Corradini to enlist syndicalists in his cause, however, FSI members steered well clear.

The war provoked FSI members to evaluate not only the relationship between their class and ethnic loyalties, but also their perspective on war, in particular, and on the use of violence, in general. FSI attitudes toward violence were shaped by a number of different factors, including the arguments of Georges Sorel, the role of violent conflict in Italian history, and Federation members' own personal experiences. When they discussed violence as an abstraction, Italian American syndicalists expressed a wide range of opinions. Certain of them were concerned that violence could be too sweeping or counterproductive.

When violence was a matter of strike or oppositional strategy, and especially an assertion of courage and masculine bravado, however, FSI members were of one mind. This would become all the more clear when the Lawrence strike began in the midst of their protest against the war. Drawn together by the very real necessity for physical courage, and buoyed by the prospect of success in Lawrence, FSI members were more steadfastly opposed to the war than were their fellow syndicalists across the ocean. Federation members' reaction to the war in Tripoli did not foreshadow the eventual split in the Italian and Italian American movements over Italian intervention in World War I the way it did among Italian syndicalists. Nonetheless, the issues the war raised for Italian American syndicalists would be continually debated in the FSI during coming years.

To analyze the nature of the FSI's response to the war, one must know something of the war itself. The rejuvenation of the FSI at the beginning of the second decade of the twentieth century coincided with the rekindling of Italy's ambition to enter the ranks of the "great powers" through an imperialist war. The Italian prime minister at the time, Giovanni Giolitti, knew a nation could not be considered a great power no

matter what its other accomplishments, if it did not have colonial possessions. England and France controlled most of the African territories
along the Mediterranean. The Ottoman Empire at this point still included the Balkan states—including Serbia, Bulgaria, and Montene-
gro—as well as the two African provinces of Tripoli and Cyrenaica, or
Libya, as the Italians referred to the two territories. But this empire was
crumbling, rent with internal disputes, and increasingly threatened by
other imperial powers, and both the Austro-Hungarian Empire and
Russia had ambitions in the Balkan states. The United States, one of the
newest entrants into the class of world powers, was colonizing the Philip-
pines and exerting its influence over its neighbors in Central America.[7]
By 1911, Italy was also once again attempting to break into the ranks of
the imperial powers.

If anything, Italy felt the need to assert itself as an imperial power
even more profoundly than its European neighbors or the United States.
Italy was a member of the Triple Alliance with Germany and the Austro-Hungarian Empire, but the word *alliance* was misleading. It was
more a league of mutual distrust. Italian misgivings about the Austrians
dated back to the *Risorgimento,* and they hardly held Germany in higher
esteem.[8] A unified Italy, as opposed to a very loosely affiliated set of
duchies, republics, and kingdoms, had only existed since 1861, and the
new nation was well aware of its lack of power and wealth compared to
its imperial neighbors. Austria's unwillingness to return two "unredeemed" territories, Trentino and Trieste—territories that Italy claimed
belonged to it after the *Risorgimento*—was a constant reminder both of
how Italy had been bullied before unification and how limited its international standing still was. Italy's membership in the alliance was purely
a matter of keeping its enemies in sight. Despite the negative incentives
that drew the countries together, the alliance, formed in 1882, had already been renewed three times by 1911.

But by that year, fifty years after it had unified, Italy was convinced
that in order to hold its own in the alliance, it had to lay claim to a territorial possession. An Englishman who was sympathetic both to imperialism in general, and to Italy's efforts to enter the ranks of world powers, in particular, explained at the time that it was necessary for Italy to
stand up for itself. He wrote, "Italy is not to blame for the 'big stick'
which is the universal policy today—the smaller nations always stand
to lose in such a game; but Italy certainly cannot be blamed for making

an effort to save herself from being crushed under the heel of one of the contending leviathans."[9] Giolitti, his eyes focused on Africa as Crispi's had been, chose Libya as a suitable conquest, with the port town of Tripoli as the point of entry.[10]

Libya at that time was one of the last remnants of the Ottoman Empire. Italy seemingly had a vested interest in not tampering with the Ottoman Empire, since any disruption in the region of the Mediterranean would presumably benefit the more powerful nations of Germany and Austria. Nonetheless, Giolitti reasoned that if the Ottoman Empire was going to lose its territorial possessions anyway, Italy should take steps to ensure that it, rather than any other nation, was the beneficiary. Its choice of Libya was a reflection of its power relative to the other great powers. Most of Libya was a desert, and even the more fertile land by the Mediterranean would require considerable investment before it began to return a profit. Despite these disadvantages, Italy set its sights on Libya, in large part because it was the last African territory on the Mediterranean coast to which it could lay a claim.

While Italy was certainly concerned about its relation to the other great powers, it was also renewing the goal of finding an outlet for emigration. One of Italy's primary motivations for its conquest of Libya was the hope that it could provide an area of settlement for increasingly impoverished southern Italians, and thus put an end to the "southern problem" in Italy. Since the *Risorgimento,* the Italian North had been developing industrially at a much faster pace than had the South. There was a small industrial base emerging in the southern regions of Italy, but southern Italy by the turn of the century was still essentially an agricultural region with a largely peasant population that was being squeezed by the increasing scarcity of land and the collapse of cottage industries. To make matters worse, southern Italy was hit by a series of economic and natural disasters in the first decade of the twentieth century. High tariffs passed to protect northern Italian industries effectively crippled what industry there was in the South. Then the vineyards in Calabria, Apulia, and Sicily, the core of much of the South's economy, were crushed by a blight and by tariffs and competition from France and the United States. Many southern Italians began to leave Italy in search of a livelihood. Initially, they looked for seasonal labor in nearby European countries, but eventually they broadened their search and migrated to the United States and South America.[11] By the time of the

Libyan war, over three percent of the population of southern Italy was migrating every year; by 1910, 5,547,746 Italians were living outside Italy. Most of these émigrés were not abjectly impoverished day laborers; they were usually middle-level peasants or even owners of small plots of land. The Italian government hoped that once Libya was captured, it would stem the tide of southern Italian migration by encouraging them to settle closer to home than New York or Buenos Aires.[12]

With this incentive, Italy began to make economic inroads in Libya as early as 1905, a policy which led it into war six years later. The head of the Bank of Rome had apparently been trying to sponsor an Italian occupation of Tripoli for some time to secure his bank's investment in the area. In fact, Enrico Corradini, the leader of the adamantly imperialist Associazione Nazionalista Italiana (ANI) wrote him a letter complimenting the Bank of Rome for being "daring and serious" in the "peaceful penetration" of Libya.[13] The Roman Catholic Church was also promoting Italian imperialism at this time through its financial cooperation with the Bank of Rome. As one historian of modern Italy has noted, "The Roman Catholic Church early began to play a major part in the finances of Liberal Italy both through small local banks and cooperatives and through major agencies, especially the Banco di Roma. This last by 1910 was a veritable agent, or even propellant, of Italian imperialism, with major interests in Libya and Egypt...."[14] While in Libya, Bank of Rome officers and Italian officials antagonized, and were antagonized by, Turkish officials. The Turkish government grew increasingly disgruntled about Italy's economic and physical presence in its colony. Meanwhile, in Italy support for a military invasion was growing because of perceived limitations being placed on Italian business interests. The official reason for Italy's war in Libya was the apparent assassination in the fall of 1911 of two Italian officials in Tripoli. A minister in Giolitti's cabinet announced that Italy could not allow its citizens abroad to be harassed by citizens or governments of other countries, and Italy declared war.[15]

Little in this war went as the Italian government planned. Italy began bombarding Tripoli on October 1, 1911; when the nearly forty-five thousand Italian troops occupied the city a week later, they expected to be able to separate the Turks from the Libyans without any trouble. On October 23, Italian troops were surprised by a counterattack launched not only by the Turks, but by the Libyans, as well. Italy, far from being perceived as a liberating force by the Libyans, was considered an infidel invader, and Muslim leaders in Libya declared a jihad against it.[16]

Italian troops had taken a series of coastal towns in the first half of October, but then the invasion stalled. The Italians did not want to be drawn inland in a fight against the Turks and Libyans, so they set up defensive positions in Tripoli and in the other coastal towns they had occupied. Giolitti declared outright annexation of Libya in November 1911, but it was an empty gesture because the war had reached a virtual standstill. Nor did much change after the annexation.

But despite the unwillingness of the Italians to move the war inland, and despite the fact that the war had been a virtual stalemate for months, the Ottoman Empire was simply too weak to hold on to Libya. In July 1912, the Turks and Italians began to negotiate a peace settlement. The Turks procrastinated for months, but eventually the pressures of their problems in the Balkan states became too distracting, and they signed the Treaty of Lausanne with Italy on October 8, 1912. Italy formally annexed Libya (after having already done so in violation of international law the previous November) immediately after the treaty was signed.[17]

When the war began, FSI members immediately threw themselves into antiwar efforts, trying to make their voices heard and to educate fellow immigrants in Italian American communities. Speakers and organizers toured the country to arouse antiwar sentiment and to confront prowar Italian Americans. Reports from various Federation section meetings—there were by this point fifty-five sections affiliated with the FSI—regularly included news of debates between antiwar syndicalists and prowar patriots. Edmondo Rossoni went on a nationwide tour, speaking against the war in towns all over New Jersey, Pennsylvania, Ohio, Oregon, and California, and Arturo Giovannitti ventured into Connecticut to denounce the war. FSI members cajoled their more patriotic fellow immigrants endlessly, goading them to return to Italy to fight if they were so supportive of the war rather than remain in the safety of their homes in the United States. "You patriots, enthusiastic admirers of the Libyan venture," exclaimed a syndicalist during a protest meeting, "what the hell are you yelling about from a distance of 5000 miles? Go get your heads broken by the Turks. . . . It will be a gain for the human species."[18]

Their efforts bore some fruit, although most people in Italian American colonies continued to support the war. At the very least, they managed to initiate debates at public meetings where support for the war would otherwise have gone unquestioned. These debates were often very combative. FSI sections in Kensington, Illinois; Trenton, New Jersey; Youngstown, Ohio; Franklin, Massachusetts; and San Francisco—usually towns where Rossoni or another Federation organizer had spoken—sent reports of clashes between their members and prowar Italian Americans. There were even signs that their protests against the war were a matter of grave concern for the Italian government. Rossoni worried the Italian consulate so much that it slanderously accused him of participating in a plot to assassinate the king of Italy.[19] But realizing that they would not be able to stop Italy's invasion of Tripoli, Federation members from the start extended their critique of Italy well beyond the boundaries of the war itself.

The greatest significance of their protest against the war for FSI members was that it compelled them to address, and to reshape, their relationship to Italy and to the United States. They remained closely connected to the Italian Left. But they also took steps to distinguish themselves from their transatlantic allies and to extend discussion of the war beyond their immigrant community. This reworking of their relationships to both Italian leftists and the American Left and labor movement would have a profound effect on how the FSI approached the Lawrence strike, in which they would play such a crucial role.

In many ways, the FSI's opposition to the war underscored their continuing connections to Italy and to the Italian syndicalist movement. Italian American syndicalists maintained links to correspondents in Italy who kept them informed of the progress of the war and opposition to it in their native country. The FSI's strategy in opposing the war drew on the essential elements of Italian syndicalism: anticapitalism, antiimperialism, antimilitarism, and anticlericalism. FSI members also took up the defense of southern Italy, an issue vital to many Italian syndicalists. They focused much of their ire on Giolitti's claim that Italy's imperialist enterprise would have a "civilizing" effect on Tripoli, responding that the war was caused by the utter failure of the major institutions of power in Italy—the government, the bourgeoisie, and the Catholic Church—to "civilize" much of southern Italy.

Federation members, like Italian syndicalists, recognized that Italy was attempting to enter the ranks of imperial powers and that its imperialist venture was, like those of other capitalist nations, simply an extension of its economic system. Alceste de Ambris made precisely this argument in an article in the Italian syndicalist newspaper *Pagine libere* titled "Against Colonial Brigandage and for the Interests of the Proletariat."[20] One of the first in the FSI to articulate the connection between capitalism and imperialism was Giovanni di Gregorio, a Sicilian who had been a member of the Federation since its earliest days.[21] In a letter written in English to the *New York Journal,* a conservative American newspaper, di Gregorio outlined the way in which imperialism in Italy, in the United States, and throughout the world was an inevitable outgrowth of capitalism. He wrote,

> After the laboring fellow citizens have been fleeced by their capitalist brothers, often members of the same creed and church, the latter may find it possible to exploit others in foreign lands, may think there are other fields for investment (a polite word for plunder) outside of their country's boundaries, and ... they will proceed to the conquest of the new promised land, by graceful means if possible, through missionaries and commercial and consular agents, or by force of arms if necessary and feasible.[22]

Italy's invasion of Libya had proceeded in exactly this manner, and the further examples di Gregorio gave were informed by his awareness of the workings of imperialism in Italy and worldwide. "Look at the latest wars," he declared. "[T]he one between this country and Spain, the Boer War, the Russo-Japanese carnage, the Turco-Italian *opera buffa,* all tell the same tale: new markets, new fields of exploitation were wanted in each case."[23] Capitalists in any country, when the markets in their own lands were glutted, would inevitably seek markets in other countries. If they could not expand peacefully, they would do so forcefully.

The rationale that Italy, like many other imperial nations, gave for its invasion was that it would civilize Tripoli. But as Giovannitti pointed out in an article he wrote (also in English) for the *International Socialist Review* titled "The Brigandage of Tripoli," this goal was nothing more than a means to capitalist exploitation. He noted that "the excuse is always the same: Civilization—an elastic and malleable word which may mean ... the Bible or the public school, the cannon or the locomotive, but which, [*sic*] ultimately signifies nothing but capitalism, whether it be investments, taxation or pure and simple highway robbery."[24] The goal of imperial ventures was never to "civilize" the invaded countries—it was to capture territory or resources. Indeed, throughout the war, FSI members called into question the very meaning of civilization in a capitalist society.

Maintaining steadfastly their antimilitarism, so central to many of them as members of the Italian syndicalist movement before they migrated, FSI members repeatedly emphasized the enormous irony inherent in the idea of Italy civilizing Tripoli through a brutally violent war. Fortunato Vezzoli, who had left Italy to avoid obligatory military service, ridiculed the hypocrisy of the leaders of a militarized state seeking to rationalize their conquest. Writing under the pen name Bifolco, he argued that while civilization should be defined as the antithesis of barbarity, in modern times it signified little more than sophistication in methods of killing. In an article titled "The Crimes of Civilization," he traced the development of armaments from the wooden club to modern dirigibles and airplanes. The irony was that once a people became skilled in the "art of killing" large numbers of their enemies, those enemies were labeled barbarians. "Between a barbarian who doesn't kill anybody, and a 'civilized' man who kills hundreds of his brothers," he asked, "who is civilized and who is the barbarian?"[25] The end result of Italy's victory, which Vezzoli saw as inevitable, given its superior fire power, would be a Libya that had achieved a "civilized" capacity to kill.

Turning to other issues central to the FSI and Italian syndicalist opposition to the war, Vezzoli concluded that Italy's militarism would impose capitalism and Catholicism on a population in Libya that had no desire for either.

> The fruits of this war used as a means to civilize will be taxes and priests. The conquered people will remain bitter towards their invaders. Their lost liberty will cause them to forever arm themselves. With melancholy they will remember the days in which they were free, the days in which they controlled their own destiny. They will soon say, as the red-skins now say—"we were better off when we were worse off."[26]

Just as Native Americans, the "red-skins," had met defeat in the United States, so would the Arabs in Libya, according to Vezzoli. Arguments that the Arabs would actually benefit from their defeat—that they would become more civilized—were farcical. Rather, they would have an alien religion and economic system imposed on them under force of arms.

FSI members, like many Italian syndicalists concerned about the dire state of southern Italy, devoted most of their energy to exploring the implications of the war for the impoverished region. They forcefully rejected the argument that Tripoli would provide a nearby outlet for the vast number of southern Italians migrating to the United States and South America every year. Giovannitti argued, echoing Crispi's words of more than two decades earlier, that the Italian government and bourgeoisie worried that "all those who emigrate to [sic] the United States are entirely lost to the mother country."[27] The reason they were emigrating, and the reason the war was being fought, Giovannitti added, was because the Italian bourgeoisie had failed; it had been unable to find any other solution to the southern problem in Italy. He explained,

> The Italian bourgeoisie having, through their utter lack of courage and capacity, been unable to create industries adequate to the necessity and even to apply modern systems to farming [so] that the land might have grown more productive, have been left to face a desperate problem. . . . After years of discussion, scheming and heavy thinking they have been able to find only one solution: to depopulate the country.[28]

Rather than developing their own country, the Italian bourgeoisie had invaded Tripoli in the hope that they could convince southern Italians to continue to migrate—but to settle closer to Italy, so that they would not be lost as labor resources.

Giovannitti's analysis of southern Italy was taken up by others in the FSI who argued that both the government and the bourgeoisie in Italy were trying to use the war to camouflage their deficiencies with regard to solving problems in their own country. Federation members insisted that, once again, the hypocrisy of Italy's civilizing mission in Tripoli was glaringly evident; Italy's government and bourgeoisie could not hope to civilize another land when they had already utterly failed in their own country. They argued that it was ludicrous for the Italian government to invest money in a war that could be so much better spent in southern Italy itself. Italy's first census, in 1910, revealed the abject poverty of much of southern Italy. In an article titled "The Glories of Italy," Vezzoli cited figures from the census to make his point. In the southern regions of Italy there were 1,254 communities with nonpotable water; 4,877 were without sewers; 5,995 had no meat; 600 had no doctors; 366 had no cemeteries; and 154 were infected with malaria.[29]

Many FSI members were able to draw on bitter personal experience in indicting the Italian government for its neglect of the South. As in the Italian syndicalist movement, many members of the Federation had been born in southern Italy. Several of them wrote about the war and the region in which they had been born in a special issue of *Il Proletario* in early January 1912. Calabrian Leonardo Frisina, for example, described living conditions in his native region and took the Italian government to task for misdirecting its efforts. Even the conservative patriotic Italian newspaper *Corriere della Sera*, Frisina argued, agreed that colonizing Tripoli would take much too long to be of any use to southern Italians. "We agree," he wrote, "with the idea that hundreds of years will pass before the colonization of Tripoli is realized—just as many years passed before the surveys were made to build the streets in Calabria."[30] The poverty and ever-present danger of disease in the South, Frisina argued, was the government's responsibility.

> If after three years it hasn't been possible to repair the buildings destroyed by the earthquake, and after 18 years not a half-mile of street has been built between Acquaro and Sinopoli which are the two major cities in Reggio Calabria, and if the elimination of malaria has not yet been realized in the most advanced cities in Reggio Calabria—including Gioia which is Calabria's New York, then I must ask you what type of civility does our government think it has? . . . Just when misery compels the people to ask for help from the King, he responds by imposing new taxes which he uses, in turn, to wage war in some foreign land. . . . He is slapping an entire population in the face. . . . What does he care if there are no streets in Calabria? What does he care if farmers have to carry their products on their backs when in Milan the fastest cars in the world are being built? What does he care if Calabrians are walking around barefoot when the rest of Italy is producing the world's finest shoes? And if in that region there still exist towns that lack schools and electricity, it is surely not Giolitti's fault—he has never even been to Calabria!!![31]

Southern Italy had not only been allowed to remain undeveloped, Frisina argued, with the authority of one born and raised there. It had also been taxed and its young men had been drafted to fight to help sustain northern Italy's industrial development. Despite the dreams of certain southern Italians—including some socialists—that their efforts on behalf of Italy would finally be rewarded with settlements in Libya, Frisina warned that only deeper poverty and continued inequality between northern and southern Italy awaited them.

Italian American syndicalists' memories of life in southern Italy evoked their angriest expressions of anticlericalism. The FSI also condemned the Catholic Church for the underdevelopment of southern Italy. FSI members, like Italian syndicalists, were united by their adamant opposition to Catholicism. Because of the church, they argued, much of the population of southern Italy was not only poor, but also undereducated and consumed by religious superstition. Sicilian Giovanni Gianchino declared, "[T]hese people were buried in the coffin of ignorance and superstition 20 centuries ago and no one has dared bring civilization to the land...."[32] He described the feast of St. Alto, in which the population of an entire town in Sicily ran nearly naked (clothed, he said, only with "a small flower that covers the sexual organs") through the town to a church in the hope that they would be visited by a miracle. He lamented, "If any strangers happened upon this town and saw the hordes of naked men and women running through the streets, they would think they were not in Italy, but among the cannibals of central Africa." "I am not like ... others," he concluded, "who think that the Middle Ages are over."[33] The church had not only failed to civilize southern Italy—it had kept its population mired in ignorance. This view of the church as a debilitating and regressive institution in southern Italy was shared by many in the FSI. When Giovannitti offered a contemptuous tally of the "fruits of Italian civilization" that would be exported to Tripoli, the Catholic Church headed the list. Italy could offer "the Roman Catholic religion," he wrote, "with thousands of priests and monks that for 15 centuries have turned the 'queen of the world' into an illiterate mendicant."[34]

The FSI drew on the key elements of Italian syndicalism in attacking the war, stressing for their fellow immigrants the failures of the major forces in their lives. The Italian government had not been able to provide for the basic needs of many of its citizens; instead it merely recruited them to fight in a war that would benefit only the Italian—and especially the northern Italian—bourgeoisie. These Italian capitalists who would profit from the war had no interest in investing in bettering the lives of their fellow citizens. They did not even want them to remain in the country—they just wanted the often desperate southern Italians close enough to Italy to continue to provide a cheap labor pool. And the

Catholic Church, far from bringing enlightenment to the peasants and neophyte industrial workers of the South, provided only empty and irrelevant ritual. Unfortunately, the FSI also shared a more detrimental perspective with many Italian syndicalists: contempt for southern Italians themselves.

As Giovanni Gianchino's scathing commentary on religious ritual indicated, FSI members' analysis of the failures of Italian authorities in southern Italy inevitably had implications for the population living there. Gianchino likened the "hordes of naked men and women running through the streets" during a religious ritual to "cannibals in central Africa."[35] Leonardo Frisina made the same acrid comparison. The article he reproduced from a patriotic Italian newspaper defined at least certain southern Italians in explicitly racial terms. Titled "The Africans of Calabria," the article speculated that some Calabrians might have been descendants of immigrants from Africa. The author of this article hedged on this assertion, stating, "[A]s far as the question of their origin is concerned, we do not wish to address it because we are not professional historians." But he was not at all squeamish about drawing a conclusion: "We can simply say that Darwin proved this year that the inhabitants are more closely related to the chimpanzee than they are to Adam and Eve."[36]

Perhaps even more disturbing than this article, which Frisina saw fit to reprint, and more revealing of the contempt in which he held southern Italian peasants—not to mention the Africans to whom they were being compared—was how willingly he embraced the author's conclusions. Frisina prefaced the article by declaring,

> We thought we were the only radicals to extol the upside-down Italian civilization. But we were wrong. . . . When, a few months ago, we said that some uncivilized areas in Calabria still exist, we were labeled as dissatisfied socialists. Now . . . he who illustrates that which our modest pens have written is neither a socialist nor an anarchist.[37]

By repeatedly emphasizing the continuing poverty of southern Italy, FSI members were able to connect the Italian ruling class's fallacious rhetoric about "civilizing" Tripoli with its dismal lack of success in Italy. But, as in Frisina's article, it was all too easy to extend this critique of southern Italian poverty to include extremely disparaging assessments of southern Italians themselves—assessments which also revealed the racism of certain FSI members.

This attitude once again linked FSI members to the Italian syndicalist movement. Leaders of the movement in Italy routinely criticized the failures of the Italian government and the Catholic Church in southern Italy; socialist leaders' refusal to acknowledge or confront the southern problem had been one of the reasons for the syndicalists' split with them. But many syndicalists had grave reservations about the capacity of southern Italian peasants as a revolutionary force. There were, of course, syndicalist strongholds in the South. There was a vibrant movement in Apulia (funded in large part by contributions from migrants living in the United States).[38] Nonetheless, although many syndicalists were born in the South, they often made their way north as they were drawn more deeply into the movement. As a leading authority on Italian syndicalism argued, "a disaffected southerner was not bound to believe the southern peasantry could play a central role in solving Italy's problems. Their southern experience convinced the syndicalists that the Italian problem was deeper than the [socialist] reformists thought, but precisely for this reason, they felt that the solution required something radically new, which they found to be developing almost exclusively in the North."[39] Arturo Labriola, for example, made his way to Milan from his native Naples when he grew too frustrated with the limits of political possibility in his native city. His return to Naples coincided with his growing disillusionment with syndicalism.[40]

It is likely that Frisina and the author of the article on the Catholic Church, who shared Italian syndicalist leaders' disparaging attitude toward southern Italians, were more extreme in their views than most members of the FSI. Both of these men were only occasional contributors to *Il Proletario*; the leaders of the FSI who wrote on southern Italians were much more temperate in their views. They recognized that most of the immigrants to the United States were from the southern regions of Italy, and their writings reflected this awareness. Giovannitti noted only that the southern Italian immigrants had, because of their continuing poverty in Italy, become alienated from the land. He wrote, "[T]he Italian peasant, which gives the highest percentage of emigration, has lost its characteristics, and having developed at home a sullen hatred for the land which has been such a cruel step-mother to him, he has refrained from agriculture and invaded the industrial fields [in the United States]."[41] But the fact that articles portraying southern Italians as backward and even barbaric appeared in *Il Proletario*, whether they were representative of views of most FSI members or not, made it clear that the syndicalists in the FSI were themselves somewhat alienated, if not from the land where they were born, then from the people they were seeking to organize.

Though several aspects of the FSI's critique of the war linked it to the Italian syndicalist movement, by 1911 it was no longer a mere arm of Italian syndicalism in the United States. Giovannitti and di Gregorio's articles in English were early indications that at least certain FSI members were striving to establish a political identity beyond even the Italian American communities in which they lived. Giovannitti wrote his critique of the war for a leading theoretical journal of the American Left. Di Gregorio sent his article on imperialism to a right-wing newspaper in the city in which he lived. These were steps, however small, past the insularity that had largely characterized the FSI during its first decade.

The clearest indication that the FSI was no longer an outpost organization was that its campaign against the war marked the first time the Federation was able to avoid being drawn into a factional dispute waged within the Italian Left. Because their movement was in transition, even crisis, as the war in Tripoli began, syndicalists in Italy ended up deeply divided over how to react. By 1911, they were forced to face the fact that their movement had been faltering for a number of years. Though the general strikes in 1904 had been waged with enormous enthusiasm, the syndicalists had found it difficult to maintain their momentum. The Socialists' establishment and domination of the CGL in 1906 had weakened syndicalism as a national movement, compelling syndicalists to concentrate their energies on areas of regional strength. The general strike in Parma in 1908, which the Socialists and the CGL had refused to support, had ended in a bitter defeat in a crucial syndicalist stronghold. Certain syndicalists, Arturo Labriola among them, started to question whether Italy, and specifically the Italian proletariat, was prepared for syndicalism. Labriola, one of the founders of Italian syndicalism, had supported the syndicalists' split with the PSI in 1907 only half-heartedly. He had responded similarly to the 1908 Parma strike, warning that excessive use of the general strike—the most important of syndicalist tactics—would further damage the proletariat's opinion of syndicalism.[42]

When Italy invaded Tripoli, Labriola and several other intellectuals shocked their fellow syndicalists by supporting the war effort. Discouraged by their struggling movement and by what they perceived as Italian workers' apathy and lack of militance, they looked to the war as a source of rejuvenation. Labriola argued that a war was exactly what the proletariat needed to shake it out of its lethargy. He insisted,

> Oh my comrades, do you know why the proletariat is not fit to make a revolution? For precisely the same reasons that it is not fit to wage war. Let the proletariat get used to fighting seriously, and then you will see that it will learn to strike the bourgeoisie itself! Make it possible for us to break out of our customary stinking laziness! Today perhaps there is no enterprise more revolutionary than this attempt in Italy.... War will impose on us new, more precise problems, having greater importance and more enduring consequences than those to which we are accustomed. It will be a tremendous and painful experience, but under that pedagogy we will remake ourselves.[43]

Labriola saw the war as a way to strengthen an Italian proletariat growing too weak and decadent to fight for its own interests. His sense that, under Giolitti, the proletariat (and Italy as a whole) had become too soft was shared by syndicalist intellectuals Paolo Orano and Angelo Olivetti. Orano expressed the hope that the war would strengthen both the proletariat and the bourgeoisie, and thus sharpen the class conflict that would lead to a revolution.[44]

These syndicalist supporters of the war were joined by anarchist Libero Tancredi. Tancredi, who frequently appeared in syndicalist newspapers and at syndicalist meetings, returned to Italy from the United States as the war began. He shared an increasing conviction that a revolution was not about to begin soon. He, too, thought that the war would increase the proletariat's ardor for combat and enhance its ability to fight a revolution.[45]

The support of Labriola, Orano, Olivetti, and Tancredi for the war deeply angered many syndicalists and disrupted the movement. Enrico Leone, for example, was vehement in his opposition to the conflict. In a book analyzing the war, *Espansionismo e colonie,* he insisted that there was no way this imperialist venture could benefit the proletariat or help the syndicalists achieve their ends. He was concerned about Italian workers' seeming lack of militance, but he argued that Italy's war had nothing to offer them or to teach them. Disagreement over how to react to the war also interrupted the publication of *Pagine libere,* by 1911 the leading syndicalist newspaper in Italy. Citing irreconcilable differences with the prowar editors on the staff, Alceste de Ambris, one of the editors, left the newspaper.

Those syndicalists identified by Zeev Sternhell as members of the new generation of activists—De Ambris, Filippo Corridoni, and Michele Bianchi, for example—were ardently opposed to the war. De Ambris attacked Labriola, Orano, and Olivetti bitterly, calling them false revolutionaries and accusing them of supporting an action that would strengthen the bourgeois state.[46] He, Corridoni, Leone, and numerous other syndicalists waged an angry, though unsuccessful, general strike against the war during its first months. They were joined by Benito Mussolini, then the new leader of the revolutionary Left in the PSI, who led demonstrators' efforts to stop troop trains from leaving Milan.[47]

The split in the Italian syndicalist movement over the war foreshadowed the much deeper and more debilitating chasm that the issue of Italy's intervention in World War I would create among both Italian and Italian American syndicalists. In 1911 and 1912 there were only a few Italian syndicalist intellectuals who were already so discouraged and so disillusioned that they were willing to encourage workers to spill their blood to revitalize themselves. By 1915, when Italy entered World War I, there would be many more who had reached that desultory state of mind.

The transnational FSI distinguished itself from the Italian syndicalist movement in its leadership's unified opposition to the war. Its most prominent members—Giovannitti, Rossoni, Vezzoli, and di Gregorio among them—all staunchly opposed Italy's imperialist venture. Having just reconstituted their Federation as a syndicalist institution, they had little reason to feel the pessimism that Labriola and other Italian prowar syndicalists felt. None of the leading members of the Italian American syndicalist movement abandoned their antimilitarist principles.

There is evidence that some rank-and-file members of the FSI supported the war. A letter from an FSI section in Monongahela, Pennsylvania, in early 1912, addressed to "ex-comrade" Zaira Tonnarelli took him to task for backing the war. The secretaries of the section wrote condemning first the prowar faction in Italy, then their former comrade. "All or almost all of the noted intellectuals [Labriola, Orano, Tancredi] wanted to voice their opinions and have succeeded in confusing the proletariat (that has nothing to gain from the war) and has rendered

them incapable of opposing the blood bath." They continued, addressing Tonnarelli,

> You side with those who approve of the war—we, with those who
> oppose it. You walk alongside the *prominenti*—the doctors, the priests
> and the bankers. We, alongside the workers. We were once held together
> by a strong bond.... You are now sinking into oblivion—as have others.
> We are ready to break off the friendship with whomever in the interest of
> the faith for which we are fighting and that we love so much.
>   Without bearing a grudge.[48]

Clearly Tonnarelli was not alone in his decision. But just as clearly, his
choice did not evoke the anger that syndicalist support for the war did
in Italy. The authors were prepared to see their former friend disappear,
but they held no grudges against him. Disagreements over the war existed only on the local level in the FSI, and did not produce any of the
rancor they did in Italy.

The FSI stood distinct from the Italian syndicalist movement not
only in its nearly unanimous opposition to the war, but also in the arguments its members made against the war. In its arguments the FSI established itself as a transnational political community—its members
protested against the war not only in terms drawn from and familiar to
Italian syndicalists, but also as immigrants struggling to find purchase
in a new home. They refuted the Italian government's claim that Tripoli
would solve the southern problem not only by critiquing its failure in
the southern regions of Italy, but also by drawing on personal experience in rejecting Tripoli as a potential lure from immigrants.

As migrants themselves, many of whom had lived and worked not
just in the United States but in Europe and South America, as well, they
were able to evaluate and dismiss Tripoli as a safety valve. They argued
that even if southern Italy had not so badly needed the resources that
were being invested in the war, Libya still would have been a poor choice
for a colony. It simply lacked the resources to provide a viable outlet for
Italian emigration. As writers in *Il Proletario* pointed out, there was little chance that the deserts of Libya could provide a home for people
who were peasants or, at most, first-generation industrial workers. Even
if they could be persuaded to immigrate to Libya, it would still require a
massive amount of money to make the area livable for them. Oscar
Mazzitelli, a Calabrian who had migrated to the United States just two

years earlier, echoed Frisina's earlier angry assessment of conditions in southern Italy, asking, "Besides the expenses incurred in the war, the state will have to provide the money necessary to build up Tripoli. . . . Where will this money be found when they don't even have enough money to build schools and roads here in Italy?" He concluded, "[I]f southern Italians are obliged to emigrate to Tripoli, they will be damned to live in hellish conditions."[49]

If Italy needed an emigration outlet, Vezzoli agreed, Libya was not the place to look. "It is the boasted necessity [of the Italian government]," he wrote,

> to conquer lands to give vent to emigration. . . . I would think . . . it would be necessary to conquer places like New York or Buenos Aires where there is room for emigration. But a land like Africa lacks streets and means for survival (like southern Italy!!!) . . . The government can go ahead and conquer all of Africa, but the emigrants that want to go to New York and Montevideo will *never* go to Tripoli and Massaua.[50]

Vezzoli, Mazzitelli, and the other FSI syndicalists were right. Libya would never live up to Italy's expectations as a colony. After thirty years of state-funded colonization efforts, Libya in 1940 would have an Italian population of only one hundred ten thousand.[51] Rather than investing in southern Italy, the Italian government and bourgeoisie were squandering money on a fruitless war.

Despite its success in military terms, Italy's war in Tripoli was so ill-conceived and so clearly an effort to avoid facing severe domestic problems that Italian American syndicalists, and those Italian syndicalists who remained opposed to the war, had little difficulty using it to critique the Italian government and capitalist and religious leaders. But the war also evoked difficult ideological and cultural questions. The war compelled Italian American syndicalists to confront nettlesome questions about their relationship to their native country. As syndicalists, they stood as advocates of international working-class solidarity; nevertheless, during the course of the war it became clear that they remained attached to Italy in complex, and at times seemingly contradictory, ways.

As FSI members strove for a new relationship to the Italian Left— and to the American Left, once the Lawrence strike began—they were compelled to face the vexing question of what being Italian meant to them. During the course of the war Federation members expressed increasingly complex perceptions of their connection to their homeland and of patriotism and nationalism. In doing so they confronted the possibility of tension between their ethnic and class identities, between their advocacy of international revolution and the enduring importance of their ethnic affiliations and loyalties. This was an issue they would continue to face throughout their political careers.

At the outset of the war it appeared that FSI members were going to maintain a strictly internationalist reading of the war—that they were going to argue that workers should not be loyal to any country, but only to other workers. In November 1911, just over a month into the war, a story appeared in two installments in *Il Proletario* titled "The Tale of One Condemned to Death." The story, in all likelihood created by Fortunato Vezzoli, concerned an immigrant from Sicily. This character's father had been a soldier in Garibaldi's army during the struggle to unite Italy and free it from Austria's rule in the mid-nineteenth century. Even though the Sicilian had been in the United States for fifteen years, at the beginning of his tale he was still fiercely loyal to his homeland. He was working in an armaments factory along with immigrants from many other countries, including Turkey.

The Italian and Turkish immigrants had always left each other alone—until the war began. Once the war broke out, they began to harangue each other daily. Finally, one day a Turkish immigrant confronted the Italian immigrant directly about Italy's invasion. It made no sense for the Italians to invade another country, he pointed out, when conditions in Italy itself were so bad. Echoing the FSI's arguments against the war almost exactly, he pointed out:

> You want to rape the deserts of Africa while at home you have huge amounts of uncultivated land due to government inefficiency and capitalist greed. You have immense swamps to drain, nude people to dress; you have to deal with tuberculosis, old people need housing, children need education, and all the money needed to do these things is spent on the most vicious of crimes: war.[52]

To make matters worse for the Sicilian, the Turk's critique of Italy's government and capitalists was seconded by an Italian American radical. When the Sicilian appealed to the radical on the basis of his national heritage, he replied, "Neither you nor your Italianness interest me." Pushed to his limits by continued affronts from the Turk, the Sicilian shot and killed his Turkish coworker.[53]

But after the murder, the Sicilian came to understand that the Turk (and the Italian American radical) were absolutely right. The tale ends with him telling the Turk he killed, "[Y]ou could not be my enemy. You were a simple laborer like me. Your faith made you better than me. . . . I believed that the venture in Tripoli was a continuation of Garibaldi's war. How wrong I was!!! The atrocious deception that made me love my homeland has turned me into a murderer." His final request was that he be buried next to his victim with a sign above their graves that read, "Here lie two victims of capitalist society."[54]

This was an archetypal socialist conversion tale, and one that fits neatly with arguments scholars like Todd Gitlin have made about immigrants' involvement in Old Left movements. A vehemently patriotic worker realizes that he has more in common with workers of other nations, even those with whom his nation is at war, than he does with the capitalists of his own country. It also arguably fit neatly with FSI members' perception of how best to fight against the war. Even if Vezzoli did not actually invent the story—he claimed that he was recounting a story that had been told to him—it could not have served his and his fellow syndicalists' purposes any better. The editors at Il Proletario and the leaders of various sections of the FSI realized that something had to be done to combat the considerable support for the war among Italian immigrants in the United States. But like most of these conversion stories, it was very simplistic. The Sicilian worker at the beginning of the tale could not have been more patriotic. He murdered a man who insulted his country, and then protested that although he was being executed in the United States for his act, in Italy he would have been hailed as a hero. Yet by the end of the tale his conversion was complete—he wanted to be buried with the man he had killed.

Life, and the realities of patriotism and nationalism, even for class-conscious FSI members, were rarely that simple. The war in Tripoli forced Federation members to come to grips with the sense of Italianità that the immigrant in the tale rejected with such certainty and ease. There were two articles, in particular—one by Fortunato Vezzoli in May 1912, and another by Giovanni di Gregorio a year later—that attempted to define how patriotism actually operated in class terms. Both men rejected patriotism that was jingoistic, oppressive, or militaristic. "We are unpatriotic," Vezzoli declared. "[W]e despise every flag that symbolizes oppression and war. . . ." Syndicalists were unpatriotic, di

Gregorio explained, "[i]f with this word one intends blind obedience to those who govern a country... [and the] fanatical readiness to disembowel opponents that the laws... require...."[55] But neither man could dismiss love of his country entirely, and di Gregorio argued that the sense of patriotism could actually be something of value. He wrote, "Patriotism signifies love of country... love for the land where one is born and raised and for its inhabitants. What is important is that the patriot must direct energies to securing the moral, intellectual and material elevation of his country."[56]

Unfortunately, the ruling class had distorted the definition of patriotism, which had come to mean little more than support for wars and rulers and, for the wealthy and powerful, a means to personal aggrandizement. Those without power in society were expected to show their patriotism by not questioning their rulers. di Gregorio explained,

> Good patriots do not grumble over public money squandered by heads of state and their families. Good patriots do not oppose or evade the burdens imposed on them by the wars waged by ambitious politicians.... Good patriots do not strike to better their conditions or get angry with the police, the judicial system, the authorities, the press and the clergy that attempt to suffocate the workers' spirit of rebellion and to cut off any chance they might have for success.[57]

As di Gregorio pointed out, any efforts on the part of workers to better their conditions were often combated with charges of antipatriotism. Using examples from the United States, he pointed to efforts on the part of civil and military authorities during strikes in Paterson and Lawrence to label the strikers and the IWW as unpatriotic to undercut the support their public support.

But the patriotism of the ruling class was hypocritical. Vezzoli argued the point best in an article titled "I Senza Patria!" in which he declared that the ruling class, "who prefer foreign workers over national ones because foreign workers are more capable, can teach us some interesting lessons on how to be unpatriotic." Go into the homes of the capitalists, he proclaimed, and

> [y]ou will find columns of marble from Carrara, on the stairs and on the floors you will find Turkish rugs, on the walls paintings by Italian artists mischievously stolen from some museum. You will see Persian tapestries, French champagne and Chinese porcelain. You will smell French cuisine served by English or Swedish servants.... Parisian material cut from

material from London and Japanese silk for the women will help me finish my painting of the most loathsome international capitalist system.... For these people their country is even greater because they can go wherever the dollar will take them.... They have the liberty to go to [Lake] Como.... For the winter there are the barbaric countries of Africa that the civil governments have attempted to civilize so the capitalists, after their autumn weariness, might go to pass the frigid months in Cairo or Tripoli.[58]

The ruling class was patriotic only in terms that suited it—in defending symbols such as the flag and in supporting military conquests that more often than not would benefit them directly. But in more concrete terms, Vezzoli argued, it was the syndicalists and others like them who were the true patriots.

> We are the only eternal poets of internationalism that feel relieved when we hear some street musician playing a piece by Verdi or Mascagni. We are the ones without a country who spend our money in our friends' stores or even deposit it in the banks owned by our compatriots. We are the ones who smoke cigars from Mulberry Street and who eat the food cooked in Italian restaurants. We continue to swallow the things that drove us out of our own countries.[59]

Both men ended up qualifying or even dismissing their own brand of patriotism. Di Gregorio declared, "It is one hundred times better to be considered unpatriotic than to be a symbol of vile power."[60] Vezzoli concluded his piece by arguing that perhaps the syndicalists should make more of an effort to imitate the ruling class by being people without a country in fact as well as symbol.

What is compelling here is that although none of the Italian American syndicalists supported the war, it made them reexamine their feelings about their native country. Each writer ended his article by dismissing any kind of patriotic feelings. But clearly they did remain loyal to their home country in one way or another, and there were aspects of patriotism that they saw as potentially valuable. At this point, unlike during World War I, their ethnic and class identities, their manifestations of patriotism and internationalism, were not seen in absolute terms, or as necessarily mutually exclusive.

It is important to distinguish between the sort of patriotism and ethnic attachment Vezzoli and di Gregorio were discussing, and Nationalism, an ideology that was beginning to find support in Italy in the years

before the war. In December 1910 Enrico Corradini had held the inaugural congress of the ANI in Florence. In the late nineteenth century
and the early twentieth century, as Eric Hobsbawm has described in
Nations and Nationalism, a number of nationalist organizations formed
in countries throughout Europe.[61] The ANI was, like most of these associations, right-wing and xenophobic. Corradini argued that Italy needed
an authoritarian state that would engage in foreign conquests—such as
the war in Tripoli. He called for efforts to instill national pride in Italian
citizens. But that is not what was most compelling and, to the syndicalists, challenging about this organization.

At the ANI's inaugural congress, Corradini argued that Italy was
"morally and materially" a proletarian nation.[62] He argued that because
of Italy's social instability and poverty, and because it lacked what he
described as "moral unity," his country's standing internationally was
analogous to the position of the proletariat in the class hierarchy. He
explained, "There are nations in a condition of inferiority in relation to
others, just as there are classes that are in a condition of inferiority in
relation to other classes. Italy is a proletarian nation: emigration demonstrates this sufficiently."[63] His conscious cooptation of Marxist vocabulary was part of his blatant effort to appeal to Italian socialists, and especially syndicalists.

Though Corradini's assertion was largely cynical rhetorical maneu-
vering, there were potentially exploitable points of connection between
his movement and the syndicalists. As Giuliano Procacci has argued,
nationalism and syndicalism emerged in Italy at roughly the same time,
and for some of the same reasons. Adherents of both ideologies shared
contempt for Giolitti's leadership, and for the softness and ineffectiveness of bourgeois institutions in Giolittian Italy.[64] Corradini was an admirer of certain aspects of socialism, and he respected syndicalist leaders' efforts to instill a fighting spirit in the proletariat. At the congress he
proclaimed, "Just as socialism taught the proletariat the value of class
struggle . . . so we nationalists must instruct Italy in the value of the international struggle."[65]

Corradini's open appeal for an alliance with Italian syndicalists was
not entirely unsuccessful. He published articles in syndicalist Paolo
Orano's review *La Lupa* in 1910 in which he strove to draw connections
between the two ideologies.[66] During the war in Tripoli, Angelo Olivetti,

a prowar syndicalist, compared syndicalism and nationalism favorably, arguing that both "are doctrines of energy and will which accept neither the idea nor the practice of compromise."[67] The syndicalists who expressed interest in nationalism in the years before World War I were the exception, however. Arturo Labriola dismissed Corradini's ideas in an article in *La Lupa* titled "I due nazionalismi" in 1910. He argued, "To the nationalism of the contractors and the military industries is opposed cultural nationalism, supported by the syndicalists, which creates a feeling of nationhood among the workers and interests them in the conservation of the assets they have in common with the whole country."[68] Like his fellow syndicalists in the United States, Labriola recognized the reality, and even the utility, of a "cultural nationalism." Even after he decided to support the war, he still argued that Corradini's enthusiastic prowar stance was simply a cloud cover for fulfilling bourgeois interests.[69]

The syndicalists in the FSI had no interest in Corradini's form of nationalism. It was not even taken very seriously in the pages of *Il Proletario*. For example, Alberto Argentieri, an active member of the FSI in 1910 and 1911 before returning to Italy, undermined the nationalists by pointing out flaws in their ideological coherence. As an *Il Proletario* war correspondent he wrote regularly from Italy, keeping FSI members informed about the war and the home front. At the end of 1911 he wrote a scathing passage on a group of nationalists who were putting together a collection for wounded soldiers from their own province. "Here is what feelings of Italianness amount to in Lombardy," he wrote. "They don't have the mental capacity to hide their regionalism."[70]

FSI syndicalists also rejected Corradini and the Nationalists' efforts to revitalize Italians' sense of their own history. The Nationalists hoped that a victory would be a first step toward constructing a powerful "third" Italy that could compare favorably to ancient Rome and Italy during the Renaissance. FSI members and their correspondents from Italy often expressed a sense of despair about the state of Italian society and its standing internationally that could have come from Corradini himself. But they refused to accept the argument that the conquest of Tripoli would have any consequence. Argentieri again articulated most clearly what many FSI members writing in *Il Proletario* felt: "Everyone knows the Americans laugh in the face of those who speak in the name of Columbus, Dante, Marcone, and Garibaldi, those who think that they are admired by all of Europe after having defeated a few unarmed boats."[71]

Despite their opposition to Corradinian Nationalism, their attachment to Italy—their "cultural nationalism" in Labriola's terms—continued to exert a strong pull on them. Many of them still dreamed of living in Italy and felt they had been forced to leave. Nicola Vecchi inserted himself into the discussion during his short stay in the United States. Vecchi, a syndicalist from Modena, fled Italy after being arrested. He spent some of 1912 and 1913 in the United States and briefly edited *Il Proletario* with Edmondo Rossoni.[72] Vecchi wanted his fellow revolutionaries to return to Italy during the war. He wanted to return precisely to reclaim a homeland that was being usurped by nationalists and imperialists. "They don't want us there," he declared, "and that is exactly why we want to return there."[73] Vecchi intended to return to Italy once charges against him were resolved; his call for massive remigration must be understood in that context. Evidently, though, his appeal resonated with certain other FSI members. Giovannitti, commenting on his piece as editor of the paper, exclaimed, "I applaud Vecchi's plea with all of my heart. Let us go now!"[74] Giovannitti had left Italy about a decade earlier. Despite Vecchi's plea and his response, he never returned to the country of his birth. Nonetheless, Vecchi had touched an emotional chord in Giovannitti, raising an issue that was crucial to the editor and to many in the FSI.

If Corradini imagined Italy as an international power, Italian American syndicalists created their own image of Italy as a nation that lived up to the ideals of the *Risorgimento*.[75] This was the Italy they envisioned when opposing the war. The reference to Garibaldi in Vezzoli's conversion story had been a pointed one—one element of the Sicilian's conversion was his realization that the war in Tripoli had nothing to do with the struggles his father and Garibaldi had waged.[76]

Numerous articles reinforced this disparity during the war. One published at the end of 1912 addressed Gustave Hervé's expulsion from Italy. Hervé, a French syndicalist, was in the process abandoning the absolute antimilitarism and antiparliamentarism for which he had been known. Nonetheless, he still harkened back to a vision of a better Italy that FSI members shared. He spoke about coming to Italy to take part in an antiwar demonstration because of

a secret sympathy for my Latin sister, for Garibaldi's country. It was in Rome where Mazzini spoke for the first time in clear terms about the United States of Europe about eighty years ago. It was then an idealistic idea of a country where steam and electricity were not yet present, but the vision of a genius of a man. I was ready to go to that same Rome where Mazzini spoke for the first time about young Europe, proclaiming a European-wide anti-war movement.[77]

Hervé was arrested soon after entering Italy and forced to return to France. There, he related in the article, he came across another symbol of the *Risorgimento,* now living in exile. "In France," he wrote, "there is a man who fought alongside Garibaldi but is no longer allowed to step foot in Italy—the country that he founded with his own blood. He is a venerable old gentleman, but he would still know how to get things done in Italy. His name is Amilcare Cipriani."[78] Cipriani's exile, to Hervé and to FSI members, was further proof of how far Italy had strayed from the original vision of those who had fought to unite it. Cipriani had voiced the same opinion in an interview with Alceste de Ambris. He had vigorously denounced the war, proclaiming, "The piracy in Tripoli dishonors all Italians. I, who have fought to make Italy, am ashamed to be Italian."[79]

It was this vision of Italy that FSI members sought to recapture when battling to make Italian heroes their own in Italian American communities. Just before the war began, for example, Giovannitti, Rossoni, Raimondo Fazio, Joseph Ettor, Libero Tancredi, and several other FSI members staged a protest in Washington Square in New York City at the base of a statue of Garibaldi. Two New York *prominenti* were staging a patriotic celebration, but the Italian American syndicalists refused to relinquish their own claim to Garibaldi's legacy. They refused to leave the park and end their protest until Giovannitti and several others were arrested.[80] When Mario Rapisardi, the famous radical Italian poet, died, FSI members in New York who attended a commemoration protested that the wealthy members of the community sat in the front seats that would have belonged to Rapisardi's family, had they been there. "The radicals who attended," commented the *Il Proletario* correspondent from New York, "demonstrated that they belonged to that family...."[81]

Eric Hobsbawm has commented that nationalists and internationalists (as well as religious leaders) were attempting to reach and recruit the same population, the working class, in the early twentieth century and that at times workers would find appeal in each, combining these seemingly contradictory ideologies. He argued: "[T]he various principles on which the political appeal to the masses were based—notably the class appeal of the socialists, the confessional appeal of religious denominations and the appeal of nationality were not mutually exclusive. There was not even a sharp line distinguishing one from the other. . . ."[82] In the years before World War I, FSI members grappling with the relationship between internationalism and cultural nationalism in their own lives certainly found this to be true. Vezzoli and di Gregorio, for example, were perfectly content to lay their deep cultural attachment to Italy and their internationalist ethos side by side rather than worrying about reconciling them.

To their benefit, FSI members' profound connection to Italy and their vision of what Italy should be enabled them to enter the debate on the war in Italian American communities not just as radicals, but as fellow Italians. When members of an FSI local in New Kensington, Pennsylvania, took over a prowar meeting and demanded to be heard, and when Giovannitti and the others protested at the base of Garibaldi's statue, they were fighting against what they saw Italy becoming.[83] When Vezzoli and di Gregorio declared themselves to be more patriotic than the wealthier classes, they were fighting for the legacy and for the future of Italy. In doing so, they were fighting for a place, and even a position of leadership, in the Italian American community, as well.

The relationship between FSI members' ethnic and class identities, and the implications of their lingering attachment to Italy, were not the only issues they faced during the war. Although they were solidly opposed to Italy's conquest, the conflict compelled Federation members to evaluate the utility of violence in achieving their ends, and ultimately its implications for their masculinity. This issue would become all the more critical once the strike in Lawrence began.

As a matter of praxis, on the streets and during strikes, the FSI's perspective on violence was fairly straightforward. When Italian American syndicalists resorted to violence, more often than not it was both a matter of strategy and an exertion of masculine resolve and courage. On a theoretical level, FSI thinking on violence was less unified and was informed by a number of different sources—ideological, historical, and personal.

The potential value of violence as a means to transform society was an issue central to syndicalism as an ideology. Just before the war in Tripoli began, Georges Sorel published his seminal *Reflections on Violence*.

He justified proletarian violence, "something very beautiful and very heroic," as necessary to combat the force used by the state to buttress the existing order. Rejecting positivist notions about the inevitability of socialist revolution, he argued that syndicalists had to construct myths consciously—especially the myth of the general strike—to prepare workers psychologically to overthrow capitalism and the state.[84]

Sorel had been known to syndicalists and other leftists in Italy since the turn of the century, when he and Arturo Labriola first began to correspond. Indeed, David Roberts has argued convincingly that Sorel's earlier works had a greater impact on Italian syndicalists than his *Reflections on Violence*. They were influenced more, for example, by "Avenir socialiste des syndicats," which appeared in Italy in 1898, in which Sorel argued that labor unions would be the agents of moral development for the proletariat. Nonetheless, even if Italian syndicalists did not accept wholeheartedly Sorel's later arguments about violence and the psychological value of myths, they could not ignore the issues he raised. Roberts describes their vantage point: "The final expropriation of capitalism would probably be violent, and the proletariat would succeed only if more powerful than its adversaries. But violence was simply the moment of transition in revolution, the final test of proletarian capacities; it was not, in itself, creative."[85] While they might not have agreed with Sorel about the "creative" value of violence, in other words, and having dismissed the relevance of socialist electoral efforts, they all had to agree that the revolution would of necessity be violent. Italian syndicalists had already faced the violence of the state on several occasions, especially when the *carabinieri* intervened during the general strikes in 1904 and 1908.

They—and FSI syndicalists—were prepared for the inevitability of violent rebellion by a long history of armed struggle for liberation in Italy that predated the Italian Left. *Risorgimento* heroes such as Garibaldi and Mazzini had led armies to unite Italy and free it from occupation by external forces. The anarchists, who had led the Italian Left from the founding of the "black" international in 1864 until the founding of the Italian Socialist Party in 1892, had harkened back to these men when explaining their own perspective on violence. Malatesta explained, "Even if we had not become anarchists with the First International, it would have been enough for us to be democrats to adopt armed revolt against oppression.... When [the Italian anarchists] passed over to the International, they taught us nothing in this camp that had not [already] been learned from Mazzini and Garibaldi."[86] The anarchists themselves had led numerous armed insurrections in the 1870s. For Italian American syndicalists, violent opposition to oppression was at once a theoretical abstraction and a practice with deep roots in Italian history.

For Nicola Vecchi, his own immediate personal experience led to musings on the subject of violence reminiscent of Sorel. Vecchi, who collaborated closely with syndicalists Filippo Corridoni and Ottavio Dinale, had been involved in a violent demonstration in Modena in September 1911 against the war.[87] Once in the United States, he contrasted the violence of Italy's imperialism with that of the revolutionary workers' movement in Sorellian terms. "It [the war in Tripoli] is not our war," he wrote. "It is not our violence. Our violence, beautiful in its disarray, is something different. It is the violence of revolting slaves, of those who know neither a King nor a God, of those without a country."[88] During the war in Tripoli there was not the profound disagreement about the use of violence within the Federation that there would be during World War I. But discussing violence in abstract terms such as Vecchi's, FSI members were not of one mind.

Few in the FSI at this point spoke of the potential of proletarian violence in such glowing and romantic terms. Already during the Italo-Turkish war there were those who foresaw where a glorification of violence could lead the syndicalists. Giovannitti, for one, warned that it could lead to an indiscriminate celebration of violence for its own sake. There were signs that this was already happening in the syndicalist movement. This, he argued, was at the root of certain syndicalists' support for the war: ". . . in the haste of exaggerating proletarian violence [certain syndicalists] have united in sentimentalizing violence so that today there is no difference between brute force and conscious force—instead they praise all violence, from wherever it comes—whether it be the violence of an entire army against a tribe of malnourished cretins or the violence of one citizen against another."[89]

If Giovannitti was concerned by a growing tendency among some syndicalists to embrace any and all violence, there were some syndicalists who emerged from Italy's war with Tripoli even more wary of, and disillusioned with, violence than he was. Fortunato Vezzoli, who was deeply affected by the war, concluded that any syndicalist strategies that included advocacy of violence would be unsuccessful. He wrote, "Suffrage, strikes or bombs can not help us obtain victory.... The workers need to ... oppose the military.... We are too weak to arm ourselves. Therefore we must work to disarm [our enemies] with the force of our anti-militarist organization...."[90] Antimilitarism, not violence or the newly granted suffrage in Italy, was the best strategy.

These syndicalists' wariness of uncritical calls for violence did not translate into an unwillingness to meet violence with violence when they deemed it necessary. Even these Federation members insisted on the utility of violence. Giovannitti explained this in a piece explaining syndicalist doctrine he wrote for the liberal *Independent* just after the Lawrence strike. He noted,

> ... if Syndicalism does not openly advocate violence, as some anarchists do, it is neither because of a moral predisposition against it, nor on account of fear, but simply because, having a vaster and more complex conception of the class war, it refuses to believe in the myth of any single omnipotent method of action. Violence, moreover, being the extreme outward expression of a moral reaction created by outside situations, is objective and instinctive and not subjective and artificial.[91]

Giovannitti, in this convoluted passage, was expressing a perspective that unified FSI syndicalists in these years. They regarded violence and physical confrontation as viable, if not singular, tools, and as essential displays of courage.

If they were divided on the issue of violence in abstract terms, all of them understood the necessity of fearlessness and masculine resolve, of facing violence unflinchingly and even eagerly. Giovannitti's hasty dismissal of the possibility that fear informed syndicalists' attitudes on violence was reinforced by the numerous fistfights that broke out in the aftermath of FSI antiwar meetings across the country. The issues of violence and masculine resolve would also be central to the FSI's involvement in the Lawrence strike.

At Lawrence, FSI members would make a point of distinguishing themselves from the more cautious IWW. IWW leaders often resorted to the rhetoric of violence. The strikes and free speech fights they led, moreover, often resulted in violence. But the IWW rarely initiated violent confrontation. At Lawrence, as in virtually every strike they led, IWW leaders urged caution and restraint, arguing that the proletariat was no match for the military power of the state.[92] The FSI would be far more confrontational during the strike and the trial that followed it.

In the course of the war, during which the strike in Lawrence began, Federation members acted as transnational radicals. Like syndicalists in Italy, they were able to use the conflict to critique sharply the major institutions involved in the war—the state, bourgeois capitalists, and the Catholic Church—focusing particularly on their failures in southern Italy. But they distinguished themselves from their compatriots in Italy not only by refusing to be drawn into their bitter debate over the war and by criticizing, as immigrants themselves, Tripoli as a potential emigration outlet, but also by participating simultaneously in the Lawrence strike. In their critique of the war as syndicalists and as emigrants from Italy, they also faced the complex juxtaposition between their class and ethnic identities, revealing their ambiguous perspective on questions of nationalism and patriotism. They also confronted the nature and necessity of proletarian violence. If they disagreed on the issue in abstract terms, they found common ground in advocating violence as a strike strategy, and especially as an assertion of masculine resolve and courage. The class and ethnic imperatives in their lives would not create the dilemmas at Lawrence that they would during World War I. But their perspective on violence and their assertions of masculinity, as well as their uncertain relationship to southern Italian immigrant workers, would.

CHAPTER THREE

The Lawrence Strike of 1912

When Carlo Tresca arrived in Lawrence in May 1912, he was elated by the possibilities that the strike waged by unskilled immigrants and the defense campaign to free imprisoned strike leaders seemed to offer. Tresca, soon known as the "Bull of Lawrence" because of his tenacity and courage, declared, "To me Lawrence was the beginning of a new era; with Lawrence I joined the army of revolutionary workers for a real and greater struggle. With Lawrence I found a better place in the great trench of class war."[1]

Tresca's expectations were more than shared by syndicalists in the FSI. Still mired in frustration over the war in Tripoli, still hovering on the fringes of both the Italian American community and the American labor movement, FSI members recognized the Lawrence strike as an unprecedented opportunity to assert themselves and to assist their fellow immigrants. Their protest against the war in Tripoli brought to the fore Federation members' fluid relationship to the Italian Left and to Italian political culture. Their participation in the Lawrence strike simultaneously did the same for their relationship to the American Left and American culture generally. The strike, which erupted in January 1912, brought the FSI face to face with the American working class for the first time. Working with the IWW and aided by invaluable networks constructed by women across ethnic lines, the transnational Federation contributed to the spirit of innovation that characterized the strike. The FSI's impact at Lawrence far exceeded its numbers, and its success imbued Italian American syndicalists with a sense of limitless optimism about the potential of their ideology. They helped the striking immigrants create a movement inspiring to its participants and astounding to on-lookers at the time. Though ultimately short-lived, the Lawrence strike provided the impoverished, neglected immigrant workers who partici-pated with a sense of hope and dignity that had rarely been a part of their lives.[2]

FSI members' effort to put their ideology into practice revealed the promise, but also the boundaries, of Italian American syndicalism.[3] Dur-ing the strike, and especially during the trials of organizers Joseph Ettor and Arturo Giovannitti and striker Joseph Caruso that followed the strike, FSI members were again engaged in the process of reformulat-ing, often consciously and explicitly, the core elements of their identity. They retained and drew on their transnational connections to Italian al-lies. The FSI created links between the American and European working classes; not only would Italian allies support their efforts in Lawrence, but those allies would themselves be affected by what transpired in the textile town. Events in Lawrence also enabled them to establish a new relationship to the Italian immigrant population and to argue with re-newed vigor for their version of radical ethnicity. Facilitating commu-nication between the Italian strikers and the IWW, FSI members reached, briefly, the apex of their influence in their ethnic community. In the process, they took on issues central to their ethnic and class identities, namely the pernicious influence of regionalism among Italians and the potential promise of a general strike against the state on behalf of the imprisoned strike leaders.

In so doing they created a unique form of syndicalism, forged of ideas and strategies drawn from the political cultures of both Italy and the United States and from the cumulative memory of past labor strug-gles in both countries. It was markedly more anarchistic and confronta-tional than syndicalist tendencies in the IWW. It was also rooted in a masculinist ethos that united them through the shared imperative for courage in the face of violence. Their consuming effort to assert their masculinity was, however, a double-edged sword. It united them, but also impaired their ability to recognize the distinctive contribution women workers were making at Lawrence and in the American labor movement in general. The version of syndicalism FSI members forged at Lawrence had implications for their relationship, not only to women workers and strikers, but also to the American Left. Their participation in the strike and the trial revealed complex and varied attitudes not only toward the IWW, but also toward the American Socialist Party and American culture generally.

Lawrence was an appropriate place for FSI members' first meaningful engagement with American society. It was a city built by immigrants, and by the turn of the century it was defined by its immigrant cultures. The Irish were among the first to arrive, recruited by mill owners who needed roads and canals to transport their goods. Between 1860 and 1890, numerous mills rose on the banks of the Merrimack and Spicket Rivers, their work forces composed largely of English, Scotch, French Canadians, and Germans. As the city and the mills expanded, so did the need for cheap labor. Mill owners sent labor agents abroad to find people to brave the voyage to the United States. By the time of the strike in 1912, Lawrence was a mosaic of ethnicities—Italians, Franco-Belgians, Poles, Russian Jews, Lithuanians, Ukrainians, Greeks, Portuguese, Syrians, Turks, and Armenians all worked side by side, tending looms or combing or sorting cloth. Among the newest arrivals, the Italians were the largest group—by 1920, they would constitute almost half of the immigrant textile workers in the city.[4] Despite their numbers, however, Lawrence was an extremely hostile home.

The Italian immigrants FSI members worked to organize met with considerable contempt, often expressed in racial terms, as they sought employment and shelter in Lawrence. Even older immigrant groups such as the Irish complained that the Italians were ruining the city because they and other recent arrivals were forced by their poverty into overcrowded tenements.[5] Instances of abuse and scornful treatment of Italians and other new immigrants at the workplace abounded. Workers testifying at a congressional hearing held during the strike related how overseers in the mills swore at men, women, and children alike, called them "ignorant Dagoes and Hunkies," and treated them like "dumb cattle."[6] Community leaders in Lawrence referred to Italians as a race distinct from, and inferior to, themselves. When Joseph Ettor was arrested with Giovannitti, a Boston paper enthusiastically reported that "the passing out of Ettor means the ascendancy of the white-skinned races in Lawrence."[7]

This perspective on Italians extended well beyond the city limits. Southern and eastern European immigrants generally were often treated as suspect aliens before, and especially during, World War I. Certain social scientists defined these new immigrants as distinct races.[8] Academics alarmed by the influx of migrants placed the new populations above Asians and Africans in the hierarchy of race, but well below northern and western Europeans. Among the "races" of Europe, in other words, southern and eastern Europeans ranked at the very bottom. In a recent essay, James Barrett and David Roediger have argued that these populations were characterized as "inbetween peoples" racially.[9] Even among this scorned population, Italians, and especially southern Italians, were often singled out as the most contemptible.[10]

Southern Italians, like the antebellum Irish who were compelled to establish their "whiteness," were the most maligned migrants of their time.[11] Sociological works in the first decades of the century defined southern Italians as the lowest of the European races and advised Anglo-Saxons not to intermarry with them. One study conducted by a group of social scientists ranked southern Italians ninth among ten racial and ethnic groups in the United States; blacks were ranked tenth.[12]

Southern Italian immigrants at times experienced attitudes and treatment that were more comparable to nonwhite groups than to other European immigrants. Their experiences were linked closely—at times physically—to those of blacks. They were recruited to work on plantations as a spur to uncooperative ex-slaves. In the segregated South in the late nineteenth and early twentieth centuries, they worked side by side with blacks and their children often attended the same schools that black children attended, acts initially encouraged by, but ultimately alarming, to many southern whites. Southern Italians suspected of crimes were occasionally lynched, a punishment reserved almost exclusively for blacks in the United States. In the most famous instance, eleven Italians held in a New Orleans prison on suspicion of killing a local law officer were dragged from their cells and lynched in 1891.[13]

However—and this is a crucial caveat—Italians were defined in racial terms with respect to other European immigrants rather than to nonwhites. They were "inbetween peoples." Comparisons of Italians' experience of prejudice in the United States with that of African Americans or any other nonwhite group break down quickly. Italian immigrants did not endure the hardships that identity as a nonwhite person imposed in the United States. They were not denied the right to naturalize; in fact, contemporaries criticized them for not naturalizing quickly enough.[14] They were not segregated from the native-born American population, or from other immigrant groups, to the extent most people of African, Asian, and Mexican heritage have been historically. Italian immigrants did not face the same hardships as those defined clearly as nonwhite.

Within this context, authorities in Lawrence—and beyond—regarded Italian Americans in racialized terms. They had higher standing than non-Europeans, but they were seen as markedly inferior to leading citizens and public officials. The contempt with which Italian immigrants—and FSI members—were treated at Lawrence because of their ethnic identity would have an enormous bearing on how they would approach the strike and defense campaign.

The beleaguered but sizable community of Italian workers in Lawrence instigated the strike over a pay cut early in 1912. Massachusetts legislators had just passed a law decreasing the number of hours in the work week. Mill employers responded by speeding up their machines to make up for the lost hours and cutting their employees' pay. A committee of Italians, led by local activist Angelo Rocco, had anticipated the pay cuts. Meeting just before the pay cuts were announced, the committee agreed to strike if they went into effect. As textile workers milled about on January 12, unsure of how to react to the small, but nonetheless devastating pay cut, Rocco's committee swung into action. They went from mill to mill, calling out other workers, cutting long belts that powered the machines, and in some mills smashing motors that ran the belts and throwing bolts of cloth to the floor. By the end of the week, twenty thousand workers had joined the strike.[15]

The IWW had maintained a small and, until 1912, largely ineffective presence at Lawrence since Elizabeth Gurley Flynn's early efforts to organize there in 1907. Immediately after the strike began, Rocco sent a telegram to Joseph Ettor requesting that the IWW organizer come to Lawrence to lead the strike. Ettor was an obvious choice for Rocco—he had stayed at Rocco's house during an earlier visit in 1910.[16]

With Ettor's arrival, the IWW entered the battle in Lawrence, and on the East Coast of the United States, in earnest. Ettor, a second-generation Italian born in Brooklyn and raised in San Francisco, had been an IWW organizer since 1906. He, like the IWW itself, began his career in the West, working a series of jobs in San Francisco and organizing a lumber workers' strike in Portland, Oregon, in 1907. In its first years, the IWW was based in the western United States where it organized miners,

lumberjacks, sawmill workers, and dockworkers. By the end of the first
decade of the century, the union was attempting to spread its philosophy among immigrant workers in the eastern United States, and Ettor
was among those leading the way. Before Lawrence, he was involved in
helping striking steel workers in McKee's Rock, Pennsylvania, in 1909,
and in strikes of shoemakers and Western Union messengers in Brooklyn and other parts of New York City.[17]

By 1912, Ettor was well known among both immigrant workers and
their employers. Though his nickname was "Smilin' Joe," beneath his
cheerful demeanor was a sharp mind and a keen talent for organizing
workers that their bosses and the AFL dismissed as unorganizable. Only
twenty-six at the time of the strike, he spoke English, Italian, and Polish
and understood Hungarian and Yiddish.[18] A first lieutenant in the Massachusetts National Guard begrudgingly described Ettor as "a man of
unlimited physical vitality and a wonderful capacity for leadership. . . ."
Ettor "in a few days had become the idol of the working class of all
races, who believed every word of his incendiary speeches."[19] Small
wonder the workers in Lawrence greeted his arrival so enthusiastically.

Ettor realized how crucial the Italian workers would be to the strike—
they outnumbered the strikers in every other ethnic group—and so he
sent quickly for his friend Arturo Giovannitti. Giovannitti was just twenty-
eight at the time of the strike, but like Ettor, he was already a man of
varied talents. The *Il Proletario* editor was a gifted writer, orator, and
poet; during the Lawrence strike he would earn the unofficial title of
"poet of the working class."

Ettor's decision to send for Giovannitti indicated how important the
FSI was to the IWW in Lawrence. It also ensured that FSI members' encounter with American society would not be characterized entirely by
hostility. They would find Americans who, however marginalized themselves, shared much with them ideologically. Many Federation members
had felt an affinity for the IWW from its founding in 1905. Tresca had
celebrated its opening convention in *Il Proletario*. The sense of connection between the two organizations grew even stronger after the FSI
officially embraced syndicalism in 1911.

Even if Wobbly leaders usually defined their ideology as industrial
unionism rather than syndicalism, the IWW and the FSI shared much
in ideological and tactical terms. They rejected electoral politics as a
means to revolution, calling for direct action and general strikes by mil-

itant unions. Leaders of both believed in industrial unionism as the principle for organizing workers in the United States. This was not always the case for syndicalist unions in Europe, including those in Italy. Member unions of the CGT in France often organized around particular skills, and there were both industrial and craft unions in Italy that defined themselves as syndicalist.[20] The IWW and the FSI were firm industrial unionists because of the exclusivity and conservatism of the AFL hierarchy and many of its member unions—virtually all of them organized along craft lines—and the vast number of semiskilled and unskilled jobs held by Italian and other second-wave immigrants. The AFL at this point was controlled by Samuel Gompers, a believer in "pure and simple" unionism and in organizing skilled workers by individual craft. It was virtually closed to Italians and other immigrants.[21]

IWW leaders believed that their message would make sense to the immigrants in Lawrence. Not only were these workers largely excluded from the major labor federation in the country, but the majority of Italians and other immigrants in Lawrence (and in the entire United States) were also not American citizens at this time. They did not vote; the electoral struggle was irrelevant to them. The IWW's and the FSI's philosophy would allow these immigrants to use the power they had: to withhold their work, and to show the strength of their numbers in the streets. It was the FSI that would communicate this ideology—infused by an ethnic identity both imposed by xenophobic Americans and forged by historical memory and ongoing connections to Italy—to the already angry Italians of Lawrence.

Federation members were just as eager to bring syndicalism to their fellow immigrants and to the American labor movement as was the IWW. By its own admission, the FSI's syndicalism was still an untried theory, and by the eve of the strike in Lawrence, FSI members knew that their doctrine needed a practical test. It was especially apparent to those who had experienced syndicalist struggles in Italy. In November 1911, for example, Edmondo Rossoni, who had been in the United States for just over a year, gave an assessment of the IWW. He declared that "it is worth one thousand times more than the AFL. That is because it represents—even though it cannot yet practice what it preaches—the method of direct action and class struggle."[22] This assessment spoke to the FSI's sense of the still unrealized promise of syndicalism.

Just before the strike, Giovannitti had been serializing Emile Pouget's *Sabotage*, which he had translated from French to Italian, in *Il Proletario*. Pouget, editor of the CGT's newspaper, had written a treatise advocating workers' interference with the process of production as a means of protest. This included anything from studied inefficiency—"soldiering" on the job—to disabling or even destroying machinery. Giovannitti published sections from *Sabotage* each week from December 1, 1911, to January 19, 1912. In the last issue, Pouget's work was overshadowed by the announcement that Italian immigrant textile workers had cut belts on machinery in Lawrence mills and declared themselves on strike. The strike was the opportunity for which Federation members had been waiting.

FSI members declared that a "class war" was being fought in Lawrence; it was not hollow rhetoric. The confrontation was violent from the start. The mill owners relied on the help of members of the state militia to put down the strike. Twenty-five hundred soldiers, along with private guards hired by the mill owners, turned Lawrence into an armed camp. Soldiers were ordered to regard three or more people congregating in public as a crowd, and therefore subject to arrest. Strikers were arrested by the hundreds and were beaten if they tried to resist. Even *Il Progresso Italo-Americano*, with whose editor FSI members had been waging a running battle for years, protested the physical abuse the strikers were enduring at the hands of the police and militia.[23] Women strikers were not spared the soldiers' wrath. Two pregnant Italian women picketers were beaten so badly they miscarried.[24] The strategy of the soldiers, as one of them related it, was to "hit the women on the hips and arms. We don't want to break any woman's head."[25] One woman, Anna Lo Pizzo, was killed by a policeman's bullet early in the strike; it was her death that Lawrence authorities attempted to blame on Ettor, Giovannitti, and Caruso. Another striker, a Syrian named John Rami, was killed when a militia member stabbed him in the back with his bayonet.

Always the fear and anger of community leaders was mixed with contempt for the strikers, not only as workers, but especially as immigrants. One judge who regularly handed out the harshest penalties possible to the strikers explained, "These men, mostly foreigners, do not mean to be offenders. They do not . . . know the laws. Therefore the only way we can teach them is to deal out the severest sentences."[26] In other words, he considered the strikers too ignorant to fathom the implications of their participation in the strike; they could only be made to understand through punishment.

Faced with this fierce opposition, the strikers and the IWW created strike strategies that were among the most resourceful and inventive in American labor history. To overcome an injunction against strikers standing on picket lines in front of the mills, for example, the IWW and the strikers formed moving picket lines. If a dozen people were no longer allowed to stand in place to protest, IWW leaders said, then hundreds, even thousands, of strikers would circle endlessly around the entire complex of mills.[27]

The creation of interethnic trust and unity was crucial to the strike. Without cooperation and coordination between nationality groups, the strike could not have lasted a week. Most visibly, the IWW organized numerous parades and demonstrations. The logic was that the strikers would maintain their sense of determination if they could see the strength of their numbers regularly in the streets. During the parades the strikers further solidified their ties by singing. They sang songs they invented during the strike, calling each ethnic group out to the picket lines, and complimenting or goading respective nationalities according to their dedication to the strike. They sang the "Internationale" at every demonstration; the song rang out in as many as twenty-five different languages at a time. The Lawrence strike was, in the words of liberal journalist Ray Stannard Baker, "the first strike I ever saw which sang."[28]

Though the strikers sang class anthems as one, the range of languages made it clear that the IWW could not ignore their ethnic identities and assume that they shared an uncomplicated universalist class consciousness. Given these linguistic differences alone, the possibility for miscommunication was too great. Rather than organizing picketing, food, financial, and other necessary committees primarily by shop or by occupation, therefore, Joseph Ettor built them along ethnic lines—two delegates each from twenty-seven different ethnic groups. This ensured that everyone involved would have a voice during the strike. Nothing of the sort had previously been attempted.

Equally new to many of the immigrant strikers was the sense of dignity in facing American authorities that the IWW instilled in them, and the respect that the union demanded from opponents in Lawrence. At one point, a legislative committee headed by future president Calvin Coolidge walked into a meeting of the strike committee with their hats still on their heads. "Take off your hats!" Ettor commanded to the cheers of every striker present.[29] The IWW convinced the strikers that they deserved to be treated as equals by local and even national leaders.

A large proportion of the strikers were women, and as Ardis Cameron has argued, they were critical to the strike's success. Even before the strike, women from a variety of nationalities established female networks in the public and semipublic spaces of their crowded, multiethnic neighborhoods. These networks provided support systems for women without relatives nearby and for those forced by economic necessity both to tend to their families and to work for wages. The links they formed across ethnic lines meant that the women strikers in 1912 were not a chaotic mass waiting to be unified by strike leaders, as many labor historians have argued. Indeed, Cameron asserts they deserved most of the credit for creating ties among the strikers from various immigrant groups. These female networks also greatly facilitated the day-to-day work of the strike, from soup kitchens to picket lines to scab patrols.[30] Bill Haywood and the IWW admitted as much. Haywood acknowledged the central role that women across ethnic lines played in the strike years later, stating flatly, "The women won the strike."[31]

The FSI contributed to the innovation and resourcefulness that drove the strike, drawing on the memories and the accumulated experience of struggles in Italy. The strikers' greatest concern was the safety of their children. Even when working, the strikers lived hand to mouth; once the strike began, food was immediately scarce. Moreover, the soldiers in Lawrence showed little discrimination when they swung their clubs. The FSI and other Italian strikers who had experience with the labor movement in Italy suggested a "children's exodus." As numerous scholars, particularly Italian historians, have pointed out, in the old country it had long been a practice to send the children out of town during labor disputes. During the syndicalist-led Parma strike in 1908, for example, children had been sent to stay with sympathizers in Tuscany, Liguria, and Lombardy.[32] With the help of the FSI and the IWW, the first two groups of children left Lawrence on February 10 and 17. They were sent to homes in Connecticut, Vermont, and Pennsylvania; in New

York, the FSI and the Socialist Party organized a demonstration to greet a trainload of strikers' children.[33]

FSI members, witnessing the reception the children received, swelled with ethnic pride. One of them commented, "[W]e Italian radicals have given a totally Latin stamp to the demonstrations in the streets."[34] Throughout the strike, and especially the trial that followed it, FSI members recognized the importance of connections to their homeland and the implications of their ethnic identity. Indeed, these connections had a formative influence on how they conducted the strike and protest during the trial.

The experience the FSI brought to the strike, the cumulative wisdom of working-class struggles, enabled Federation members to have an impact far beyond their relatively small numbers. The children's exodus, in particular, an idea imported from Italy, constituted a turning point in the strike. When the children arrived in New York, their malnutrition and poverty drew national attention to the Lawrence strike for the first time. Margaret Sanger, then working as a nurse in New York, recorded her shock at their appearance. "They were pale, emaciated, dejected children. I have seen the children of other industries. I have worked in the slums of New York, but I have never found children who were so uniformly ill-nourished, ill-fed and ill-clothed. There was not a stitch of wool on their bodies."[35] The painful irony of barely clad children living in the country's leading textile city was inescapable. Dismayed Lawrence authorities tried to thwart the exodus. The next time a group of children arrived at the Lawrence train station, on February 24, the police were waiting. They waded into the crowd of frightened mothers and children, clubbing the women and trying to take their sons and daughters from them on the pretense that they were neglecting their children by sending them out of the city.[36] Even those unsympathetic to the strikers could not ignore such outrageous conduct by the Lawrence police. The national attention it received resulted in an enormous increase in financial contributions to the strikers, and eventually led to a congressional investigation of working conditions in Lawrence. Buoyed by additional funds and by public sympathy that the FSI had, albeit unwittingly, swung the strikers' way with the suggested children's exodus, the mill workers forced virtually all of their employers to come to terms within a month.

The victory, the culmination of a wave of uprisings initiated by un-skilled immigrant workers in textile mills and garment factories be-tween 1909 and 1912, was a tremendous achievement.[37] Never had so many immigrants from so many different countries been able to unite and win their demands. Eugene Debs, leader of the Socialist Party, called it "the most decisive and far-reaching ever won by organized workers."

The success was all the more impressive in that the strikers won de-spite the fact that AFL leaders not only refused to help them, but ac-tively worked to defeat the strike. The AFL's conduct at the Lawrence strike was reprehensible. The AFL-affiliate union there, the United Tex-tile Workers, was led by John Golden. Golden, a longtime enemy of the IWW, had come to Lawrence at the request of city officials to help end the strike. He had refused even to acknowledge that the IWW was lead-ing the strike. In an article titled "The Worst Enemy," one FSI member noted, "Golden said that if the *padroni* were to recognize the IWW, the AFL would do everything in its power to oppose any solution to the strike and would render impossible the lives of the workers. . . ."[38] While perhaps overstated, this assertion captured Golden's antipathy toward the IWW and the strikers. It also proved to FSI members that they had been fully justified in calling the AFL the "American Assassination of Labor."[39] Federation members—and in Lawrence, the strikers, as well—saw the AFL as part of the power structure they were fighting.[40]

The strike was not a victory solely for workers in Lawrence. It spawned a series of strikes against mills in nearby towns such as Lowell and New Bedford. By April 1, two hundred seventy-five thousand textile workers in the surrounding area won pay increases, and certain FSI members began to believe that the battle in Lawrence could spark a general strike in the industry.[41]

The general strike was at the core of syndicalist strategy and FSI members' optimism that a revolution was about to erupt. They believed that the awakening of proletarian consciousness would come through a series of ever larger, ever more confrontational strikes. These would cul-minate in general strikes large enough to halt production in key indus-tries and enable the workers in these industries to assume control of the means of production. Many in the FSI saw the spread of textile strikes beyond Lawrence, and the strikes being waged concurrently in other in-dustries, as proof of the viability of their strategy. The strike was more than a moment of opposition to unfair working conditions; it was a blueprint for the future. Edmondo Rossoni boasted,

> We won because we knew how to bring out the enthusiasm and solidarity in the workers of America . . . and reached them even though they were controlled by the *padroni*. It was an awesome struggle. . . . It will represent the principle of a new era. From now on the *padroni* will have to face a new army made up of rebellious workers. From now on the AFL has lost control of the workers. Today begins the historic story of the proletariat in America.[42]

To Rossoni and the other members of the FSI, the strike had proved that workers in the United States would no longer be willing to put up with the accommodationist AFL. Rather than the AFL cutting deals with the mill owners, Rossoni declared that "the workers instead saw at their side—through the work of organizers of the IWW—men who, rather than hurrying to finish the agitation, sharpened the hostility of the strikers. . . . The Lawrence strike wrote an unerasable page in history."[43]

This sense of optimism pervaded the FSI. Throughout May and June, writers for *Il Proletario* covered strikes being waged not only by textile workers, but also by hotel and maritime workers. By the end of June, Rossoni boasted, "It is the Hour of Revolutionary Syndicalism."[44] A month later, Albino Braida, one of the rare theorists in the FSI, voiced his agreement with Rossoni. Touting the effectiveness of the general strike, he announced, "The great strike is becoming more dreaded and fatal for the *padroni*. If tomorrow these strikes reach such a colossal potentiality that capitalism will not be able to tolerate the power we are gaining in the factories, then we will obtain in the not-so-distant future the instruments of production and distribution."[45] Together with the IWW, the FSI had introduced to workers in Lawrence, and in the entire country, a new, more confrontational, and more effective form of labor organizing. For the moment, there seemed to be no limit to what they could achieve.

In Lawrence itself, the end of the strike was not the end of the battle; the defense campaign on behalf of Ettor, Giovannitti, and Caruso that followed the settlement was even more momentous for the immigrant mill workers, the IWW, and especially the FSI than the strike had been. Early in the strike, on January 29, a series of parades had been organized by the general strike committee. When police tried to stop one of the parades, fighting broke out between them and the strikers. Shots were fired, and a striker named Anna Lo Pizzo was killed. Scores of witnesses identified a policeman named Benoit as the man who had fired the fatal bullet, but the police seized the opportunity to try to break the strike.[46] They arrested Caruso and accused him of killing Lo Pizzo, and they arrested Giovannitti and Ettor, who until that point had been leading the strike, for complicity in the murder. The trial of the three men would last for almost a year after the end of the strike itself.

To the FSI and the IWW, the defense campaign for the three prisoners assumed even greater importance than the strike. FSI members and their allies during the strike recognized that the true test of their strength, and of the ideology of syndicalism that they had worked to introduce in Lawrence, would be the effort to free the imprisoned strike leaders. In May 1912, two months after the strike had been settled, Carlo Tresca arrived in Lawrence to lead efforts to free Ettor, Giovannitti, and Caruso. He announced, "Now it remains to prove that practice can correspond to theory and to demonstrate that the union can truly assume the defense of its members."[47] Tresca was editing his own newspaper, L'Avvenire, and working among Italian immigrant miners in New Kensington, Pennsylvania. In all likelihood, he would have come to Lawrence sooner, but he had been in jail following a scurrilous libel conviction.[48] As he realized, however, it was the defense campaign, as much as the strike, that constituted the moment of reckoning.

It was a challenge to which the FSI in many ways responded ably. Federation syndicalists were instrumental in attempting to free the prisoners. In the course of their efforts, they not only reaffirmed their relationship to allies in Italy, but also assumed a leading role in Italian migrant colonies across the United States. In doing so, they confronted one of the most complex aspects of their ethnic identity—the ongoing problem of regionalism among Italians and Italian migrants. They also organized a general strike during the trial, once again drawing on historical memory and allies in Italy for the force of will to wage a strike against the state.

FSI members were inspired by the Herculean effort Carlo Tresca made to convert the enthusiasm the textile workers had shown during the strike into support for Ettor, Giovannitti, and Caruso. To get these workers, who had returned to work months before, back out into the streets, Tresca organized a series of meetings and events in the summer months. Unable to obtain a permit to meet from the police, Tresca rented a square surrounded by apartment buildings for one of the first meetings. To communicate to this ethnically diverse population, he recruited not only Elizabeth Gurley Flynn, but also speakers from a number of nationality groups to address workers from eight different platforms. According to local newspapers, the crowd swelled to thirteen thousand people. He managed to get a permit for one meeting by holding a funeral for Anna Lo Pizzo; though she had been buried months before, workers in Lawrence had not yet publicly mourned her death. According to Tresca, fifteen thousand textile workers marched to the cemetery to cover her grave with flowers. He next arranged bail money for Bill Haywood, who had been arrested for his involvement in the strike; Tresca then rented trains to take four thousand people to Boston to greet Haywood after his release from jail. Twenty thousand people in Lawrence saw Haywood's welcoming committee off at the train station; these four thousand became part of a crowd of twenty-five thousand people who heard Haywood speak at the Boston Common on September 14. The same day, two weeks before the prisoners' trial began, a meeting in New York City attracted fifty thousand people.[49] Tresca, working with the leaders of other nationality groups, continued throughout the summer and early fall to draw thousands of people out of the textile mills in Lawrence and to generate support for the prisoners in other cities.[50]

FSI members complemented Tresca's work by turning to their allies in Italy. Soon after the strike, IWW member Justus Ebert boasted that "the Lawrence textile revolt reverberated throughout the industrial world."[51] The transnational FSI lent truth to this statement by encouraging and reporting the active support of sympathizers in Italy, thus making the revolt in Lawrence truly an international phenomenon. Rossoni, who took over as editor of *Il Proletario* after Giovannitti's arrest, regularly corresponded with Italian radical papers. He sent progress reports on the strike and the trial, and urged them to do all that they could to help. Throughout the defense campaign, Rossoni and other FSI members cheered on supporters of the prisoners who were emerging throughout Italy, and especially in the Italian radical community. Every major city in Italy had an Ettor-Giovannitti defense fund. Leftist newspapers in Sestri Ponente, Corpi, Parma, Milan, and all over Italy followed the trial closely. In *Lotta Operaia,* published in Sestri Ponente, for example, editor Antonio Negro demanded Ettor and Giovannitti's release throughout the summer of 1912. Alceste de Ambris also issued ardent and repeated calls from the chamber of labor in Parma and in *L'Internazionale* for workers in Italy to take to the streets to demand that they be freed.[52]

Echoing De Ambris's insistence that direct action was needed, workers' groups in numerous cities attempted to start general strikes. For example, the chamber of labor in Bologna organized demonstrations in coordination with newspapers such as *L'Avanti!* and *L'Internazionale*. *Avanti!* editor Benito Mussolini called for Italian workers in Milan to burn down the American consulate if Ettor and Giovannitti were not freed. The editor of *Lotta Operaia* called for a mass walkout in Sestri Ponente, and Giovannitti's brother Aristede tried to organize a general strike in his hometown. In Modena, Giovannitti was made a candidate for the chamber of deputies in an effort to keep his name in the national press in Italy.[53]

One measure of the impact of the FSI during the strike and trial was that transnational connections between it and the Italian Left did not flow just one way; events in Lawrence reverberated in Italy. While Italian leftists were demanding the strike leaders' release from prison, they were themselves affected by the defense campaign. Many syndicalists saw the strike and the trial as a vindication of their ideology and even as a model for future actions. They saw at Lawrence tactics like the children's exodus they had utilized in Parma in 1908; they heard calls for revolutionary industrial unions and direct action that they had themselves voiced in strikes in Italy.[54] Anarchist Leda Rafanelli was convinced that the strike and trial, and the insurgence of the immigrant working class in Lawrence, could only inspire workers everywhere. She wrote, "[T]he victory will be much more than the freeing of the two men . . . it has more value to the entire proletarian cause. . . . It will be an argument of conviction as well as an example. . . . [W]e will know how and how much the bourgeoisie fears the working population's return to being a lion, after years of being like a pack animal; and [that will be] an example for our continual battles."[55] She urged Italian workers to follow the example to free political prisoners such as Maria Rygier, an Apulian syndicalist then facing charges in Italy. "I would like for, following the example, the Italian proletariat . . . to look towards the prison walls where Maria Rygier is in agony, and for that look to be as sharp as a blade."[56]

For Italian syndicalists and radicals like Rafanelli, Lawrence was an inspiration and an exemplar.

Federation participation in the defense campaign established its reputation not only among allies in Italy, but also among Italian immigrants in the United States. Edwin Fenton noted years ago that the strike and trial "united the Italian American community as no issue had done since the turn of the century."[57] The FSI reached its greatest prominence among its fellow immigrants; for the moment, the Federation's version of ethnicity was ascendant in the Italian American community.

This ascendance manifested itself in several ways. First, Giovannitti, even more than Ettor, captured the attention of the nation during his stay in prison. While in his cell, Giovannitti wrote almost a dozen poems that were immediately and widely circulated. The poignancy of one poem, titled "The Walker," compelled one writer for the liberal journal *Current Opinion* to write, "He has the soul of a great poet, the fervor of a prophet and, added to these, the courage and power of initiative that mark the man of action and the organizer of great crusades.... This jail experience of Giovannitti's has given the world one of the greatest poems ever produced in the English language."[58] In much of the Italian American community, concern for Giovannitti rose to the level of hero worship. One apocryphal story tells of how in many Italian immigrant homes after the strike, pictures of two men adorned the mantles—Jesus Christ and Giovannitti.[59]

Second, and this underscores the signal importance of ethnic identity to their efforts, the strike leaders garnered the support of certain *prominenti* in Lawrence (and beyond) through appeals as fellow Italians. One reason Tresca was considered such a good "fixer" at Lawrence was his ability to convince *prominenti* in town to help the mill workers and Ettor and Giovannitti—in essence, to advance the class struggle—on the basis of their shared ethnicity. He convinced an Italian banker, for example, to provide bail money for Bill Haywood, arguing that it would help free the Italian men being held in prison. "To Mr. Pitocchelli the two prisoners were not class-war prisoners," Tresca reflected years later. "They were victims of race prejudice. I let him talk."[60] Pitocchelli had apparently done well in the United States; he had accrued wealth and a degree of social standing. Nonetheless, he remained so keenly aware of the contempt with which Italian immigrants were regarded that he was willing to act against his own class interests to defend, not just them, but Bill Haywood, as well. Tresca appealed to a shared sense of *Italianità* again when convincing potential witnesses among the *prominenti*—including a Doctor Calitri, who would help Tresca sneak into Lawrence during the 1919 strike—to provide testimony favorable to the defendants.[61]

Tresca may have sounded cynical about appeals to a shared sense of ethnic identity when he mentioned that he "let [Pitocchelli] talk" about racial prejudice. But the sense of *Italianità* Italian American syndicalists brought to Lawrence was essential to their capacity to lead their fellow Italians. The IWW was eager to free the prisoners, but it was Italian textile workers, urged on by the FSI and Tresca, who issued the most adamant calls for action on the prisoners' behalf. They appealed to these workers not only in class terms, but specifically as fellow Italians who had to endure the slurs hurled at them in Lawrence. Federation members bristled when they and other Italians were referred to as dagoes. They warned protesters repeatedly, as Fortunato Vezzoli did, that "these police are racists and because of this are treating the prisoners with brutality."[62]

It was obvious that FSI members took great pride in having inspired the Italian American workers who participated in the strike and fought for the release of the men in prison. "It is an impudent lie," Rossoni declared, responding to an article questioning Italian immigrant workers' commitment, "that the Italians don't care about the cause to liberate Ettor and Giovannitti. In Lawrence, in all of New England, in all of America there are those who are giving major moral and financial support to the cause. They possess an enthusiasm and a passion that are unknown to other nationalities that don't have our temperament and our fervor for combat."[63] As Rossoni recognized, Italian immigrants' ardent support of Ettor and Giovannitti was rooted not only in their class identity, but also in their ethnic identity. Italians led the defense campaign because to them the prisoners were not only fellow workers, but fellow countrymen, as well.

In their appeals to Italian immigrant workers in Lawrence, Federation members worked to overcome regional distinctions between them that were evident even in the structure of the neighborhoods. One woman, a child at the time of the strike, remembered years later, "The Naples people and the Sicilian, they kind of stayed by themselves. The Sicilian took the section of Lawrence near the lower end, near the Everett Mills. And the Naple [*sic*] people took over the side after the Common."[64]

FSI members, in warning about racist police brutalizing Italians, and in comparing Italians favorably to other nationalities, worked to submerge regional identities within a larger Italian identity during the strike and trial. This effort was reinforced by the IWW strike leadership which, through its organizational structure and its songs, identified workers by their nation of origin.

The FSI found it difficult to eliminate regionalism—particularly distinctions between northern and southern Italians—completely. Most Italian immigrants in Lawrence were from southern regions, and evidence suggests that certain northern Italians in and around the FSI remained aloof from these workers they were striving to organize. Even while praising their tenacity and passion, for example, Rossoni referred to the Italian strikers as having displayed the "unchained wrath of our Southern mobs."[65] A relatively innocent comparison, his use of the phrase "Southern mobs" nonetheless did reveal the sense of distance he felt from the strikers, and even, in a sense, his perception of them as an undefined and unthinking mass. They were not the sophisticated workers that Rossoni had worked with in Milan.

Libero Tancredi was even more explicit about differences between organizing southern and northern Italians. Between 1908 and 1910, Tancredi had worked as an organizer in Wilkes Barre, New York and Chicago and contributed regularly to both *Il Proletario* and Galleani's *Cronaca Sovversiva*. Comparing Italian radicals in the United States and Italy, he observed that "the latter carry out their actions among the cultivated masses." He added bluntly, "[O]fficial radicalism within the Italian peninsula is primarily a Nordic phenomenon."[66] The former group, the Italian radicals in America, "instead, has in front of them the illiterate mass, encouraged to emigrate by a government that fears ragamuffin turbulence...."[67] Despite his condescension, he did not reject the worthiness of the strikers' efforts. Tancredi offered words of encouragement and support for the workers in Lawrence, expressing his "profound and sincere admiration—whether in defeat or victory."[68]

Nonetheless, the appearance of his disparaging view of southern Italians in an article that was supposedly intended to encourage the strikers revealed a great deal about how southern Italians were regarded by Italian leftists. Even the syndicalists, who had been openly critical of socialists for ignoring the population in the South, had themselves focused their attention on northern Italy. Tancredi articulated what was implicit in their actions. Southern Italians were "illiterate . . . ragamuffins" to whom leftists—and the Italian government—wanted to devote little energy. Only Tancredi, however, was this openly critical of southern Italians' capacities in the pages of *Il Proletario.*

FSI leaders did not have the luxury to make demeaning regional distinctions—nor did most of them seem to want to. Many Federation members were themselves from southern Italy. Tancredi's comments were more than counterbalanced by the fact that the most prominent of the strike leaders were southern Italians. Giovannitti and Tresca, both adored and defended by the Italian workers at Lawrence, were born in Molise and Abruzzi, respectively. The bonds they formed with the southern Italians during the strike and the defense campaign lasted for decades. Even if regionalism did not disappear completely at Lawrence, at times it could actually enhance the FSI's efforts to lead their fellow immigrants.

Their efforts to generate support for the prisoners culminated in FSI members, Tresca, and the IWW calling for a general strike to demand that the prisoners be released. Rossoni announced, "For the first time in the United States we will conduct a general strike—for the sake of Ettor and Giovannitti—and this will act as a formidable weapon that will demonstrate the immense force of the proletariat. . . ."[69] It was an audacious plan. Unlike the meetings and demonstrations during the summer, which had been held on workers' days off, this was a call for them to abandon the mills again.

More importantly, and to the consternation of IWW leaders, it was being directed against the state rather than private employers. Years after the strike, Elizabeth Gurley Flynn, who with Haywood had replaced Ettor as organizer for the IWW at Lawrence, still remembered the fervor of the Italian strike leaders and workers. Haywood publicly backed the idea of the strike. In September he declared, "Open the jail doors or we will close the mill gates."[70] But behind the scenes, he expressed trepidation to Tresca—he felt it was too risky to foment a strike that was not directed against a private employer.

FSI leaders—and Italian workers—were far more eager. Rossoni, in particular, presented a version of class struggle that was once again informed by ethnic identity. He was openly critical of the IWW's stance on the strike, accusing the union of passivity and uncertainty at a crucial moment.[71] The call for a general strike worried even Ettor and Giovannitti, who wrote a letter to FSI members before the strike urging caution. "It was a dangerous gamble, they felt," Flynn recalled, one "never before attempted in this country as far as we knew—a political general strike with demands directed not to the employer, but to the state. They felt that the risk of failure was too great, on the one hand, and the temper of the workers, particularly the Italians, too explosive, on the other. . . ."[72] The Italian strikers, led by the FSI and Tresca, downplayed Ettor and Giovannitti's advice. Flynn surmised, "It was evident that the Italian workers believed that since Ettor and Giovannitti were in prison they could not safely encourage a general strike, and it is likely that their foreign language orators managed to convey this idea to them."[73] They apparently did not need much convincing.

Despite Haywood's and the prisoners' hesitation, the strike was not canceled; in fact, it began early. It was supposed to begin September 30, the first day of the trial. Ettor and Giovannitti had been right about the temperament of the textile workers, however—they began to leave the mills by the thousands on September 27. Once again, Italian workers were the most visible and forceful of the participants during the protest strike, which stretched to three days. When police tried to arrest Tresca on September 29, his fellow immigrants formed a human wedge and forced him out of their hands.[74]

Italian immigrants outside Lawrence also answered the call for the general strike, once again linked to the prisoners by a shared ethnic as well as class identity. In Lynn, Massachusetts, five hundred shoe makers marched; in Quincy, twelve hundred quarry workers left work for a day; in Belle Vernon, Pennsylvania, five thousand miners demonstrated; in South Barre, Massachusetts, five hundred workers walked out of the Barre Wool Company to support the cause.[75]

The primary result of the FSI's increased prominence and of the very conscious test of its ideology at Lawrence was a uniquely Italian American—a transnational—form of syndicalism, which revealed both the potential and, ultimately, the limits of the FSI as a revolutionary organization. Italian American syndicalism, more anarchistic and violent than syndicalist tendencies in the IWW, was forged by experiences and influences in both the United States and Italy. The often fiercely masculine environment in and around the FSI, the enormous emphasis placed on courage, extended at Lawrence to an enthusiasm for violent rhetoric and confrontations. Italian American syndicalists' enthusiasm for violence and vehement antistatism, both sustained and supported by allies in Italy, distinguished the FSI from the IWW.

An aura of masculine bravado surrounded the Italian American syndicalists' presence in Lawrence. They had disagreed during philosophical discussions on violence while opposing the war in Tripoli. In Lawrence, they were firmly united by the masculine imperatives of ardor and fearlessness and by their contempt for those who did not meet these standards. Federation members routinely accused Lawrence authorities and mill owners of cowardice in their dealings with the strikers and their leaders. Their greatest act of cowardice, of course, was locking up Ettor and Giovannitti. Rossoni stated bluntly, "You are cowards. You conspire in the shadows. You are afraid of admitting you are thieves protected by the law. You fear letting the world know that you put to trial[,] you condemn and you kill by raising the gallows to safeguard your privileges and your rights."[76] In the FSI, there were few accusations worse than lack of courage.

To Federation members, bravery in the violent environment of Lawrence—in the face of arrests, death threats, and vigilantes—was of the utmost importance. According to his son, who was told stories of the strike by his mother, Giovannitti had been worried about his own safety in Lawrence when first called. His female companion, a Russian Jew named Carolina Zaikener, had urged him to go. When she offered to go with him, however, he said no. He would not assuage his fear through the reassuring presence of a woman. Giovannitti went to Lawrence alone and withstood nine months in prison facing a life sentence, defiantly translating Emile Pouget's *Sabotage* into English and writing poetry in his cell.[77] (Despite their enormous emphasis on courage in the face of physical confrontation, there was clearly room within the Italian American construction of masculinity at this point for artistic and intellectual expression.) Tresca remembered, "Giovannitti was more powerful and manly than Jesus"—a comment that reinforced the connection not only between Giovannitti and Jesus as icons during the trial, but also between masculinity and heroism.[78]

For Tresca and many FSI members, courage at Lawrence extended to an enthusiastic embrace of violent opposition to the imprisonment of Ettor, Giovannitti, and Caruso. Their perspective on violence as praxis was not simply an assertion of masculinity; it was also part of their strategy to empower their fellow immigrants. They had no hope of stopping the violent carnage in Tripoli; this confrontation in Lawrence was "their violence." Rossoni made this clear in an article titled "May First of the War." Addressing the mill owners and authorities in Lawrence, he blared, "Ours is an open war at high peak. We confess that to you. We will tell you to your faces: it is a war for the demolition of your system of propriety and of exploitation that we want."[79] He issued a call to workers in Lawrence: "If you are not cowards join us in saying: We want all who have been persecuted and imprisoned by those scoundrels to be freed. Freed at any price. Either everybody in prison or everybody free! . . . We will see who flees and who bravely stays at their place in the battle."[80]

Rossoni's call was taken up by others writing in *Il Proletario*, even by Fortunato Vezzoli, who had expressed hesitation about using violence during the campaign against the war in Tripoli. Again, abstract discussion was one thing; action in the midst of struggle was another altogether. Declaring that "as for the means—not one of them should be abandoned," Vezzoli called for unity among all radicals and among all Italian immigrants, but refused to dismiss the utility of violent confrontation.[81] Bellalma Forzata Spezia warned of an "explosion of anger from all the legions of the free and the honest" if Ettor and Giovannitti were not freed.[82] Forzata Spezia was one of the few women in the movement, and by 1912 a regular contributor of articles and poems to *Il Proletario*.

Allies in Italy reinforced FSI members' calls for confrontation, and for violent opposition to free the imprisoned strike leaders. In mid-September, preparing for the beginning of the trial, Rossoni and the FSI put out a special issue of *Il Proletario*. They printed fifty thousand copies of the September 14 issue, and sold them in blocks of from one hundred to five thousand copies. The special issue, published the day of the mass meetings in Boston and New York, two weeks before the trial began, contained messages of support from syndicalists and other radicals in the United States and Europe. The feature articles were urgent, angry pieces written by Italian radicals. Alceste De Ambris, Rossoni's longtime friend, goaded the strikers, telling them they were being too sentimental and not recognizing what could happen to the men in jail. "We must look to our workers' solidarity to find a means of defense," he declared, "learning to oppose violence with violence, reprisal with reprisal."[83] Leda Rafanelli, who had contributed articles in the past to both *Il Proletario* and *Cronaca Sovversiva*, issued a call to arms to the strikers. She wrote, "[C]omrades, the wish to be able to win this battle that is yours… moves you towards war. You will know how to face the bourgeoisie and impose your will. The bourgeoisie is vile to the population and it trembles when the winds of the storm start blowing. Shake violently under the gust and bring it to the ground."[84] The message from these radicals in Italy was unmistakable. The FSI and the strikers had shown their strength against mill owners during the strike. They shouldn't be afraid to use it, these Italian radicals insisted, in whatever way possible to free their imprisoned leaders.

Their stance on violence, reinforced by fellow radicals in Italy, was not simply rhetorical flourish for Tresca and for FSI members. Tresca later recalled that during the trial, Lawrence remained an intensely violent environment. Nonetheless, he led demonstration after demonstration in the face of constant threats against his life and pleas for caution from Flynn and Haywood. Vigilante groups opposed to the continuous demonstrations roamed the streets at night. When a Polish IWW member was found slain near his home one morning, Tresca was sure that vigilantes were responsible. Over Haywood's objections, Tresca organized a funeral march, despite the fact that he and Haywood were both worried that the march would be attacked by vigilantes and the police.

The march went smoothly, but threats against Tresca and Haywood increased. Haywood began receiving death threats almost daily, and Tresca began carrying a gun when he walked the streets of Lawrence. He later said, "It was civil war, and in war time guns play their part."[85] In one instance, recounted with relish in his autobiography, he walked the streets of Lawrence, armed with a pistol, staring down vigilantes after newspapers had reported he had been chased out of town.[86] In mid-October a friendly reporter informed Haywood that vigilantes were planning to lynch him and Tresca the next day. The two men spent the night in an Italian section of Lawrence called Il forte Makalle, which was known for being hostile to and impenetrable by the police. Haywood slept surrounded by six young armed Italians. Tresca summoned allies from nearby towns to help protect him and Haywood; the Providence group had a shoot-out with men already protecting the protest leaders before they were identified as friends. By that point sympathizers among the Italian immigrants in surrounding towns were arriving, prepared to take the offensive and spurred on by a flier declaring, "Come and carry a gun with you. Come to Salem to get Ettor and Giovannitti out." When someone released the flier to the newspapers, the atmosphere around the courthouse reached a fever pitch. Finally, Fred Moore, lawyer for the prisoners, convinced Tresca to intervene. Certain that they would fare poorly in an armed battle, he talked the armed protesters into giving up their arms—"on the floor of Mr. Moore's office guns lay in great number," he later recalled—and declaring a truce.[87]

The FSI's willingness to face and even encourage violent confrontation, forged by its members' experiences at Lawrence and bolstered by allies in Italy, distinguished it from the IWW. Tresca and FSI leaders had to coax and cajole IWW leaders into supporting the demonstrations and especially the general strike for Ettor and Giovannitti. During the trial, their perspective toward violence constituted one of the distinctive elements of Italian American syndicalism.

This was especially true since the IWW was consciously trying to downplay its reputation for violence and extremism in Lawrence. "Real Labor War Now in Lawrence," the *New York Times* had warned when the IWW arrived at the start of the conflict. Mill owners tried immediately to take advantage of this reputation. Before Ettor was arrested, certain mill owners hatched a plot to implicate him and other IWW leaders in plans to blow up several local institutions. According to Angelo Rocco, the plot was discovered because John Breen, a member of the Lawrence school board and son of a former mayor, had left his name and address on one of the packages of dynamite.[88]

But from the beginning of the conflict, IWW organizers discouraged the strikers from using violence to gain their ends. Ettor told the strikers, "By all means make this strike as peaceful as possible. In the last analysis, all the blood spilled will be your own."[89] To a large extent, this advice was heeded. The strikers did not abstain from physical confrontations completely. Women strikers confronted and often assaulted scabs and their relatives. Numerous women were arrested for battling with the police, throwing red pepper at them, and even swinging an occasional lead pipe. Nonetheless, these women's exploits paled in comparison to the deaths of Anna Lo Pizzo and John Rami and the beatings the children suffered when trying to leave town. In celebrating the strikers' victory, Haywood was able to exclaim, "Passive, with folded arms, the strikers won."[90]

After the strike was over, the IWW described the strike in terms that would appeal to the mainstream in the United States. In *The Trial of a New Society,* Justus Ebert contrasted the dismal living conditions of the mill workers with the opulent living standards of the mill owners, concluding that "the benefits of industrial living go not to [the strikers], but to the Woods, Turners, et al., who live in wasteful extravagance upon their merciless exploitation, regardless of common decency and in defiance of the social spirit of the times."[91] It was the callous mill owners, not the strikers or the IWW, who were out of step with American society.

In contrast to the IWW, FSI members had little interest in presenting themselves in palatable terms to the American mainstream. Throughout the defense campaign, they were much more openly antistatist than their allies in the IWW and remained profoundly distrustful of the court's capacity to render a fair verdict. This was another marked difference between the two organizations at Lawrence. In part because of continued contact with anarchists and syndicalists in Italy, in part because of their own experience in the textile town and in the United States generally, the FSI was more anarchistic than the IWW.

Haywood and the IWW had been hesitant about the demonstrations on behalf of Ettor, Giovannitti, and Caruso, which they recognized as protests against the state itself, but Federation members had no qualms about presenting the battle in such stark terms. In mid-April, just after the case was sent to a grand jury, an article by syndicalist Giacomo Li Causi, who had arrived in Brooklyn about a year earlier from Marsala in Sicily, appeared in *Il Proletario* titled "The State Sustains Capitalism: A Proposal on the Lawrence Strike."[92] The article was a direct assault on the state. The author exclaimed, "[T]he state makes martyrs, it is the executioner of the proletarian class.... Capitalism apparently has in the state an extremely powerful guard dog."[93] The state had intervened against the workers in Lawrence, he explained, before the bosses had even asked for help. The police arrested Ettor and Giovannitti instead the policeman who actually shot Anna Lo Pizzo, because they wanted to defeat the strike. Li Causi elaborated, "Because Ettor and Giovannitti were the leaders, the souls of the strike, and since the strike had to suffocate, [the police] bit it in the head." Only one alternative was left. "Nothing remains for the proletariat to do but to combat the state without rest—until it is demolished."[94] If the state refused to protect downtrodden workers, and even lent unsolicited support to those who continued to oppress them, Li Causi argued, the only option was to enlarge the battle to include it.

Though no other Federation members issued such bold challenges, the pages of *Il Proletario* were filled with distrust of the state and especially of the courts. Tresca expressed the wariness of the judicial system that FSI members shared simply and clearly soon after his arrival in Lawrence: "[T]he judges are the defenders of capitalist exploitation, of the *padroni*'s rights."[95] As Albino Braida pointed out, the state simply reinforced the will and power of the capitalists. "Social force," he wrote, "does not derive from the ballot-bearing crowd that goes every year to the polls, but rather from an even smaller minority than this, the capitalist class. . . . To vote outside of the factory where the vote doesn't touch the point of social force is not worth a thing. It is always he who has the factory that also has the power to make laws. Politics by itself is nothing," he concluded, "it reflects only the economic force that it has behind it."[96] That was the reason that revolutionary industrial unionism, syndicalism as manifested in the United States, was the only effective strategy to fight for power in society. That was also why the FSI and Tresca organized protests in the streets and, ultimately, the general strike for Ettor and Giovannitti. These were the only ways that capitalists and the state could be effectively combated.

The FSI's antistatism at Lawrence, like its stance on violence, was encouraged and augmented by radicals in Italy. The articles Italian anarchists like Tancredi wrote for *Il Proletario* reinforced FSI members' arguments that the state and capitalism were interdependent in the United States. Tancredi delivered a scathing indictment of the role of the state in the United States in an article titled "The Glory of Disgrace." "America," he asserted, "is the most genuine land of capitalism and thus the most showy, [and it] lacks cultural and historical tradition to smooth off its edges. Its state was born on the grounds of capitalism—not inherited, as it was in Europe. This organism is the slave of absolute capitalism. . . ."[97] Because capitalism had not emerged from a feudal system as it had in Europe, the state and capitalism in the United States were inextricably intertwined. Alceste de Ambris urged the protesters to abandon their ingrained reverence for the courts and judges. "In reality," de Ambris insisted, "[the judge] is nothing more than the most refined and hypocritical hired killer of the class that pays him."[98] Despite the façade of objectivity and fairness that judges might present, they were beholden to the capitalist class.

FSI members' extreme distrust of the state, one of the unique elements of its syndicalist vision, was not rooted solely in their ties to syndicalists and anarchists in Italy; it was also a logical outgrowth of their own experience as Italian immigrants during the strike. Federation members had seen their fellow immigrants sentenced time and again as severely as possible, solely on the basis of their ethnicity. Italian men and women were regularly given six months in jail for "rioting" and one-hundred-dollar fines for "intimidation" by a judge who thought that "foreigners" needed to be taught the laws of the United States.[99] What chance did Ettor, Giovannitti, and Caruso stand to receive a fair trial on murder charges? It was a question Italian radicals had faced in the past, and which they would face three times within a single decade, with Tresca's arrest on fabricated murder charges in 1916 and with Sacco and Vanzetti's arrest in 1920.

Unlike the Sacco and Vanzetti case, however, the trial of Ettor, Giovannitti, and Caruso did not end tragically. The general strike organized by the FSI and given cautious endorsement by the IWW, the international outpouring of support for them, and the flimsiness of the state's case resulted in acquittals for all three men in November 1912.

The Federation's particular version of syndicalism contributed to victory in the strike and trial, but it also had decidedly less advantageous results. Italian American syndicalists' unflinching courage in the face of violence, and their strident antistatism, were essential to their leadership of the protest. But they did not even recognize women's participation at Lawrence, much less come to grips with the implications of that participation. The strike and trial also had complex—and at times dire—implications for FSI members' relationships to the American Left and American society more broadly.

Despite their success in creating support for the prisoners, Federation members' masculine ethos, particularly their perspective on women, cast a shadow over their achievements at Lawrence. It also ultimately limited the potential of the Federation's efforts in the years before World War I. Most FSI members—most Italian American leftists—found it difficult, if not impossible, to perceive women as fellow workers. Vecchi had described the revolutionaries' "cult of the woman" in the letter he wrote to the queen of Italy to protest the war in Tripoli. Women, in this construction, could be mothers, sisters, or daughters—but little else.[100]

This was the world view, not just of FSI members, but also of the Italian American socialists analyzed by Virginia Yans-McLaughlin in her work on Italian immigrants in Buffalo. Some emphasized the need to direct propaganda efforts toward the women in the Italian American community; certain of them were outspoken advocates of birth control as a potential aid to women. But ultimately these socialists chose not to challenge the traditional roles assigned to women. "The Socialist emphasis on motherly and wifely roles," Yans-McLaughlin noted, "indicates both an insensitivity to the 'woman question' and a political concession to immigrant conservatism."[101] Either out of shared belief or a decision not to challenge tradition, Italian American socialists in Buffalo accepted these circumscribed roles for women in their community.

This attitude pervaded the FSI. Giovannitti, for example, wrote an article in June 1911 titled "The Woman and the Gallows." It concerned a woman condemned to death in Canada despite the fact that she was pregnant. Giovannitti objected to the sentence, arguing that the woman should have her child before she was killed. He closed the article with a more general statement on women's rights. Insisting "I am not a feminist," and admitting to ambivalence on the issue of the "so-called emancipation of woman," he concluded, "but . . . a woman who has five children has the rights of five lives and . . . one who doesn't have the right to make a law doesn't have the duty to submit to it either."[102] Couched in a critique of women's lack of suffrage that fit comfortably with the syndicalist dismissal of electoral politics was the same perspective Vecchi expressed. To the extent that women had a claim to any rights in society—the five lives Giovannitti enumerated included each child's, but not her own—they were derived primarily, if not solely, from their roles as wives and, especially, as mothers. Raimondo Fazio dismissed the issue of women's suffrage even more abruptly. In an article titled "Women, Suffrage, and Industrial Organization," he characterized the suffrage movement as a bourgeois distraction from the far more pressing need to organize effective unions.[103] This was not a surprising perspective from a syndicalist. It was significant, nonetheless, that this was the only article of any length focusing on women that appeared in *Il*

Proletario during the entire strike and trial. If FSI members could not perceive the utility of granting women suffrage, neither could they see the merit in addressing their potential as union members.

The dominant image of woman as wife and mother was counterbalanced by Italian American leftists' frequent depictions and pursuit of women as objects of sexual desire or conquest. Many prominent Italian American leftists—often young men in their twenties—had (and at times nurtured) reputations as ladies' men or womanizers. Anarchist Luigi Galleani, known for his sartorial splendor, was also reputedly known for working his charms on the women (including, on occasion, the wives of fellow immigrants) in Barre, Vermont. Giovannitti, according to Haywood, had been reluctant to come to Lawrence when first called because he hadn't wanted to leave his "sweetheart."[104] Tresca had been in trouble more than once, both with the FSI and with the law, for his dalliances with (often very young) women. He began a passionate affair with Elizabeth Gurley Flynn at Lawrence, made famous when the police discovered a series of inscriptions he wrote to Flynn inside a copy of Gabriele D'Annunzio's *Maiden on the Rocks*. He left his wife, Helga, who finally sued for divorce years later. Tresca eventually had an affair, and a child, with Flynn's sister.[105]

There is evidence, beyond Tresca's and Galleani's apparent infidelities, that at least one member of the FSI considered adultery a virtually inevitable result of a normal man's sex drive. Syndicalist G. A. Andaloro presented this perspective in an article Giovannitti published in *Il Proletario* in December 1911 titled "Proletarian Tragedies." The tragedy in this case was that an Italian immigrant worker had been robbed of his life's savings while on his deathbed in a Philadelphia hospital. The circumstances of the theft were truly remarkable. The worker, "pushed by bourgeois greed to distance himself from his wife and family," had committed adultery and caught a venereal disease. "In one of those moments in which the lunacy of sex perverts reason," Andaloro lamented, "he fell in the whirlpool that sweeps away adolescence. He, like many other workers whose most glorious instinct is to find the channels of love open, was punished for his weakness." Worse, he couldn't figure out who to turn to for help in finding a cure. "In the orgasm of his own moral responsibility towards the company he did not know how to fight the disease he [had] acquired, nor where to turn for advice." Finally, he registered in a hospital under an alias to avoid discovery by his wife. But he had waited too long, and died before the disease could be treated. When his friends arrived, his belongings—a gold chain and two hundred dollars—were gone. "His wife is now alone in raising their children," Andaloro concluded indignantly, "because the greedy bourgeois hospital staff decided to keep the money that he worked so hard to earn. When will it end?"[106] Andaloro's outrage was directed at the "greedy bourgeois" hospital workers for leaving the worker's wife and family impoverished. The worker's sexual appetites went unquestioned, since these appetites were like those of "many other workers whose most glorious instinct is to find the channels of love open." This limited view of women's roles and capacities—wife and mother or sexual object— had a lengthy history in the FSI and the Italian American Left.

In practical terms, at Lawrence and in other strikes in which the FSI participated, Federation members were all but blind to the implications of women's involvement in labor activism. Certainly, FSI members—not to mention Carlo Tresca—respected and admired Elizabeth Gurley Flynn, a crucial presence at Lawrence. Indeed, her articles were often serialized in *Il Proletario.* The women strikers themselves, however, were seemingly invisible to FSI members. As Arturo Caroti had discovered during the garment workers strikes in New York, Italian American women were very difficult to organize in the years before World War I. They were often vital to their families' economic survival, and usually faced cultural and religious imperatives against labor activism.

Ardis Cameron's argument about the importance of women in winning the strike in Lawrence and Haywood's acknowledgement of their centrality are therefore all the more compelling in this context. Several scholars have analyzed the gender politics of the IWW and argued that it, too, was characterized by a masculinist ethos.[107] Nonetheless, Haywood recognized that women workers were not only actively engaged in the strike, but vital to its success. In contrast, FSI members scarcely realized that women were involved at all. Women strikers received scant attention in *Il Proletario.* Giovannitti had run a two-part piece titled "Women and Syndicalism" by Flynn in the paper before the strike. But the only time women in Lawrence were addressed specifically during the entire strike and trial was in a condescending filler piece titled "Women Praying," which mocked a group of women seen praying for Ettor and Giovannitti's release.[108]

At Lawrence, the FSI was not only plagued by its perspective on women workers. It was also dragged back into the squabbles of the American Left as it became increasingly intolerant of the more reform-minded Socialist Party's efforts there. As the FSI had confronted the state more stridently and outspokenly, prodded in that direction by Italian anarchists and syndicalists, its relationship with the SPA (and with Italian American socialists, which had never been very good) became openly antagonistic. Though FSI members' syndicalism was not identical to the IWW's revolutionary industrial unionism, they never ceased to consider the IWW the best hope for workers in the United States. As relations between the Socialists and the IWW deteriorated during the defense campaign, the FSI was drawn so deeply into the conflict in defending its ally that it confronted the Socialists even more angrily than the IWW itself did.

FSI members had followed relations between the IWW and the SPA since before the strike and, embittered by their own past experiences in Italy and within their own organization, had concluded that cooperation between the two organizations could not last. In this way, FSI members' ties to Italian political life led to a stand that would ultimately work against them. Days before the strike began, Giovannitti wrote a prescient cautionary article titled "The Crises in the Socialist Party" in *Il Proletario*. "Recently in the Socialist Party," Giovannitti wrote, "a revolutionary stream favorable to the IWW has appeared. If this stream . . . continues to grow, [it] will eventually provoke a crisis."[109] He realized that the problem was that the socialists and the revolutionary industrial unionists in the SPA were advocating increasingly divergent tactics. He explained, "The question that needs to be resolved is . . . between politics and anti-parliamentarianism"—between socialists, who advocated revolution through the ballot box, and IWW advocates, who called for revolution through direct action at the work place. He warned, "This minority group [i.e., the Wobbly elements] will drag the Socialist Party into the open battlefield."[110]

Recalling the conflict between syndicalists and socialists in Italy, Giovannitti sensed that the battle would be traumatic, especially for the relatively young SPA. He noted:

> The Socialist Party of America is going through roughly the same situation that the Italian Socialist Party went through six or seven years ago that provoked their break from the syndicalists. The only difference

is that the Italian Socialist Party was already mature and . . . was better able to resist the crisis. The American Socialist party has no force of cohesion and will probably not survive the collision of ideas unharmed.[111]

Given this dire assessment of the SPA's future, it was not surprising that Federation members regarded the socialists warily at Lawrence.

The Socialist Party supported the strike, but never won the FSI's trust. Party members collected money for the strikers, and the socialist daily, the *New York Call,* donated profits from a special issue on the strike to the strike fund. Socialist Congressman Victor Berger issued the call for a congressional investigation into police violence during the children's exodus and requested that a delegation of strikers be sent from Lawrence to Washington to testify. But despite the strike leaders' decision to honor Berger's request, according to *Il Proletario,* delegates were expecting little more than to face a "parliamentary investigation."[112] Raimondo Fazio, by 1912 both an IWW organizer and an FSI member, was among the delegates. He argued with socialists all the way to Washington, questioning the value of the committee hearings. He thought the committee should have come to Lawrence to witness what was happening to the strikers instead of remaining in Washington. "Nothing will be resolved," he told them. "They can't force the *padroni* to adhere to any rules."[113] His opinion was shared by other delegates. "We came here," one of them declared, "to make sure that the political socialists do not miserably drown the great proletarian battle that represents such a great point in the history of the struggle of America's working class."[114] They were going to Washington precisely because of their distrust of Berger and the investigative committee. The tension between the FSI and the SPA was exacerbated by the deplorable conduct of the AFL at the strike because in the eyes of FSI members, parliamentary socialism and support for the AFL went hand in hand.[115]

There were other reasons for the FSI's lack of faith in the Socialist Party. At the same time the SPA was helping the strikers, there were socialist sections working to remove Haywood from the National Executive Committee of the party, and even to remove the IWW supporters from the party itself. Haywood had angered certain Socialists in December 1911 when he endorsed a vaguely defined policy of sabotage in the work place.[116] One socialist section had proposed a resolution at that point to expel him. But no one was willing to second such a resolution until Haywood, angered by the beating of children by the Lawrence police, firmly rejected electoral politics, declaring, "I will not vote again."[117]

The repercussions were felt just two months later at the Socialist Party convention in May. A resolution was introduced calling for the expulsion of any party member who opposed electoral politics or advocated sabotage or violence during strikes. Any doubts that this resolution was directed against the IWW were dispelled by Victor Berger. Defending the resolution, he declared, "[T]he trouble with our party is that we have men in our councils...who use our political organization—our Socialist Party—as a cloak for what they call direct action, for IWWism, sabotage and syndicalism. It is anarchism by a new name...." He concluded, "The IWW can go to hell."[118]

Haywood was soon charged with having violated this resolution; in February 1913 he was recalled from the party's National Executive Committee. Haywood's removal did not result in a mass exit of revolutionary industrial unionists from the Socialist Party. Many of them preferred to continue the fight within the organization. But the resolution against sabotage and the vote against Haywood severely limited future cooperation between the Socialist Party and the IWW.

The FSI reacted to the conflict quickly and angrily—in fact, far more quickly and much more adamantly than the IWW did. In an article titled "Towards the Light," published in *Il Proletario* on the same day in March 1912 that celebrated victory in the strike, the FSI unleashed an attack on the Socialists. An Italian American parliamentary socialist had complained that the FSI "didn't publicize the Socialist Party which supported and defended the workers' cause in the Lawrence strike."[119] FSI syndicalists, according to the author, had bided their time, waiting for a justification of their attitudes. News of an early effort to expel Haywood was ample proof that their attitude had been warranted. Assuming, prematurely though presciently, that efforts to remove Haywood would be successful, the syndicalist explained,

> Today Haywood is the next to be thrown out of the National Executive Committee of the Socialist Party because he has defended the Lawrence strikers.... Today the Socialist Party has declared itself officially opposed to the direction of the Lawrence strike.... Therefore we were right when we were attacking that Party because it wasn't responding to the necessity of a class struggle.[120]

In March 1912, when this article was written, Haywood was still lauding the Socialists' contributions to the strike. Even at the Socialist convention in May, when the antisabotage resolution passed, Haywood congratulated the Socialists on another resolution advocating unionizing along industrial lines.[121] He was not expelled from the party until early 1913. FSI members angrily severed their relations with the Socialists fully nine months before Haywood and the IWW did. To the FSI, if not to the IWW by this point, syndicalism (or revolutionary industrial unionism) and parliamentary socialism were absolutely incompatible.

In this sense, the Lawrence strike and defense campaign, which revealed the enormous possibilities of the FSI's vision of syndicalism, also revealed its limitations. The FSI would be constrained not only in seeking a place within the American labor movement, but also in competing with other versions of (radical) ethnicity within Italian American communities. Federation members could not have foreseen the consequences of their hasty condemnation of the Socialist Party, and thus of virtually all the nonsyndicalist elements in the American labor movement. They had no way of knowing that within a year, the IWW would virtually abandon its efforts to organize immigrants on the East Coast.

Nor was the FSI solely responsible for syndicalists' sour relations with the Socialists. For example, shortly after the end of the defense campaign in Lawrence, two leading Italian American socialists and AFL organizers, brothers August and Frank Bellanca, began publishing attacks against the IWW and the FSI. In language guaranteed to raise the syndicalists' ire, one of them accused the IWW of cowardice and treachery to the working class and called Giovannitti the "buffoon of Lawrence." When Ettor, Giovannitti, and Oscar Mazzarella visited the Bellancas to demand a retraction, the meeting ended in a fistfight.[122]

An opportunity at Lawrence for joint action between the FSI, the IWW, and the Socialist Party, and even of reconciliation between Italian American syndicalists and socialists, was lost. This would not help FSI efforts to exert leadership in its own ethnic community. Moreover, after the IWW's virtually complete withdrawal from the East Coast after 1913, it became immensely more difficult for the FSI to maintain a foothold in the American labor movement.

The FSI's relationship to the working class in the United States was affected not only by infighting among American radicals, but also by the range of attitudes Federation members expressed toward the United States. Even as the transnational syndicalists protested Italy's war in Tripoli, their efforts in Lawrence marked a new sense of engagement, not only in the American radical community and labor movement, but in American culture in general. In a sense, the FSI members' experience of the strike and trial paralleled, though was not identical to, the experiences of the strikers themselves.

Peppino Ortoleva has described how, in the aftermath of the general strike, the immigrant work force in Lawrence was presented with a choice about their relationship to American culture. At the general strike, a group of anarchists from Boston had hoisted a banner proclaiming, "No God, No Master." Father O'Reilly, Catholic leader and long-standing opponent of the strike, quickly seized the opportunity the brash banner presented. He organized a counterdemonstration called "For God and Country," cleverly scheduling it for Columbus Day to compound Italian immigrants' interest in the event. In so doing, Ortoleva argued, O'Reilly offered the mill workers a decision: unity on the basis of equality in the name of America, or self-exclusion. Certain historians have argued that the massive turnout for O'Reilly's parade signaled the mill workers' change of heart, and that it marked the distance between the revolutionary fervor of the FSI and the IWW and the ends of the workers themselves. But, as Ortoleva argues, there was a logic to the workers' decision to march with O'Reilly. Much of the bitterness they felt toward Lawrence authorities, much of what had sparked the strike, was these immigrant workers' realization that they were not really welcome in the United States. They were tolerated because their labor was needed, but regarded with disdain by their employers. This was what the IWW had fought by arguing that the strikers were the "real Americans," and this was the sentiment that O'Reilly tapped into with his parade. In large part because of their victory in the strike, immigrant workers in Lawrence could use the Columbus parade to assert their right to be in the United States.[123]

In a sense, the strike and trial offered FSI members a similar choice about their relationship to American—and to Italian—culture. Federation members were not about to march in a parade celebrating God and the United States; they organized a march of their own on the same day, with disappointing results. But the strike victory offered them their best chance to establish a place for themselves in the American labor movement. It was counterbalanced by FSI members' connections to Italian radicals, who affected them profoundly.

Not surprisingly, there was a range of choices transnational FSI members made about American society, and, in effect, about how to balance their ethnic and class identities, at Lawrence. Certain Federation members' continued involvement with Italian political life led to their rejection of American culture. But other FSI syndicalists emerged from the Lawrence strike feeling enormously optimistic about their lives in the United States.

Edmondo Rossoni, still closely connected to Italy, was not drawn to American culture and the labor movement by his experience at Lawrence. Having arrived in the United States in 1911, he would ultimately leave the country for good in 1915.[124] Rossoni spent much of September and October 1912 editing *Il Proletario* and touring Italian communities to generate support for the prisoners. When he returned to Lawrence in mid-November, he sensed the atmosphere in the city had changed drastically. He recalled earlier in the defense campaign seeing strikers everywhere wearing buttons that said "Don't be a scab" or that had pictures of Ettor and Giovannitti on them. "Now it is impossible," he lamented, "to walk around without seeing the people of Lawrence decorated with American colors and American flags hung in windows. It is becoming more and more difficult to see people with IWW or Ettor and Giovannitti buttons."[125] In a sense, Rossoni's comment reflected a realistic concern that the IWW and the FSI were losing influence among the workers after the "For God and Country" campaign.

But it also spoke to his perception of the place both he and the FSI occupied in American society. The strikers had been waving American flags, asserting that they, too, had a right to a voice in the United States, from day one of the strike. In Rossoni's view, nonetheless, support for the IWW and the prisoners, and for American patriotism, were mutually exclusive.

Rossoni had expressed his alienation from American culture and capitalism two months earlier. He had declared, "No one will ever be able to believe in the freedom of America. We have always said that capitalism—monarchical or republican—is the same everywhere. Capitalism in the United States does not avoid the rule! . . . In truth, in no other country in the world is the worker's life so neglected as in the land of the dollar."[126] Disputing claims that American citizens enjoyed greater liberties than elsewhere, Rossoni argued the "land of the dollar" was more inhumane than the nations of Europe. The difference lay in the brashness of capitalists in the United States. "Here," he fumed, "the capitalists—who have the most vulgar appetites, and have a wallet full of dollars where their heart should be, and where their brains should be yet another wallet—are the most brutal, and the most wild."[127] The United States and unrestrained capitalism were one and the same. Rossoni was one of the many FSI members arrested during the strike. But unlike many of his fellow syndicalists, he had decided to skip bail and return to Italy. He left in early January 1913, accompanied by Nicola Vecchi, who had issued the call to FSI members to return to Italy during the war in Tripoli and had always intended to return himself.

Libero Tancredi, one of the Italian anarchists who had encouraged the general strike for the prisoners from Italy, reached the same conclusion as Rossoni even earlier. His decision to return to Italy in 1910, after two years in the United States, was final, and was rooted in his disparaging view of American culture. Tancredi declared, "the United States does not have a culture other than that of industrial and commercial spasms. . . . America knows only three verbs . . . produce, consume, sell— most of all sell."[128] Like Rossoni, Tancredi saw the United States only through its economic system. He closed his indictment by confessing, "I would like to be able to persuade myself that America is less American than I know it to be."[129]

Like Tancredi, Rossoni's bitterness about American culture, and his devotion to Italy, eventually compelled him to leave the United States permanently. And like others who would abandon internationalism during World War I, Rossoni became a staunch defender of Italian intervention in the war. He resigned his editorship of *Il Proletario* in 1915 and left the Federation. He briefly edited a nationalist, prointerventionist paper in New York called *L'Italia Nostra* [*Our Italy*], and then returned to Italy. Like Tancredi, he eventually joined Mussolini and the Fascist Party. A speech Rossoni delivered at the first Congress of Fascist Unions in Italy in 1922 revealed that his future path was based at least in part on his memory of the disillusionment he experienced upon witnessing the treatment of Italian immigrants in the United States. He explained, "[W]e have seen our workers exploited and held in low regard not only by the capitalists but also by the revolutionary comrades of other countries.

We therefore know from experience how internationalism is nothing but fiction and hypocrisy."[130] Rossoni may have been exaggerating the extent to which his anger and frustration over the treatment of Italians in the United States—and in the American Left—contributed to his decision to join the fascists.

His comment was nonetheless enormously revealing. He was speaking in explicit terms—and drawing an extreme conclusion—about the efforts to balance ethnic and class identities in which all FSI members were engaged. Although they didn't necessarily reach the same conclusions, FSI members at Lawrence, and recurrently throughout their political careers in the United States, consciously reconfigured the relationships between these identities. They each did so when waging strikes, leading protests, deciding whether to stay in the United States, and deciding whether to join—or leave—unions or radical organizations.

It is unlikely that the Lawrence strike alone convinced either Rossoni or Tancredi to join the fascist movement after World War I. Indeed, Tancredi had already decided to remain in Italy before his article on American culture appeared in *Il Proletario*. But especially for Rossoni, this first real immersion in the American labor movement and in American culture led to a heightened awareness of ethnic discrimination and a sense of disappointment in class terms. It did little to draw them further into life in the United States.

In contrast to Rossoni and Tancredi, however, others in and around the FSI saw reasons at Lawrence to increase their commitment to the working class in the United States. Tresca's experiences in 1912 served to broaden his sense of class identity and to intensify his connection to the United States and to the American working class. Before the strike, Tresca had had his sights set more on Italy than on the United States. In his autobiography, he reflected on his activities before 1912:

> In my past years of agitation and propaganda work among the Italian immigrants, living and fighting in a world which was a slice of the mother country transplanted by virtue of economic necessity and the spirit of adventure . . . had been for me a matter of marshaling the Italian workers as compatriots rather than as part of the world's workers.[131]

Tresca moved beyond primarily ethnic concerns, embraced the multiethnic strike at Lawrence, and found the sense of connection to the world's workers that he had been seeking. It was for him, "the beginning of a new era."[132] The man whose only English after over eight years in the United States was, by his own sentimental reckoning, the phrases "I fix" and "guilty," finally felt a real sense of connection to the American working class.

Arturo Giovannitti reacted similarly to his experiences at Lawrence. Like Tresca, he came away feeling a firmer sense of connection to the American working class, and even, in the arrested strike leader's case, to American culture in general. The eloquent speech he made to the jury at his trial revealed how the strike had affected his feelings about the United States. He began by declaring, "It is the first time in my life that I speak publicly in your wonderful language, and it is the most solemn moment of my life."[133] This was not really true—he said later it was an attempt to get the jurors' sympathy. All his comments certainly reflected an awareness of the fact that he was facing a potential death sentence. But, unlike Rossoni or Tancredi, he was still able to see the United States as more than an oppressive economic system. He told the jury,

> When I came to this country it was because I thought that really I was coming to a better and a freer land than my own. It was not exactly hunger that drove me out of my house. . . . I thought I could visit the world and I desired coming here for that purpose. I have no grudge against this country. I have no grudge against the American flag. I have no grudge against your patriotism. . . . They say you are a free and wonderful country. I say that politically you are, and my best compliments and congratulations for it. But I say you cannot be half free and half slave, and economically all the working class in the United States are as much slaves now as the Negroes were forty and fifty years ago.[134]

Both Tresca and Giovannitti found something in the American labor movement—and, in Giovannitti's case, in the culture itself—in Lawrence that convinced them that their efforts in the United States would not be wasted.

Of course, for FSI members the question of maintaining connections to Italy and a sense of *Italianità*, on the one hand, and establishing a place in the American labor movement and in the culture more broadly, on the other, was never simply a matter of choosing one or the other option. Because the strike and trial were being conducted at the same time as Italy's war in Tripoli, FSI members were testing their connections to the American labor movement at the exact moment they were reevaluating their feelings toward Italy. In the years before World War I in this transnational immigrant community, members were able to—

were compelled to—maintain and reconcile connections to both cultures at the same time.

FSI member Giovanni di Gregorio's reaction at Lawrence in particular illustrates the complexity of a transnational existence. Di Gregorio, who wrote articles in both English and Italian evaluating *Italianità* and patriotism during the war in Tripoli, commented regularly in *Il Proletario* on the strike and the trial. All of the articles he wrote—on the children's exodus, on the AFL, on the congressional hearings, on demonstrations during the trial—were in English and were signed John di Gregorio.[135] But despite his willingness to learn and communicate in English, in many ways he remained sharply critical of American culture, and especially of American socialists. Like Fazio, di Gregorio dismissed the congressional hearings as a virtually useless gesture, commenting that "the capitalists and their trusted friends: legislative, judicial, clerical and military, think along the same lines all over the world."[136] On May Day, Rossoni had an altercation with a group of American socialists at a gathering in New York City. The socialists, already disturbed that Rossoni was speaking, were further dismayed when some of his enthusiastic listeners tore down American flags that organizers had hung for the meeting. Di Gregorio, writing in English, defended Rossoni and ridiculed the American version of socialism on display that day. "It is providential that there are foreigners here to inject the proper spirit into the workers, to maintain the traditional uncompromising attitude of international socialism and to slap in the face any milk and water body that attempts to misrepresent or misguide socialism or cover it with ridicule. Is there any other country," he continued, "where the national flag is carried side by side with the socialist emblem, outside of places where the latter is outlawed unless it is chaperoned by the former?"[137] Regardless of their particular perspective on American culture, or the degree to which they chose to immerse themselves in it, FSI members in 1912 were still united not only by their syndicalist beliefs and but also by their shared sense of being "foreigners" in the United States.

The Lawrence strike and the defense campaign were seminal events in the history of the Federation. Lawrence was the high point of the organization's unionizing efforts and of its implementation of its unique construction of syndicalism. FSI members created a transnational syndicalism that offered fellow immigrants an alternative to the exclusive AFL. They introduced innovative strike strategies, drawing on connections to Italian allies and on their own accumulated experience of labor struggles. They infused the strike with a stridency unmatched even by the IWW. They assumed leadership, if briefly, of their immigrant community and presented to it their radical version of ethnicity. Not simply seeking assistance from leftist allies in Italy, they inspired their counterparts in their native land with their success. In doing so, they made a substantial contribution to Italian Americans and to the American and Italian working classes.

But its experience at Lawrence also delineated and foreshadowed the FSI's shortcomings. The Federation's trenchant antistatism affected the organization for good and ill. Its lack of faith in the state to conduct a fair trial helped produce the first general strike against the state in American history. If this strike did not directly impact the outcome of the trial, at the very least it kept the prisoners and their fate in the public eye. But FSI antistatism also drew it back into factional feuds within the American Left that ultimately contributed to its isolation from the American labor movement. Its members' experience at Lawrence demanded redefinition and reformulation within the FSI, revealing tensions rooted in regional loyalties and compelling confrontation not only with American employers, but also with the state.

The strike and defense campaign also revealed the intricate relationship between FSI members' ethnic and class identities. Events in Lawrence exposed the complexity of FSI members' views of American culture— at the same moment they were articulating equally complex views of Italy in protesting the war in Tripoli. Federation members were not of one mind about the promise of the American working class or about their feelings toward the United States and Italy after Lawrence. These issues would not disappear; in fact, they would reemerge very shortly after the defense campaign was over, when the debate on Italy's entrance into World War I began. FSI members' attitudes toward the United States and Italy, and their efforts to maintain the delicate balance between their ethnic and class identities, foreshadowed whether they would return to Italy or not. They also foreshadowed the ideological splits that would emerge during the Federation's debates about intervention in World War I.

The FSI's perspective on gender issues in Lawrence particularly had implications for the organization—and for Italian American syndicalists generally—in two ways. First, the failure to recognize the growing importance of women in the work force limited the potential of the movement and would plague these syndicalists until after World War I. Second, if such a perspective on gender provided a shared set of assumptions within the FSI on standards for masculinity at Lawrence, even this sense of agreement would break down soon after the strike. Once World War I began, arguments over these standards would constitute an essential part of the debilitating debate on Italy's intervention.

CHAPTER FOUR

Nationalism and Masculinity Splinter the FSI

In April 1915, Edmondo Rossoni issued a call to action to syndicalists in the FSI. He declared, "[I]n this Springtime of rebirth, there is ... a more useful activity that calls to us and seems pressing, and it is in this field that we must not be sluggards, lukewarm and barren of enthusiasm and faith, armchair [philosophers]."[1] It was just two years after the syndicalists' enormous victories in Lawrence, Massachusetts, and the wave of strikes by immigrant workers in the United States showed no signs of abating. But the "more useful activity" Rossoni was referring to was not organizing workers or participating in strikes; his declaration was not meant to encourage fellow syndicalists. Rather, Rossoni's article was one of the last he would write for *Il Proletario*. It was a call for Federation members to support Italian intervention in World War I on the side of the Triple Entente (France, England, and Russia) and an accusation directed against neutralists in the FSI who disagreed vehemently with him. A month after he wrote the article, pointedly titled "Waste of Time," Rossoni left the FSI and began to publish *L'Italia Nostra* [*Our Italy*], a nationalist newspaper. He soon returned to Italy to join the Italian army. He eventually became the head of the Confederazione Nazionale delle Corporazioni Sindacali (CNCS), the national confederation of fascist unions.

Unfortunately for the FSI, the success and the sense of possibility that they and the IWW experienced in Lawrence had been short-lived. In the next year and a half, before World War I began, the FSI endured two major defeats. The first was the loss of a strike in Paterson, New Jersey, in 1913. The defeat all but ended IWW organizing efforts on the East Coast of the United States. The second was the collapse of Red Week in Italy in June 1914, when a potentially revolutionary moment slipped through Italian syndicalists' fingers. These setbacks left FSI syndicalists shaken by the stark realization that their vision of a new civilization, seemingly so close in Lawrence, was no longer within reach. The ten-month intervention debate, lasting from August 1914 until Italy entered the war in May 1915, was conducted in an aura of despair within both the FSI and Italian syndicalist circles.

FSI syndicalists had long battled in their immigrant communities, and within their own organization, as well, for their particular vision of ethnic identity. Serrati fought against the influence of exploitative colonial elite from the moment he founded the Federation. Others, including Tresca and Giovannitti, followed his lead. During the war in Tripoli, FSI members faced the challenge posed by nationalists in Italy and in Italian American communities. Syndicalists vied with parliamentary socialists, first for control of the FSI, then in other organizations. FSI syndicalists' challenge to the various ideologies within the Italian American community—religious, entrepreneurial, socialist, nationalist, assimilationist—reached its apex during the struggle in Lawrence. But soon after, syndicalists in the Federation would square off against each other in an ideological battle—between two versions of ethnic identity—that would have enormous consequences within the FSI and the Italian American community as a whole.

The Federation split into two camps: the interventionists argued that Italy should join the war; the neutralists argued the war was a battle between capitalist nations. The two sides disagreed over how to react to the enormous violence the war had unleashed and over whether the war had created enough unrest to make a revolution possible. Interventionists claimed that the war might actually advance the cause of syndicalism by weakening their political foes. They spent the first months of the debate insisting that they were not, despite the neutralists' accusations, betraying their revolutionary principles.

But the interventionists' argument that they remained true to syndicalist principles and to the cause of international revolution broke down as the debate raised the recurrent tension between nationalism and internationalism in the FSI to the boiling point. FSI members had always exhibited ethnic pride, and had debated the implications of "cultural nationalism" when protesting the war in Tripoli. During the war, the interventionists, having witnessed socialist parties throughout Europe rush to vote for war credits, grew impatient with the neutralists' arguments about the need to educate workers about international solidarity.

The faith that many interventionists had had in internationalism and syndicalism weakened and finally collapsed as they succumbed to the increasing allure of a far more chauvinistic nationalism. The political nationalism that Rossoni and many interventionists embraced during the war exalted Italy as a polity, even while remaining critical of it. The exaltation of their homeland brought them closer ideologically to Corradini, the head of the ANI, than to the more benign cultural nationalism FSI members had expressed earlier.

Not only their shared faith in syndicalism and internationalism, but also the ideal of a virile community—which FSI leaders had shared, for better and worse, at Lawrence—broke down during the intervention debate. In arguing for the war, the interventionists reworked previously accepted standards of masculine behavior in the FSI. At Lawrence, masculinity had meant facing violence and imprisonment unflinchingly and not relying on women for emotional support. It had meant being unafraid to meet violence with violence, or even to initiate violent confrontations in the name of the working class and revolution. But now the interventionists took a dramatic leap in their embrace of violence, reveling in the bloodbath of the war. They begged the neutralists not to appear weak before the bourgeoisie, and when this did not work, taunted them for lacking revolutionary ardor, courage, and even sexual prowess. As before, such capacities were linked in the minds of these FSI members. But now they were deployed to uphold a far more brutal conception of masculinity.

The issue of what constituted masculine behavior was not the sole cause of the rupture of the FSI, but it contributed substantially to it. FSI members were not only debating masculinity on a literal level by evaluating who was showing true courage or cowardice—always a crucial measure of worthiness within the revolutionary Federation. The issue of masculinity was also being debated on a rhetorical level; the discourse of masculinity was frequently the language through which the battle over intervention and the viability of international revolution was fought. Thus the issue of masculinity became closely intertwined with these other issues, and with the emergent nationalism of many interventionists.[2]

To Rossoni and his followers, ultimately the capacity to embrace the bloodshed of the war and revolutionary capacity were one and the same. Rossoni interpreted the neutralists' opposition to the war as a failure of will and courage. He and other interventionists accused the neutralists of flinching in the face of violence—a tendency de Ambris had discerned among Italian syndicalists even before the war. By the end of the debate, Rossoni concluded that the syndicalist movement could not be revived; it was dominated not by men of action, but by intellectuals immobilized by the war, and thus rendered unworthy and incapable as revolutionaries.

Faced with the neutralists, who refused to abandon antimilitarism, international revolution, or the previously accepted standards of masculinity, the interventionists lost faith in internationalism and in the FSI. Many of these "long-distance nationalists," certain that the Federation could no longer be a revolutionary and virile community, left the organization.[3] Searching for a new virile community, Rossoni and other syndicalist interventionists joined ranks with a collection of disgruntled Italian leftists, nationalists, and other antibourgeois elements who were seeking to remake, while glorifying, Italy and its population. Rossoni and those who followed his lead were no longer *i senza patria*. His form of nationalism appeared in terse language on *L'Italia Nostra*'s masthead: "The Fatherland is not to be denied, but conquered."

The intervention debate played, with calamitous results, on tendencies long extant within the FSI. Transnational connections kept FSI syndicalists closely tied to Italy. These connections, and the hostility and distrust with which Italians were so often greeted in the United States, ensured that Federation syndicalists' ethnic identity would remain central even as they sought a class-based revolution. They had always placed enormous emphasis on masculinity and on enthusiasm for violence. Each of these elements—their intense connections to Italy and their emphasis on ethnic identity and especially on masculinity—contained the seeds of potential corruption, especially when certain members became convinced that the potential of the FSI and syndicalism had played itself out. Each of them had, to one extent or another, strengthened the FSI. Reconfigured, they virtually destroyed the FSI, and led a number of disillusioned radicals into the fascist movement.

To understand the syndicalists' reaction to the war, it is necessary first to examine the context within which they acted—the setbacks they suffered just before the war, after brief moments of enormous promise. Though the Lawrence strike had not produced the sustained general strike many FSI members had anticipated, in the following year the immigrant-led strike wave was still going strong. Throughout 1913 FSI members participated in the strikes erupting all around them. Giovannitti, after a brief rest following his imprisonment, rejoined Ettor and Tresca to lead a hotel workers' strike that began in New York City on New Year's Eve. By the spring, Italian American syndicalists were helping to lead strikes waged by barbers in New York and Brooklyn; day workers and brick layers in New York; tailors in New York, Baltimore, and Providence, Rhode Island; and stonecutters and marble workers in Massachusetts. In early May, Giovannitti and Ettor were again reunited during an iron workers' strike in Hopedale, Massachusetts. Giovannitti was arrested again, though he was released after a brief trial. Throughout these months, *Il Proletario* featured numerous articles supporting these conflicts and hailing other strikes being waged by tailors in Seattle, by bricklayers in Philadelphia, by porters in New Orleans, and by silk workers in New London, Connecticut.[4]

The strike in which FSI members invested most of their energy—and which proved to be the most disappointing—began early in February in Paterson. When more than twenty-five thousand silk workers went out on strike in the New Jersey city, the IWW and members of the FSI, eager to build on their recent success in Lawrence, rushed to the city. The IWW anticipated that victory in Paterson would establish its permanent presence on the East Coast. Instead, the crushing defeat the IWW, the FSI, and the strikers suffered virtually marked the end of Wobbly efforts in that region.[5]

The IWW and the FSI arrived in Paterson full of enthusiasm and confidence, and quickly attempted to implement strategies that had worked so well in Lawrence. They established worker-led strike committees so that the strikers would lead their own fight and so that everyone in this multiethnic work force would have representation. Elizabeth Gurley Flynn conducted weekly meetings for women strikers. As in Lawrence, IWW leaders buoyed the strikers through regular meetings at which William Haywood, Flynn, Tresca, and others exhorted them to continue their struggle. Giovannitti and other FSI members, drawing on both their ethnic and class identities as they had in Lawrence, kept the large contingent of Italian workers unified. The IWW also held frequent parades and even a circus. Having learned in Lawrence that singing could help unify workers of different nationalities, Haywood announced early in the strike, "We're going to learn how to sing in Paterson. . . . We're going to learn to sing, in many different languages."[6] As in Lawrence, the IWW and the FSI called for a general strike, hoping to spread the strike to nearby mills in Pennsylvania, and the FSI attempted to organize a children's exodus from the city.

If anything, the IWW and the FSI relied too heavily on their experience in Lawrence. Especially early in the conflict, certain strike leaders seemed to forget where they were. In Lawrence textile production was dominated by several large mills, and the IWW and the FSI had railed continuously against the "wool trust." In a speech to Italian strikers in Paterson Giovannitti told them they had to stand firm against the "silk trust," despite the fact that in Paterson there were literally hundreds of shops of various sizes producing silk, and thus no powerful trust to oppose. An IWW leader gave a speech in which he, as a Paterson newspaper described it, "continually referred to Lawrence, until Miss Flynn had to prompt him several times. It seems that . . . the speaker did not realize that he had ceased his activities in Lawrence."[7]

But the syndicalists soon discovered that strategies they had employed in Lawrence could not be carried intact to New Jersey. The childrens' exodus did not arouse nearly the enthusiasm it had in Lawrence. Even more damaging, the IWW could not spread its call for a general strike to nearby Pennsylvania towns. This was a crucial blow to the strike, because the Pennsylvania mill owners were able to undermine the strike—and their Paterson competitors—by increasing silk production.[8]

The syndicalists did not admit defeat easily, however, and with the help of Greenwich Village intellectuals, they recaptured their spirit of innovation. By 1913 Greenwich Village was a mecca of cultural and political radicalism. Advocates of socialism, syndicalism, anarchism, free love, and free verse gathered in the bohemian neighborhood to celebrate their rejection of social mores and the existing economic system. The irreverent *The Masses* had strongly supported the IWW in Lawrence, and Haywood had been an honored guest at Mabel Dodge's salon gatherings, which brought together radicals of all stripes to debate the means of political and social change.[9] At one salon meeting, Haywood was lamenting that the strike in Paterson was not going well—the strikers were short on funds, and the publicity they were getting was entirely unsympathetic. Dodge suggested that the IWW, with her help and with the help of John Reed, the Harvard cheerleader-turned-leftist journalist, bring the strike to New York by staging a pageant. Haywood agreed to the idea enthusiastically, and by late spring plans had begun to recreate the strike on stage at Madison Square Garden.[10]

Giovannitti and Tresca agreed to help. The experiences of both men in Lawrence had redefined their perspective on American culture. After 1912, each was drawn increasingly to the atmosphere of artistic and political experimentation in the Village. Giovannitti, editor of *Il Proletario* before his arrest in Lawrence, edited the paper again briefly in 1913. But thereafter he immersed himself in Greenwich Village, contributing to *The Masses* and starting *Il Fuoco* (*The Fire*), a magazine of political and cultural criticism. Although the FSI gave only nominal attention to the pageant, Giovannitti was a member of the executive committee that planned the event.[11] Tresca appeared in three of the six scenes, recreating speeches he had made to the strikers.[12]

By all accounts, the pageant on June 7 was a stunning artistic success. Even newspapers hostile to the IWW agreed that nothing like it had ever been attempted. Over one thousand strikers brought their struggle to life before an overflow audience in Madison Square Garden. They recreated the police beatings and arrests they had faced and even reenacted a funeral that was held for a striker who was killed. The pageant blurred the lines between artistic performance and political action as the strikers—and the audience—cheered speeches by Tresca, Haywood, and Flynn and booed the actors who played scabs and police. Once again, the syndicalists, with assistance from intellectual allies in New York, had redefined the possibilities of labor organizing.

As an artistic endeavor and as a publicity event, the pageant was an unquestioned success, but ultimately it could not rescue the faltering strike in Paterson. Some IWW leaders, Flynn foremost among them, even blamed the pageant for the collapse of the strike. Despite promises that it would raise funds for the financially strained strikers, the pageant lost money, instead. Moreover, Flynn noted later, the pageant had diverted the attention of the strikers who participated from the real battle in Paterson and aroused jealously among those strikers left behind.[13] Though the strikers held on for almost two more months, they could not overcome the failure to spread the strike to Pennsylvania and the determination of the mill owners not to allow another IWW victory on the East

Coast. By early August they returned to work with little to show for their twenty-two week strike.[14]

Try as they might, neither the IWW nor the FSI could deny the enormity of this defeat. Even after the strikers returned to work, Ettor refused to accept the outcome. Writing in the IWW weekly *Solidarity*, he put the word "defeat" in quotation marks, insisting that "[t]he Paterson struggle is not over."[15] FSI member Giovanni di Gregorio argued, with a note of desperation, that it was "necessary to disprove the idea that the strike ended in a fiasco."[16] But Justus Ebert, who had hailed the beginning of a new era in labor organizing after Lawrence, bluntly stated that, after Paterson, the IWW was "in many respects, a lamentable failure."[17] Even di Gregorio had to admit that the syndicalists did not have a guaranteed formula for success. He wrote, "The Paterson strike . . . teaches one lesson, that is, that there is no 'cocksure' method yet devised or devisable under the present system by which a strike can be won. . . ."[18] IWW and FSI members admitted that the implications of the defeat extended far beyond the silk-producing city. They had arrived in Paterson with the same tactics and vigor that had produced a victory in Lawrence, had again created new forms of class struggle, but had failed. It was a defeat not just for the strikers, but for syndicalism, as well.

In Italy, too, the syndicalists' optimism was waning. In November 1912, they had formally split from the CGL, which was still dominated by socialists, and formed the Unione Sindacale Italiana [USI]. Though within a month the USI had 100,000 members, the CGL still had a membership between three and four times as large. Nor did USI membership approach the peak of syndicalist numerical strength; in late 1907, syndicalist unions in Italy had represented 200,000 workers.[19] In May and June of 1913, syndicalist Filippo Corridoni, head of the newly established Unione Sindacale Milanese (USM) led a general strike in Milan. Initially the strike seemed promising, even winning the support of *Avanti!* editor Benito Mussolini. But eventually the strike was defeated by employer lockouts and by the opposition of reformist socialists.

The assistance of FSI syndicalists did little to salvage the faltering movement. Back in Italy after his arrest in Lawrence, Rossoni had led the strike with Corridoni. The two men initiated another general strike in August, but the defeat this time was even more resounding. Rossoni was arrested and fled to Lugano, Switzerland, and Corridoni was left with the USM bleeding funds and members.[20]

The series of strikes labeled Red Week, which occurred in Italy in June 1914, ironically also dealt a serious blow to Italian syndicalists. The widespread uprising began on June 7, when police in Ancona fired on workers demonstrating against militarism and killed three people. The call for a general strike, backed by the Socialist Party and the CGL, spread to nearly every major city in the country. Many revolutionaries considered the uprising the closest Italy had yet come to a revolution. The aim of most strikers was not more pay or fewer hours—it was to overthrow the government. This was an astounding opportunity for Italian radicals, and many responded admirably. Socialists, syndicalists, republicans, and anarchists dropped their differences to work together during the conflict—something they had not done during the general strikes in Milan a year earlier.[21]

But the strikes ended well short of revolution, and Italian radicals faced disappointment and even embarrassment. Key elements of the workforce failed to participate in the strike. *Avanti!*, the socialist daily and the radicals' primary means of communication, was itself shut down by a strike. Clearly, no one was prepared to take command of the uprising, which had surprised not only government officials, but working-class leaders, as well.

This led to stark realizations for Italian syndicalists. Alceste de Ambris, who participated in the strike, admitted that the workers had surprised their own leaders. For all of their rhetoric, the radicals were unprepared because they had not really believed that the workers would revolt. As a result, no one coordinated the strikes nationally, and strikers could organize only in their local areas.[22]

De Ambris was particularly disturbed, foreshadowing the central importance of masculinity in the intervention debate, by Italian syndicalists' apparent unwillingness to use violence on anything more than a rhetorical level. In Parma, for example, when strikers began throwing stones and threatening other forms of attack against local authorities, the syndicalists called off the strike in its second day.[23] This type of decision, de Ambris insisted, revealed a profound flaw in syndicalist thinking and tactics. In an article titled "Contradictions," he voiced his frustration:

> We that feel the absolute necessity of violence for the solution of
> social conflicts, we find ourselves continuously caught up in a tragic
> contradiction. All year long, there is preaching about the duty to act
> heroically... but when the hoped-for moment of proletarian reawakening

comes . . . it is we that run to contain this proud impulse, to dam the
storm of contempt. In this way we deny in one day all the propaganda
spread throughout long months. . . . [L]et's admit our guilt, let's confess
to it and purge ourselves. The contradiction is revealed, and it cannot
and should not endure.[24]

The syndicalists' unwillingness to do more than speak of violence exposed their trepidations about leading a revolution at all.[25] The doubt
de Ambris expressed would resonate throughout the intervention debate,
ultimately expanding to doubts about the masculine resolve of opponents of the war.

Faced with defeats in Paterson and during Red Week in Italy, Rossoni
was beginning to share de Ambris' doubts about the possibility of a syndicalist revolution. Rossoni, back in the United States by late 1913 and editor of *Il Proletario* by early 1914, signaled his agreement with de Ambris
by publishing his article on Red Week on page one of the FSI weekly in
early July. At the outset of the war, de Ambris and Rossoni were contemplating the possibility that their fellow syndicalists, having failed to take
advantage when workers of either country exhibited revolutionary (or
at least oppositional) impulses, lacked revolutionary will themselves.

There were other signs of de Ambris's and Rossoni's disillusionment.
Both had attended the International Syndicalist Congress in London in
1913, de Ambris as a delegate from the USI, and Rossoni as a USM delegate.[26] They fought so vehemently with German delegates that one of
them accused de Ambris of not wanting a syndicalist international. Anticipating his rejection of internationalism and his invectives against
the Germans during the war, de Ambris replied caustically that he wanted
an international, just not with the Germans or the Dutch. De Ambris
fiercely opposed a resolution to create an information bureau in Amsterdam, arguing that its placement there would "condemn it to sterility."[27]
Unable to convince the other delegates, de Ambris angrily bolted the
congress. Rossoni wrote later in *Il Proletario* that the congress had been
a disaster.[28]

This is the context within which Italian American syndicalists' reaction
to World War I must be understood. The war did not mean inevitable
disaster for the FSI. The wave of immigrant strikes beginning at the
end of the first decade of the twentieth century, into which Federation
members had launched themselves in Lawrence and Paterson, did not
abate when the war began or even when the United States entered the

war in 1917. Despite increasing repression of labor organizers, the number of strikes, their average duration and the number of strikers involved all reached their peak between 1916 and 1922.[29] There was still, during and after the war, a large body of workers in the United States who might have been receptive to the FSI's message.

But defeats in Paterson and during Red Week, compounded by the disappointing International Syndicalist Congress, left the FSI—and their syndicalist allies in Italy—shaken and uncertain. The implications of those setbacks were twofold. First, they made it clear that syndicalism had failed to establish—or, in Italy, to maintain—a firm base of support or any lasting institutions among workers in either country. Second, the collapse of Red Week left not only Rossoni and de Ambris, but also many leading syndicalists in Italy, deeply disillusioned. FSI members attempted to draw on transnational connections, as they had to great effect only two years earlier, but the syndicalists to whom they looked for advice already had profound doubts about the efficacy of their ideology. When Italian American syndicalists looked homeward for guidance during the war, as immigrant leftists throughout the United States did, it had dire consequences. The FSI had shown its potential to lead Italian American immigrants during the Lawrence strike, but ensuing setbacks left Federation members and their allies in Italy ill-prepared to deal with the war.

This war was a historical moment when the power of nationalism—either loyalty to existing states or to those that might emerge out of the conflict—was enormously compelling. It was a moment when international working-class solidarity crumbled, despite the promises of socialist parties world-wide to remain true to internationalist principles if war erupted. Socialists in Germany and France voted immediately, over the shocked protests of a tiny number of their comrades, to support their respective nations in the war. Facing strongly prowar populations, socialists of both nations searched desperately for some way to support the war and still maintain their principles. Ultimately, they argued that socialism would suffer severely if their respective countries were overrun by backward, autocratic powers. In France, socialists argued that Germany under the Kaiser was still—at least in part—a feudal state; in Germany, leaders of the socialist party feared a defeat by czarist Russia.[30]

In the United States, not just Italian American syndicalists, but immigrant leftists in general had long struggled to reconcile the imperatives of their ethnic and class identities. When World War I began, many immigrant radical organizations were badly damaged by disagreements over whether to push for international working-class solidarity or to use the war to promote independence for their homeland. The Yugoslav Socialist Federation, for example, was split in two by right-wing socialist Etbin Kristen. Kristen traveled to the United States in 1914 to convince fellow Slovenes, as well as Croats and Serbs, that the only way to ensure a united, independent Yugoslav state was to fight Austro-Hungary.[31] Many in the Polish Socialist Federation fell under the sway of right-wing socialist Jozef Pilsudski, who put together "legions" of Polish-American volunteers to fight alongside Germany and Austro-Hungary for an independent Poland. The Polish Socialist Federation virtually collapsed when Pilsudski's followers were expelled from the antiwar Socialist Party of America.[32]

Italy didn't join the war until May 1915; for the ten months after August 1914, its potential involvement sparked enormous disagreement both at home and in overseas Italian immigrant communities. Most Italians—along with the parliament and the prime minister at the time—opposed Italian intervention in the war. The memory of the costly, and largely unsuccessful, war in Tripoli was still fresh. Moreover, Italy was still a member of the Triple Alliance with Germany and Austro-Hungary, which obligated its members to support each other in wars of defense. But distrust of their "allies" ran so deep among Italians that there was no chance that Italy would join the war on the side of Triple Alliance. The choice in Italy was whether to remain neutral or to ally with the Triple Entente. When the PSI came out against the war, with only a few—if very prominent—dissenters such as Benito Mussolini, it was able to do so with the support of much of the nation. Even in May 1915, just days before Italy entered the war on the side of the Triple Entente, the socialists were able to draw thousands of Italian workers to an antiwar rally.[33]

Among syndicalists in Italy and in the FSI, however, there were many more who argued for Italy's intervention in the war. As David Roberts notes in *The Syndicalist Tradition and Italian Fascism*, "the leading syndicalists [in Italy] came out for intervention quickly and almost unanimously."[34] Arturo Labriola and Angelo Olivetti both became interventionists. This was not shocking; both men had backed Italy's war in Tripoli.

Far more surprising was the decision by a number of the younger, more activist contingent of syndicalists to support intervention. Increasingly disillusioned about the prospect of international working-class solidarity, and hoping that war would reinvigorate the Italian working class, de Ambris and Rossoni were among the first syndicalists on either side of the ocean to publicly support Italian intervention. Their pronouncements just days into the war—Rossoni's in *Il Proletario* and de Ambris's at a USM meeting in Milan—shocked many syndicalists. During the war in Tripoli, both had been arrested in Italy for antimilitarist agitation. Nonetheless, now they argued strongly for intervention, and both were prominent participants in the debate within the FSI from the first. Rossoni, editor of *Il Proletario* throughout the battle in the organization, reprinted the prointervention speech his friend gave in Milan on page one of the paper.[35]

The interventionists, headed by Rossoni and de Ambris, were opposed by those in the Federation who insisted that Italy remain neutral. The neutralists argued that the responsibility of radicals confronted by the disastrous world war was to educate and convince workers that international solidarity was still possible, and that they had nothing to gain—and everything to lose—if they fought in the war. They were led by Flavio Venanzi, whose mentor Enrico Leone also remained opposed to the war. Venanzi had become an increasingly important member of the FSI in recent years. He had been *Il Proletario*'s correspondent during Ettor, Giovannitti, and Caruso's trial; during the debate, he was the managing editor of the paper. Like his close friend Giovannitti, his interests extended beyond the political world of the FSI. He was an omnivorous reader and writer who produced articles and essays not only on syndicalism, but also on art and literature.[36] He taught Helen Keller Italian by reading to her from Dante. During the debate, he wrote passionately against intervention whenever he could. But he was an unimposing man. FSI historian Mario de Ciampis said of him, "in meeting Venanzi no one could take him for a subversive."[37] He was frail, and was often ashen-faced from battling health problems; he would die of pneumonia in 1920 at age thirty-seven. He did not have the commanding presence necessary to stand up to Rossoni. Venanzi shared leadership of the neutralists with Giovanni Baldazzi, a recent arrival who had been an electrician in Bologna, and with Giuseppe Cannata, a chemist and autodidact from Sicily, who was a much more confident orator than Venanzi.[38]

Initially, the interventionists in the FSI and in Italy denied that their support for the war constituted a rejection of internationalism and an embrace of nationalism. Indeed, even after the debate they maintained they were still good, if misunderstood, syndicalists. This was de Ambris's argument when he addressed the USM conference in Milan in September 1914. He explained,

> Nothing is less dogmatic than syndicalism whose force derives from the possibility of nimbly adapting the action to the concrete fact without the obstruction of rigid doctrines. . . . No boldness of conception, no contradiction can scare the syndicalist who does not fear falling into heresy for the fact that Syndicalism is not Orthodox—and he who tries to secure orthodoxy only demonstrates his lack of Syndicalist qualities.[39]

This was an ironic perspective on the ideology, given that de Ambris himself had presented a motion at the International Syndicalist Congress defining the contours of international syndicalism. There, too, he had described syndicalism as a flexible ideology, but had insisted there were certain core principles: direct action, the general strike, proletarian violence—and antimilitarism.[40]

Nonetheless, he and Rossoni now rejected antimilitarism, rationalizing that the turmoil of the war would actually help the cause of syndicalism and international revolution. The failure of the socialist parties that were members of the Second International to resist the war, Rossoni argued, might finally reveal the fallacy of parliamentary socialism. He raised this argument throughout the debate. The German socialists, who had dominated the Second International, were social democrats. Rossoni argued, "[W]e believe that syndicalism itself has gained a great deal from the failure of Teutonic [i.e., German] socialism that has poisoned up until yesterday the entire international workers' movement."[41] With the collapse of the German-dominated Second International, parliamentary socialists would no longer impede the cause of the revolution. De Ambris, for his part, tried to convince the neutralists that the war, precisely because of its destructiveness, might end militarism. "Perhaps because of its enormity," he wrote, "and because of the frightful violence of death and misery that it brings, it will be the most efficacious propaganda against the militarism that brought us the war."[42] The war would destroy parliamentary socialism and bolster the arguments of the antimilitarists, thus advancing the goals of syndicalism.

Even early in the debate, though, the interventionists' impatience with calls for international working-class solidarity was growing. Both Rossoni and de Ambris accused the neutralists of being unwilling to face reality. "Insurrection rather than war. It's our idea, but today it has sunk," Rossoni declared in his first article on the war. "Not because we wanted it to, but because the reality of things made it fail. We have anxiously awaited the announcement of a general strike in all nations. It did not happen."[43] It was futile, Rossoni insisted, for the neutralists to launch any meaningful opposition to the war. He declared,

> Our theories are very beautiful, but it is necessary to see where they end up, and in what measure they have an influence today on society. Let's try not to live in a fantasy world. . . . Let's try to understand that there are certain powers . . . whose movements are not controlled by our wills in the middle-class world, the collision of which may quicken or stop depending on whether these forces or those forces have the upper hand, and this collision may quicken or stop the historical course of human destiny much more than our little committee meetings held by the thousands.[44]

Rossoni was already concerned that the FSI was suffering from inertia and holding futile meetings rather than acting. From the start, by contrast, he was convinced that no appeals to internationalism could stop the war. Nor was he certain, even at this point, that international working-class solidarity was worth trying to salvage.

His growing despair about internationalism was rooted at least in part in his deepening rage—expressed in class and especially in ethnic terms—over the treatment of Italian immigrants in the United States. He had always been fiercely protective of Italian workers. The same could be said, of course, of every member of the FSI. But the intensity of Rossoni's anger over the treatment of Italian immigrants distinguished him. He had made a tour of Italian immigrant colonies in 1911, and reported: "I have been traveling among the Italian colonies in this republic of the dollar for more than one year. . . . I have made the same disheartening discoveries everywhere and at all times: impoverished Italians are the garbage . . . of American social life and are victims of two-sided exploitation: the more common one by capitalism and the one particular to the fact that they are Italians."[45] They were exploited and held in contempt not only by the bourgeoisie, but, even worse, also by fellow workers and leaders of supposedly international working-class organizations. Like all

in the FSI, Rossoni regarded the implications of ethnic and class identity for Italian immigrants and for the syndicalists themselves as inseparable. But his frustration took him in a different direction than most
FSI members. Rossoni's disillusionment with internationalism, evident
before the war, would grow as the war progressed. His resentment
about the treatment of Italian immigrants in the United States would
culminate, in a sense, in his angry speech before a Fascist Congress in
1922.

De Ambris, like Rossoni, argued that the neutralists were being unre-
alistic in their approach to the war. Every effort to prevent the war had
failed, he insisted.

> [A]ll the sentimental and logical constructions aimed at guaranteeing us
> international peace have fallen like the wall of Jericho at the first sounds
> of war.... Today the war is a reality... all the proletarian and capitalist
> interests are worth nothing trying to stop it.... Faced with this truth it
> would be absurd to profess a rediscovery of our duty and class interest.
> We need to examine objectively the phenomenon in its entirety—
> putting aside all of our prejudices.[46]

De Ambris, Rossoni and the other interventionists used their control
over *Il Proletario* to dominate the debate in its first months. They argued
that the prospects for internationalism had disappeared as working classes
had leapt to defend their nations, and as socialists had abandoned their
resolutions to oppose the war almost as quickly.[47]

De Ambris and Rossoni argued that the only possible response to the
war was to support France and her allies against Germany and Austro-
Hungary. Alceste de Ambris had shown his distrust of the Germans at
the International Syndicalist Congress in 1913. Now he expressed undiluted contempt for them and for the Austro-Hungarians. As far as he
was concerned, Germany and Austro-Hungary were responsible for starting the war. He proclaimed, "[E]verybody knows who wanted the war.
Published documents did nothing but strengthen the unanimous conviction that attributes the responsibility to the central empires Germany
and Austria/Hungary."[48] Even more importantly, de Ambris and Rossoni
argued that France, on the one hand, and Germany and Austro-Hungary on the other, represented two very different cultures. Rossoni regarded the war as a struggle between "two civilizations and two tendencies," and de Ambris made the contrast explicit: "Germany... is not a
bourgeois nation but a type of two-headed monster, a bourgeois-feudal

state where the most bizarre anachronisms are possible."[49] Germany, in other words, was still—at least in part—a feudal state. Thus the fight against Germany and Austro-Hungary was, in this sense, against a corrupt anachronism. If the Allies failed to defeat this power, de Ambris and the interventionists warned that the result would be the regression of the entire social order of Europe.

If Germany was the most archaic nation in Europe, according to the interventionists, France was the most advanced. The interventionists, particularly Rossoni, were unabashedly sympathetic to France. "We are decidedly Francophile," he declared, "and in consequence, sympathizers with the Allies."[50] He hailed France as the birthplace of the best of revolutionary thought. This was a perspective shared by anarchists in Italy and elsewhere who became interventionists. Rossoni published an article by Libero Tancredi in October which pointed out that the revered Russian anarchist Peter Kropotkin had written years before that he would happily fight on the side of France against Germany.[51] Tancredi reminded *Il Proletario* readers that the "worst of the [revolutionary] defeats of 1870–1871 were caused by the intellectual eclipse of France." The Franco-Germanic war had forced the French to concentrate all of their energy on protecting their country, and had therefore "paralyzed revolutionary thought."[52] Rossoni, too, defended France's revolutionary heritage—it was the birthplace of syndicalism.[53]

The neutralists in the FSI, in stark contrast to the interventionists, clung ardently to their internationalist principles. For them, there was little difference between two groups of capitalist industrial nations at war with each other. Although Venanzi was a managing editor of *Il Proletario*, with Rossoni as editor the neutralists had to struggle to make their voice heard in its pages.[54] Nonetheless, they were gradually able to stake out their adamant opposition to the war, a stance that not only set them at odds with the interventionists, but also, once the United States entered the war, would leave them vulnerable to repression, arrests, and deportations.

In mid-August, Cannata presented his interpretation of the war. He argued that "Europe today is dominated by a group of industrial nations, relatively well developed. What the capitalist in each one of these nations needs is a wide field where he may be able to sell his products and acquire new goods."[55] Outlining the imperialist adventures of all of the major participants in the war, he continued

Today... a limit has been reached. The capitalists have no new worlds to conquer. It follows logically thus that there should be a struggle for lands already conquered.... Today Germany, more than any other nation, feels the need to expand territorially.... Today the German middle class has thrown prudence to the winds, so as to entrust to violence their economic invasion, and England, Russia and France will very determinedly stand in the way of the appalling German colossus, and the great war will decide everything.[56]

Although Cannata closed by arguing that the proletariat of all of these nations had no investment in the war, his emphasis on German imperialism indicated the extent of Rossoni's editorial control. Indeed, Rossoni agreed with the gist of his article. In an editorial note, he stated that "this article is not contradictory with our thought because it... limits itself to a general background of the war."[57]

But when Rossoni went on a lecture tour in September, Venanzi took advantage of his absence and published an article declaring his opposition both to the war and to the interventionists in no uncertain terms. He declared,

The current war in Europe has motives that are too profound, both political and economic, for the proletariat to get any possible advantage out of it. To start coming out with capricious hair-splitting distinctions to keep the responsibility for the war on this or that nation... is not a reliable method nor does it justify anyone.... All of the modern nations have contributed so that the enormous fire would leap and spread everywhere.[58]

It was irrelevant, Venanzi and the neutralists argued, to blame one or another nation for the war. The war was being fought between capitalists battling over increasingly scarce resources, and the proletariat of every nation would pay the price for the war and reap none of the benefits. Venanzi also rejected Rossoni's assertion that the war could advance the revolution, pointing out that, historically, wars had been followed by periods of severe repression.[59] The war could only harm both the workers of every nation involved and the cause of international revolution.

The neutralists insisted that the only possible response to the war was to present to workers the true causes of the conflict. In an article bemoaning the state of the revolutionary movement among Italian radicals in the United States, Giovanni Baldazzi made clear his disagreement with the interventionists' manipulation of the flexibility of syndicalism.

He asserted it was "necessary not so much to modify the principles and the tactics as to infuse them with a more spiritual and intimate quality that . . . is still lacking in them: education."[60] Venanzi wrote, "[I]t is urgent, even if it means repeating the same old arguments, that we explain continuously to the workers the deep causes of the war."[61] These men hoped that an educated working class would see that their interests would not be served by the war, and that they would therefore reject it.

There is no overestimating the neutralists' anger at what they saw as the interventionists' betrayal of their class principles. Venanzi argued the interventionists had been swayed by the effort of the middle class in Italy to maintain harmony between the classes in support of the war. He declared, "[I]t is not possible to make justifications . . . for that which we believe is against the vital interests of the proletariat."[62] He continued, "[W]hoever attempts . . . to reconcile the antithetical terms of the conflict between capital and labor is outside the directive of the revolutionary movement and falls blindly into utopianism."[63] Syndicalism may have been a flexible ideology, but as far as Venanzi and the neutralists were concerned, it was not flexible enough to include calls for intervention.

Because their influence over the paper's editorial policy was circumscribed, and because many of the Italian immigrants they sought to reach were unable to read, the neutralists extended their battle with the interventionists to lecture halls, saloons, and clubs where Italian Americans congregated. In these gathering places they clashed with the interventionists fiercely, at times even violently. Carlo Tresca berated Rossoni as a "war-mongering buffoon" at one meeting, and at another neutralists had to be physically restrained from attacking Rossoni.[64] They were supported by several sections of the FSI—including the interstate Federation of Massachusetts, Rhode Island, and Connecticut as well as the San Francisco branch—that opposed the war and called for Rossoni's resignation.[65]

Their efforts to reach the Italian immigrant population were complemented by the powerful voice of Italian American anarchist Luigi Galleani. In the middle of 1912, Galleani had moved his *Cronaca Sovversiva* from Barre, Vermont, to Lynn, Massachusetts, where he continued to lead a small but fiercely loyal following of antiorganizational anarchists that included Nicola Sacco and Bartolomeo Vanzetti.[66] On lecture tours and in his paper, Galleani berated de Ambris and Rossoni as traitors and beseeched his fellow immigrants to oppose a war in which they would die so that the ruling classes could fill their coffers. "The war is just a business affair," he thundered in one of a series of articles against the war. "On it the lights of civilization, the flags of progress, the national prides are being poured, only to hide the shameless betrayal that comes down to this: it is fought for the advancement of the great thieves, who will require the necessary tribute of veneration and blood from the proletariat."[67] For Galleani, as for FSI neutralists, there could be no compromise with war advocates.

Though unable to keep Italy out of the war, the neutralists and Galleani may have had an impact on the Italian immigrant population in the United States. When Italy joined the war and began to call Italian immigrants back home for military service, only about 15 percent of Italian Americans eligible for service responded. Moreover, while many Italian Americans bought Italian war bonds, their subscription rates were considerably lower than in Brazil and Argentina, the two other nations in the hemisphere with sizable Italian immigrant populations.[68]

Nonetheless, the debate was devastating to the FSI's effectiveness as a workers' organization. Local and national FSI leaders spent all of their time arguing about the war and virtually abandoned efforts to organize workers. Local secretaries reported that the debate was the only thing being discussed, and that fistfights had broken out over the issue in meetings. The FSI began to lose entire sections, their members irreconcilably split over the war. By late October 1914, the FSI was so paralyzed by the debate that its National Executive Committee met to address the issue. The committee was receiving complaints about Rossoni regularly from various FSI sections and realized that some sort of stand on the debate was necessary. But the committee itself was split between Rossoni's opponents and supporters. It even took the neutralists to task for unfairly hounding the interventionist editor. However, the National Executive Committee did ask both Rossoni and Venanzi, in particular, to tone down their battle in the pages of the newspaper.[69] Little was written about intervention, pro or con, for the next two months.

But the issue could not be buried indefinitely, and when Rossoni renewed the debate in January 1915, it was clear that it would ultimately splinter the FSI. From a certain perspective, it seems puzzling that this debate was so wrenching and ruinous. The war in Tripoli—in which Italy's ambitions were explicitly imperialist—had been supported by certain Italian and, in lesser numbers, Italian American syndicalists. But this debate over Italy's attempted naked land grab had not been as destructive to the syndicalist movement in either country. Rather, it was the issue of Italy's entry into a war in which the issues, at least according to the interventionists, were far more complex that hobbled syndicalism in the FSI and in Italy.

This debate was so debilitating because, ultimately, intervention was not the sole issue, although it was certainly the catalyst for the battle. The disagreement over whether Italy should enter the war, isolated from other disagreements the war created, was not enough to ruin the FSI. Many FSI members supported Rossoni's interventionism—some admired his organizing abilities, and some agreed with his logic. But not all of them followed him when he left the Federation. In fact, one of the men who replaced Rossoni as editor was himself an interventionist.

Especially by the end of the debate, Rossoni and certain other interventionists explicitly rejected internationalism and began to fight for revolution as nationalists. But this issue alone, although certainly crucial, would not mortally wound the FSI, either. There were some who agreed with Rossoni on this issue as well who remained in the Federation; certain FSI members after 1915, for example, contributed articles to both *Il Proletario* and Rossoni's *L'Italia Nostra*.

Disagreement over questions of intervention and of nationalism and internationalism was so destructive to the FSI because these questions became closely intertwined not just with each other, but also with the issue of masculinity. A crucial question after the beginning of 1915 was whether the Federation, which had struck fear in the hearts of the middle class in Lawrence, could brave the test of courage that the interventionists were certain the war posed. At Lawrence, the aura of masculine bravado that pervaded the FSI had produced acts of great courage, but had also impaired its members' ability to recognize the potential of women workers. During the wartime debate, disagreement over standards of masculinity within the FSI produced unmitigated disaster. This issue went right to the core of the FSI's viability as a revolutionary organization. In the months before Italy entered the war, Rossoni and other interventionists goaded and tested FSI neutralists to see if they still constituted a virile community and found them wanting. This contributed substantially to Rossoni's final rejection of internationalism and to his decision to leave the Federation and seek another means to remake society.

In December 1914, in an article in *Il Proletario* titled "Women and the War," Odilla Bioletto focused on an indisputable problem with the syndicalist movement. "Women are overlooked in this movement," she explained, "The profoundness of women's capacities are never considered properly."[70] Bioletto, by 1916 the secretary of the Federazione femminile socialista in Turin, was discussing the syndicalist movement in Italy. There is no evidence that she ever visited the United States.[71] But she could just as easily have been talking about the FSI and the Italian American radicals who associated themselves with it.

In a recent biography of Elizabeth Gurley Flynn, Helen Camp described Flynn's discomfort with the "machismo community" that constituted Tresca's Italian radical friends.[72] Flynn, committed for decades to the labor movement as a syndicalist and then as a communist, was also Tresca's lover between 1912 and 1925. Flynn noted later that "[t]here were practically no women in the Italian movement—anarchist or socialist. Whatever homes I went into with Carlo the women were always in the background, cooking in the kitchen, and seldom even sitting down to eat with the men."[73] The degree of Flynn's discomfort is debatable—she was apparently comfortable enough in this community to be called "one of the finest products . . . Italians have yet been able to offer to America" by Michael Gold in a commemoration in 1926.[74]

Nor was the syndicalist movement entirely male. There were women who rose to prominence both in Italy and in the Italian American movement. Maria Rygier, for example, was one of the leading syndicalist speakers in Apulia.[75] Leda Rafanelli, anarchist and free love advocate, agitated and wrote numerous pamphlets on revolution and workers' rights in Italy. She also contributed to *Il Proletario,* including the article during the Lawrence strike hailing the strikers and calling for Rygier's release from prison.[76] Angiolina Algeri, born in Reggio Emilia, was a less renowned syndicalist. She lived most of her life in Pennsylvania, and before the war traveled to conferences and met with Italian American radicals such as Tresca, Giovannitti, and Galleani. She remained a correspondent of Rossoni's—if an increasingly wary one—after he left the FSI and returned to Italy.[77]

Bellalma Forzata Spezia was particularly significant because she eventually participated in the virile community Rossoni sought outside the FSI. Born in Modena on January 1, 1877, Forzata Spezia had been a member of the FSI since at least 1907. Over the years she had contributed nu-

merous articles and poems to *Il Proletario* on syndicalism, women's issues, and events in Italy; she also ran a radical publishing house in West
Hoboken, New Jersey, with her husband.[78] Like most interventionists,
she had once been an antimilitarist; beginning in 1909, she was a member of the agitation committee of the International Anti-Militarist Alliance.[79] Like Rossoni, however, she not only became an interventionist
during the war, but also abandoned the cause of international revolution. She did not appear in *Il Proletario* during the debate, but once
Rossoni left the FSI, she began writing articles and poems supporting
the war and endorsing Italian nationalism for *L'Italia Nostra.*

Despite the participation of these few women in the syndicalist movement, Flynn's description of the Italian American Left was not unjusti-
fied. One result of the virtual absence of women in the movement was
the gendered rhetoric through which FSI members described and evaluated their revolutionary prowess. At Lawrence, this vocabulary had
united them. During the wartime debate, as their shared criteria for
masculine behavior broke down, it was used in accusations against one
another.

Tancredi was one interventionist who used gendered language and
imagery in *Il Proletario* to point to what he perceived as the failures of
the syndicalist movement and of the entire Italian Left. Tancredi, who
had spent time in the United States and had contributed enthusiastically
to *Il Proletario* during the Lawrence strike, had also supported Italy's
war in Tripoli.

His endorsement of this earlier conflict had produced a break with
the Left. When Tancredi reappeared in the pages of *Il Proletario* in October 1914, however, he was utterly dismayed by the state of international
revolution. He wrote,

> We are just now concluding in Italy especially, and in the Latin countries
> in general, a period of relaxation in which everything was a comedy
> more or less conscious and shameful . . . [a] period in which nothing was
> serious or sacred because skepticism had emptied everything so it was
> without spirit and without faith. . . . Oh, the revolution, once of the
> dignity of a gentle woman who one loves and desires in silence, now
> fallen to the level of a worthless whore. . . .[80]

Tancredi's use of the virgin/whore dichotomy was a familiar part of the
vocabulary of Italian and Italian American leftists. This usage, especially his metaphorical depiction of woman revolution as a prostitute,

also had ample historical precedent. Maurice Agulhon has described "an old and well-established tradition of the denigration of popular revolutionary movements, in which the role of the goddess of Liberty [or, in Tancredi's usage, woman revolution] can only be played by a woman of 'easy virtue.'"[81] Tancredi's symbolic woman revolution had been pristine—gentle, dignified, and badly in need of protection. His description of the revolution as a "fallen" woman reflected his growing skepticism about the syndicalist movement.

As Rossoni would just months later, Tancredi had lost faith in his revolutionary community. Leftists in Italy had not protected woman revolution; they had failed as revolutionaries. He made his accusation explicit, blaming their failure on

> the disorientation [of] the subversive parties . . . who are incapable of finding in their very distant origins and traditions the courage for a courageous redemption. . . . Thus they find their usefulness whining disapproval of those who save themselves from the senseless shipwreck, of those . . . [who] live with a generous heart, magnanimously, rather than suffocating it in the name of rigidity. . . .[82]

Like de Ambris, Tancredi indicted Italian neutralist internationalists for shrouding their confusion in doctrinaire responses to the war and for attacking the interventionists who responded more flexibly and realistically. Their lack of courage and their inflexibility dictated their responses to the war.

Publishing Tancredi's critiques of Italian neutralists in *Il Proletario*, Rossoni extended his indictment to FSI neutralists. He wrote a preface to Tancredi's piece, endorsing his argument and confronting the Federation neutralists by cautioning, "May the 'puritans' not be scandalized and not misinterpret the lively tone used by Tancredi. . . ."[83] By October, Rossoni was involved in a gendered discourse—and through Tancredi, a transnational discourse—drawing on interventionist arguments in Italy to help him combat his opponents in the Federation.

The issue of masculinity in the FSI was far more than just a matter of gendered language being deployed in a political debate. It provided a vocabulary Federation members used to discuss revolutionary capacity and the viability of internationalism.[84] But it also constituted an issue in its own right. The question of whether the interventionists or the neutralists were showing true masculine resolve was a critical element of the debate.

Rossoni saw the neutralists' stance as unwillingness to act as decisively and courageously in response to the war as they had in Lawrence. Numerous scholars, Gail Bederman most recently, have discussed the new threats to their masculinity that middle-class men in the United States faced in the first years of the twentieth century, including the feminist movement, narrowing career opportunities, and increasing tolerance in the medical community of homosexuality. Foremost among these challenges were those posed by immigrant and working-class men, particularly when they waged confrontational and violent labor actions.[85] FSI members in Lawrence had relished the threat that they consciously posed to the bourgeois social order. Giovannitti had thundered in the *Independent* after the strike, "Outside of [scabbery], any and all means are right and permissible on the sole condition that they bring results disastrous to the master class and advantageous to the proletariat. However shocking this may sound to pious, God-fearing souls, it nevertheless reflects the entire attitude of the Syndicalist movement in connection with the class struggle."[86] He and fellow syndicalists had not shied from violence during the strike and the defense campaign. They had faced imprisonment and beatings, and had encouraged the strikers to engage in direct confrontation with authorities in the city.

Though the interventionists' standard of masculine conduct changed fundamentally during the war, they continued to agree with the neutralists on certain principles. They were united, for example, by their contempt for pacifism. Rossoni, relating pacifism to Christ's command to love one's neighbor, sneered, "His maxim would not be a thing to reject if Christ had not taught men too well to cry. Many among the advanced thinkers risk falling into the same degeneracy, but it is truly a disaster if the revolutionaries, the innovators, learn nothing but to cry or to whine. . . ."[87] This was predictable for Rossoni. Many of the neutralists, however, felt much the same way. Venanzi gave a speech at Faneuil Hall in Boston dismissing what he called "the decadence of pacifism." He insisted that opponents of the war needed to prepare for "a new war, more tremendous, more intense, more just." He repeated what certain syndicalist opponents of the war in Tripoli had argued, that "proletarian violence will be creative; the hero will be the producer. . . ."[88]

This was not enough for Rossoni and the interventionists, who insisted that enthusiastic support for the bloodletting of the war was now the minimum standard for masculine resolve in the FSI. Margaret Randolph

Higonnet has argued that "total war has acted as a clarifying moment, one that has revealed systems of gender in flux, and thus highlighted their workings."[89] The upheaval of the war, the interventionists argued, compelled a reconfiguration—and an enormous intensification—of masculine behavior in the FSI. From the first, Rossoni implored the neutralists not to let the middle class "have the fact of our cowardice in moments of danger" to use against them.[90] There was only one way to prevent this: ending discussion, seeking action at any cost, and exalting in the bloodshed and violence of the world war as curatives for society.

From the first, Rossoni had made it clear that massive bloodshed did not intimidate him. "Life is not sacred," he had written in August 1914. "Yes, I see the fertile countrysides devastated, the cities destroyed, mountains of corpses unburied and the rivers red with human blood, but I am not afraid. I think that those poor human machines that obeyed the order to kill or to let themselves be killed had nothing in their breasts or had only foolish lies there."[91] Nor was he intimidated by the prospect of a massive number of deaths during the war. He concluded that "[l]ife that has no worth may be crushed with impunity."[92] With increasing insistence, he called on the neutralists to match his level of fearlessness.

By early 1915, he was nearly convinced that the neutralists were incapable of doing this. In an article titled "Liberty and Blood," which was published in *Il Proletario* in January, Rossoni explicitly drew a line between the opponents of the war and the interventionists. The neutralists were cowering behind their principles. Only the interventionists still constituted a virile community courageous enough to continue to fight a revolution. "Humanitarian friend," he wrote,

> don't cry, don't be horrified if I should become drunk with blood, if I ask for revenge and not tears. . . . [W]e want iron and bread, war and revolution, and on top of all that, liberty. Liberty is not just a pretty woman with lipstick and rouge that a great yell would make faint. Rather, she is a strong woman with strong breasts and a rough voice, with fire in her eyes, who becomes drunk at the sight of bloody conflicts amidst the clamor of the populace, the smell of gunpowder and the rumbling of the cannon. And she offers her sturdy pelvis only to men as strong as she is, and she wants to be embraced only by arms covered with blood.[93]

This disturbing passage was based on a poem titled "La Curée" ("The Bandwagon") by nineteenth-century French poet Auguste Barbier. Barbier's poem, which lauded a symbolic Woman Liberty, described her as

> A strong woman, stout bosom'd
> With raucous voice and rough charm...
> She strides forward with confidence,
> Rejoicing in the clamour of the people, the bloody conflicts...
> The smell of gunpowder... and the rumbling cannons

and as one

> Who takes her lovers only from among the masses,
> Who gives her sturdy body only to men as strong as herself
> and who wants to be embraced by arms red with blood[94]

Clearly, the woman who symbolized liberty in this passage was not the chaste, dignified figure in need of protection that Tancredi had presented, nor was she the figure that George Mosse and others have described as more typical of the symbolic women deployed by defenders of both revolutions and nations.[95] If anything, Woman Liberty here was reminiscent of Marianne, the sexually charged—and, in Delacroix's painting, equally strong-breasted—symbol of the French revolution. Eric Hobsbawm has speculated that Barbier may have had this painting in mind when he wrote the poem.[96] Whether or not Rossoni was evoking the image of Marianne, his choice of the poem underscored his identity as a francophile. His choice, and his reworking Barbier's poem, also suggested a great deal more.

Rossoni's image of Woman Liberty, borrowed from Barbier, was so forceful that it was arguably homoerotic. She wore neither lipstick nor rouge; strong-breasted and rough-voiced, she reveled in bloodshed and violence just like the interventionists. Seen in the light of Mosse's work on fascism, this could hint at Rossoni's eventual role as a leading member of the early Fascist Party. Mosse has analyzed the homoeroticism latent in both modern nationalism and fascism: "Any discussion of fascism and sexuality must always return to the worship of masculinity.... Fascism ... threatened to bring to the surface that homoeroticism which had been a part of modern nationalism from the beginning."[97] However, this implies too uncomplicated a relationship between fascism and homoeroticism, and too simple a conception of what constituted homoerotic behavior in the Italian immigrant community.[98] George Chauncey, in his work on gay culture in New York City, argued that homosexuality was far more prevalent among Italian immigrants there than among many other immigrant groups. However, within this immigrant community, only certain behavior was labeled homosexual. Being sexually penetrated by another man was considered a homosexual act, but sexually penetrating another man was not.[99] Following this logic, since Woman Liberty—even if strikingly unfeminine in certain ways—was making herself available to men as strong as she, those men would not have construed their activity as homosexual.

This forceful woman, if not a homoerotic symbol, could also reflect the possible inclusion of women in the virile community; the interventionists were largely, but not exclusively, male. But this possibility, too, is ambiguous at best. Woman Liberty was a figure of strength in that she was able to choose to whom she would offer her pelvis. She was, however, also drunk (albeit with the sight of blood) and satisfying multiple partners, which would have made her a dubious icon for women in the syndicalist movement.

Whether Rossoni intended any of these meanings or not, his use of this reworked poem with its vivid sexual imagery made one point clearly: His faith in the courage and the viability of the FSI was disappearing, or had disappeared altogether. Though both the syndicalist and the French poet reveled in militance and even carnage, Rossoni's Woman Liberty, unlike Barbier's, did not choose her lovers "from among the masses."

The context within which Rossoni presented the poem underscored the distance between his message and Barbier's original exaltation of the proletariat. The woman in each passage selected lovers only from among those who accepted the bloodshed of war, whose arms were "covered with blood." But Woman Liberty in Barbier's poem was choosing from among those fighting for a working-class revolution. In Rossoni's reworking, only those who wanted to fight in the war would be suitable partners. His fellow FSI members who continued to oppose the war were failing a test of manhood.

This argument reflected the standards of Italian immigrant men, who constituted an important element of the "bachelor subculture" of New York City, where *Il Proletario* was published. In Chauncey's analysis, this immigrant subculture was composed not only of the many single immigrant men living in the city, but also the married men who associated with them. He argued that in this subculture, "[s]exual prowess with women was . . . [an] important sign of manliness, but such prowess was significant not only as an indication of a man's ability to dominate women but also as evidence of his *relative* virility compared to other men's; manliness in this world was confirmed by other men and in rela-

Strikers in Lawrence in 1912 square off against armed private guards. Archives of Labor and Urban Affairs, Wayne State University.

Edmondo Rossoni, a central figure in the Federazione Socialista Italiana, eventually left the United States and joined Mussolini's Fascist Party. Immigration History Research Center, Minneapolis.

Arturo Giovannitti (here) and Joseph Ettor were arrested on fabricated murder charges while leading the Lawrence strike in 1912. Archives of Labor and Urban Affairs, Wayne State University.

At a demonstration in 1912 on behalf of Ettor and Giovannitti, women strikers circulate copies of the newspapers of the Federazione Socialista Italiana, Industrial Workers of the World, and Socialist Party. Though virtually ignored by Italian American radicals, women's participation in the strike and defense campaign were critically important. Archives of Labor and Urban Affairs, Wayne State University.

This cartoon from *Collier's Weekly* indicates how police violence during the "children's exodus" from Lawrence provoked nationwide indignation. This children's exodus recreated an Italian leftist tradition in the United States. Archives of Labor and Urban Affairs, Wayne State University.

AI SOCIALISTI DEL RE

NEW YORK   15 Dicembre 1918   Numero Unico

Drawn by Boardman Robinson

— *Maesta', non tremate, il "lavoro" e' con voi!*

Cover of *Ai Socialisti del Re (To the King's Socialists)*, a single-issue newspaper that brought together a wide range of Italian American leftists to protest the arrival of a reactionary Italian Workers Mission in the United States in 1918. Immigration History Research Center, Minneapolis.

The members of the Italian Workers Mission, which visited the United States as guests of Samuel Gompers in 1918. Many of the members had been allies of Italian American leftists before World War I; several would soon join forces with Benito Mussolini. Alceste de Ambris is seated second from the right. Immigration History Research Center, Minneapolis.

Anthony Capraro, just after having been beaten by vigilantes in Lawrence in 1919 for his role in sneaking Carlo Tresca into the city to deliver a speech to strikers. Immigration History Research Center, Minneapolis.

Carlo Tresca speaking on behalf of Sacco and Vanzetti. Tresca was the first in the Italian American community to draw attention to the arrests of the two anarchists. Tamiment Institute Library, New York University; Roberta Bobba/Peter Martin Collection.

Carlo Tresca, assassinated by an unknown assailant in New York City in 1943. Archives of Labor and Urban Affairs, Wayne State University.

tion to other men, not by women."[100] Rossoni was delineating a community of virile, revolutionary men united by the shared penetration of a woman. It was a community of men who had proved their masculinity by supporting the war. Chauncey argues that a sense of manhood had to be constantly earned in the bachelor subculture. Though he was speaking to the risk of being stigmatized as homosexual, his insight sheds light on the distinction Rossoni was making. In Chauncey's words, "The men in this culture regarded manhood as a hard-won accomplishment, not a given, and as a continuum, not an absolute value or characteristic.... They constantly had to prove their manhood, and often sought to demonstrate that they were more manly than their rivals."[101] Rossoni and the interventionists had asserted their masculinity by embracing the war (and Woman Liberty); the neutralists had not.

Two things emerged clearly the day Rossoni's article appeared, as the issues of masculinity and internationalism intertwined in the debate. One was that neutralists were not part of the community of virile revolutionaries that he envisioned. They were the "humanitarian friends" Rossoni derided, the ones who were "horrified" by his lust "for revenge and not tears." Their failure to support the war had rendered them impotent as revolutionaries; they had not earned the embrace, much less the sturdy pelvis, of Woman Liberty. Second, Rossoni already had profound doubts that this community could be internationalist rather than nationalist. On January 30, the day his *Il Proletario* article appeared, Rossoni took a step away from internationalism and toward nationalism by filing the necessary paperwork for mailing privileges for his nationalist newspaper *L'Italia Nostra*.

Rossoni's move showed that he was not at all confident that he would be able to change the neutralists' minds. It also signaled his conclusion that if he could not redirect the movement, he would no longer be able to work within it. He was convinced that the cause of neutralism would ruin the syndicalist movement and end his hope that it could constitute his virile community. For the next five months after "Liberty and Blood" appeared, Rossoni nonetheless strove to change the course of the movement.

He concluded in those months that the neutralists could not respond appropriately, and that the syndicalist movement was imperiled, because it—and specifically the FSI—was dominated by intellectuals. The role of intellectuals in the Left had long been a matter of concern for syndicalists. Syndicalist theorist Georges Sorel had been openly contemptuous of intellectuals' capacity to lead the movement.[102] Enrico Leone, Venanzi's mentor, had also been wary of intellectual leadership on the Left. FSI members apparently shared his uneasiness—Leone's articles on the subject appeared several times in *Il Proletario* between 1909 and 1913. In an early article, Leone warned that the dominance of intellectuals would lead to socialism's "degeneration into the swamp of a sterile party parliamentarism."[103] Little more than a year before World War I began, another Leone article warned of the dire consequences of intellectual domination of the movement.[104]

Now Rossoni turned this concern into an accusation against Leone's student Venanzi and the other neutralists, protesting that the FSI was being ruined by intellectuals. Venanzi was the perfect foil for Rossoni—he was indisputably an intellectual, and was physically wan and unimposing, as well. Even early in debate, Rossoni had been too eager for action to tolerate Venanzi's entreaties for education and discussion on the war. In October, he had complained that "for several weeks now he [Venanzi] has been afflicting us with his stultifying internationalist lessons. . . . I feel as if I'm still in the classroom."[105]

By the new year, Rossoni had concluded that the neutralists' emphasis on education—on intellectualizing about the war—was not simply boring. It was undermining the syndicalist movement. He ended "Liberty and Blood" by insisting that the time had come to stop discussing the war; it was time to take action—seemingly, any action—rather than stand still. "Stagnant immobility is ruin," he blared. "Ardor is for the strong and movement is salvation."[106] The neutralists' unwillingness to do anything more than discuss the war was proof that they did not merit inclusion in the virile community Rossoni sought.

He would continue to berate intellectuals until he finally left the FSI. In an *Il Proletario* article on May Day, Rossoni bemoaned the effete and ineffective intellectualizing in the organization from which he would soon leave, writing, ". . . where there is a semi-intellectual or intellectual chatterbox, spontaneity and pure class interest inevitably becomes suffocated."[107] He added, more pointedly, "People object that even the syndicalist movement is currently inspired and guided by intellectuals. This is a sorrowful truth."[108] As long as intellectuals continued to rule the syndicalist movement, "the spontaneity of sentiment and pure class interest"—and, by implication, Rossoni himself—would be "suffocated."

The irony of Rossoni's objection to intellectuals' domination of the movement underscored its connection to the issue of masculinity. The distinction that Rossoni drew between himself and the interventionists—virile men and women of action—on the one hand, and the impotent neutralist intellectuals, on the other, was largely illusory. Venanzi aside, Rossoni and the interventionists were more aptly described as the intellectuals of the movement. Virtually all of them had more formal education than the neutralists.[109] Indeed, these accusations went both ways. Another FSI neutralist would later describe Rossoni and the interventionists as "dilettante intellectual revolutionaries in great part scoundrels and...injurious to the interests of the working class."[110] Rossoni's labeling of the neutralists as intellectuals and "chatterboxes" had little to do with their education. Rossoni's aim was again to contrast his opponents' passivity with the interventionists' lust for action.

The neutralists resisted Rossoni and the interventionists' accusations of cowardice, reasserting previously shared masculine imperatives of antimilitarism and internationalism. If in somewhat less strenuous language, they insisted that it was they, not the interventionists, who were exhibiting true courage. Venanzi insisted that "the science of the new socialists knows nothing but a society divided in two parts, [workers and capitalists]....And between these two groups stand people who are lazy, ignorant, eloquent and stupid, who make appeals to general cowardice so as to make the turmoil of the civil war disappear."[111] There was no mistaking who Venanzi was talking about with his counteraccusations of cowardice.

Fortunato Vezzoli responded similarly, arguing that the neutralists were "Against Today's War, for the War of Tomorrow."[112] He had no fear of war. But war between nations could never benefit the proletariat—only the war between the classes could. He thrust the onus of cowardice back on Rossoni and his allies. "For those who have become interventionists," Vezzoli declared, "the situation is easy, because if Italy does not intervene, they have good arguments with which to attack the government, and if on the other hand war breaks out, it means the triumph of their strange revolutionism."[113] For the "pure internationalists," as Vezzoli called his comrades, the stakes were much larger. "If they stay firm and rebel," there was a great risk that, "just as traitors, they will be shot or reduced to silence in the corner of some prison or sent to die in the front lines, struck by the musket fire of those whose lives they devoted themselves to saving."[114] The neutralists' opposition to the war was itself a courageous act. Indeed, certain of them lamented that they had been assaulted when they spoke against the war by some of the same people they had been organizing as strikers just months earlier.

The neutralists' ethos of masculinity and courage—their determination to remain true to their ideals rather than changing course—was shared by many in the American Left and in the labor movement who opposed the war. These American allies routinely voiced their opposition to the war, and their dismay about those who succumbed to their nations' calls to battle, in expressly masculine terms. For example, in the *International Socialist Review* one writer denounced European socialists who were fighting in the war. He lamented, "Instead of expressing their manhood, instead of expressing their courage, instead of expressing their education, instead of expressing their hatred of capitalism, like millions of sheep, they followed the tinkling, deluding bells of their insane leaders, and flocked into the armies, to slaughter and be slaughtered!"[115] Here, as among neutralist FSI members, internationalism, education, antimilitarism, and courage were spoken of in the same breath. Another socialist warned fellow revolutionaries, "To those of you who are afraid, I beg of you to go your way while there is yet time to retire gracefully, for in the times that are coming we will have little use and less respect for cowards."[116] Antiwar socialists saw opposition to the war as proof of their masculinity and courage. So did IWW members; one IWW sticker put out during the war insisted, "Don't be a soldier. Be a man. Join the I.W.W. and fight on the job for yourself and your class."[117]

Unfortunately, the battle in the FSI did not constitute part of the larger debate among leftists in the United States. One severely damaging aspect of the debate for the neutralists was that it was conducted in isolation from the American radical community. The *International Socialist Review* provides a telling example of the invisibility of the FSI and their syndicalist counterparts in Italy during the intervention debate. This journal's editors, active supporters of syndicalism and industrial unionism, had hailed the role of the FSI during the Lawrence strike. Once the war began, there appeared a regular column on the European Left in which the editors tried to keep careful track of advocates and opponents of the war. Fully six months after his call for Italian intervention in the war, de Ambris was identified in this column as an opponent of the war.[118] The editors of the *International Socialist Review* could not have made this mistake had they been aware of the battle raging in the FSI. The FSI's isolation during the debate had two consequences. First, the neutralists were unable to draw on the support of like-minded American radicals. Second, after the debate ended, the syndicalists who remained in the Federation had to face the prospect of rebuilding not only their organization, but also ties to the American radical community that had been so painstakingly forged during prewar strikes.

Isolated from the American Left and confronted with the interventionists' accusations of cowardice, certain neutralists continued to attack Rossoni physically when he spoke publicly in favor of the war. A group of neutralists called the Liberty Group boasted of their assault: "[P]unches were flying from every direction. . . . Rossoni was bleeding from his nose and head as were his followers who were seeking to defend him."[119] Neutralists at Rossoni's speeches denounced him and challenged him to leave the FSI and join the Italian army.

Edmondo Rossoni finally left the FSI in June 1915, one month after Italy entered the war. The National Executive Committee had voted to expel him in May. Although initially he was reluctant to give up his editorship, neutralist Giuseppe Cannata and Quadrio Muratori, an interventionist, convinced him to let them move the paper, now deeply in debt, to Boston.[120]

Rossoni moved to Brooklyn and began putting out the weekly *L'Italia Nostra*. He took with him a number of longtime contributors to *Il Proletario*. Forzata Spezia, for example, wrote for *L'Italia Nostra* throughout its run in the United States. Her pieces in the newspaper revealed the same perspective on nationalism and on the internationalist movement that she and Rossoni had just left. She was convinced that to remain true to antimilitarism and internationalism was to condemn the movement to impotence. In a piece titled "È Tornata!" she wrote, "Denying the homeland, the right of independence, of nationality and of defense of the populace" was "rationalizing a eunuch doctrine of resignation and of collective tolerance of outrages and of the vexations of the strongest. . . ."[121] The strongest in the syndicalist movement—she and Rossoni among them—had had to leave the FSI or be rendered powerless.

After publishing *L'Italia Nostra* for a year, Rossoni returned to Italy in April 1916 to join the army. Many of his fellow syndicalist interventionists, including de Ambris, had enlisted days after Italy entered the war. Of the fifty or so most prominent syndicalist leaders who volunteered, thirty-six were sent to the front. Six syndicalists at the front were killed, including Filippo Corridoni, who had led the 1913 strikes in Milan as the head of USM; nine more were wounded within six months. Some of the syndicalists, instructed by the Italian government to continue to look after union matters, saw no active duty. Rossoni was among these. He was assigned to the National Committee for Industrial Mobilization and toured factories in northern Italy to convince workers to continue producing war materiel.[122]

In Italy, Rossoni joined the virile community he had been seeking from across an ocean. His discontent, and the gendered language he used in expressing it, were shared by interventionist syndicalists like de Ambris and Tancredi and by a diverse group of discontented leftists, nationalists, avant-garde artists in the Futurist movement, and followers of the poet and war hero Gabriele D'Annunzio in Italy. All were growing increasingly frustrated with the impotence and softness of the Left, of the bourgeoisie, of parliamentary government, and of Italian society as a whole. Numerous scholars have analyzed these various dissidents' criticisms of Italian society and their desire to recreate Italy. Many, if not most, ended up in the Fascist Party. Indeed, as Zeev Sternhell has argued, revolutionary syndicalists, Futurists, and nationalists were central to the emergence of fascist ideology: "This total synthesis infused fascism, giving it its character of a movement of rebellion and revolt: of cultural revolt, and afterward, political revolt."[123]

One who did not join the Fascist Party was de Ambris. Although close to joining the fascists for a time, he ultimately broke with Mussolini. During and just after the war, de Ambris was a leader of the Unione Italiana del Lavoro (UIL), seeking to organize war veterans into a revolutionary vanguard.[124] Like Rossoni, he continued to insist that his nationalism was still a revolutionary impulse. As a leader of this union, and with several future fascists, he made a tour of the United States in 1918. After he returned, he stated that he would join the fascists if his affiliation with the UIL did not prevent him from doing so. He regarded fascism as the "only Italian political movement that efficiently and energetically contrasts the niggardly incapacity of the ruling classes and the demagogy of the socialist materialists."[125] However, he chose instead to ally himself with the poet Gabriele D'Annunzio. De Ambris was an enthusiastic advocate of D'Annunzio's occupation of Fiume, one of Italy's "unredeemed territories," in 1919. De Ambris traveled to Fiume, and helped pen the Carta del Carnaro, the constitution of D'Annunzio's brief governance of the territory.

Both de Ambris and D'Annunzio had a significant influence on the fascist movement. The constitution they wrote together, according to David Roberts, "became the single most important vehicle of syndicalist influence on the young veterans in fascism."[126] D'Annunzio joined the fascists in 1919, and the pageantry and drama of his occupation of Fiume provided a model for Mussolini's march on Rome. But the future duce and the poet had a falling out. D'Annunzio never renewed his membership, and de Ambris died in 1935 an antifascist exile in France.[127]

Rossoni and many other syndicalists, on the other hand, were quick to join the fascist movement. As Sternhell noted, "Not all revolutionary syndicalists became Fascists, but most syndicalist leaders were among the founders of the fascist movement."[128] Rossoni was head of Mussolini's labor unions, the CNCS, until 1928.[129] Tancredi was particularly important to the emergence of fascism because of his key role in Mussolini's decision to support intervention. In early October 1914, Mussolini was still editor of L'Avanti! He was still defending, though increasingly unconvincingly, Italian neutrality. Tancredi wrote him an open letter, insisting that he clarify his position on the war. Days later, Tancredi left to fight for Italy in France, and Mussolini renounced his insistence on absolute neutrality.[130] Tancredi, like Rossoni, joined the Fascist Party in its early days. It is unclear whether Bellalma Forzata Spezia ever joined the Fascist Party. But by 1928 she was living in Rome with her son and working as a translator.[131]

As scholars such as Victoria De Grazia and Barbara Spackman have argued, the reassertion of masculinity was not only a component of the new civilization that certain syndicalist interventionists and other future fascists sought—it was central to it. De Grazia described them as the "discordant voices" of an "exasperated masculinism . . . raised in the name of building a 'New Italy.'"[132] Spackman, commenting on Sternhell's work, explained that "Zeev Sternhell . . . lists virility as one of many qualities and cults which characterize the 'new civilization' desired by fascism, yet those cults in fact read like dictionary entries for a single master term. The cults of youth, of duty, sacrifice and heroic virtues, of strength, obedience and authority, of physical strength and sexuality, of war and brutality: all are inflections of that master term, virility."[133] Rossoni's reworking of masculinity during the debate—his sexual imagery, glorification of war and violence, ardor for action and change, and utter contempt for the "cowardly" neutralists—was inextricably tied to his rejection of internationalism and his embrace of nationalism. It also connected him and FSI interventionists to elements in Italy that would form the core of the fascist movement.

Rossoni and the interventionists who joined him left behind an FSI still deeply divided over the war, and in a state of considerable confusion. When the National Executive Committee voted to expel Rossoni, for example, they also voted for Venanzi's expulsion, though he was guilty only of maintaining steadfastly the principles of antimilitarism and internationalism.

Not every interventionist left the FSI with Rossoni. *Il Proletario* was coedited after Rossoni's departure by neutralist Cannata and interventionist Muratori; both agreed to quell discussion on the war. For others, dealing with the split was at best a balancing act and at worst an emotionally wrenching, and even impossible, task. Interventionist Duilio Mari, a Chicago bricklayer, remained in the FSI but refused to break with Rossoni. He served as Chicago correspondent for both *Il Proletario* and *L'Italia Nostra*. Nor did he abandon syndicalism. He served as the head of the Italian Defense Committee for the IWW after the massive wave of war-inspired arrests in 1919.[134]

For some, like Angelo Faggi, this balancing act was far more difficult. Faggi, by 1916 the editor of *Il Proletario,* had been greeted by Rossoni when he arrived in New York at the height of the debate in March 1915. He came to the United States with a long history of radical organizing behind him. He was propaganda secretary of the Parma chamber of labor during the general strike in 1908, and undoubtedly worked with de Ambris there. He became secretary of the chamber of labor in Piacenza in 1909. He fled Italy after being arrested for leading protests against the war in Tripoli. Late in 1912, in yet another example of transnational labor protests, he was expelled from Switzerland for leading demonstrations among Italian workers there for Ettor and Giovannitti. Though sympathetic to the interventionists, as editor he produced *Il Proletario* as an antiwar paper. But even after the war, Faggi found it more difficult than Mari to maintain contacts with both groups. He felt compelled to write a letter in late December 1918 to Armando Borghi, head of the antiwar USI from which de Ambris and his followers had split, justifying a sympathetic letter he had written to Rossoni. He explained that he had praised France so effusively to the ex–FSI leader only to get his letter past the censors, and assured him that de Ambris and his cohort appalled him. It was only because so many IWWs and other syndicalists—including Faggi himself—were facing wartime prosecution that he was reaching out to radicals of all tendencies.[135]

For still others, the split was even more wrenching and the resolution longer and more painstaking. Giovanni Baldazzi also arrived in New York during the debate, in October 1914. He battled the interventionists until Italy entered the war. Soon after Rossoni left the FSI, Baldazzi wrote a letter to Borghi bemoaning the critical condition of the FSI. The blame, he concluded, rested with Rossoni, whose behavior had disgusted so many comrades in the Federation. Nonetheless, Baldazzi's emotional ties to certain interventionists were impossible to break. He was shaken by the death of his friend Filippo Corridoni when he was killed at the front early in the war. Baldazzi confessed in another letter to Borghi, in January 1916, that "the notice of Corridoni's death has profoundly affected me. He was the only one among the many militants I met in Milan who inspired me with . . . sincere affection and admiration."[136]

Despite early opposition to Rossoni and the interventionists, Baldazzi ended up in the Fascist Party. But he took a circuitous route. He remained in the United States, where he organized Italian immigrant workers until arrested in 1917. After the mass arrests and trial of IWW members, he was deported. By 1924 he was in Rome working as editor of Stirpe, a fascist corporatist newspaper under Rossoni's guidance.[137]

This wide range of responses to the intervention crisis spoke to the complexity of identity and militance in the FSI. The fluid juxtaposition of class, ethnic, and gender identities created the possibility of a nationalist impulse. It also produced a sense among some FSI members that nationalism—even political nationalism—and syndicalism were not necessarily mutually exclusive. Even those who, like Rossoni, decide to leave the FSI continued to insist (if unconvincingly) that they had reconceptualized, rather than abandoned, their relationship to syndicalism and revolution.

Even after the most disillusioned interventionists had left, few in the FSI were confident about the future of syndicalism. During the debate, organizing activity had ground almost to a standstill and membership in the Federation had plummeted. In an article titled "Our Problems," Giuseppe Cannata argued that "the IWW in the United States is a premature organization." According to Cannata, most important problem syndicalists faced was the hostility of the "natives" toward syndicalist ideology. "The difficulties," he explained, "lie in the character of the American proletariat, which is made up of indifferent and unconscious people who have no subversive traditions and who lack the capacity to make any revolutionary organization function."[138] In examining their problems, much less in searching for a solution, the complex relationship between their ethnic and class identities continued to define members of the FSI.

Though Rossoni had been unable to convince FSI neutralists that proof of masculinity and courage lay in supporting intervention, after his departure many FSI members argued that they needed to strengthen their masculine resolve. Badly out of touch with the people they were trying to organize, they sought to reinvigorate their movement by reasserting their own standards for masculinity and recapturing the bravado that had sustained them in Lawrence. By the end of the debate, searching for a way to get back in touch with the working class in the United States, certain neutralists began to suggest increasingly militant solutions. Many agreed—as they always had—with Rossoni's warnings about the dangers of a movement dominated by intellectuals. They argued that the Federation had lost its vigor by overemphasizing education at the expense of action. Some even argued that the FSI needed to go underground to regain its revolutionary vitality.

The most startling advocate of this position was Fortunato Vezzoli, who had argued during the war in Tripoli that it was futile for the working class to fight violence with violence. Now, in the aftermath of the world war, Vezzoli argued that the FSI and syndicalism would not succeed until

> in the place of academies and talk, are substituted facts and actions. . . .
> We need to go back to the clandestine way of doing things, to secret
> societies. . . . We should not worry about whether our comrade knows or
> doesn't know about the iron law of salary, about historical materialism,
> or the works of Marx, but we should ask him only if he is ready to fight
> and die for the proletarian revolution.[139]

For Vezzoli and others, the organization had become entirely too complacent, even too legitimate. FSI members had to make syndicalism a truly revolutionary movement again.

For some in the FSI, the condition of their organization after the debate was too much to bear. After Venanzi's expulsion, Giovannitti, who had already distanced himself during the debate, severed his ties with the Federation completely.[140] At least one FSI member gave up all hope. In the spring of 1915, Vezzoli, who had issued a call to action two months earlier, killed himself. This was the state of the FSI after the ten-month debate on intervention. Among its leaders, the generation of men who had led it to its greatest triumph in Lawrence, Vezzoli was dead, Venanzi and Rossoni had been expelled, and Giovannitti had left of his own will.

Several more members, having wreaked havoc in the movement, abandoned it in the name of Italy and the war. Their ideological shift meant that they rejected the version of ethnicity for which they and fellow FSI members had fought. It revealed the contradictions inherent in Federation members' transnationalism and in the extent to which their ethnic identity, and especially their masculinity, informed their lives. At Lawrence, each of these tendencies had worked, though certainly not to the same extent, to the advantage of the FSI and syndicalism. But faced with a world war, a number of Federation members drew on these same tendencies to justify their abandonment of their ideology and their organization.

Italian American syndicalists would continue to make an impact on the American labor movement. But their brief moment of coherent action through the FSI was indisputably over. Recent arrivals such as Faggi and Baldazzi would be left to try, largely unsuccessfully, to pick up the pieces of an organization that had ceased to be the focal point of revolutionary efforts to organize Italian immigrants.

Part II
Transnational Syndicalism after the FSI

CHAPTER FIVE

The Mainstreaming of Italian American Syndicalism

In the summer of 1916, the FSI was eager to put the intervention debate behind it and return to organizing workers. As one Federation member noted, there was ample opportunity to do so—workers everywhere were initiating strikes. He wrote, "[T]he workers have now returned to face their enemy: capitalism. The strikes . . . have been going on in a most unusual manner—assuming a character of open rebellion at times. . . . The agitations are becoming more intense; there is a little discontent everywhere. The time is now—so what are we waiting for?"[1] His impatience was understandable. The end of the intervention debate in the FSI coincided with a surge in the American economy, spurred by war contracts from embattled nations and by the "preparedness" campaign in the United States. The war increased demand for production and expanded the labor market enormously for workers in the United States by limiting European immigration.

The result was a reinvigoration of the unprecedented strike wave that would stretch from 1909 to 1922. In this new phase of the strike wave, workers struck in virtually every industry in the country; never, since that time in American history, has the number of strikes or the number of strikers involved in them been equaled. Union membership during these years nearly doubled and, most important for Italian American syndicalists, many of the workers now flocking into unions were immigrants previously ignored by or alienated from AFL organizers.[2] Many strikes were conducted under the auspices of the IWW. Even more were waged, especially on the East Coast, by radical unions such as the ACWA, which operated independent of both the AFL and the IWW. Despite the intense repression that would accompany the United States's entry into the conflict, radicals and immigrant workers alike saw these years during and just after the war as a period of enormous opportunity.

Italian American syndicalists in 1916 saw two possible directions for their energies. One was to affiliate themselves with the IWW, as they had so successfully in Lawrence in 1912. Their other option was to participate in the "new unionism" that was redefining the American labor movement during the strike wave by allying themselves with the independent radical unions that emerged in this period. Both directions required Italian American syndicalists to rework their relationship to the American labor movement and to reconcile, yet again, the relationship between their ethnic identity and their class identity in the aftermath of the intervention debate.

The FSI took the first route, attempting to rejuvenate not only its relationship with the Wobblies, but also its relationship with its allies in Italy.[3] The FSI threw itself, for example, into an IWW-led strike in the Mesabi Iron Range in 1916. Its members drew on old strategies and strengths, resurrecting the fearlessness in the face of violence that had defined its leadership in Lawrence. Federation members also introduced new strategies at Mesabi, helping workers build more stable, lasting institutions. The IWW was itself going through a rejuvenation; both organizations were rethinking, in similar ways, their approaches to organizing workers. But the Federation's decision had a deleterious, if largely unforeseeable, effect. During the strike Federation members made several stark realizations: The IWW was redirecting its organizing efforts away from the FSI's center of power; the war had dramatically decreased contact with fellow radicals in Italy; and they were now estranged from many former leaders of their organization.

Although Italian American syndicalists made a critical contribution at Mesabi, the FSI could claim no credit. Carlo Tresca, whose distance from the FSI grew during the strike, was arrested on a fabricated murder charge. Once again, an Italian American syndicalist risked his life to draw attention to the plight of maligned immigrant workers. Wartime censorship made it difficult to benefit from international support for Tresca. Nonetheless, the trial was widely publicized, and allies in Europe followed it as closely as possible. The FSI rallied support for Tresca, but the organization was no longer the force it had been in Lawrence. By the end of the strike and Tresca's trial, the FSI was utterly isolated from its former sources of strength and was little more than a branch of the IWW. Small wonder that by the end of the year Giuseppe Cannata would reflect that 1916 would "be remembered . . . as the year of missed opportunities."[4] The FSI's attempt to regain its strength, much less its leadership of the Italian American working class, foundered finally at Mesabi.

The second possible route for Italian American syndicalists, affiliation with independent radical unions, proved much more fruitful. The IWW was no longer the only union in the United States espousing syndicalist ideas of industrial unionism and workers' control of their industries. During this strike wave, adherents of the "new unionism" replaced the Wobblies as the predominant voices of radical unionism. This was especially true in the garment and textile industries, where, alongside the IWW—and, in Baltimore in 1916, in direct competition with it—unions such as the ACWA emerged. The ACWA attracted not only most garment workers in the industry, but also many of the most prominent and capable former members of the FSI.[5] For former FSI members drawn to it, and for many members of the union, the ACWA offered the first opportunity to work and organize regularly within an organization with broad appeal in the American working class. It provided ex–FSI members with the chance to move beyond their old organization and to integrate themselves into the American labor movement to an unprecedented extent.

Their involvement with the ACWA enabled Italian American syndicalists to rethink several key aspects of their relationship to the labor movement. Former FSI members like Giovannitti recognized in new ways the importance of building enduring relationships with activists and workers from other ethnic groups. They also moved, if haltingly, toward a new perspective on the gender politics that had so limited the FSI's potential. This greatly enhanced chances for success in a heavily immigrant industry where women constituted an increasing proportion of the work force.[6] They remained committed to assisting Italian immigrants, and they continued to define themselves, and to be defined, as Italians. Indeed, their participation in new unions such as the ACWA meant collaboration with other Italian American radicals who had long been adversaries. This new spirit of cooperation would have enormous implications in a few short years. But their involvement in the ACWA also enabled them to broaden their commitment to the working class in the United States as a whole.

The ex–FSI members who allied themselves to the ACWA, Giovannitti and Tresca foremost among them, used this larger though more moderate organization to ensure that Italian American syndicalism would endure. In the ACWA their syndicalist ideas could still have an impact on the American working class in an increasingly suppressive society. Syndicalism was one of many political philosophies and radical formulations in the ACWA, and after strikes in Baltimore in which the IWW opposed the ACWA, it was not held in extremely high regard. Nonetheless, these former FSI members proved ardent supporters of the new union. Their support enabled Giovannitti and Tresca to return to Lawrence in 1919, this time during a strike waged by the ACWA rather than the IWW.

In Lawrence, Tresca and Giovannitti affected profoundly the course of 1919 strike. They energized the strikers by evoking powerful memories of the 1912 strike. A speech Tresca gave to a surprised and delighted crowd proved a turning point in the strike. The Lawrence strike exemplified how far labor activists, including Giovannitti, had come in building a multiethnic union and in at least realizing the importance of galvanizing women workers. But it also revealed the evolution of leftist politics in the workers' movement, where syndicalism was one of many radical ideologies espoused by organizers. Syndicalism would have a place in the new unionism of the ACWA, albeit a contributory place and, as time went on, a less and less influential one.

During the transitional years and beyond, ex–FSI members' transnationalism remained a constant in their lives. Their connections to Italy did not end. Italian American syndicalists' involvement in new unions and their newfound unity with other Italian American radicals (the subject of this chapter) would prove invaluable when they immersed themselves in the battle (the subject of the next chapter) against fascism in Italy and in Italian American communities.

The Mesabi Iron Range strike in 1916 marked an opportunity for the FSI after the intervention debate to participate in the resurgence of strikes by unskilled workers. The multiethnic striking miners were attempting to take advantage of the favorable labor market and the increasing demand for war production. Two factors, however, made organizing these miners unusually daunting. First, the miners were not concentrated in a single town; fifty thousand people inhabited five Minnesota frontier communities, of which Virginia and Hibbing were the largest. Coordinating the efforts of these strikers was difficult, at best. Second, U.S. Steel owned and operated the mines. The enormously wealthy and powerful corporation had up to that point successfully resisted every effort to organize its workers.

The IWW and the FSI leapt at the opportunity to help the strikers. Both organizations were adapting to changes the war was producing in the economy and in the work force in the United States. Considering the obstacles the strikers and syndicalists faced, especially the enormous power of U.S. Steel, the strike was a considerable success. Beginning in early June, the strikers held out for nearly five months. Although compelled to return to work without having all of their demands met, they intimidated their employers into making concessions. By February 1917, wages had risen and working conditions had improved not only at Mesabi, but throughout the entire mining industry.[7] For the IWW, at least, the strike was a promising new beginning after many disappointments.

Both the FSI and the IWW were changing their organizational philosophies when the strike erupted. Despite the defeat in Paterson in 1913 and a depressed American economy between 1913 and 1915, the IWW was revitalized by 1916. Due largely to a revised strategy, it had enjoyed considerable success in organizing agricultural workers in the Midwest. The IWW was, as a convention delegate put it late that year, "passing out of the purely propaganda stage and . . . entering the stage of constructive organization."[8] The Wobblies' new approach was embodied by organizer Walter Nef, who brought thousands of migratory wheat harvesters and much-needed funds into the IWW-affiliate Agricultural Workers Organization in 1915 and 1916. In earlier years, the IWW had emphasized the strike, the moment of rebellion, rather than the long-term effects of a strike. Nef focused on creating a stable union in the wheat fields by building a treasury to finance strikes and emphasizing immediate demands over future revolution.[9] The IWW sent Nef to the iron range to help lead the strike.

The FSI in 1916 was eager to renew its commitment to organizing workers and to resuscitate its transnational connections to Italian allies still active in the syndicalist movement. Federation members were active in strikes in Philadelphia and Old Forge, Pennsylvania, and in Lackawanna, New York early in the year.[10] The FSI also began efforts to rebuild connections to syndicalists in Italy and elsewhere in Europe. In January, Giovanni Baldazzi wrote to Armando Borghi, head of the USI, about finding a columnist to write for *Il Proletario* on European, and especially Italian, unions and politics.[11] That spring, the National Executive Committee of the FSI replaced editors Giuseppe Cannata and Quadrio Muratori, who had taken the paper over from Rossoni, with Angelo Faggi. Though Faggi had organized with De Ambris in Parma, and had been greeted by Rossoni entering the United States, he was deeply committed to syndicalism and to the FSI.

Faggi's appointment as editor reflected Federation members' determination to confront the bitter lessons of the intervention debate and to provide a sense of closure to it. Faggi, like many other FSI syndicalists, had had international experience as a radical organizer. He had participated in radical circles in Italy, Switzerland, and France before coming to the United States in 1913. But unlike virtually every previous *Il Proletario* editor—Giovannitti and Rossoni are prime examples—he was not a scholar or a learned man. The FSI's choice of Faggi as editor may have been a response to Rossoni's accusations, and to Federation members' own discomfort, about intellectuals dominating the syndicalist movement. A stonecutter by trade, Faggi seemed much better suited to labor organizing than to propagandizing.[12] His international experience as a labor organizer immediately paid off for the Federation. Faggi reorganized sections that had dissolved during the intervention debate. While certain sections were lost for good, Faggi returned both the FSI and *Il Proletario* to solvency.

His strategy—less talk about the war, less propagandizing, and more organizing—brought the FSI to Mesabi. In a July 1916 article on the strike he conceded that antiwar propaganda had its place. But he declared, "The organization that can contribute in transforming the workers' sentiments through oral propaganda, and that works towards this goal . . . of uniting the workers of various nations, is more effective when it embarks on the war against capitalism. . . . [L]et us work towards the organization of the workers. Down with the war now and always, but also long live the workers' organization."[13] It was an attitude which merged well with the IWW's new priorities.

The Mesabi strike was one of the first events after the intervention debate that enabled the Federation to concentrate anew on building workers' organizations. Its members strove to publicize the strike and to help the strikers. News of the strike and, later, of meetings and demonstrations for Tresca and the other prisoners, dominated the pages of *Il Proletario* for the last six months of 1916. Faggi had Efrom Bartoletti, an FSI member living in the Mesabi Range, act as a correspondent for the paper. Bartoletti sent regular reports on how the strikers, and Tresca and the other detainees, were faring. Like so many in the Federation, Bartoletti had a penchant for poetry. He dedicated a poem of his own to the striking miners called "The Rebels of Minnesota" in his report to *Il Proletario*.[14] Clearly, the strike had captured the imaginations of Federation members.

The tough mining towns of the Mesabi Range were an ideal venue for Federation members to reassert their masculine prowess after Rossoni's condemnation of them. The FSI brought to the strike the same willingness to meet violence with violence it had displayed in Lawrence, and with good reason. Employers in Mesabi controlled most local sheriff's offices and police departments and had hired an additional five hundred fifty private guards. These guards attacked strikers when they held demonstrations in June in the towns of Hibbing and Virginia. In the latter town, the guards fired on the strikers, killing a Croatian IWW member named John Alar.[15] FSI members urged the strikers to defend themselves. In an article titled "Long Live the IWW," Faggi described the end the FSI sought in the Mesabi strike. "The worker... starts to see an enemy in the boss... and he begins to get used to thinking that he has the right to strike [him] in all [his] vital parts: beating up scabs, sabotaging machines and fighting violence with violence."[16] As in Lawrence, this assertion of masculinity was central to FSI members' participation in the strike.

As in the earlier strike, however, the FSI's conduct was not simply masculine bravado. FSI syndicalists saw violence as a way to establish their own bravery, but as a strategy they also recognized it as the last resort of the disempowered. The striking miners, like unskilled and semi-skilled workers across the country, faced violent suppression, disenfranchisement, and exclusion from "respectable" mainstream unions. The only way they could fight for their rights, FSI organizers recognized, was to use direct, and even violent, action against their employers.

FSI members still placed great faith in the general strike as a means to power for the strikers, and as the vehicle for instigating syndicalist revolution. Especially after Tresca's arrest, *Il Proletario* featured frequent calls for a general strike. One unsigned article summed up FSI sentiment: "The proletariat has no greater weapon in its struggle. Let us use this weapon in this solemn moment to reach our goals: victory for the miners, and freedom for the incarcerated. . . . He who is without faith in the general strike is without faith in the revolution."[17] Tresca wrote to *Il Proletario* from his jail cell to build enthusiasm among the strikers for a general strike. He exclaimed, "The Steel trust recognizes its power—the government, the magistrate, the press and the church. Yet you, the workers of America, do not know how to use yours. . . . The general strike is our weapon. Let's use it."[18] These syndicalists still believed firmly that the general strike and direct action were the most effective tools that workers had.

Despite its continued advocacy of the general strike and violent opposition, the FSI, like the IWW, approached the Mesabi strike with a changed conception of what a single act of rebellion could achieve. Federation members still had great faith in the power of strikes. But gone was the unquestioning faith in the power of a strike alone to produce a revolutionary mentality in the working class. One syndicalist from a Federation section in Milford, Massachusetts, Saverio Piesco, summed up this new awareness. He stated,

> A strike . . . if made on the grounds of the class struggle, provides the workers with the opportunity to recognize their enemy, but it cannot eradicate their prejudices. After a strike, the worker that gives up, that no longer participates in meetings, that loses contact with his comrades, forgets worker solidarity and the memories of past struggles. The sacrifices and violence must always be remembered. This duty can only be carried out through class organization.[19]

Strikes might awaken workers' class consciousness. But Piesco, a shoemaker who had been an FSI member since 1909, when he arrived in the United States, was now convinced that only a strong organization could keep them class conscious.[20]

FSI leaders echoed this sentiment throughout the strike. In mid-August, when strikers' energy was waning and the strike had reached a crisis point, the importance of organization was stressed repeatedly in *Il Proletario*. As one Federation writer noted,

It is the life of the industrial trade unions, the struggle between boss and
worker through which the workers see the functions of the state, the
policemen, the priest and militarism[,] that contribute in developing the
workers' class conscience.... It is useless to graze in hopes and ideologies.
The organized force of capitalism needs [to be met by] another real
force, and this can only come from the trade union.[21]

The IWW and the FSI were each moving past the stage of propagandizing among workers to the stage of constructing unions through which
workers could galvanize their strength and their oppositional energy
over time.

Despite the FSI's revamped philosophy and its renewed ties to the
IWW, participation at Mesabi did not constitute a new beginning for
the organization. Even its connection to the IWW, so critical at Lawrence,
was now evidence of the FSI's marginalization in the American labor
movement. In Lawrence in 1912, the FSI and the IWW had functioned
as independent organizations. But at Mesabi, the FSI invested itself so
thoroughly in the fate of the IWW that during the strike *Il Proletario* often sounded more like an IWW than an FSI organ.[22] On a certain level
this made sense. The strike was in the Midwest, where the IWW already
had considerable experience and where the FSI had virtually no history.
Moreover, it was a miners' strike. Again, the IWW had drawn much of
its strength from miners in its early days—the Western Federation of
Miners had been a central participant in its founding. The FSI, by contrast, organized primarily among urban workers. So it was logical that
the Federation, out of its milieu, would identify so closely with the IWW
during the strike.

But for the FSI, the Mesabi Range strike was a harbinger of things to
come. The strike was part of the IWW's geographical reorientation. The
Wobblies had virtually abandoned organizing on the East Coast and
turned their sights back to the West Coast. The FSI had strong sections
in California, but was essentially an East Coast organization. *Il Proletario*
had moved several times, but had never left that part of the United States.
The Federation, therefore, found itself in a strange and unfortunate situation—drawing closer to an organization that was pulling further away
from the FSI's own sources of strength and support.

Tresca's prominent role in the Mesabi strike also marked the FSI's
falling stature among immigrant workers, even as it provided ample
proof of Italian American syndicalists' continuing impact on the Amer-

ican labor movement. In Lawrence, Giovannitti, a Federation member, had been the focal point of the defense campaign and the hero of Italian strikers. In Mesabi, they called upon Tresca, the fiercely independent radical organizer, to defend their interests. As Giovannitti had, Tresca became the rallying point for the immigrant workers when he was falsely accused of murder. In doing so, he helped publicize the workers' cause while continuing to fight for syndicalism as a viable strategy.

Tresca was arrested in early July, after police raided the home of a striker named Masonovich while supposedly looking for an illegal still. They assaulted Masonovich and his wife, and the couple and their boarders, also strikers, fought back. During the scuffle, gunshots wounded a number of boarders and killed a deputy. Afterward, the police arrested not only the Masonoviches and their boarders, but also Carlo Tresca and two IWW leaders for murder. Tresca and the Wobbly leaders were taken while asleep in their hotel rooms, despite the fact that they had not even been in the same town as the Masonoviches at the time of the shootout.[23]

The FSI labored arduously for Tresca's release, raising funds at meetings of Federation sections and pleading in *Il Proletario* with the Mesabi miners not to become complacent about the outcome of his trial. "We must once again repeat our complaint," Faggi wrote in late October, "the Pro-Tresca movement is exhausted and is being conducted with very little energy. . . . [T]he movement as a whole . . . does not understand the real danger that faces our imprisoned comrades. . . . Their condition is much worse than that of Ettor and Giovannitti."[24] FSI members continued to worry about Tresca and the other prisoners until they were acquitted in December. Unlike in Lawrence, a policeman had been killed in Mesabi. There was also confusion about whether the death penalty was still in effect in Minnesota.

The concern about Tresca's fate was understandable, given his long history with the FSI. During his time as editor of *Il Proletario*, between 1904 and 1906, Tresca had had considerable influence on the ideological direction of the FSI. He had helped revive an organization rocked by ideological confusion and scandal and guided it toward its eventual embrace of industrial unionism and syndicalism. Though by 1916 Tresca had not been a member of the FSI for ten years, he had been critical to the defense campaign for Ettor, Giovannitti, and Caruso at Lawrence in 1912.

Tresca's prominence in the strike was logical—like many in the IWW, and unlike FSI leaders, he had a history of working among miners. In western Pennsylvania, where he moved after leaving the FSI, he organized Italian Americans working in the mines.[25] But the former Federation member's central role at Mesabi, like the FSI's relationship to the IWW, again revealed the Federation's marginalization in the American labor movement.

Within the Italian American community, as well, the FSI found itself challenged by other leftists, including its former leaders. As they had during the defense campaign for Ettor, Giovannitti, and Caruso, radicals across the spectrum of the Italian American Left protested against Tresca's imprisonment. Although the tensions between them never disappeared completely, syndicalists, socialists, and anarchists spoke from the same platforms to insist on Tresca's release. While syndicalism remained a powerful ideology in the Italian immigrant Left, the declining stature of the FSI itself was glaringly evident at these rallies. For example, Faggi was one of several speakers at a huge meeting in Boston in August. He had the misfortune to speak just before Giovannitti. According to *Il Proletario,* though Faggi was met with "fervid applause," "[t]he crowd soon grew impatient waiting for Arturo Giovannitti."[26] Four years earlier, the FSI had been at the forefront of the Italian American Left—and, arguably, of the American labor movement as a whole. Now, during the Mesabi strike, its leaders were being rushed off speaker's platforms by crowds calling for the poet organizer who had left his old organization.

Unfortunately for the FSI, its efforts to solicit help for Tresca from the international radical and working-class community only exacerbated its sense of isolation. Though Federation members kept in touch with their Italian allies, these transnational connections were harder to maintain and did not bolster them as they had in Lawrence. Soon after Tresca's arrest, the National Executive Committee of the FSI appealed for assistance from allies across the ocean. But the war had created a much different situation than the one the Federation had faced four years earlier. As early as August, Faggi complained that agitation for Ettor and Giovannitti had been much more intense than the support Tresca was receiving. He pointed to the inability of Italian and other European radicals to help as they had in 1912 as a central problem:

Evidently the historical moment which we are now crossing helps to weaken the agitation. The one for Ettor and Giovannitti was above all characterized by the support of all the international proletarian forces. . . . In Italy, France and Switzerland the agitation assumed perhaps a more grandiose character than in America. . . . An atmosphere saturated with passion and fervor was created—it greatly influenced the fate of the victims of the strike in Lawrence.[27]

Now Federation members had to fall back on their own resources to arouse support for the prisoners within the United States. Faggi continued, "Not much can be expected from Europe because of the tragic historical period through which they are now passing. . . . [I]f no help can be expected from Europe, we must multiply our forces to make up for the lack of European solidarity."[28] Federation members could not count on their counterparts in Italy as they had in the past. However, this did not mean that their transnational ties had been completely severed, or that their European (and especially Italian) allies had been totally silenced.

In fact, Tresca's imprisonment created an enormous uproar in Europe. Once again, the impact of Italian American syndicalists, though now outside the FSI, extended well beyond their numbers. Radicals in Italy and across Europe rushed to the defense of Tresca and his cellmates. Organizations like the Swiss Masons' Federation and the National Council of the Swiss Syndicalist Union held protest meetings, as did workers in nearly every major city in Switzerland.[29] In Italy, a wide range of organizations and leftists exerted pressure on the Italian government to intercede on behalf of Tresca and the other imprisoned Italian citizens. Railway workers in Milan and Pisa, the Young Socialists of Florence, the CGL in Milan—all tried to arouse support for Tresca. USI leader Armando Borghi called for meetings in cities across Italy to insist on Tresca's release.[30]

Often Tresca's most vehement defenders in Italy were transnationals who had spent time organizing in the United States themselves. Arturo Caroti, for example, held conferences throughout Italy for Tresca. Born in Florence in 1875, he had migrated to Philadelphia in 1905. He joined the FSI shortly after he arrived, and organized briefly for the IWW, as well. By 1907, he had left the IWW and begun organizing for the ILGWU. He returned to Italy in 1913 and won a parliament seat in Florence. Though the ideological distance had grown between Tresca and Caroti over the years, the socialist parliamentarian worked tirelessly for Tresca's release. Because of the years he had spent in the United States, *Avanti!* Bookstore asked him to prepare a pamphlet, which he titled "For Carlo Tresca," explaining the prisoner's situation.[31] Giacinto Serrati, the founder of the FSI who by 1916 was manager of *L'Avanti!*, also spoke publicly on numerous occasions at pro-Tresca meetings. So, too, did Dino Rondani, one of *Il Proletario*'s earliest editors.[32]

Once again, Italian American syndicalists made a labor struggle in the United States an international incident. The participation of the Italian Left was limited, however, not only because of the war, but also because Tresca's trial aroused the ire of the Italian government. Italian authorities were concerned that protests for Tresca would boil over into antiwar protests, and it monitored pro-Tresca meetings in Italy and correspondence between radicals in Italy and the United States very closely. The police commissioner of Milan wrote in his October report on socialist activities, "The Socialist Party is constantly trying to make a name for itself with demonstrations against the war and the Tresca case is nothing more than an excuse to keep the proletariat worked up."[33] The Milan police, using a law that had been passed the week after Italy entered the war, insisted that no "public" demonstrations be held for Tresca. All meetings had to be by invitation only, and they were attended by police officers to ensure that the law was obeyed.[34]

The FSI quickly realized that the Italian government not only would not help Tresca, it was doing what it could to discourage support for him. The Italian government had remained uninvolved in the trial of Ettor and Giovannitti. But fearful that the fight for Tresca and against the war would become intertwined in Italy, it did what it could to downplay the seriousness of Tresca's situation. A press release on his case, finally issued in mid-November, said only that the protesters were misinformed—there was no death penalty in Minnesota. Faggi protested: "Evidently the Italian government is annoyed by all of the commotion over Tresca, especially in a time of war. The Italian people are supposed to be concentrating on the war!!!"[35]

The Italian government did more than downplay the danger Tresca was confronting. Unlike in Lawrence, it attempted to disrupt pro-Tresca sentiment. For the first time, the government censored communications between Italian radicals and *Il Proletario*. Even news about meetings was occasionally prohibited. For example, about a meeting held for Tresca in Milan in September, Faggi could only report, "[E]ven though the censors impeded us from receiving information about it, we heard from various sources that it was a great success."[36]

Certain Italian officials were so concerned about the impact of Tresca's case in Italy that they launched a smear campaign against him. In September an official in the Italian embassy in Washington sent a report to the minister of foreign affairs in Rome asserting that the strike was a German and Austrian enterprise. He reported that

> the strike in the Mesaba [*sic*] Range was financed by Germany and Austria. I know from a trustworthy person who saw [Tresca] give a woman, who belongs to the IWW, a check for $20,000 through a German bank in New York. I also know that the workers who abandoned their mining jobs were almost all Austro-Hungarian.[37]

Three weeks later the same embassy official reported the woman to whom Tresca gave the money was "Evelyn Flinn"—undoubtedly Elizabeth Gurley Flynn.[38] Finally, in November this accusation was made public. Leonida Bissolati had at one time been a member of the PSI, but had been expelled for supporting Italy's war in Tripoli in 1911. By 1916 he was a member of the Italian parliament and fiercely loyal to Italy. He issued a press release stating, "Carlo Tresca could be a German emissary."[39] Little came of these accusations. But with the censorship and the monitoring of meetings in Italy, they revealed the lengths to which Italian authorities went to interfere with efforts in Italy to assist Tresca. They also revealed how difficult communication had become between radicals in the United States and in Italy. Italian American syndicalists maintained contact with Italian leftists; this was a constant in their lives. But it was now much more difficult.

As the FSI struggled to maintain connections with allies in Italy to help Tresca, it also found itself cut off from many former leaders, including Tresca himself. These ex–Federation members also felt the repercussions of their relative isolation from Italy. Tresca, after all, was the one on trial. But Tresca and fellow ex–Federation member Giovannitti had firmer connections to the American working-class community than most FSI members did. The political culture of Italy would continue to have a profound impact on their lives. At this point, however, they were forging radical identities independent of the FSI and integrating themselves further into the American labor movement.

Giovannitti's distance from the FSI by 1916 was obvious. After resigning as editor of *Il Proletario* in 1914, he had committed less and less of his time and energy to the Federation. After briefly editing the political and literary newspaper *Il Fuoco* (*The Fire*) with friend Onorio Ruotolo, he contributed to *Vita* (*Life*), the newspaper Flavio Venanzi edited after he was forced to leave the FSI. Giovannitti did not avoid contact with his old organization altogether during the Mesabi strike and Tresca's internment; he spoke at meetings with Faggi and other Italian American radicals in support of Tresca.[40] But when he wrote on Tresca, he published his articles not in *Il Proletario*, but in newspapers such as *La Lotte di Classe*, the Italian-language newspaper of the Cloak and Shirt Makers' union in New York.

Moreover, he often praised Tresca in terms that underlined both his increasing independence as a radical and the distance he felt from the FSI. In one article, he described what made Tresca so infinitely valuable as a revolutionary. In doing so, he embraced Tresca's fierce sense of independence and reveled in the ire it caused among certain other unnamed radicals:

> Carlo Tresca never bothered to write down his beliefs or to replace the oil in the lamp of consistency.... For this Tresca has always remained just beyond the reach of the radicals' favor, always suspicious in the eyes of the faithful, always reeking of sulfur and heresy to the observing friars [who] spend their lives passing back and forth from old sanctuaries to new baptistries.... However, he was always present where ever there was the din of struggle because his soul wanted him there. There was never any quarrel in ten years of agitation in which Tresca wasn't first in line.... He will always be on the go until he is condemned to collect the fruits of his struggle in prison. How can it be surprising if so many simple and generous people love him and follow him like some sort of antique thaumaturge?[41]

Tresca had got himself into trouble with his tempestuousness and lack of concern for doctrine or ideological consistency. The decisions he made at Mesabi would once again get him into trouble, this time with the IWW. But, Giovannitti argued, his integrity as a radical and the love many Italian American workers felt for him were unquestionable. It is unclear whether Giovannitti was referring to Federation members in speaking of "friars ... passing back and forth from old sanctuaries to new baptisms." But to Giovannitti, Tresca, rather than the FSI, provided the model for revolutionary action—regardless of how the FSI had reformulated its strategy and its goals.

Giovannitti was not the only former FSI member whose disaffection with the organization was obvious at Mesabi. Raimondo Fazio, who had joined the FSI at about the same time as Tresca and who had been in the thick of the Federation fight at Lawrence, was also on hand during the strike. But the articles he wrote on the strike and on Tresca never appeared in *Il Proletario*. Rather, they were published in Tresca's paper *L'Avvenire*.[42] Giovanni di Gregorio, the FSI's secretary of the defense campaign in Lawrence, now chose to write his essays on Tresca in *La Lotte di Classe*.[43]

The limitations of the FSI were evident at Mesabi. It had attempted to recapture the momentum from Lawrence through a combination of old and new strategies—emphasizing masculine courage and the general strike while calling for the creation of more lasting workers' organizations. But as it tied itself more and more closely to the IWW, and as the Wobblies shifted their energies further west, the FSI lost much of its direction and energy. The departure of its most talented leaders was the virtual death knell for the Federation.

In the years after the Mesabi strike and the defense campaign, the chasm between estranged members of the FSI and the organization only widened. One main reason for their increasing inability to cooperate with each other was the bitter disagreement between IWW leader William Haywood and Tresca, Elizabeth Gurley Flynn, and Joseph Ettor over an out-of-court settlement the three organizers had engineered. According to the terms of the settlement, three strikers, including Philip Masonovich, pleaded guilty to first-degree manslaughter; in exchange, all of the charges were dropped against Tresca and the other prisoners. At the time of the trial, no one in the IWW or the FSI protested publicly against the agreement, though as a rule the IWW did not strike deals in court. In fact, both organizations expressed enthusiasm about the settlement. Faggi announced, "We cannot describe the joy that we felt upon reading this telegram [describing the agreement].... We couldn't imagine that the outcome of the proceedings would be so favorable."[44] But the settlement apparently infuriated Haywood, who argued it had sold out the strikers, and who ultimately broke with both Tresca and IWW organizers Flynn and Ettor.

Tresca's—and Giovannitti's—estrangement from the IWW led to their final break with the organization during the mass arrests of IWW members in 1917. In September of that year, the Justice Department raided IWW offices across the country, arresting over two hundred past and present leaders and associates of the Wobblies, including Tresca and Giovannitti. Despite angry objections from other prisoners, both Tresca and Giovannitti insisted on separate trials.[45]

Because of its ties to the IWW, the FSI contributed to this disagreement with Tresca and Giovannitti in the years after the trial at Mesabi. Already losing its own identity by 1916 and still suffering financially from the intervention debate, the Federation followed Haywood's directive to foreign-language newspapers affiliated with the IWW and moved its paper to Chicago less than two years later, in May 1918. Though formal affiliation came in 1921, the FSI from that point ceased to be anything more than a section of the IWW.

Years later, as leaders of an IWW foreign-language branch, Federation members still accused Tresca of betraying the IWW during his trial in Mesabi. In December 1920, fully four years after his trial, Tresca wrote a lengthy article in *Il Martello* titled, "A Last, Exhaustive Dutiful Response to My Accusers."[46] By this point *Il Proletario* was accusing Tresca of a number of digressions against the IWW, including his request for a separate trial in 1917. It had all started, however, at Mesabi. The first accusation Tresca wearily addressed was that he had sold out three imprisoned strikers by making a deal with the authorities during his trial in 1916.[47]

By 1920, the distance between Tresca and Giovannitti and their old organization was the not just the result of the Mesabi and the IWW trials. It was also a product of the ex-Federation members' connection to the ACWA, which managed to straddle the ideological boundaries that separated the IWW and the AFL. To understand the role of former FSI members in the ACWA, and the ways in which the ideology of syndicalism was incorporated into the union, it is necessary to review briefly the history of the Amalgamated, and especially its relationship to the AFL and the IWW.

Though the ACWA would become the nemesis of the IWW, the first battle that the men and women who would establish the new union fought was with the AFL. The ACWA emerged out of conflict between members of the AFL-affiliate United Garment Workers of America (UGWA) in 1914. The UGWA, like many AFL unions, organized workers by craft and downplayed the importance of immigrant workers—especially immigrant women—who were generally less skilled than native-born workers in the industry. In the years before 1914, UGWA leadership came under increasing pressure, especially from young immigrant men and women, to broaden their organizing efforts and to organize along industrial lines.

The first rift between the UGWA and immigrant garment workers over whom it had jurisdiction occurred during a strike in Chicago in 1910. The centrality of immigrants and women in the garment industry, and UGWA leaders' contempt for them, were unmistakable. Sixty-five percent of the garment workers were foreign-born, and another 32 percent had immigrant parents; half of the workforce were women.[48] The strike began in September when sixteen Jewish and Italian women walked out of their shops to protest a wage reduction; within weeks, twenty thousand workers were on strike. The UGWA waited over a month to recognize the strike, and then did so only reluctantly. The union's slowness to react, as one UGWA leader admitted, was rooted in "a lack of faith in the possibilities of organizing these people."[49] The UGWA tried to settle the strike as quickly as possible. The settlement angered many men and women in Chicago who would eventually assume leadership roles in the ACWA, including future president Sidney Hillman and vice president Bessie Abromowitz. It also impressed upon them the importance of women workers in the industry and laid the foundation for the relatively prominent role that women would play in the leadership of the new union.

Disagreements between the UGWA and its rank and file came to a head during a 1913 strike in New York, when Jewish and Italian strike leaders once again bristled at the lack of UGWA support. Most UGWA members sympathized with the strike leaders, and by the time of the convention the following year, they were in a position to reorganize the union. UGWA leaders, fearing they would lose their union, tried to head off the rank-and-file movement by holding the convention in Nashville, Tennessee, far from the insurgents' centers of power. Delegates from the rebellious locals arrived at the convention anyway, only to find the old guard in charge and refusing to seat them. Unable to gain representation, they bolted the convention and established a new union, eventually known as the Amalgamated Clothing Workers of America.[50]

The new union was markedly different from the UGWA, not only in terms of leadership, but also in terms of ideology and strategy. The

ACWA's preamble rejected the craft orientation of the UGWA and embraced industrial unionism as the only hope for the working class. It stated, "The history of the Class struggle in this country for the past two decades amply testifies to the ineffectiveness of the form, methods and spirit of craft unionism.... The working class must accept the principles of Industrial Unionism or it is doomed to impotence."[51] But the central difference between the UGWA and the ACWA was the new union's rejection of capitalism. Its preamble continued:

> Every oppressed class in history achieved its emancipation only upon attaining economic supremacy. The same law operates also in the struggle between Capital and Labor. The industrial and inter-industrial organization built upon the solid rock of clear knowledge and class consciousness will put the organized working class in actual control of the system of production, and the working class will then be ready to take possession of it.[52]

The ultimate goal of the ACWA, according to its leaders, was to replace the capitalist system with a system of worker control.

The revolutionary goals of the ACWA reflected the political inclinations of its leaders and members. The union was an ideological hodgepodge, drawing into its ranks socialists, Bundists, syndicalists, and, after the Russian revolution, Communists.[53] Its first general secretary was Joseph Schlossberg, a Jewish immigrant from the Russian Pale of Settlement and a member of the Socialist Labor Party until 1917. The preamble of the ACWA drew from the preamble of the SLP constitution. The Italians among ACWA leaders also had radical roots; they were the parliamentary socialists Italian American syndicalists had been fighting for years. The leaders of Italian local 63 in New York City, who had been at the forefront of the 1913 strike, were all socialists. For example, brothers August and Frank Bellanca had been organizing Italian workers under the auspices of the Socialist Party for years.[54] Communist Anthony Capraro, who would represent the ACWA in Lawrence in 1919, was a former syndicalist.

Despite the radicalism of many of its leaders and its bombastic rhetoric, however, the ACWA was far more willing to work within the existing power structure than was the IWW. The young union, for example, was willing to sign contracts with employers. In the ACWA local 63 newspaper, *Il Lavoro*, Anthony Capraro staked out a middle ground between

the AFL and the IWW by explaining that the IWW did not reject contracts outright. Answering the objections raised by some ACWA members, he stated:

> This hostility towards contracts with the enemy is a direct result of an
> anti-AFL principle initiated by the IWW because the AFL made con-
> tracts and agreements with the bosses, thus shackling the workers' hands
> and feet to a certain job in a certain industry and rendering impossible
> any unified action against the manufacturers. But the IWW did not
> oppose the idea of the contract per se. That would have been the epitome
> of absurdity because the conclusion of one struggle, even if it is tempo-
> rary, is in itself an agreement.[55]

Nonetheless, the ACWA was more willing to negotiate with employers
than the IWW had ever been. IWW members argued this frequently in
objecting to the new union. One rank-and-file Wobbly writing about
the ACWA put it succinctly. The ACWA, he wrote, "recognize[s] the necessity of a contract between boss and worker—just as the AFL does. . . .
Binding the workers with the chains of a contract is vile."[56] The ACWA
was critical of AFL contracts, but to its detractors, its willingness to sign
any contract put it squarely in the ranks of mainstream unions.

This was not the only way in which the ACWA leaned toward mainstream unionism. During World War I, the union won the right to make
uniforms for American soldiers. Its leaders convinced the secretary of
war that ACWA shops could assure him steady production.[57] This com-
pliance in the war effort benefited the ACWA greatly, allowing it to dodge
charges of disloyalty that sparked the mass arrests of IWW members.

The ACWA combined elements of the vibrant radical unionism of
the prewar era with the pragmatism that enabled it to survive the Red
Scare. Perhaps the clearest indication of these two tendencies was revealed in the union's "Manifesto on the Present World Crisis to the Membership of the ACW of A," printed in its 1918 convention report. There,
side by side, ACWA leaders praised both the Russian revolution and
President Wilson. "The Russian revolution," they wrote, "was in every
respect the greatest and most far reaching of all revolts and uprisings of
the oppressed of the world against their oppressors in recorded human
history."[58] Their praise for Wilson was no less elaborate. They exclaimed,
"We joyfully take this occasion to reaffirm our attitude as repeatedly expressed in our press . . . that we stand by President Wilson in his efforts
for a democratic and durable peace, as shown by his recent addresses to

the Congress of the United States."[59] The ACWA became a hybrid union, simultaneously calling for revolution and functioning within the mainstream American labor movement.

The ACWA was at the forefront of the new unionism that defined the labor movement in the war and postwar years. It was able—in ways the IWW and the FSI were not—to combine long-term goals of transforming the political and social system of the United States with constructive union practices. A central issue to the ACWA (and to other practitioners of new unionism) was workers' control. Though the phrase was rarely used before World War I, as David Montgomery has argued, the issue of workers' control had a long history in the American labor movement. Nineteenth-century craft workers had battled their employers over workplace autonomy and control of their skills. The IWW brought the issue to unskilled workers, envisioning a series of producer cooperatives that would replace capitalist ownership. After the war, as industrialists became increasingly enthusiastic about scientific management and the "rationalization" of industrial production, the phrase became popular parlance. The ACWA and other "new" unions reacted to the deskilling of the workforce that scientific management entailed by extending their demands to include issues of production levels and shop floor supervision. And always, there was the revolutionary goal of workers' control of the means of production.[60] These short- and long-term goals of workers' control enabled the ACWA to serve as a meeting ground for its syndicalist, socialist, and unionist members.

The new unionism of the ACWA also included actively recruiting women and empowering them within the union. At the turn of the century, immigrant women seeking work began to flood the garment industry. Chicago's garment industry, in which over half of the workforce were women, was not unique. By 1905 in New York City, over 61 percent of Italian immigrant women between the ages of sixteen and twenty-one, and over 45 percent of all Italian immigrant women worked outside the home. Of these, 80 percent were employed in the "fashion" industries producing garments, millinery, and artificial flowers. By 1910 in New York, Jewish women constituted 60 percent of the garment industry work force.[61] The ACWA encouraged these women to unionize, with considerably greater success than most other labor organizations. By 1920, approximately 40 percent of Amalgamated members were women. By then, only 7 percent of all women workers in the United States were organized into unions; over half of them belonged to unions in the clothing trades.[62]

The ACWA's recruitment of women and their election to positions of power came only with considerable goading from women members and their allies. In 1915, Dorothy Jacobs, the president of a Baltimore local, protested to ACWA President Sidney Hillman that "the men [in the ACWA] are not yet awakened to the importance of organizing the women and lose sight of the fact that women are the majority in the industry."[63] Largely through Jacobs and the Bellanca brothers' efforts, resolutions calling for women organizers and a permanent women's department were introduced at every convention.[64]

The ACWA responded to these calls far better than the UGWA had. In 1916, Jacobs was elected to the general executive board—an unusually prominent position for a woman in a union, at that point—and the board called on local unions to establish women's clubs and other organizations to encourage women to join the union. In Baltimore, ACWA women formed a "girls' local" where they could discuss problems specific to women workers and prepare for union meetings. In Chicago, a Girls' Civic and Education Club formed for the same purposes.[65] As ACWA women gained influence and confidence, the resolutions on their behalf at the conventions spoke to increasingly far-reaching needs, many of which would long remain unsatisfied. At the 1922 convention, resolutions called for equal pay for women for equal work and even for the establishment of ACWA daycare facilities.[66] Nothing came of these resolutions, and ACWA efforts on behalf of women remained imperfect, but the role women played in the union was a marked improvement over most AFL unions and even over the IWW.[67]

From the first, the ACWA's new unionism posed a serious threat to both the UGWA and to the IWW. To UGWA leaders, the ACWA was a renegade union, led by people who had illegally severed their ties and were now trying to lure away garment workers. ACWA leaders denied this charge vehemently, and with good reason. The delegates who had split from the UGWA at the Nashville convention had represented fully two-thirds of the UGWA membership.[68] As one ACWA representative wrote, "Whatever the value of our actions may be, the accusation of secession can not be applied to us. We have not detached ourselves from anyone. It is physically impossible for the majority to detach itself from the minority."[69] Nonetheless, the UGWA continued to deny the right of the ACWA to exist, and the AFL accused it of practicing "dual unionism" by attempting to claim organizational territory belonging to the UGWA.

The ACWA also constituted a threat to the IWW. Although IWW strength on the East Coast was waning, it still had several strongholds in northeastern cities, especially among garment and textile workers. Moreover, the ACWA was not confining its activities to the East Coast. Its dynamic center was in Chicago, where the IWW had its central offices.[70] IWW leaders were worried that the ACWA would be recognized as a more practical, yet still revolutionary, form of industrial unionism. Both the IWW paper *Solidarity* and *Il Proletario* printed the ACWA preamble and offered scathing critiques of the organization. "If we were to stick with the concepts expressed in [the preamble]," one writer explained, "we could say that the Amalgamated is a radical proletariat organization. But it isn't. . . . The officials of the ACWA have always contradicted the words written in the preamble, trying to create divisions in the working class and fighting the true industrial unionism represented by the IWW."[71] The ACWA straddled the line between the UGWA and the IWW so successfully that, just like the UGWA, the IWW regarded the ACWA as a direct competitor. The article ended with an appeal to workers to choose the IWW over the ACWA: "Organize yourselves in a true class union—the IWW—the only organization based on the true principles of industrial unionism. The miserable conditions of your class and the incompetence of the Amalgamated will force you to join it . . . sooner or later. Why don't you do it now?"[72]

The ACWA posed such a threat to both the IWW and the AFL-affiliate UGWA, that in 1916 the two mortal enemies formed an alliance in Baltimore to destroy the ACWA. The fight between the ACWA, on the one hand, and the IWW and the UGWA, on the other, carried enormous stakes for the ACWA. The Amalgamated's organizing drive in Baltimore, one of the nation's largest men's clothing centers, constituted one of the union's first big efforts to organize the garment industry. Its fate there would affect its future in other, larger markets such as New York and Philadelphia.[73]

UGWA leaders, realizing how much hinged on the ACWA's success in Baltimore, sought to disrupt the Amalgamated's efforts there. The conflict between the ACWA and the UGWA began in January 1916 in the firm of Louis Greif and Brother, one of the three large shops manufacturing men's clothing in Baltimore. The ACWA led a short strike that was quickly resolved when Greif agreed to rehire Amalgamated workers he had fired and promised not to discriminate against ACWA members in the future.[74] But the UGWA quickly stepped in and signed another agreement with Greif requiring the skilled workers in the shop—the cutters and the trimmers—to belong to the UGWA. Even more shocking to Amalgamated workers in the shop, Greif, though staunchly antiunion, signed an agreement that all of his semiskilled and unskilled workers would be members of the IWW.[75]

This alliance between the IWW and an AFL union was virtually unprecedented. The two unions had vied for the same workers throughout the IWW's existence, especially in the garment and textile industries.[76] Even when the IWW and the FSI had captured the attention of the nation in Lawrence in 1912, the AFL affiliate in that city had fiercely opposed the radical union, even trying to circumvent the IWW by negotiating with the textile owners. Before the Baltimore strikes, the two unions had been nothing but adversaries. As one ACWA member noted sarcastically, "For the first time in their history the IWW and the AFL have reached a perfect understanding and harmonious cooperation upon the common ground of organized scabbery."[77] Frank Bellanca, long a foe of the IWW and syndicalism, wrote a scathing exposé of what he described as the IWW's history of "scabbism," which had culminated in its cooperation with the AFL.[78] The reason for this alliance was clear to Bellanca and to other Amalgamated members. The AFL and the IWW were working together to destroy the ACWA. A tailor in Baltimore testified at an ACWA convention that AFL leaders anticipated that "this present fight was going to be the last fight for the Amalgamated Clothing Workers of America. . . ."[79]

When the ACWA began picketing again at Greif and Brother, UGWA and IWW members did their best to defeat the strike. The UGWA ordered its members to remain at work, and the IWW provided replacement workers. When this did not work, UGWA and IWW members began to threaten and attack Amalgamated picketers on the streets.[80] The two unions, cooperating with one another, finally defeated the ACWA strike at the Greif firm and, in the summer of 1916, they attempted to oust the Amalgamated from another of Baltimore's largest men's clothing companies.

This time, however, the situation was reversed. Now ACWA tailors remained on the job while UGWA and IWW members picketed the shop.

Once again, the two unions quickly resorted to violence against Amalgamated members. IWW members sent letters on condolence notepaper with black borders to ACWA members who refused to join the IWW. One of them read, "You are written down in our books as a dead man if you don't stop work. Listen Friedman, you dirty scab from South America, if you keep it up I will catch you—if not today I will get you tomorrow."[81] The IWW often made good on its threats. Its members ambushed ACWA members on their way to work; several were beaten so badly they had to be hospitalized.[82]

The ACWA responded by attempting to drive skilled UGWA cutters out of yet another large shop in Baltimore. In August the ACWA placed three cutters in the midst of two hundred fifty UGWA cutters in the Sonneborn shop. That morning, when the UGWA shop chairman blew a whistle, all two hundred fifty cutters turned on the three Amalgamated workers. But this time the ACWA was prepared; Amalgamated members employed in the shop as unskilled workers converged on the UGWA cutters from every floor.

This time it was ACWA members who had initiated a violent confrontation. It was a mentality that must have been familiar to Italian American syndicalists, whose masculinity was of such enormous importance to them. ACWA members would not finally defeat the rival unions until they had proved themselves more courageous in hand-to-hand combat. One eyewitness later recalled, "At each floor... the fighters were reinforced by men of both factions until fully 2000 were engaged."[83] The fight extended into the street, and when the police arrived, they were greeted by the sight of literally thousands of workers brandishing cutting shears at each other. Dozens were hospitalized, and even more were arrested.[84]

For the ACWA, the "battle of the scissors" was the turning point. The UGWA cutters joined the ACWA, and the IWW gave up the fight.[85] At the next ACWA convention, the Baltimore local reported it had organized almost 75 percent of the men's clothing workers in the city (the Greif shop remained a UGWA stronghold). The ACWA had ensured its survival in Baltimore—and throughout the nation, as well. It was a clear signal that the impetus of radical unionism was shifting from the IWW to the new unionism of the ACWA.

Events in Baltimore made the ACWA a bitter enemy of the IWW and the FSI. FSI leader Giovanni Baldazzi traveled to Baltimore during the strikes to encourage workers to join the IWW, and Amalgamated members confronted him at every turn. They accused him of being an "ex-counterfeiter"—he had been imprisoned in Paris in 1912 for forging cash vouchers—and mocked him for the hopelessness of his mission.[86] "Baldazzi went to Baltimore," *Il Lavoro* reported, reflecting on the futility of his visit and the diminishing influence of the FSI, "with four weeks' pay in his pocket—à la Don Quixote he believes that he can lay the entire city to waste and descend into combat with all the workers at his side. And yet the workers . . . are making him look like a buffoon."[87] They challenged him at meetings to defend the IWW and gleefully reported on his inability to do so. At one meeting, an ACWA member asked Baldazzi, "If we can prove to you that the IWW's local 192 that you defend is allied with the AF of L of Baltimore with the goal of crushing the ACW of A, what would you say?"[88] His response reflected the awkwardness of the IWW's role in the strikes:

> "Answer him" could be heard from throughout the hall. I was in the front row and I heard Baldazzi say, "It's not true, it can't be." However, he mumbled these words and not everyone heard him. . . . [A]n ex-member of the IWW, Nicola Crocetti, got up and said to Baldazzi, "Yes, it's true, the IWW aligned itself with the AF of L to crush the Amalgamated. . . . Then they yelled, "Here's your proof Baldazzi! Do you still want to defend yourself?" I saw that Baldazzi didn't dare respond.[89]

The IWW and the FSI left Baltimore not only having lost the fight for control of the city, but having thoroughly embarrassed themselves, as well.

More importantly for ex-FSI members who eventually aligned themselves with the ACWA, the Baltimore strikes fueled the skepticism many ACWA members felt not only about the IWW and the FSI, but about the ideology of syndicalism. Many ACWA members had had doubts about syndicalism well before the strikes. Socialist members of the Amalgamated had had their meetings raided by IWW members, and had in turn raided IWW meetings, for up to ten years. The Bellanca brothers were long-time foes of syndicalism and of the FSI. Frank Bellanca had called the IWW traitors to the working class during the Lawrence strike and had referred to Giovannitti as the "buffoon of Lawrence."[90] It was Frank and August Bellanca who had fought Giovannitti, Ettor, and Oscar Mazzarella when the three syndicalists demanded a retraction.[91]

The Baltimore debacle left certain ACWA members and advocates firmly convinced that syndicalism was simply a historical mistake. For Girolamo Valenti, the garment strikes confirmed long-held beliefs about syndicalism. Valenti was born in Valguarnera Caropepe, Sicily, at the time of the *fasci* movement in 1892, and grew up discussing with his father the deplorable living conditions of sulfur workers in the area. He migrated to the United States in 1911 to seek a career as a journalist. He left Italy not because of economic misery or political persecution, but, as Elisabetta Vezzosi has noted, out of the same sense of adventure as Giovannitti. Unlike Giovannitti, however, Valenti affiliated himself with the reformist socialists of the FSI/SPA.[92] He became a critic of syndicalism almost immediately. After Baltimore, he reasserted that syndicalism was a historical mishap. He argued, "[S]yndicalism, this absurd and equivocal tendency, was stimulated by doctrinaires who denied the [socialist] movement, and it originated from certain ultra-reformistic errors that for a period of time troubled and corroded the European socialist parties."[93] Syndicalism would never have emerged if socialist parties in Europe had not created an opening for it by becoming too reform-oriented.

Syndicalism in the United States, Valenti and others like Frank Bellanca argued, survived only at the expense of other unions. "This is the syndicalists' absolute mandate," Valenti wrote. "They must find something to exploit—they look for even the smallest scandal or error so that they can speak ill of their competitors.... And when these tactics no longer work they resort to slander."[94] The IWW and the FSI did nothing at Baltimore to disprove these claims.

Nonetheless, the ACWA still borrowed freely from syndicalist ideology and tactics. Antisyndicalists' objections notwithstanding, the union espoused goals of unskilled workers' control of their workplace, industrial unionism and the alliance of industrial unions, and a revolutionary transformation of the economic system—all aims propounded by syndicalists in the United States.[95] Even direct action, the quintessentially syndicalist tactic of confronting employers forcefully at the point of production, was, if not generally accepted in the ACWA, at least constantly debated in the union.[96]

Despite the bitter feud in Baltimore, and despite certain Amalgamated members' outspoken opposition to syndicalism, the ACWA still attracted former members of the FSI. Unfortunately for the FSI and the

204 The Mainstreaming of Syndicalism

IWW, the ACWA sapped the strength of these two organizations by attracting men such as Giovannitti and Tresca, the shining lights of the Italian American syndicalist movement. To their minds, syndicalism was anything but a "historical mistake." It was a means to empower unskilled and disenfranchised workers, and they saw the ACWA as a way to continue to pursue that goal. It was this union through which they would have the opportunity, for example, to contribute to a second strike in Lawrence in 1919.

The ACWA also appealed to these men simply because it remained a viable organization during the Red Scare. Its wartime contract to make soldiers' uniforms enabled the union to avoid the devastating suppression that virtually every revolutionary organization in the United States faced during and after the war. The Espionage Act of 1917 and the Sedition Act of 1918 were used to imprison American radicals who spoke against the war. The postmaster general of the United States cut off second-class mailing privileges to antiwar radical newspapers, shutting down—often permanently—many leftist groups' principle means of communicating with their members.[97]

Though few radical organizations were left untouched, the IWW bore the brunt of the wartime suppression. Beginning in 1917, several western states passed antisyndicalism laws directed specifically against the Wobblies.[98] The raids in September 1917, organized by the attorney general of the United States, included virtually every city where the IWW had an office or a local. In Chicago, the site of the IWW's headquarters, 166 indictments were handed down against every IWW leader, past and present.[99] With all of its leaders in jail and its offices in disarray, the IWW could barely mount a defense, much less continue to organize workers.

The FSI was also crippled by the Red Scare. Italian American radicals, and immigrant radicals in general, were arrested and deported under the Alien Act of 1918. This act specified that anarchists, or those who believed in the violent overthrow of the government, could be expelled from the United States, but it was used against radicals of every stripe. Anarchist Emma Goldman and hundreds of members of the syndicalist Union of Russian Workers who left New York on the Buford, the "Soviet Ark," at the end of 1919, were deported under this act.[100] So were Giovanni Baldazzi, Angelo Faggi, and several other FSI members who were arrested in the IWW raid.[101] Italian American anarchist Luigi Galleani, whose career frequently intertwined with those of Federation members, was also deported, along with many of his followers. Indeed, federal and state officials' relentless pursuit of the *Galleanisti* culminated in the arrest and execution of Sacco and Vanzetti.[102]

By the end of the war, the FSI, like the IWW, could do little more than solicit support for imprisoned members. Even this was difficult—*Il Proletario* was denied mailing privileges during the war, and like many radical papers, it confused its readership by changing its name several times to elude the postmaster general's censorship. The title of the FSI paper during the months after the raids, *La Difesa* [*The Defense*], indicated the condition of the Federation. Radicals everywhere in the United States were having their careers interrupted and even ended, and syndicalists were being specifically targeted by antiradicals.

Former Federation members such as Giovannitti were drawn to the ACWA because it was a radical organization that was still actively organizing the American working class. Giovannitti's adament opposition to the war only deepened when his brother Aristede was killed at the front; he would later lose his brother Giuseppe to the war, as well. Though he avoided the FSI intervention debate, he spoke and wrote frequently against the conflict. In November 1916 he staged an antiwar play titled *Come era nel principio (Tenebre Rosse)* [*As It Was in the Beginning (Red Shadows)*] at the People's Theater in New York City.[103] Despite Giovannitti's steadfast opposition to the war, he apparently understood the ACWA's decision to manufacture uniforms as a survival tactic. In fact, he regarded the ACWA as one of the only unions after the war that enabled the American working class to maintain its self-respect. He hailed Amalgamated leaders and members as "the ones who have saved the honor, the dignity and the right of the American Proletariat to look at their European comrades without being embarrassed. They are the ones who opened an oasis of civil conscience in this arid country."[104] Despite its compromise on the war and certain members' opposition to syndicalism, Giovannitti recognized the ACWA as a way to keep organizing workers and to keep syndicalism alive.

Tresca, as usual, was much less forthcoming with praise for a specific union, but he, too, recognized the ACWA's importance. During the Baltimore strikes, before his break with the IWW, Tresca appeared at an ACWA conference at which he was introduced by Girolamo Valenti. After he spoke, FSI member Oscar Mazzitelli rose and objected to ACWA attacks against the FSI and the IWW. Asked his opinion, Tresca insisted, in the words of a correspondent at the conference, that "in spite of his sympathy for the IWW he is not antagonistic towards [the ACWA] and that it doesn't make a difference if a union fights under a red flag or a black flag."[105] This may have seemed like thin praise for the new union. But as a response to a question from an FSI member, at a conference attended by both ACWA and IWW members when the Wobblies were trying to eliminate the young union, it was clearly an endorsement of the ACWA. By the 1919 Lawrence strike, Giovannitti and Tresca had redirected their energies from the IWW and the FSI to the ACWA. The more mainstream union was the vehicle through which they could reach a broader segment of the American working class.

Their return to Lawrence exemplified the extent to which Tresca and Giovannitti were able to renew their fight for the working class. These Italian American syndicalists represented a powerful political memory for the strikers, many of whom had participated in the strike seven years earlier. As concrete links to the 1912 strike, they lent a sense of coherence and continuity to the labor struggle. But they were more than just historical memories at Lawrence. Their new, if halting, awareness of the importance of ethnic diversity and of the role of women in the strike showed how they had adapted to the changing needs of the labor movement. Their input at critical junctures proved enormously helpful to the strikers. Tresca's actions at Lawrence would contribute decisively to the resolution of the strike.

But Lawrence in 1919 also signaled unmistakably that the extreme radicalism of the IWW and FSI had been supplanted by the ideologically diverse, and more mainstream, ACWA. Syndicalism was one of many ideologies at work in Lawrence in 1919, and certain ACWA leaders were extremely wary of its advocates. Giovannitti and Tresca's experience in Lawrence indicated that syndicalists would have a role in the postwar labor movement, but a contributory one: as a motivating historical memory, and as one element of the ACWA's ideology.

Lawrence in 1919 was not drastically different from how it had been seven years earlier. It was still dominated by textile mills; its citizens were still predominantly immigrants. Wages had risen considerably since 1912, due in large part to the earlier strike, but postwar inflation was so high that once again most workers in Lawrence were living hand to mouth. Even worse, the cancellation of government war contracts had resulted in severe unemployment and underemployment.[106]

As in 1912, a wage cut led the textile workers to rebel against the mill owners. An AFL affiliate, the United Textile Workers, was waging a nationwide campaign for the eight-hour day, and it brought the fight to Lawrence in January 1919. Mill owners were eager to acquiesce, since they did not have enough orders to keep the mills running for fifty-four hours a week (the mill workers worked nine hours a day, six days a week). But they argued that if workers only worked forty-eight hours a week, then they should only be paid for forty-eight hours. On the surface, this seemed a reasonable demand. But the textile workers were so underpaid they simply could not afford the lower wages. When UTW officials endorsed the pay cut, the workers, feeling betrayed by an AFL union once again, turned elsewhere for help.[107]

This time, however, they turned to the ACWA instead of the IWW and the FSI. A committee of strikers sent a message to the ACWA which read, in part, "The workers of Lawrence will go on, unless they are utterly vanquished and cowed, to seek a real living wage, to organize 'one big union' for all the textile workers of Lawrence to take their part in preparing for the day when democracy in industry shall be realized, and the workers of the world shall own and control their own industries."[108] Their reference to the goal of "one big union"—long a catchphrase of the IWW—indicated unmistakably that in the minds of the Lawrence strikers the ACWA had replaced the IWW (and the FSI) as the most viable radical union in the country.[109] The Lawrence strike in 1912 had been the IWW and the FSI's shining moment, and the memory of the IWW was still strong in the minds of many workers there. Yet the strikers had turned to the ACWA. The fact that the ACWA was a garment workers' union, rather than a textile workers' union, made the implications all the more clear.

The organizers the ACWA sent to Lawrence in March 1919 indisputably shared the strike committee's revolutionary ideals. In fact, they represented virtually every radical tendency in the United States at the time. As usual during labor conflicts in the postwar United States, the strike leaders were red-baited relentlessly. One mill owner claimed, "Bolshevist propaganda in Lawrence is the real cause of the continuing trouble here,"[110] ignoring the pressing problems of Lawrence textile workers that had caused the strike. But fear of a Communist presence was not unwarranted, as Rudolph Vecoli notes in his work on Anthony Capraro. Capraro, an ACWA member and chairman of the crucially important finance committee, was a Communist, full of enthusiasm for the Russian revolution and for Lenin.[111] There were others involved in the strike who, if not Communists, were nonetheless supporters of the Bolshevik revolution. Ime Kaplan, a Russian Jew who was secretary of the general strike committee, had been a member of both the IWW and the Socialist Party. By 1919 he, too, was enthralled by the Russian revolution.[112]

They shared leadership of the strike with socialists like Gioacchino Artoni and Vittorio Buttis. Artoni, a founding member of *Il Proletario*, had left the FSI with Giuseppe Bertelli. By 1919, Artoni was a veteran organizer for the ACWA. He was joined there by friend and fellow socialist Vittorio Buttis. Born in Venice in 1860, by the early 1890s Buttis had been considered a dangerous socialist by Italian police authorities. He was secretary of a chamber of labor in Intra and editor of its newspaper, *L'Aurora*, before leaving for Brazil in 1911. When he arrived in the United States he joined the FSI/SPA, and in 1916 became editor of its newspaper, *La Parola del Proletario*. Though arrested in 1918 for writing antiwar articles, he was known in the organization as a voice of moderation and even as a censor of ideas he thought too extreme. He did not support the Russian revolution, even in its early years, because he considered Lenin too critical of international socialism. Nonetheless, he worked together with Capraro at Lawrence, running the soup kitchen for Italian strikers and writing a daily column on the strike published by friend Vincenzo Vacirca's *La Notizia* in Boston.[113]

There were also participants in the strike who remained committed to syndicalism. Among them was Lena Cacici, a fiery Italian woman who was a constant presence during the strike. She and the faction she led, labeled extremists by Capraro and certain other strike leaders, issued insistent calls for Tresca and Giovannitti's involvement in the strike.[114] Former FSI member Flavio Venanzi also returned to the scene of the Federation's previous glory. When he spoke to the strikers in Lawrence, they met him with rousing applause.

If Capraro was wary of syndicalists' influence in Lawrence, at least they shared a deep respect for Lenin. At this point, syndicalists such as

Venanzi and Giovannitti did not consider support for the Bolsheviks as mutually exclusive with their ideology. Venanzi wrote glowingly of Lenin in an essay titled "Lenin: The Man and His Ideas." Giovannitti was so taken by the new leader that he named a son born in 1920 Lenin.[115]

Finally, and perhaps least likely in a radical coalition that included anticlerical Communists and syndicalists, there were three Protestant ministers among the strike leaders. The best known was A. J. Muste, who would assume a prominent position in the labor movement in the 1930s. In 1919, however, none of these ministers had ever been involved in a labor strike. In his first speech to the Lawrence strikers, Muste insisted that they, too, had revolutionary aspirations. "You should learn all you can about the textile industry," he told them, "because very soon you are going to take it over for your own."[116] The ACWA had so much faith in Muste that, despite Capraro's trepidations about their Christian rhetoric, it made him the head of the new union, the Amalgamated Textile Workers of America (ATWA).[117]

The FSI did its best to assist the strikers, but it was limited to virtual observer status. It published announcements in *Il Nuovo Proletario* on the strike sent to it by the strike committee and added encouraging editorial notes like, "We would like to announce that the strike in Lawrence is going strong."[118] But Federation members spent most of their time defending their organization against claims that it and the IWW were defunct, and, even more insulting, that they had no legacy left in Lawrence. "The struggle of 1912 had no repercussions on the strikers of 1919," one Federation member paraphrased the argument, and protested, "Where did the Bolshevik columnist . . . perform the psychological exam on the strikers of Lawrence?"[119]

FSI members argued convincingly not only that vivid memories of the 1912 strike endured, but that there was a sense of continuity between the two strikes. At one meeting, the same Federation member went on to argue, the strikers had been asked to raise their hands if they had participated in the 1912 strike. He reported that "a sea of hands was raised showing their faith and the memory of innumerable sufferings of that struggle that strengthened their soul and reinforced their spirit."[120] There was more tangible evidence that the strike of 1912 had not been forgotten. Consciously imitating the earlier strike, the general strike committee organized another children's exodus to remove some of the strikers' children from harm's way. This time, however, they conducted the exodus much more quietly so as to avoid the police riot that had taken place at the train station in 1912.[121]

Of course, the most tangible evidence of the enduring influence of syndicalism were the contributions of Tresca, Giovannitti, and the other syndicalists in Lawrence. Ill health and trepidations about how his presence might anger Lawrence authorities kept Giovannitti from visiting the city during the strike. He and Tresca jointly sent a note to the strikers explaining, "[W]e believe . . . that our presence in Lawrence could perhaps irreparably damage the negotiation process that is currently in the making and that could, we believe, bring the strike to an end."[122] Nonetheless, they stressed that they were with the strikers until the end. They wrote, "All of our energies, faith and capacity are at your disposition, unconditionally and without any reserve."[123] Giovannitti did what he could from New York, writing articles for *Il Lavoro* and for Tresca's *Il Martello* and speaking at meetings in support of the strikers.

His and other syndicalists' efforts to help the strikers were possible because of their work in the ACWA forging connections with other Italian American leftists with whom they had vied for influence in their immigrant communities. This work would ensure their continuing ability to contribute to the labor movement. Their willingness to accommodate the perspective especially of assimilationist Italian American socialists—in essence, to rework, once again, the relationship between their ethnicity and their class politics—provided a basis for unity that would be crucial in the coming years. Of the former FSI members, Giovannitti had thrown himself most wholeheartedly into this effort. He had participated in ACWA-sponsored lecture series since 1917 alongside former adversary Frank Bellanca.[124] Now, assisting the Lawrence strikers, he was forging links that would draw together a wide range of Italian American leftists in the years after the strike. He was moreover, reshaping more than just his perspective on his previous adversaries.

His articles and speeches supporting the strikers showed how far Giovannitti had come in realizing the importance of two issues crucial to the ACWA and the postwar labor movement in general: consistent ethnic cohesiveness, and the central role of women in the labor force. ACWA members revealed in the "battle of the scissors" their willingness to engage in the sort of violent conflict that had characterized the FSI.

The union was nonetheless firmly committed to organizing women workers. Giovannitti attempted to follow suit, issuing impassioned calls for a
new effort to organize Italian women. "The strike has proven to us," he
proclaimed, "that the Italian women are the most active, the most ener-
getic and the most belligerent, as the police statistics demonstrate."[125]
But a strange duality existed among Italian women, who also constituted
the majority of the scabs. Giovannitti declared that the time had come
to resolve this dualism. The problem was not economic or social—it
had nothing to do with money, or with religious or educational background. Rather, it was a domestic problem. Italian women were expected
to heed the dictates of their fathers and, eventually, of their husbands.
Compelling them to obey union strictures as well would be useless. We
cannot ask them, he insisted, "to substitute one obedience for another."[126]

Italian American labor organizers had a long history of struggling to
organize Italian women workers. In the Italian American community,
women continued to face severe, culturally based restrictions placed on
their activities, particularly outside the home. Custom prohibited Italian women from venturing out unattended at night, when union meetings were often held. Italian daughters could work outside the home,
but were expected to turn their paychecks over to their fathers. Of course,
as Miriam Cohen has advised, these restrictions, and the extent to which
paternalism defined gender relations in this community, should not be
overstated. Italian women exerted considerable power within the household, and younger women often fought vigorously for increased autonomy. Nonetheless, their fathers and husbands still expected subservience.
Thus when the men in their families forbade them to participate in
strikes—as they often did, because their wages were crucial to the family's economic survival—they were expected to obey. Even if Italian
American labor organizers did not accept these cultural assumptions
and restrictions—and they usually did—they still had to combat them.
Arturo Caroti in 1909 had offered cash payments to fathers to convince
them to allow their daughters to strike. Even this had failed, because
many expected the full pay their daughters would have earned.[127]

When he addressed the issue at all during his days in the stridently
masculine FSI, Giovannitti had shared assumptions about women's subservience to men and their circumscribed role in society. He had stated
his views on their place in the Italian American family succinctly, de-

claring, "Our society has defined the woman as that member of the family who cares for her children."[128]

By 1919, involved in a strike—and a union—in which women played a crucial role, Giovannitti at least attempted to break with his own cultural assumptions. Though he addressed himself solely to men in the ACWA, he challenged them, and himself, to approach the task of organizing women from a new perspective. "Every act of liberty is always started with an act of disobedience," he insisted.

> Let us teach women to disobey. Let us expose them to the facts of which they are still ignorant—the fact that . . . the house is as much hers as it is her husband's or her father's; that she is economically liberated from every domestic tutelage. . . . Where she was a servant yesterday she will be a partner tomorrow. . . . What was once the task of suffragists and feminists is now the task of the revolutionary proletariat.[129]

This was hardly a dramatic reversal of Giovannitti's previous attitude. In fact, his assumption that women had to be taught by men to be defiant and autonomous, and his assertion that women remained ignorant about their own lives, was quite condescending. Nonetheless, he was at least aware that women's activities were not, and no longer could be, confined strictly to the home. And he was acknowledging the idea that men and women could one day become partners.

To men and women workers at Lawrence, Giovannitti remained a hero, a symbol of resistance and hope. Though unable to come to Lawrence during the strike, he visited the city several times in ensuing months to help the fledgling ATWA, the offshoot of the ACWA. His presence, as always, was electrifying. Capraro wrote to Muste at one point, "I need not say anything about the effect of Comrade Giovannitti's two wonderful speeches. He is really great."[130] One reason for Giovannitti's enduring appeal was that he was not simply evoking a powerful memory at Lawrence. He was also adapting, if slowly and imperfectly, to the changing imperatives of the labor movement.

During the strike in Lawrence, Giovannitti began to rethink not only the importance of women in the labor movement, but also of other ethnic groups. The Lawrence strike Giovannitti helped lead in 1912 had drawn together immigrants of over twenty-five different nationalities. But Giovannitti's speeches in 1919 indicated that he was realizing the importance of ethnic unity in a profoundly new way. He recounted the

effect that the presence of a group of old Jewish tailors had on him during a speech he gave in New York. He had prepared to deliver a bombastic speech to fellow Italians, but a group of older Jewish workers in
attendance made him reconsider his message. He reflected,

> I who had come with a message of defiance and scorn for everything
> that was not new and young and impudent, I was suddenly taken back to
> the years of my boyhood when I was told to honor age next to the
> memory of the great dead and to hail its crooked staff in the marching
> pageant of the people before the lilies of the virgins, the bays of the
> poets, the trophies of the warriors and the garlands of the athletes. And
> lo! The multitude disappeared before my eyes and I only saw them, the
> elders of our new state.[131]

The Jewish workers at the meeting were symbols of longevity and ma-
turity in the labor movement, and Giovannitti recognized that they had
much to teach the "young and impudent" Italian Americans among
whom he had worked all his life. Small wonder ACWA and ATWA leaders
were so glad of Giovannitti's presence in Lawrence. He had embraced
many of the ideals, including the necessity of interethnic cooperation,
upon which the organizations were built.

These shifts—in his perspectives on women workers, other ethnic
groups, and other Italian American radicals and unionists—marked a
new relationship to the American labor movement and American culture as a whole. Giovannitti retained his faith in syndicalism, and sought
to use the ACWA to keep this ideology alive. His sense of *Italianità* did
not disappear by any means; he communicated during the strike mostly
to Italians in Italian. In coming years he would participate in the creation of an Italian chamber of labor in New York and in the fight against
Italian fascism. But by 1919 he knew that to continue to fight for the
working class in the United States, he had to broaden his focus considerably. His sense of his own ethnic identity would never disappear, but
his sense of the class struggle had to continue to evolve.

ACWA organizers were not as enthusiastic about Tresca's contribution to the strike, despite the obvious place he still had in the strikers'
hearts. Lena Cacici and others began insisting that Tresca be brought to
Lawrence just two months into the strike. But Capraro told them that
the strike did not need Tresca to succeed. By April, when he wrote an
update to the ACWA headquarters, Capraro was no longer hiding his

impatience with what he called "the Tresca affair." He wrote, "This morning I was approached by a few young men who made the same old argument. The people need Tresca to guide them. . . . I quickly lost my patience and responded that if the people really feel the need to hang themselves they don't at all need Tresca to help them do so."[132] Cacici called for Tresca so insistently that at one meeting Capraro forced her to sit down and be quiet.[133]

Capraro's fears about Tresca's participation were well-founded; the syndicalist brought issues of masculinity back to the fore, and undoubtedly exacerbated tension about radicals in Lawrence. It was not just that Tresca had made such enemies of city officials in 1912, though this was certainly the case. After the 1912 strike, they had vowed he would be arrested on sight if he returned. Tresca had undoubtedly deeply wounded City Marshall O'Brien's sense of masculinity when he slapped him in the face during an encounter in 1912. The city marshall now promised he would kill Tresca if he saw him again.[134] Capraro also had to contend with the severely antiradical and antilabor atmosphere of the postwar United States. Government officials and mill owners continued to level charges of Bolshevism at the strikers. William B. Wilson, the secretary of labor, called the strike "a deliberate attempt at a social and political movement to establish soviet governments in the United States."[135] As in 1912, the elite in the city was quick to level accusations of un-American behavior. When mill owners initially refused mediation of the strike, they did so insisting, "There can be no arbitration between Americanism and Bolshevism."[136] ACWA leaders could refer back to their union's steady wartime production of soldiers' uniforms to fend off these charges. But the last thing Capraro wanted to do was to further enrage mill owners and officials in Lawrence.

Nonetheless, the calls for Tresca continued, and Capraro finally acquiesced. He insisted, however, that he be given complete control over the visit. Capraro arranged to sneak the syndicalist hero of the 1912 strike into Lawrence on May 2, 1919. In another instance that indicated the enduring memory of the earlier strike, Tresca once again reached across class lines within Lawrence's Italian American community. He convinced certain *prominenti* in Lawrence that their ethnic bonds were more important than their class differences. Tresca arrived in Lawrence in the trunk of a car owned by a doctor named Calitri, the same man he had convinced to testify for Ettor and Giovannitti during their trial. Though the doctor was opposed to the 1919 strike, he was still Tresca's *peasano*.[137] Capraro announced to the strikers that there would be a surprise at their meeting on May 2. Only Calitri and a handful of strike leaders knew of Tresca's impending visit.

The night of the meeting, strikers crowded into the carefully guarded meeting hall, eager for the surprise. The doors were sealed once the hall was full. In 1919, with the United States in the throes of the Red Scare, there were surely spies and informants in the crowd. With the doors guarded, no one could leave and tell the police that Tresca was there.

Then Capraro quieted the crowd, uttered a single word "Carlo," and Tresca climbed up from under the podium where he had been hiding. The impact on the crowd was electrifying—they cheered for ten full minutes before he even spoke. Though unfortunately no one recorded what he said once the crowd ended its ovation, the strikers' newspaper reported that he captivated them for an hour and a half, exhorting them to remain strong and unified. Then he departed a full hour before the hall doors were opened. The police, having heard rumors of Tresca's visit, were searching cars going into Lawrence at the very moment the car he was in left the city. By the time they learned about his speech, Tresca was long gone.[138]

The impact of Tresca's presence at Lawrence, however brief, was enormous. His speech and its immediate aftermath were the turning points of the strike. Furious about their role in bringing Tresca into town, a group of vigilantes kidnapped Capraro and another ACWA organizer from their hotel rooms in the dead of night and nearly killed them. The men had a noose around Capraro's neck before being frightened off by a car driving by.[139] But Tresca's electrifying speech and the assault on Capraro breathed new life into the strikers. Two weeks later, mill owners ended the strike and granted them a 15 percent wage increase.[140]

The contributions of syndicalism to the strike, and to ACWA ideology, were evident throughout the conflict. In addition to the impact that syndicalists like Tresca and Giovannitti had on the strikers, the ACWA employed syndicalist tactics in Lawrence and in other locales when organizing workers. Many strategies used by Amalgamated organizers at Lawrence in 1919 were the same ones the FSI and the IWW had used in 1912—mass picketing, organizing strike committees by ethnic group, and sending strikers' children out of the city. The IWW and the FSI were not the first to use these tactics, but they had made them famous by using them so successfully. In more general terms, the ACWA repeatedly reasserted its belief in the effectiveness of the general strike and in industrial unionism—both fundamental to syndicalism in the United States. Frank Bellanca, long a foe of syndicalism, spoke enthusiastically about Tresca's advocacy of the general strike: "Many people, including Tresca, mentioned the idea of a general strike. It is an excellent idea. . . . What other weapons can be used to combat the piratry organized by Wall Street?"[141] ACWA organizers who led the strike in Lawrence even called, albeit unsuccessfully, for the merger of the ACWA and the ATWA, a first step towards "one big union" that would encompass the entire clothing industry through every stage of production.[142]

But while ACWA members in Lawrence borrowed freely from syndicalist tactics and ideology, many remained extremely wary of syndicalists themselves. Cacici and Tresca, vocal advocates of syndicalism, were not trusted by ACWA organizers. Capraro had resisted Tresca's visit as long as he could; he then insisted on complete control over Tresca's appearance, at least in part to prevent Cacici and her faction from benefiting from it.[143]

Capraro's battle with ACWA syndicalists continued after the strike. The tension between Capraro and his fellow Communists and the syndicalists, evident in Lawrence, was exacerbated in the early 1920s by the two groups' increasingly divergent perspectives on the Bolshevik revolution. Syndicalists had been enthusiastic about the establishment of workers' soviets (workers' organizations with governing powers) early in the revolution. But Lenin soon consolidated power in Russia and called on Communists worldwide to construct vanguard political parties based on the Bolshevik Party. The Communists in the ACWA (and elsewhere in the United States) took this advice to heart, which separated them from those who merely sympathized with the Russian revolution.

In a letter to the syndicalist president of an Amalgamated local written early in the 1920s, Capraro insisted that the agent of revolution was the political party and not the union. During a strike and negotiations between owners and workers, he asserted,

> [R]evolution is not even mentioned. . . . Without the "preamble of the Amalgamated" the workers' union could not save itself from reaction. This is the horrible truth. . . . If this were not true I would be a syndicalist and I would abandon the political party whose existence presumes the limitations, from a revolutionary point of view, of the workers union.[144]

Although syndicalism, and syndicalists, continued to play a role in the ACWA, that role became increasingly embattled as the number and influence of Communists in the union grew.

Unfortunately, the ascendance of either ideology in the union soon became a moot point. By the mid-1920s, the postwar strike wave ground to a halt and the ACWA, eager to maintain its status as a "respectable" union, purged its syndicalist and Communist members. Many syndicalist contributions remained part of the ACWA's ideology, even into the New Deal years. However, they were often diluted into vague, nonrevolutionary calls for industrial unionism and "industrial democracy."[145]

The years following the intervention debate offered Italian American syndicalists two distinct avenues to reestablish and reformulate their relationships to the American labor movement. Those remaining in the FSI chose to remain linked to the IWW. They made an earnest effort to recover their momentum in organizing workers, drawing during the war years on a combination of old and new strategies. But FSI members marginalized themselves by tying their fate to the IWW as it moved away from the Federation's locus of strength. Both organizations, moreover, would succumb to the suppression of the Red Scare. Syndicalism would remain a vital ideology in the labor movement in the United States, but not through the FSI.

Rather, leading Italian American syndicalists would ally themselves with new unions such as the ACWA. Giovannitti and Tresca's participation in the ACWA enabled them to escape, if briefly, the suppression that overwhelmed the FSI and the IWW. But this second option demanded a dramatic shift in perspective on labor organizing in the United States, on the relationship between ethnic identity and class politics, and on issues of gender in the workplace. Cooperating with the ACWA, and especially participating in Lawrence in 1919, Italian American syndicalists made halting steps toward a new attitude in relation to non-Italians and women in the workforce. They also built bridges to other Italian American leftists with whom they had fought for years.

Ex–FSI members integrated their ideology into the new unionism of the ACWA and brought syndicalist ideas into the larger American labor movement. The role of syndicalism in the ACWA never went unchallenged, but its influence on the organization was unquestionable. Giovannitti, and especially Tresca, were able, moreover, to play fundamentally important roles in the second Lawrence strike, not only as powerful historical memories, but also as inspiring and maturing strike leaders.

Their immersion in the ACWA and in the American labor movement, however, did not mark the end of their involvement in Italian political culture. Nor did it indicate an abdication of the responsibility they assumed for addressing the specific needs of Italian American workers. At Lawrence in 1919 they had far fewer transnational connections to their homeland than FSI members had had during the earlier strike. But these syndicalists had not lost their passionate concern about their home country and their fellow immigrants, concerns which had led them to join the FSI early in their careers in the United States. Rather, their involvement in the ACWA opened up new avenues for approaching the problems facing Italian American workers and, as Mussolini's influence and power increased, facing Italy itself.

The spirit of cooperation they forged with many Italian American radicals and unionists in the ACWA—Capraro was an exception here, of course—would lead to the creation of an Italian chamber of labor in New York City soon after the Lawrence strike. Through this chamber, former FSI members and a variety of other Italian American radicals would reformulate their relationship to the Italian immigrant working class. The evolution of the chamber's purposes would reveal that transnational connections between Italian American leftists and their homeland remained as important, and as complex, as they had been a decade earlier. In the 1920s, it would become the vehicle through which they would battle against both the Red Scare in the United States and fascism in Italy.

CHAPTER SIX

The Italian American Left against the Postwar Reaction

In April 1923, soon after Mussolini rose to power in Italy, Arturo Giovannitti called for unity at a New York meeting hall packed with Italian American radicals and workers. "Supported by the full resources of Italy's black shirts who control all areas of the Italian government, and encouraged by the instigators of reaction in America," he entreated the crowd, "the fascists in America can be beaten only by a solid organization of the liberal, radical and constructive work force in America."[1] At this meeting of Italian American syndicalists, socialists, Communists, and unionists—a room full of former adversaries—Giovannitti articulated the desires of everyone present. He was speaking to delegates of the Anti-Fascist Alliance of North America (AFANA), established a month earlier.

Though everyone present agreed with Giovannitti, the spirit of cooperation that constituted what was then the only organized opposition to fascism in the United States was the result of several years of arduous coalition building. A series of cooperative efforts by Italian American radicals had enabled them to set aside competing versions of ethnic radicalism and build an infrastructure to battle against postwar anti-radical reaction in both the United States and Italy. Through these efforts they would redefine their relationship to the United States and prepare themselves for the battle against fascism that would dominate the rest of their lives.

The victorious Lawrence strike in 1919 had not signaled an end to Italian American leftists' transnationalism. And while cooperation between former FSI members such as Giovannitti and Tresca and Italian American union organizers such as Frank Bellanca and Anthony Capraro in the ACWA helped ensure the victory, it was not the first time that these former adversaries had worked together. In December 1918, just before the strike, they found common cause opposing a collection of former syndicalists and radicals from Italy who were interventionists during the war and were now arriving in the United States as the Italian Workers Mission. AFL leader Samuel Gompers, well known for his contempt for southern and eastern European immigrants and for his opposition to radicalism, hosted the mission. In the long term, the Italian American Left's opposition to the mission, many of whose members would soon ally themselves with the Italian fascist movement, anticipated their eventual immersion in the battle against Mussolini and his followers. More immediately, in the years after World War I—years filled both with hopes for a revolution in Italy and the specter of a nativist and antiradical reaction in the United States—former FSI members and leading Italian American unionists finally worked together to create an institution to galvanize the Italian American working class. This institution, the Italian chamber of labor of New York City, enabled Italian American radicals to build on the unity they had achieved in opposing the mission and during the Lawrence strike in 1919.

The chamber reflected its members' evolving relationships to Italy and the United States as well as the still complex relationship between their ethnic and class identities. The chamber, established in November 1919, was initially an attempt to recreate powerful working-class chambers in Italy. It did not, however, live up to its creators' expectations; it was impossible to recreate an Italian chamber of labor in the United States. The realities of a multiethnic working class rendered the chamber's original goals out of reach. Even as they came to terms with their inability to recreate an Italian institution, Italian American leftists faced the stark implications of their ethnic identity in the United States. In the postwar years they endured ongoing deportations of immigrant radicals, the "Americanization" campaign waged against immigrants, and the open-shop movement. This postwar reaction exacerbated existing problems in the Italian American working-class movement and convinced chamber leaders to revise their aims. By 1920, they began to use the chamber to confront nativists by enabling immigrants to take the process of assim-

ilation into their own hands. They encouraged fellow Italians to integrate into American society as workers through the labor movement.

This capacity to experiment with the tactics and structures that had
brought Italian American syndicalists their greatest successes characterized the evolution of the chamber. Its purposes continued to change as
Italian American leftists used it to respond to developments in both
American and Italian political culture. By the end of 1922, the chamber,
again straying far from its original purposes, became crucially important
in yet another sense. Once Mussolini rose to power in Italy, the Italian
chamber of labor of New York City, along with the fiercely independent
Carlo Tresca, would lead the antifascist movement in the United States.
Indeed, for several years Tresca and chamber members who founded the
AFANA were Mussolini's only organized opponents in the United States.

On one level, the immersion of the already struggling chamber in the
crusade against fascism signaled that ex–Federation members and their
new allies had begun a period of retrenchment and defensiveness almost
as quickly as the IWW and the FSI. But chamber members' efforts on
behalf of Italian immigrants and against fascism reflected not so much
retrenchment as their capacity to repeatedly reformulate their class and
ethnic identities in the political whirlwind of the postwar world. Their
battle against reaction in the United States and in Italy was forced upon
them. But as their response to the Italian Workers Mission, their efforts
to establish—and reorient—the chamber of labor, and their vigorous
opposition to fascism showed, it was a battle they were prepared to fight.
Italian American leftists did not simply endure the onslaught of nativists
and antiradicals in the United States. Despite small numbers, they established the antifascist movement in Italian American neighborhoods
and in the United States as a whole.

Giovannitti and other former Federation members had shown willingness to work with more mainstream Italian American union organizers
in Lawrence in 1919. But to understand how they finally created a unified
chamber of labor—and why the purposes of this organization evolved
as they did—it is necessary to backtrack to the arrival of the Italian
Workers Mission in December 1918.

Though rarely dicussed by historians, the mission had enormous implications and consequences for Italian American radicals.[2] First, it clearly

indicated the long reach of Italian politics and their continuing impact on the Italian American Left. Political alliances were still being made—and broken—across oceans. The challenging presence of the Italian ex-radicals, including several future fascists, in the mission, now guests of Gompers and speaking against them, provoked unprecedented cooperation on the Italian American Left. Former FSI syndicalists, Italian union organizers, and independent radicals such as Tresca produced a pamphlet titled *Ai Socialisti del Re* (*To the King's Socialists*). They also coordinated their efforts to confront former ally Alceste de Ambris and the other mission members throughout their tour.

Second, the mission revealed to Italian American radicals the connection between wartime interventionists and the postwar bourgeois reaction in Italy, a connection that foreshadowed the one between the bourgeois reaction and the fascist movement. In this sense their opposition to this mission anticipated their battle against fascism.

Third, by linking Gompers's nativism and antiradicalism with antiradical elements in Italy, the mission unified Italian American leftist opposition to the postwar reaction in the United States. The Italian Workers Mission assaulted both their class and ethnic sensibilities. They shared a sense of outrage at the betrayal of the working class by their former allies. They were also united as Italians in condemning the nativist host of the mission.

The Italian Workers Mission's simple goals belied the complexity not only of its members' past and future roles in Italian politics, but also of their relationship to Italian American working-class leaders. The mission's purpose was twofold. First, the mission was to tour major American industrial centers, reciprocating Gompers's visit to Italy the previous summer. Second, as a patriotic colonial newspaper described it, it was intended "to render more cordial the relationship between the organized Italian work force and that of the United States."[3]

But Italian American radicals regarded the mission as a painful reunion with men who had betrayed them and the working class. Alceste de Ambris, who with Rossoni had called for intervention even before Mussolini, led the mission. Another mission member, former syndicalist Silvano Fasulo, now edited the nationalistic *Popolo d'Italia* with Benito Mussolini. Several more, including Alceste's brother Amilcare de Ambris, had been syndicalists and/or active in the labor movement.[4] The Italian American

Left, and particularly the FSI, had once considered virtually every member of the mission an ally.

The repercussions of the intervention debate had not ended when Italy entered the war, or even when the war had ended a month earlier. When the mission arrived, the issue of intervention, which had wreaked havoc in socialist and syndicalist organizations in Italy, and from across an ocean in the FSI, as well, again reached a boil. Former Federation members and their new allies assailed mission members as traitors to their ideals and to the working class. Flavio Venanzi announced in *Ai Socialisti del Re,*

> One beautiful summer morning these men realized that capitalism is capable of promoting war . . . that socialist ideas are false . . . that the socialists, syndicalists, and anarchists are traitors and spies. . . . The Italian bourgeoisie opens its arms to the prodigal sons that joined them in the crusade against the Italian revolutionaries. Mussolini [and] de Ambris [have] tightened their allegiance with the gallows.[5]

The intervention debate had only strengthened Italian American radicals' resolve to work together. De Ambris and the other mission members did not realize, communist ACWA organizer Anthony Capraro declared, that "the greatest slaughter that history can remember possesses both scandalizing and purifying characteristics."[6] The war that had produced de Ambris and the others' betrayal had given Italian American radicals a common cause. He continued, "[W]hen the ones from Italy, in response to the attraction of betrayal, came to America . . . [i]nstead of discord among the parties, they found they had to swallow the bitter pill of finding thirst for action and . . . liberation!"[7]

The mission members did not consider themselves traitors, insisting that they had themselves been betrayed. They had argued for intervention, and had been ostracized against their will. De Ambris declared that he was "always and more than ever a syndicalist."[8] But he was by this time proposing a much different route to revolution. Together with syndicalist interventionists Edmondo Rossoni and Angelo Olivetti, de Ambris had founded the UIL in June 1918. The UIL was a direct challenge to the existing syndicalist organization in Italy, the USI, whose leaders had also issued an angry denunciation of the mission.[9] The UIL newspaper, *L'Italia Nostra,* reflected the nationalist and interventionist character of the new organization as well as Rossoni's influence. Like Rossoni's newspaper of the same name which he published in Brooklyn before he returned to Italy, the UIL paper's masthead blared: "[T]he Fatherland should not be denied, it should be conquered!"[10] The revolution UIL leaders sought was one of national, rather than international, conquest. They considered the Bolshevik revolution, and the enthusiasm it had generated among many Italian radicals, a profound menace to Italy.

UIL leaders wanted to combat both the Italian liberal parliamentary state and the existing labor organizations in Italy, which UIL members thought had acted woefully during the war. De Ambris focused on workers who were disgruntled with the USI and the PSI's antiwar stance. He focused especially on war veterans, whom he regarded as battle-hardened and potentially the new vanguard of a revolution. Rossoni's aims for the UIL were much simpler. As he explained to Mussolini late in the war, he wanted "to organize the greatest number of workers. Only then will we decide the question of methods."[11] Rossoni even proposed a merger in early 1919 between the UIL and the CGL, the national federation of chambers of labor, despite its socialist leadership. His proposal, no doubt an effort to coopt the numerical strength of the CGL, was brusquely rejected. Rossoni, despite his failed merger plans, agreed with de Ambris and the UIL that the methods and organizations of their old allies were bankrupt.

They maintained, however, that they were still revolutionaries. In March 1919, for example, the UIL would lead an occupation of a steel factory in Dalmine which ended only when fifteen hundred soldiers recaptured the factory by force. The occupation was hailed by Mussolini, who in the months just before and after the mission was encouraging UIL leaders to join him in establishing the fascist movement.[12]

Italian American leftists quickly rejected de Ambris and the other mission members' insistence that they were "renegade" and "misunderstood" radicals. Tresca derided de Ambris's claim as cynical manipulation of revolutionary ideology. In *Ai Socialisti del Re*, he wrote: "Syndicalism—now that he has taken off his mask it is easier to recognize his attitudes—was not a method of struggle and accession of the revolutionary working class, but a means to use and to prepare the market for his pliable ideas."[13] Frank Bellanca, too, berated de Ambris for abandoning his ideals. Speaking unusually sympathetically of the early years of the syndicalist movement, Bellanca reminded him, "I remember your youthful enthusiasm. . . . Orano, Monicelli and Leone were at your side and it seemed that a super human revindication glimmered in the future. But that was 1907. And in eleven years we have seen many rises and falls . . . [including] you, Orano, Sabatini, Fasulo and Rossoni."[14] De Ambris and his allies' support for the war and their nationalism placed them outside the movement.

Besieged by former comrades, de Ambris's appeal to his friend Angelo Faggi, then editor of the FSI's *Il Nuovo Proletario,* also failed. De Ambris explained, "I can excuse the slanderous attacks made against me by those who don't know me; but I can't find any excuse for you—you were so close to me and up until your departure for America (I contributed to your expenses) you demonstrated nothing but friendship and faith towards me."[15] Faggi and the FSI were isolated from the Italian American radical community. No one in the Federation contributed to the *Ai Socialisti del Re* pamphlet. Nonetheless, de Ambris was most closely allied to the FSI before the war. The interventionist's personal disclaimer did not sway Faggi. He reminded de Ambris that "you are the one who compromised our friendship by forgetting the ideals that held us together— and in doing so you violently broke our friendship."[16] Given de Ambris's choices, Faggi could only renounce him as a class traitor, as well.

Alceste de Ambris, Rossoni, and the other interventionists, in breaking with the FSI and splintering the syndicalist movement, had questioned the masculinity and courage of the neutralists, and the reappearance of accusatory masculine language and imagery underscored the enduring bitterness of the intervention debate. Contributors to *Ai Socialisti del Re* consistently referred to de Ambris as *Quattropalle*—literally, "four balls"— in all likelihood alluding to de Ambris's inflated sense of his own masculinity. Vincenzo Vacirca made even more specific reference to the taunts the interventionists had hurled during the debate. He wrote, "That which lies between us is the distance between the honest workers and the supporters of the international bourgeoisie. If we wanted to use their language, we would call them 'bitches.'"[17] But as Vacirca made clear in this invective, the burning issue now was not simply intervention, but mission members' alliance with the bourgeoisie and the ruling class in Italy and in the United States.

The participants in the mission tried to downplay their alliance with the government and with industrialists in Italy. They insisted, in fact, that they did not represent anyone in Italy. De Ambris wrote in Mussolini's *Popolo d'Italia,* "Our mission contains no official character because we are here on our own."[18] He repeated this strange admission in another interview: "We come to America not as official delegates of any particular organization."[19] There was ironic truth in this assertion. Although all of the mission members were labor organizers and editors, none could claim any substantial support in Italy. De Ambris and Rossoni's UIL had few supporters. Mussolini would not form the *Fasci di Combattimento* (the organization of the early fascist movement) until March 1919; thus Fasulo had no real following, either.[20]

But the contributors to *Ai Socialisti del Re* recognized that the mission members, once adversaries in a debate on the war within the Left, were now active agents of the bourgeois reaction. Throughout the mission's tour, Italian American radicals confronted de Ambris and the others for their association with the Italian bourgeoisie. One of them calculated the cost of the three-month tour at two hundred sixty thousand lire (twenty-four thousand dollars). He insisted, "We must pose the question—where did these men get 260,000 lire for the trip?"[21] The answer was obvious, and one of them, Pietro Allegra, stated it outright:

> The royal Italian government . . . sent a certain Workers Commission to America representing the Italian proletariat(?!) with de Ambris as spokesman. Its apparent goal is to "pay back" Gompers' visit to Italy last summer, but in reality they came to America with the underlying goal of quieting the emigrated workers and leading them away from Bolshevism.[22]

The mission was in the United States at the expense of the Italian government and of leading Italian industrialists, attempting to undermine Italian American leftists in their communities.

They had sponsored this visit precisely because virtually all of the members of the tour had abandoned their leftist ideals to support the war and were now fighting against leftists in Italy. The sponsors assumed that there was no better propaganda against radicals than the use of their ex-allies to undermine their principles. That was why, for example, when Edmondo Rossoni returned to Italy to join the Italian army after leaving the FSI, the Italian government sent him out on lecture tours, where he urged Italian workers to throw themselves wholeheartedly into the war.[23] This strategy was not lost on Italian American radicals, who frequently interrupted the mission members' meetings to reveal them to their audience as traitors and agents of oppression.

Nor were the implications of having Samuel Gompers host the mission lost on Italian American radicals, all of whom by now considered him a bourgeois collaborator and an enemy of the working class. Gompers and the AFL had long been a divisive issue for them. The split between Giovannitti, Venanzi, and the syndicalists, on the one hand, and Frank Bellanca and other Italian American union organizers, on the other hand, had been rooted in large part in disagreement over Bellanca and the others' affiliation with the AFL. The syndicalists had dismissed Bellanca's protests that he had chosen to work within the AFL to steer it away from Gompers's influence. But this was no longer an issue in 1918—Bellanca had disassociated himself from the AFL when Gompers tried to strangle the ACWA. The Italian American leftists standing opposed to the mission were of one mind about Samuel Gompers.

Gompers was perfectly suited to host the mission, because his wartime activities closely paralleled those of his Italian guests. Though long an enemy of socialists and syndicalists, he had also been an adamant antimilitarist before the war. In July 1914, he had sent essays advocating international peace to the Carnegie Peace Foundation for publication. But when the war erupted he, like the Italian ex-radicals, quickly embraced the conflict. He later wrote, "I hastened to the Carnegie Peace Foundation and withdrew the manuscript I had given them authority to publish. I was no longer a pacifist."[24] When the United States entered the war in 1917, he immediately pledged the cooperation of the labor movement.

His cooperation with the government took several forms. He was already serving with several leading industrialists on an advisory commission on preparedness established by President Wilson in 1916. Now, with the United States in the conflict, he established a War Committee on Labor to arouse working-class support for the war. In the Fall of 1917, he established the American Alliance of Labor and Democracy (AALD) to combat the antiwar efforts of the People's Council, an organization founded by American pacifists, liberals, and leftists.

It was as leader of the AALD that Gompers's wartime role most closely paralleled that of the Italian Workers Mission. Like the mission members, Gompers could not claim to represent anyone with his prowar organization—he had no official authorization to establish the AALD or to name himself its head.[25] In fact, he founded the AALD because he feared the antiwar movement was undermining his authority in the AFL. By August 1917, People's Council leaders had announced that AFL locals were joining them at the rate of one a day.[26] But like the Italian Workers Mission, Gompers received considerable financial support from his government. George Creel's Committee on Public Information quietly sponsored Gompers's trip to Europe, including his visit to Italy in October 1918.[27]

Gompers, like the members of the Italian Workers Mission, was working at the behest of his government to disrupt the activities of radicals and other opponents of the war. He refused, as AALD leader, to protest against the suppression of free speech and the deportations during the war, and might even have encouraged government attacks against his IWW rivals. Bill Haywood claimed years later that Gompers had aroused the Justice Department's interest in the Wobblies.[28] While this claim may have been overblown, Gompers's fear of radicals, especially after the Russian revolution, was indisputable. After the revolution, he later wrote, "There followed a world-wide Socialist offensive to control public opinion. Should labor be lured by the Russian will-o'-the-wisp, the gains of years would be lost. . . . I had no choice but to assume leadership to protect American labor and American institutions."[29] It was in his perceived role as the "protector" of American labor that Gompers was serving as host for the former radicals in the Italian Workers Mission.

The Italian American Left was appalled, but not surprised, by the mission's connection to this man. Gompers proudly declared himself an ally of the American bourgeoisie. He refused to lend assistance to the hundreds of IWWs and other political prisoners who had opposed the war, and he was staunchly anti-Bolshevist. "Homage to Gompers!", Venanzi cried, to the man "who shackled the wrists of America's workers with the heaviest chains of moral servitude . . . the man that refused his solidarity to liberate the war's political victims . . . the man who wants to suppress and suffocate true democracy in Russia." Venanzi was dismayed, but he expected nothing more. He added, "This is . . . the only man that can hold the Commission's hands."[30] Gompers was a fitting host for the sordid mission members.

Carlo Tresca reinforced Venanzi's assertion, arguing that Gompers and de Ambris were very much alike. There were, in Tresca's words, "some remarkable spiritual affinities."[31] Both men were former radicals—de Ambris had of course been a syndicalist, and Gompers had been mentored by an old anarchist in his early days in the cigar factories. Both had abandoned the radicalism of their youth, however, and in Tresca's mind, both were now equally dangerous to the working class. Tresca argued that de Ambris had much to learn from Gompers. "It is true that [de Ambris] does not lack ability.... He succeeded in uniting the renegades, the deserters and the wanderers in the areas of production and politics. But this is not enough. Gompers does it better; Samuel succeeds in doing more." So, Tresca averred, "the Honorable *Quattropalle* studies and learns from Gompers how to crush solidarity among the workers."[32]

Gompers's connection to the mission enabled Italian American radicals to solidify their ties not only in class terms, but also in ethnic terms. Though an immigrant himself, Gompers had been calling for immigration restriction since his first days as president of the AFL. He reflected in his memoirs,

> [N]ever for a moment did I think of myself as an alien. I spoke the same language as the citizens of the United States.... Instinctively, I thought of those speaking other languages as the foreigners.... it was without a question that I accepted American customs and American institutions and the American life. To my mind the foreigner was the one who did not identify with American life and purposes.[33]

In 1891 he had called for limits on immigration at the AFL convention, beseeching the delegates to support his efforts to find "relief from this pressing evil."[34] Gompers would continue to press for immigration restriction for the next three decades.

Gompers directed his efforts against Italians and others from southern and eastern Europe, "where lower standards of life and work prevailed. As these immigrants flooded basic industries," he wrote, "they threatened to destroy our standards."[35] His opposition to immigration, and his contempt for immigrants, intensified during the war. In December 1918, while hosting the Italian Workers Mission, he met with an AFL committee and resolved to push for a national law banning any immigration into the country for at least two years.[36]

Given Gompers and the AFL's attitude toward immigrants, the mission's association with him was an insult not only to Italian American radicals, but to all Italian Americans. Bellanca declared, "He who believes that the AF of L represents the workers' soul, the organ of resistance for the organized Italians, is deceiving himself, and the more he deceives himself, the more he demonstrates his ignorance concerning... the terrible anti-Italian sentiment of the men that support the organization."[37] Italian Americans had never found a home in the AFL, Bellanca insisted, because Gompers not only did not want them in his union, he did not want them in the United States. Gompers inadvertently helped Italian American leftists galvanize on the basis of ethnic identity. They would draw on this sense of unity as they adapted their chamber of labor to the needs of Italian immigrants.

The Italian Workers Mission's visit brought to the fore all of the issues that Italian American leftists would face in the postwar era. They regarded the mission as an expedition to the United States on behalf of the Italian government to learn how to suppress the increasingly revolutionary Italian working class more effectively, hosted by a man who was an enemy of both radicals and Italians. While they took heart that the mission members were vastly outnumbered—at least at this point— by revolutionary forces in Italy, the Italian American Left glimpsed in the mission the first inklings of a reactionary movement that would culminate in Mussolini's victory in 1922. Moreover, the very issues for which they took Gompers to task—his antiradicalism and his nativism— would become national passions during the years after the war.

Responding to the Italian Workers Mission and its host, Italian American radicals cooperated with each other, united on the basis of shared class and ethnic identity, in unprecedented ways. When the strike erupted in Lawrence in 1919, the men who had opposed the mission were ready once again to work together. A unified Italian American Left would defend themselves against the Red Scare and postwar nativism and eventually battle against the fascist movement.[38] In more immediate terms, their cooperation would be institutionalized in the Italian chamber of labor in New York City in late 1919.

Chambers of labor, a relatively recent phenomenon in Italy, had proved very effective, and the Italian American Left made several efforts to recreate them. There were at least four attempts to start a chamber of labor in New York City before the war, each undermined by doctrinal disputes. The first call for a chamber of labor came from Tresca in 1905, the year after he arrived in the United States. Despite his advocacy of syndicalism, he regarded Italian immigrants as the most exploited workers in New York City, and argued that he and other Italian American leftists and unionists had to put aside their doctrinal differences and work together. Tresca thought the chamber could circumvent the corrupt hiring practices of opportunistic *padroni* and strengthen the position of Italian immigrants generally. But differences between syndicalists and socialists were too great to overcome.

Tresca was not alone in arguing before the war for cooperation among Italian American leftists on the basis of shared ethnic identity. Edmondo Rossoni (at that point still a respected FSI member) raised the idea again in 1911. Like Tresca, he had only been in the country a year when he proposed a chamber of labor in New York to unite organizers and activists, regardless of political or even religious orientation. Both men had witnessed the power of chambers of labor in Italy—Rossoni had been a member of the Milan chamber since 1907. But when Frank Bellanca insisted that all chamber members adhere to the AFL's principles, Rossoni and the syndicalists abandoned the idea.[39] There were attempts to form a chamber in 1913 and 1914, the last by Bellanca himself, though again factional disputes scuttled the efforts.[40] These repeated efforts to recreate an Italian chamber of labor in the United States, especially in the face of such obvious deterrents, underlined the potency of the idea.

Particularly during the *biennio rosso* (the two red years) of 1919 and 1920, when left-wing revolution in Italy seemed imminent, the Italian chambers of labor were worth emulating. Though Mussolini founded the fascist movement in March 1919, the chambers of labor, along with the PSI, were the most powerful institutions in the country. The trauma of postwar inflation and unemployment vaulted the socialists into an enviable position. At the end of 1919, two million Italians were out of work, and by the middle of 1920, prices were almost six times higher than before the war.[41] Angry workers turned to the PSI and the CGL to regain what the faltering economy had taken from them. In 1919, the PSI captured 156 seats in parliament, by far the most of any single party running. The following year, the party won majorities in over two thousand communes—nearly a quarter of the total number in the country. Membership in the CGL, under two hundred fifty thousand in 1918, peaked at over two million by the fall of 1920.[42]

The CGL exerted its strength in numerous ways during these two years. It led strikes involving millions of workers in virtually every industry in the country and, in July 1919, helped sponsor a twenty-four-hour general strike to express sympathy with the Russian revolution. During food riots in northern and central Italy in June 1919, chambers of labor set up food committees with local officials. They took over stores and established affordable food prices.[43] In the notoriously radical provinces of Ferrara and Bologna, chambers of labor dictated working conditions and wages to local industrialists and often even the choice of crop to large landowners.[44]

During the *biennio rosso,* the number of strikes, led not only by the PSI and the CGL but also by syndicalists and anarchists, reached record levels. Membership in the syndicalist USI reached its peak at the end of 1919. At its December congress, delegates represented over one thousand locals—including twenty-two local chambers of labor—and over three hundred thousand members. Seeking to initiate the general strike that would spark a revolution, the leaders of the USI participated in numerous strikes in the postwar years. Among their numbers, further evidence that transnational connections continued to run both ways, were former FSI members who had returned to Italy. For example, Angelo Faggi, deported from the United States in 1919, led a strike among agricultural workers as secretary of the chamber of labor in Sestri Ponente.[45] A far larger conflict began in June 1920 in Ancona; when two divisions of Italian soldiers mutinied, the USI and a group of anarchists led by Errico Malatesta rushed to their defense. Within days, the entire city was in revolt; strikers captured the armory and began to distribute weapons. The rebellion, however, deflated by the CGL's refusal to call for a national general strike, was quickly crushed.[46]

One of the things that would cripple leftists' potential power in Italy in the years after the war was their disunity. The USI, on the one hand, and the PSI and the CGL, on the other, consistently worked at cross-purposes—when they were not openly combating each other. PSI leadership was buoyed by electoral successes, and CGL leaders' confidence was swelled by the power individual chambers were able to exert. They saw little benefit, and considerable potential damage, in the direct and often violent confrontations called for by the USI and the anarchists. PSI and CGL leaders earned the contempt of the USI by refusing to foment revolution as general strikes erupted during the *biennio rosso.* In the general strikes in July 1919 and in Ancona in June 1920, for example, the PSI and the CGL, confident that they would be able to assume leadership of Italy on their own terms, worked to defuse any potential revolutionary fervor.[47] Despite the furious impatience of USI leaders, in 1920, with the PSI firmly entrenched in parliament and the CGL dictating the terms of employment in certain provinces, there were few in Italy or in

Italian American communities who questioned the inevitability of a Left-led revolution.

The climax of the *biennio rosso*, when over four hundred thousand workers occupied factories and shipyards in September 1920, began as a routine wage dispute at the Fiat automobile company in Turin.[48] It escalated when workers, worried about a lockout, took over the factory themselves. The idea spread throughout Italy, and soon metallurgists and shipyard workers followed suit. Workers in these industries ran the factories themselves for the next four weeks. They fed themselves by setting up "communist kitchens," and in Turin, they continued to produce automobiles. These workers insisted they were building cars more quickly than they had before the strike. The occupation produced panic among Italian industrialists, especially after reports from certain factories that workers were beginning to make weapons.[49]

But the occupation of the factories did not produce a revolution. Prime Minister Giolitti reacted to the occupation with the remarkable calmness that he had brought to previous labor disputes. Ignoring demands from industrialists that he recapture the factories by force, he simply waited the strikers out. He put his police at key strategic points and told the strikers, "[T]he post offices, the telephone service, . . . the Prefecture and the Bank of Italy are all in my hands." To factory owners, he asked, "If I use the police and the troops to occupy the factories, who will there be to guard the really vital places for me?"[50] His strategy, to let the workers realize for themselves the futility of their actions, worked perfectly. Though the USI argued that this was the start of the revolution, CGL leaders interpreted the occupations as defensive measures against intransigent industrialists. They were afraid the revolution would not be successful, and that even if it succeeded, countries opposed to it would cut off vitally necessary food exports to Italy.[51]

The occupations were defeated not only because of the CGL's reticence, but also because of PSI leaders' failure of will. PSI leaders agreed with the syndicalist USI—which had been shut out of strike meetings by the CGL—that the occupations could be the first step toward revolution. But they refused to accept the CGL's offer to take control of the situation.[52] The occupation died of natural causes. In early October the humiliated workers left the factories, with only a vague and ultimately unfulfilled promise from Giolitti that workers would have some degree of control over their industries.[53]

Few foresaw that the failure of the occupation of the factories would mark the end of the *biennio rosso* and the possibilities for the Left in Italy; many Italian American leftists remained convinced that revolution in Italy was virtually inevitable. In late October 1920, Giovannitti gave a speech hailing the achievements of the Italian proletariat, the PSI, and the CGL. Only in Italy had a general strike been called in support of the Russian revolution. Unlike in the United States, he declared enviously, in Italy the Socialist Party and unions worked in concert with each other. "Can you imagine," he asked, "the executive committee of the Socialist party... order[ing] Gompers to declare a general strike among all of the unions affiliated with the AF of L?"[54] The CGL and the PSI's hesitancy during the occupations would contribute to the Left's downfall in Italy, but this was not yet evident at the end of 1920. Giovannitti saw the two organizations working in concert and simply disagreeing over strategy. Moreover, he agreed with CGL leaders that the time was not right for revolution. He declared, "[A] premature revolution could prove disastrous."[55] What was important to Giovannitti was that the spirit of cooperation between the socialists and the unions in Italy differed dramatically from the situation in the United States, where the Left and the AFL were enemies.[56]

If Giovannitti and other Italian American leftists continued to draw inspiration from Italian Left institutions at the end of the *biennio rosso,* it had been even easier to do so at its onset, in 1919. At that moment he and his fellow radicals were again seeking to establish a chamber of labor in New York City. It was clear that a new type of organization was necessary. They sought to create an association of unions that could pool their efforts and help Italian immigrants attempting to organize themselves.

In August 1919, ex–FSI member Raimondo Fazio wrote an article calling for this new association. He realized that the days of factionalized groups such as the FSI were over and that a more inclusive form of organization was necessary to reach Italian American workers. He wrote, "A political group can be formed by individuals; a circle, catholic or anarchist or republican or syndicalist, can survive with individual adhesion. But an association that can work to build and provide for the needs of an entire mass, must be an aggregate in which the persons that make it up must also be formed into aggregates—the entire entity must be made up of interlocking bodies."[57] He continued, reflecting on his experience in the FSI,

A crowd of individuals can make a sensation, but it can not influence the relations between foreigners and natives.... Only a Chamber of Labor that is the Federation of existing workers' institutions can achieve such a goal. Only a Chamber of Labor that—like the one that is in formation—accepts entire unions and organizations can hope to triumph over the conditions that affect the workers.[58]

"Crowds of individuals" like the FSI had achieved certain successes, but the only way Italian American workers could exert any lasting influence was by unifying existing unions long separated by factional disputes.

Its leaders thought of the chamber from the first in both class and ethnic terms. They saw it as a means both to provide, at long last, an institutional base of strength for Italian working-class immigrants and to fight antiradicalism and nativism in the United States. When Giovannitti, Venanzi, and the other ex–FSI syndicalists met with the Italian leaders of the powerful New York clothing workers unions in the summer of 1919, they knew what was necessary to make the chamber of labor a powerful institution. They would have to help the unions comprising the chamber, but not impose their will on them. Most important, they would have to build on their sense of ethnic unity, avoiding the partisan disputes that had ruined efforts at cooperation before the war. Venanzi summed it up in an article in Frank Bellanca's *Il Lavoro* in late August 1919. He wrote, "[T]he Chamber of Labor will have to guarantee the complete autonomy of the unions in all of the struggles fought for the betterment of the workers without interference or the imposition . . . of a given program thought better than another."[59] There could be no more arguments between syndicalists and socialists, or between those still affiliated with the AFL and those who had broken with it—either years before, in the case of the syndicalists, or recently, in the case of the ACWA leaders.

The Italian chamber of labor of New York was launched in November 1919 with ambitious goals and expectations. At its initial meeting, the chamber united twenty-four union locals from the area, including ten in the clothing industry. On the first executive committee were Giovannitti, selected as secretary of the chamber; Salvatore Ninfo, an ILGWU vice president who was appointed treasurer; Frank Bellanca, editor of *Il Lavoro* and an ACWA organizer; Anthony Capraro of the ATWA; Raffaele Rende, director of *La Giustizia* and ILGWU organizer; Luigi Antonini, general organizer for ILGWU local 25; Gioacchino Artoni, ACWA organizer; and Pietro Maddii, FSI/SPA secretary.[60] Its goal was to forge a unified Italian American working-class movement. As Venanzi put it, the chamber was to be "a new organization that is capable of coordinating the actions and movements of America's immigrant working class."[61] In this sense, the new chamber was trying to function in the United States like chambers of labor in Italy.[62]

Chamber leaders were primarily trying to educate Italian immigrants about class and immigration issues and to provide financial assistance to them whenever possible. The leaders of the chamber strove to inform Italian American workers about socialism, about immigration, and about the rapid political and economic changes occurring in the United States and in the world. Venanzi, who spearheaded the chamber's educational efforts, argued that Italian Americans—and other immigrant workers— needed an organization that would study labor conditions and the problems immigrants faced, and then make its findings available to its members. Venanzi declared that issues specific to immigrants' lives had been neglected for too long. "When have they been the subject of a study? And when have practical suggestions been proposed? The few pieces of research and observation of the conditions of the emigrants in America do not contain enough information to serve as a basis for change or a remedy."[63] The chamber of labor also sponsored conferences organized by Giovannitti and others on topics ranging from industrial unionism and cooperativism, to the workers' movements in the United States and Italy, to art and literature.[64]

The chamber also sought to educate Italian immigrants about the workings of corporations and capitalist economies. Venanzi wrote articles for affiliated unions' newspapers, explaining how the world economy had changed since the war, critiquing "bourgeois" science, and explaining the connection between stocks and profits.[65] Part of the process of educating immigrants was studying changes in the industries in which they worked. Again Venanzi noted, "[K]nowledge of the conditions of an industry, prices, the cost of material, profits and salaries, the opportune moment for an agitation, the abundance or scarcity of the work force . . . is an essential part of the plan of attack or defense of the proletariat organization."[66] The chamber office was open to anyone seeking advice or statistics on working conditions and industries in the New York area. Italian union members, of course, were especially encouraged to visit—its officers promised that "special treatment will be granted to those Italian immigrants who possess the Italian unionist card."[67]

The goals of the Italian chamber of labor—to function as an educational resource for Italians and other immigrants and to help finance their strikes and labor protests—were noble ones. Considering its limited resources, in its first two years the chamber did remarkably well. A year after it was established Bellanca asserted, "Today the Chamber of Labor is regarded with sympathy and respect by the workers of other countries and is beginning to be considered a real element in the unionist school."[68] As Giovannitti pointed out at the second annual congress, the chamber had offered assistance not only to New York unions, but also to unions as far away as Philadelphia, Boston, Baltimore, and Rochester. Giovannitti declared, "I challenge anyone to cite one case in which any organization asked for help or collaboration and didn't immediately receive it."[69] Though the chamber of labor clearly had an ethnic orientation, it was nonetheless committed to the class struggle. Founded to help Italian American workers, it had unhesitatingly used its limited resources to help the entire working class in the United States.

Unfortunately, the chamber's task was difficult, at best, because the organization was founded when the massive strike wave, begun in 1909 and reinvigorated in 1916, was starting to decline. Strike activity nationally did not drop off until 1922, but by 1920 the momentum and enthusiasm from earlier strikes had all but disappeared. There had been a sense, not only in Lawrence in 1919, but also in other strikes that year—the enormous steel strike and especially the Seattle general strike, for example—that a new economic and social order was within reach. The Lawrence strike had drawn syndicalists, socialists, Communists, and even leftist religious leaders into a fairly stable alliance. Steel workers had struck at the heart of the notoriously antiunion U.S. Steel Corporation; at its height, the strike involved a quarter of a million workers. In Seattle in early 1919, a shipyard strike became a truly revolutionary situation when workers took control of the city for a week, setting up community kitchens and collective butcher shops and laundries and administering the telephone directories, dairies, and hospitals themselves.[70] But the steel strike and the Seattle general strike were defeated, and the revolutionary energy of the strike wave waned in the following year as the economy slumped and unemployment rose. By 1922, 20 percent of non–farm workers in the United States were out of work. In strikes waged when the chamber of labor was most active, workers were simply trying to maintain their wages and their right to organize.[71]

Moreover, the fears aroused by the postwar strikes, and especially the involvement of immigrants in them, raised antiradicalism and nativism to a fevered pitch in the United States. The perception that immigrant radicals were attempting to "bolshevize" the United States was widespread. Strike leaders had been red-baited at Lawrence. During the steel strike, the *Chicago Tribune* declared, "[T]he decision [the strike compels] means a choice between the American system and the Russian—individual liberty or the dictatorship of the proletariat."[72] The Federal government's response to this perceived danger came quickly. Early in 1920, Attorney General A. Mitchell Palmer orchestrated a series of raids that resulted in the arrest of over ten thousand radicals and unionists. He also expanded the Bureau of Investigation, and placed J. Edgar Hoover in charge of its "alien radical" division. Congress passed an immigration act in 1920 that not only limited the number of immigrants who could enter the country, but also simplified prosecution of immigrants arrested in the Palmer raids. The new law made even possession of radical literature a deportable offense.[73] Only a small percentage of the arrests resulted in deportations. Lawyers representing radicals became increasingly sophisticated at defeating charges against their clients, and public outrage at the excesses of the raids spread by the early 1920s. Nonetheless, it was these raids and constant harassment of radicals generally that compelled organizations such as the IWW and the FSI to spend all their resources on defending their members.[74]

Federal efforts were complemented on the local level by attempts to coerce the immigrant population to "Americanize." The quest to Americanize immigrants—to instill in them a sense of American culture and values—had been largely the domain of liberal intellectuals before the war. The efforts of people such as Jane Addams and Frances Kellor, who headed the Committee for Immigrants in America, were mostly well-intentioned and benevolent. Once the war began, however, the Americanization campaign expanded enormously and changed drastically. Previously, Americanizers had sought to help immigrants adapt to their new homes; now, they protected the country against potentially disloyal "foreign" elements. As one movement spokesman described it, "We have found that our forces for assimilating this foreign element have not been working.... We have suddenly been made to realize that ... many of these ... are not strangers to the hand that stabs in the dark or the lips that betray with a kiss."[75] This movement pervaded American society—numerous business organizations, women's clubs, fraternal organizations, patriotic organizations, and local chambers of commerce all echoed the call of "America First." The AALD, Gompers's vehicle for rousing support for the war, won federal backing precisely because he presented his organization as an "attempt to Americanize the labor movement."[76]

The Americanization campaign continued unabated after the war, now tinged with antiradical and antilabor fervor. Fear of immigrants, working-class advocates, and radicals merged in an increasingly panicked atmosphere. One clear example of the intermingling of nativism and antiradicalism was the report on "revolutionary radicalism" issued by the New York state legislature's Committee on Seditious Activities. The report was the product of committee chairman Clayton Lusk's two-year investigation into radical activities in New York. Almost half of the forty-five-hundred-page report dealt with Americanization as a cure for radicalism.[77] Many business leaders took advantage of both this patriotic fervor and rising unemployment to attack union gains made in the strike wave during and immediately after the war. They launched an "open-shop" campaign and referred to it as the "American plan."

Advocates of the open shop, too, combined antiradicalism and nativism in assaulting unions. They argued that complacent workers were truly American, and that workers who wanted to join a union were un-American—usually, dangerous foreigners. As one advocate put it in July 1920, less than a year after the chamber's establishment, the

> real issue, is that of the open or closed shop. The old controversies concerning hours of work, wages, collective bargaining, relations between employers and unions, are subordinated to the most fundamental fact of all—that of the absolute irresponsible dictatorship of a few men (usually of foreign birth), who desire to run labor in this country on the basis of the class struggle of Continental Europe.... They forget that the whole basis of American democracy is that of absolute denial of class interests.... Not only is their own attitude un-American, but so also is the closed shop.[78]

As unemployment grew, so did the open-shop campaign. By the end of 1920 there were open-shop associations in two hundred forty cities in forty-four states. The number of unionized workers in the United States decreased dramatically. The AFL, despite Gompers' eager cooperation during the war, and despite his longstanding opposition to foreign influences in the labor movement, lost 25 percent of its members during the peak years of the open-shop campaign between 1920 and 1923.[79]

This is the atmosphere in which the chamber of labor attempted to function in the early 1920s. Chamber members were unrepentant immigrant radicals, "foreign" advocates of a unified and powerful (largely immigrant) working class; they represented everything that advocates of deportation, Americanizers, and open-shop boosters feared and despised. Moreover, chamber members were unreservedly enthusiastic about the Soviet experiment in its early days. Chamber members often looked to the Russian revolution for inspiration. For Giovannitti, especially, the Bolshevik revolution was a regular point of reference. When Venanzi, one of his oldest and closest friends, died of pneumonia at age thirty-seven, Giovannitti blamed the Western nations' efforts to undermine the new Russian state. He wrote, "The doctor, a good and strong man . . . said that he died of pneumonia. . . . But I, his comrade and his friend . . . know very well that it was the blockade of Russia that killed him."[80] Some of the Chamber's most notable achievements came in combating the opposition of the United States to Russia. It organized a Workers' Alliance to provide economic assistance for Russia, an organization that would eventually have five hundred thousand members. It also worked behind the scenes at the United States Senate, sending a delegation to lobby for the resumption of trade between Russia and the United States.[81] Its efforts on behalf of the Russian revolution aside, even Giovannitti admitted the chamber was a struggling organization.

As the working class in the United States grew weaker, the problems inherent in chamber members' attempt to recreate an essentially Italian institution in a multiethnic working-class community multiplied. Giovannitti confessed that 1921 had been a year "bristling with difficulties, full of conflicts, saturated with errors, and not at all immune to discouragement and mistrust."[82] The chamber had little success following the example of Italian chambers of labor. Leonard Frisina, an old FSI member, argued that "a true Chamber of Labor based on the one[s] in Italy is not possible here in New York," and Giovannitti could only agree. "All of the concrete elements are lacking. We lack the direct control over the member organizations, the majority of whom consider us an auxiliary body that should obey and not lead."[83] The chamber of labor in New York had nothing near the power or authority of chambers of labor in Italy. Giovannitti explained, "[W]e need the right and power to declare strikes, to regulate labor, to interfere directly in the internal proceedings of labor." This was impossible in the United States because the American working class was simply too diverse. He admitted that "from a strictly unionist point of view, here in this multi-racial and heterogeneous land, a strictly and essentially Italian Chamber of Labor would be incongruous."[84] The chamber of labor as it existed, had limitations.

Though this was an *Italian* chamber of labor, developed to galvanize the Italian American working class, Giovannitti and other chamber members realized that it was essential to expand both the chamber's and Italian immigrants' participation and power in the American labor movement. Frank Bellanca brought the same awareness of ethnic issues to the chamber that he had revealed in his critique of Gompers during the visit of the Italian Workers Mission. He argued that the chamber "did not only have to explain its program to the Italian elements . . . but also [to] the American workers' movement that is composed of workers from the most far-away countries."[85] The need to expand the chamber's influence was obvious. As Bellanca pointed out, "[N]o industry in America can claim to be represented by one sole linguistic group."[86] Bellanca and other ACWA organizers knew that even in this union where the Italians had considerable power, their success or failure hinged on their relationships to native-born, Jewish, and southern and eastern European workers.

Italian American radicals were once again compelled to reconfigure the relationship between their ethnic and class identities, between their *Italianità* and their radical aspirations. Ex–Federation members and other chamber members concluded that to have any lasting influence in the diverse American working class, they would have to directly confront the increasing pressure on immigrants to assimilate into American culture. Having endured accusations from opponents who considered immigrants, unions, and Bolshevism as synonymous and equally alien, they knew that they were going to have to take Americanization into their own hands.

This impulse anticipated the efforts of labor organizers in the 1930s, usually in the CIO, to promote union membership and labor activism as avenues to Americanization. George Sánchez has argued that Chicana and Chicano activists used militant garment and cannery unions

to facilitate Mexicans' integration into American society while still maintaining an oppositional edge. Gary Gerstle has made a similar argument
about textile unions as Americanizing agents for French Canadians in
Woonsocket, Rhode Island, though he emphasizes that the strategy ultimately defused the unionists' militancy.[87]

There was no such dilution of revolutionary ardor among chamber
leaders. Like union organizers would in the 1930s, they approached the
matter of Americanization by reading ethnic identity through the lens
of class. To a much greater extent than many future CIO organizers,
they hoped that the process of Americanization, if immigrants themselves were agents of their own assimilation, could have profoundly radical results. Ex–FSI member Giovanni di Gregorio articulated this perspective most clearly. Writing in English and signing his name "John di
Gregorio," he argued that the cries for Americanization had singular
aims: to align "the foolish and b[i]goted ones among the American
workers against the foreign born workers, and to cow and subjugate
the latter to the will of the master class and to make them subservient
tools of exploiters and tyrants."[88] He continued, "The question of Americanization is, like many other questions . . . a class question. It has the
sole purpose of advancing the interests of the wealth-owning class and
of making the milking, fleecing and shearing of the workers much easier."[89] But, di Gregorio argued, Americanization in the hands of the immigrants themselves, and guided by organizations such as the Italian
chamber of labor, would not lead to acquiescence. As he put it, "[F]or-
tunately for the working people, the more the foreigners become Americanized, the worse it is for the profit-taking class; the more they become
assimilated, the more they ask; the more they become enlightened, the
more they fight the tyranny and the poverty imposed upon them."[90]
This premise was at the root of chamber members' efforts to integrate
Italian immigrant workers into the American working class.

The notion that participation in the American labor movement would
facilitate Americanization and assimilation was one many members had
brought with them into the chamber of labor. Ex–FSI member Raimondo
Fazio, discussing the chamber three months before its founding meeting, argued that one of its purposes was "to destroy the abstentionist
and separatist prejudices, to acclimatize our labor force and make it
able to participate in the complex American system."[91] This realization

was only reinforced as the chamber faced the complexities of helping Italian immigrants.

By the end of the chamber's first year, many chamber leaders considered enhancing communication and interaction between Italian immigrants and other workers their central task. Giovannitti explained this clearly, insisting that "[w]e must ... adapt ourselves to the environment. ... We need to validate the Italian workers' movement, make it more fluid, more amalgamatable, and able to struggle in a more disciplined way so that its influence penetrates even the most inaccessible centers of the American movement."[92] The only way to break through the barriers imposed by conservative, often antiimmigrant unions in the AFL was to help Italian immigrants realize their potential power in the American working class.

Giovannitti concluded, "[W]e must educate in order to survive."[93] This emphasis on education was an explicit part of chamber leaders' efforts to guide the process of Americanization themselves. In late 1922 Giovannitti made a firm step in this direction, accepting a position as head of the ILGWU's educational department—"one of our old dreams come true," an ILGWU official declared. Giovannitti began to offer English courses, as well as classes in Italian on labor strategy and history.[94] The ILGWU was one of the few socialist unions in the AFL, and many of its members were Jewish or Italian immigrants. Nonetheless, Giovannitti's decision to affiliate himself with any member union of the AFL, against which he had struggled for so long, signaled his commitment to helping Italian immigrants empower themselves in the labor movement. He joined Italian American socialists like the Bellanca brothers and Luigi Antonini, who had participated in "new unions" such as the ACWA and the ILGWU and their educational efforts since before the war.[95]

These acculturative efforts were the only alternative for the chamber, given the diverse American working class and postwar intolerance. It had proved impossible to transport an effective organization in one country to another where the cultural and ideological terrain was quite different. As an organization fighting for workers' rights, the chamber of labor had gone from being a cultural carryover to actually being an agent of Italian immigrants' assimilation into American society.

Giovannitti had insisted in its second year that "the Italian Chamber of Labor of New York is no longer an infant. It is now a virile adolescent and is ready to enter the battle against capitalism in the name of the so-cial revolution."[96] Even in an atmosphere of nativism and antiradicalism, the chamber had strived to engage in this struggle in a meaningful way. Giovannitti, Bellanca, and the other chamber members realized follow-ing the example of chambers of labor in Italy too closely was not prac-tical or even useful. Their efforts to help Italian immigrants assimilate into the American working class was a clear sign that the chamber of labor of New York was able to adapt and readapt its role to the realities of postwar American society.

Unfortunately, the fledgling efforts of the chamber of labor were cut short by the triumph of Mussolini's fascist movement, which again complicated chamber members' relationships to their home and adopted countries. Assimilation efforts did not end, but they ceased to be the singular or even the primary focus of the chamber. Its members' eyes had never left Italy, and there was no more important time to focus on developments there than in the early 1920s.

The end of the occupation of the factories in October 1920 ended any possibility of a left-wing revolution in Italy, but this was not the percep-tion of the Italian bourgeoisie. They were horrified by leftists' power and by Giolitti's apparent unwillingness to act on their behalf. In early 1921, they responded to this perceived threat by funding *squadristi* in the socialist-dominated provinces of central Italy. The *squadristi* were groups of ex-soldiers, college students, and antisocialist peasants who launched violent attacks against the socialists in the next two years. In the first six months of 1921 alone they managed to destroy 119 chambers of labor, 107 cooperatives, and 83 peasant league offices.[97]

Mussolini did not ally himself with the *squadristi* immediately. As late as 1919, his fascists had run for parliament on a leftist platform vir-tually indistinguishable from the PSI's platform. Mussolini was still un-successfully beseeching the UIL, led by de Ambris and Rossoni, to merge with his fascist movement. UIL members had much in common with the fascists in 1919. Both were wary of premature revolution; UIL lead-ers were growing convinced, like Mussolini, that the proletariat was in-capable of leading a revolution in Italy; both the UIL and the fascists considered Bolshevism the greatest threat to Italy. But the UIL rejected the merger with the fascists. Ironically, given their eventual relationships to fascism, de Ambris was more interested in the merger than Rossoni.

The former FSI leader adamantly opposed involvement in any movement participating in parliamentary politics.[98]

Mussolini gained political strength in 1920 and 1921 by dropping leftist elements of the fascist platform, playing on the Italian bourgeoisie's fears, allying himself to the *squadristi,* and convincing Italian industrialists to fund his *Popolo d'Italia.* Giolitti, recognizing Mussolini's control over the *squadristi,* offered to include the fascists on the government ticket in the 1921 elections. He hoped to coopt this insurgent group, as he had the Socialist Party in the years before the war, by including it in the government. It almost worked with Mussolini—the fascists won thirty-five seats in parliament, and three months later, Mussolini proposed a "pact of pacification" with the socialists. But this proposed truce infuriated *squadristi* leaders, and Mussolini nearly lost control of the fascist movement. In September he began again to support the violent actions of the *squadristi,* and the following month he officially incorporated them into the newly founded Fascist Party. By the end of 1921, the party had two hundred thousand members, including a private army in the form of the *squadristi.*[99]

Many Italians—including some former allies—regarded Mussolini at this point as little more than an agent of the antiradical bourgeois reaction in Italy. De Ambris, for example, had remained a fascist sympathizer until Mussolini turned his back on Gabriele D'Annunzio's occupation of Fiume. D'Annunzio, the nationally renowned poet and self-proclaimed war hero, led a band of "legionnaires" who occupied the unredeemed city of Fiume for a year after the war. The poet captured the imagination of many Italians, including de Ambris, who became D'Annunzio's chief of staff and authored the Carta del Carnaro, the constitution of the new state. D'Annunzio and Mussolini were in close contact during the occupation, and de Ambris was convinced that a coalition of the two men's followers was possible. But Mussolini, wary of the poet's popularity, ultimately agreed to help Giolitti control the impact of the occupation—this was one of the ways the fascists gained a foothold in parliament. De Ambris broke with the future fascist leader. When Mussolini founded the Fascist Party in November 1921, both de Ambris and UIL leader Angelo Olivetti dismissed it as just another political party.[100]

Syndicalists in the USI saw Mussolini in the same light, as a powerful tool of reaction, not a viable force in his own right. Unfortunately, USI leaders maintained this stance even after Mussolini led his march on Rome. In a letter to *Il Proletario* in December 1922, USI leaders commented that they had not opposed Mussolini's assumption of power, choosing to remain uninvolved in a "bourgeois conflict."[101]

Tresca was the first one in the Italian American Left—and in the Italian American community as a whole—to raise an alarm about fascism. But because of Mussolini's close ties with industrialists in Italy, and because of his brief cooperation with Giolitti, Tresca and others on the Italian American Left, like the USI, did not initially perceive fascism to be a threat in and of itself. They labeled Mussolini and the fascists a brutish arm of the bourgeoisie. Tresca delivered this assessment in *Il Martello* as the *squadristi* rampaged through Italy in early 1921. "What is [fascism]? ... Mercenary troops—the heart of the white guard of the Italian bourgeoisie. Cowards, these fascists that murder and destroy to protect their bosses' safes."[102] In the pages of *Il Lavoro*, the perception was identical. One writer argued, "Fascism is not a political association. It is simply an extension of the bourgeoisie[;] it is its body guard, whose only task is to tame the working class. ... Fascism represents violence— it is the unleashing of the most bestial instincts."[103]

Whether the fascists were the henchmen of the bourgeoisie or a threat in their own right, however, they were wreaking havoc in socialist strongholds in Italy, and Tresca and others urged the Italian Left to meet the fascists' violence with violence of their own. The writer in *Il Lavoro* insisted, "We say that the violence, more now than ever, requires a proletarian response—they must unite in the struggle and beat the fascists in the battlefield."[104] As late as August 1922, Tresca still believed a revolution was possible. He felt it was possible because he believed that Italy's workers would eventually stand up to the fascists, even if it meant the possibility of a war with them. He wrote, "Italy's untamable proletariat will return to the front lines, it will challenge fascism. It will be very difficult to conquer Italy, it will be very expensive, but it will soon belong to the proletariat."[105]

Tresca's optimism was little more than wishful thinking. Given the mantle of legitimacy by Giolitti in the May 1921 elections, Mussolini and the *squadristi* in his Fascist Party only had to wait until they had enough strength to gain control of socialist strongholds in northern Italian cities. By May 1922, the Fascist Party counted over three hundred thousand members, and that summer it launched its assault. In July the *squadristi* rampaged through socialist-held towns in northern Italy. In one instance, Rossoni and Libero Tancredi led a group that broke up a general strike in Genoa; the fascists took control of the city less than a month later.[106] An attempted national general strike by Italian leftists failed dismally, and days later, the fascists attacked Milan, the last major city under socialist control. On August 4, after three hours of street fighting, the fascists broke up the printing presses of the socialists' daily *L'Avanti* and burned their buildings.[107]

Now no one could prevent Mussolini from assuming power. No longer having to settle for shared leadership, he declined an offer to participate in a new government coalition. In October, after the king of Italy refused to declare a state of martial law, Mussolini was invited to form a new government. Though the intimidating *squadristi* had given him his muscle, and though he would soon declare himself dictator of Italy, Mussolini did not have to fight his way into the capital city of Italy. He rode into Rome on the train, arriving early on the morning of October 29, and assumed power at the invitation of the king.[108]

Many Italian American leftists greeted Mussolini's rise to power with derision. In October 1922, he threatened the life of Paolo Valera, a frequent contributor to Carlo Tresca's newspaper. Tresca replied to Mussolini, "You threaten Paolo Valera—a man who is defenseless against your armies. Cowards and barbarians. Only barbarians make threats against a man like Paolo Valera who tells the bitter truth."[109] He was not the only one on the Italian American Left who scorned Mussolini and mocked his pretensions. An *Il Lavoro* correspondent, who somehow got an audience with Mussolini just after he took power, wrote that Mussolini went to extremes to adopt a Napoleonesque stance, complete with military headgear and his hands grasped firmly behind his back. But he was not completely comfortable with this stance yet. The correspondent wrote that Mussolini paced constantly during their meeting, "every now and then passing by a mirror to see if he really looked like Napoleon. He walked and talked, and every now and then he changed the position of his hands, but a subtle whisper by Bianchi [a former syndicalist, now his aide] quickly corrected the situation."[110] Despite their jibes, however, chamber leaders and other Italian American leftists soon realized that fascism endangered not only Italians, but Italian Americans, as well.

Having gained control of Italy, the fascists quickly asserted themselves in the Italian American community.[111] They gained control, for example, of the Dante Alighieri Society. Ostensibly a literary society, founded in 1890 to promote awareness in the United States of the richness of Italian history and heritage, the society was a steadfast defender of Mussolini from the 1920s through the 1940s. Other societies and organizations followed suit. The Italian Historical Society, Casa Italiana, and the Italian Library of Information, run by D'Annunzio's son, all functioned as fascist propagandists.[112]

The fascists also gained the support of the powerful Sons of Italy, though this caused great consternation within the organization. Giovanni Di Silvestro, formerly a socialist and Tresca's ally, had by 1922 long since abandoned his radical principles and become the Supreme Venerable of the Sons of Italy. Following the "March on Rome," he declared at the organization's convention that "the Order of the Sons of Italy must take inspiration from Fascism."[113] Delegates voted to send a telegram to Mussolini which read, "While Fascism under your leadership lifts Italy up in the Roman way, the 300,000 members of the Order of the Sons of Italy send you their greetings and good wishes.... The new Government, gathering together the youthful energies of the country for fecund and efficient work, will instantly renew confidence and prestige abroad."[114] In January 1923, the Fascist Party in Italy announced the formation of a secretariat general of the *fasci* abroad, which declared Di Silvestro's *fascio* in New York City the "Central Fascio of the Italian Fasci in North America."[115] Di Silvestro's actions, however, outraged many in the organization. One state branch—ironically, the New York chapter—split from the Sons of Italy and formed a separate fraternity. But as John Diggins has noted, "despite the initial dissension the Sons of Italy... became an important source of Fascist propaganda."[116]

The fascists' staunchest organizational support in the United States came from the Fascist League of North America (FLNA). By the time it was dissolved in 1929, following accusations that it was run through, and by, the Italian government, it had eighty branches across the country and a membership of twelve thousand five hundred.[117] During the years of its existence, the FLNA had its headquarters in New York City; the fascist stronghold in the United States was also where Italian American leftists had established their chamber of labor.

The Italian chamber of labor, once based on Italian chambers, then an agent of assimilation, responded immediately to this new challenge. In March 1923, it invited all representatives of workers' organizations to come together to fight fascism. Giovannitti declared, "The Italian Chamber of Labor is well aware of the task that it must perform for the Italian working class. It cannot remain unfeeling to the appeal launched by Italy's organized labor force to the Italian workers living abroad; nor can it ignore the challenges and insults launched by the fascists of New York, Boston, Philadelphia, etc."[118] He continued, "While every day we are welcoming more and more workers who have been chased away from their homes for having refused to prostitute themselves for the Italian dictatorship, here in America a group of renegades is trying to poison the consciences of our weakest comrades and build the first fascist bands that will raze our sacred institutions to the ground."[119] The battle against fascism was no longer confined to Italy; it was now in the Italian American Left's community, threatening its own institutions. In April, opponents of fascism attended two huge meetings held by the Italian chamber of labor.

Representatives of more than one hundred fifty thousand Italian American workers drew up plans for the AFANA, the first organized opposition to fascism in the United States. Again, a small group of Italian American leftists sought to shape the political culture of both Italy and the United States. If not completely successful, they achieved far more than their numbers would have suggested was possible. Attending the meetings were several former members of FSI—Giovannitti, Giovanni di Gregorio, Giuseppe Cannata, and Leonardo Frisina—and virtually all of the Italian leaders of the clothing and hotel workers' unions in New York. Elated chamber leaders exclaimed, "In these two meetings, [the representatives] succeeded in creating what they didn't know how to create in the past months and years: the unification of all the healthy, militant forces in the workers' movement."[120] The meeting had brought together rival unions and battling leftist factions that the Italian chamber of labor had not been able to convince to put aside their differences. In their elation, however, the chamber leaders downplayed the fact that their organization had paved the way for this show of unity and strength. Without its work building an infrastructure in the three previous years, there would have been little hope of responding so quickly or in such great numbers to the arrival of fascism in the United States.

It was fortunate that the Italian American Left was able to respond as it did, because Mussolini had many advantages. He had the backing of the Sons of Italy, of numerous other Italian American organizations, and of the three largest Italian American newspapers in the country.[121] Many Italian Americans believed Mussolini would reclaim for Italy a sense of pride and dignity that it had not enjoyed since the days of the Roman empire. Many regarded him as a man who, in Di Silvestro's words, "has assumed for Himself the hard task of giving back to Italy that spiritual discipline, which is the foundation for her economic rebirth and for her prestige abroad."[122] The newly formed AFANA faced an uphill battle.

The Italian American chamber leaders who founded the AFANA were the only people fighting against fascism in the United States in the early 1920s. Necessarily, their energies were rerouted by this fight. When called upon, they still attempted to assist striking Italian immigrants.[123] They finally established a daily Italian-language labor newspaper titled *Il Nuovo Mondo* in 1925. But this newspaper quickly became a voice of antifascism. In this guise its importance cannot be overestimated. Because Mussolini had by then shut down all opposition papers in Italy, it became the only Italian-language antifascist daily in the world.[124] The magnitude of the struggle against fascism, and their place in it, was not lost on them. It was a battle that consumed them.

On a certain level, the AFANA leaders' immersion in antifascist activity constituted a setback to their hopes of integrating themselves and Italian immigrants into American society. It turned their attention back to Italy, and led to frequent physical confrontations with fascist supporters in the United States—confrontations deemed "un-American" even by some of their native-born allies on the Left. In the first years of the 1920s, there were regular street battles between fascists and antifascists. When a celebrated fascist Italian aviator toured the United States in 1924, for example, antifascists met him at every stop. A banquet the Italian Fascist Society of Philadelphia gave in his honor ended in a brick-throwing riot. The next day, in New York City, he and the Italian consul were pelted with tomatoes as they entered the Metropolitan Opera House.

But Italian American antifascists, and Tresca in particular, saw—and often themselves embodied—connections between the reactions in Italy and the United States. Tresca and the AFANA's efforts to combat Mussolini raised considerable ire. Fascists in New York made several attempts on Tresca's life, including one instance when they tried to bomb his office. The offices of both Tresca's *Il Martello* and the antifascist *Il Nuovo Mondo* were raided and destroyed several times by fascists. In

May 1923, Mussolini himself initiated an effort to silence Tresca and the antifascists. The Italian embassy sent a letter to the State Department accusing Tresca, Giovannitti, and other "notorious Italian labor agitators" in the New York area of attacking the Italian government. Weeks later, Tresca was arrested for sending Margaret Sanger's birth control advertisements through the mail in *Il Martello,* and for mailing a book called *The Art of Preventing Childbirth* to people who requested it. He was sentenced to a year and a day in a federal penitentiary, and served four months.[125]

After his release Tresca continued to rail against fascism in his newspaper and to battle fascists physically in the streets. As a friend recalled years later, "Carlo had groups in all parts of the country. Here in New York there were maybe several hundred. They'd break up fascist meetings with baseball bats."[126] Despite Tresca and his friends' use of a consummately American weapon in fighting the fascists, their actions shocked some American allies. Max Eastman took Tresca to task for his "un-American" behavior. Tresca's vantage point reflected the lesson of his prison sentence, prompted by the Italian embassy and handed down by the United States government. It also revealed clearly the perspective that he and his fellow antifascists on the Italian American Left had earned in their years of shifting identities and watching both American and Italian society evolve.

His work, and the work of Italian American leftists generally, was not only to battle fascism in their own communities, but to convince their American allies that this was not simply an "ethnic" issue. It had dire implications for anyone involved in the class struggle. Tresca told Eastman,

> We don't argue with the Fascists. When they offer to debate, we say we'll debate when our brothers in Italy have a free press and the right to speak and meet in the streets. Until then, we do our arguing with guns. You Americans think this is very Latin and far away. You fool yourselves. Fascism is already here in embryo and it can't be stopped except with out and out war.[127]

Tresca and other Italian American Leftists continued to battle the fascists themselves. The war between the fascists and antifascists claimed over a dozen lives in New York City alone.[128]

Street fights against fascists, though the most visible form of opposition, were not the antifascists' only means they used to comat fascism. At their meetings in the spring of 1923, the antifascists of the Italian

American Left put together plans to confront fascism within and beyond the Italian American community. The AFANA established an information and publicity office to distribute news of fascist atrocities in Italy and in the United States. The chamber of labor proposed to publish a biweekly bulletin for the same purpose. The AFANA also sponsored antifascist demonstrations "in every corner of the country" and sent its speakers—Giovannitti among them—free of charge to any local branch that requested them.[129]

Throughout the 1920s, they fought Mussolini's attempts to convince Italian immigrants to send their money to Italian banks. Giovanni di Gregorio, for example, wrote articles explaining that because of Mussolini the economy in Italy was too unstable to be trusted. All of the rich capitalists in Italy, he pointed out, had their money in Swiss banks.[130] While his entreaties had little immediate impact, he and other antifascists continued to urge Italian immigrants to hold onto their money. By 1928, the *New York World Telegram* reported, "We have verified that the anti-fascist propaganda . . . has had the effect of making Italians, resident in America, abandon Italian banks. Thus it is said that last year the money sent home by Italian immigrants diminished by a billion lire."[131]

AFANA members continued to solicit support from native-born Americans and fellow labor leaders in combating fascism. They recognized Mussolini's considerable popularity among Americans. Giovanni di Gregorio, reflecting bitterly on the history of oppression in the United States, lamented, "The Americans, save a few rare exceptions, approve of Italian fascism because it relates to the spirit that has animated them from the time that they deported the Quakers to the present day in which they approve of violence against blacks . . . and workers."[132] Nonetheless, AFANA members strove to change American opinion. Frank Bellanca, for example, sent regular releases to the American press to convince editors to change the tone of their reporting on fascism. The AFANA also led a public campaign to convince Nicholas Murray Butler, president of Columbia University, to fire a fascist faculty member.[133]

Tresca and AFANA members brought fascism into the national spotlight in the United States by arguing that the rise of fascism in Italy, and nativism and the Red Scare in the United States, were both part of the same reaction. Tresca's arrest by federal agents had attracted the attention of American liberals. Margaret Sanger and the American Civil Liberties Union helped Tresca with his defense; H. L. Mencken ran the same birth-control ad in his paper to protest Tresca's arrest and sentence.[134] A writer in the *Nation* asked whether the government was acting as an "agent of the Mussolini dictatorship," and a *New Republic* writer noted that the district attorney admitted that the complaint against Tresca had originated in the Italian embassy.[135]

Federal prosecution of Italian American antifascists—and many American industrialists' enthusiasm about Mussolini—helped immigrant antifascists' convince American leftists and labor leaders there were connections between fascism and the postwar reaction in the United States. Their warnings to American allies that fascism was part of a worldwide reaction—that, as an ACWA leader put it, the "enemies of labor everywhere have greeted the Fascisti as saviors of Society"—finally began to pay off.[136] In 1924, Elizabeth Gurley Flynn toured the country lecturing on "The Fascista [*sic*] Menace in America" and holding conferences on connections between the Ku Klux Klan, the American Legion, and the fascists in Italy.[137] At a protest rally in Carnegie Hall sponsored by the Italian chamber of labor and the AFANA, Flynn accused American oil interests of covert dealings with the Italian government that would "have made the Teapot Dome scandals look sick." A socialist judge at the meeting told the crowd that the chant of "Abbasso Mussolini!" (Down with Mussolini!) was not sufficient—"Abbasso capitalismo!" was necessary.[138] Tresca and the AFANA had achieved a crucial goal—fascism was no longer strictly an ethnic issue confined within the Italian American community.

Even AFL leaders rallied to support Italian American antifascists. Gompers was an admirer of Mussolini, but when he died in 1924, he was replaced as AFL president by William Green, who was an outspoken opponent of fascism. He assured an AFANA convention in 1926 that the AFL "will stand with you and work with you until we have succeeded in driving Fascism from the face of the earth." At the AFL convention that year, he helped pass a resolution condemning fascism.[139] This resolution again symbolized the antifascists' tremendous accomplishment. In Mussolini's first years, the Italian American radicals in the AFANA made their cause a national issue in the United States.

Considering the forces arrayed against them—the Italian government, the United States government, many Italian American editors and other *prominenti,* and violent fascist mobs—the vigor with which the antifascists waged their fight against fascism was little short of remarkable. In later years, Tresca boasted that because of his intimidation tactics, fascists refused to hold open meetings in New York. Another Italian antifascist from Chicago made a similar claim. After he and other antifascists confronted a fascist parade, he declared, "In a very short time the fascists disappeared. We never heard from them again. They never attempted again to parade in Chicago."[140]

Unfortunately, Italian American radicals' leadership of the antifascist movement was short-lived. The coalition of syndicalists, socialists, and Communists in AFANA soon fell apart. Distrust between political factions returned to plague them once again. This time the divisions were caused primarily by the rivalry between Communists, on the one hand, and socialists and syndicalists, on the other. The first edition of the Italian American Communists' newspaper, *L'Alba Nuova* (*The New Dawn*), had appeared in September 1921. Editor Anthony Capraro, with the assistance of Giuseppe Cannata and another ex-*Il Proletario* editor, Antonio Presi, combined calls for a Bolshevik-style revolution with polemics against syndicalism and socialism. The issue of whether to affiliate with the Third International, headquartered in Moscow, split the ranks of both the FSI and the FSI/SPA (just as it did the PSI and the USI). After its establishment in December 1921, entire sections of the FSI went over to the Communist Workers Party of America. As Rudolph Vecoli has argued, the timing of FSI leaders' decision to merge formally with the IWW in 1921 had much to do with the burgeoning strength of Italian American Communists.[141]

The Communists' peaceful coexistence within the antifascist movement did not last long. Both Cannata and Presi were founding members of the AFANA. But socialists and syndicalists in the AFANA, wary of the Communist presence from the start, had their worst fears confirmed in 1926 when the Communist faction assumed control of the organization. Valenti and Ninfo led a withdrawal of anticommunists from the AFANA and established the Anti-Fascist Federation for the Freedom of Italy.[142] The Communists, among them Cannata and ex-syndicalist Pietro Allegra, cemented their control over the AFANA.

Despite their factionalism, Italian American leftists never gave up their fight against Mussolini. Tresca devoted his life to opposing fascism until his assassination in 1943. The struggle Giovannitti, di Gregorio, Tresca, and other ex-members of the FSI initiated with Frank Bellanca and Italian American trade unionists against fascism began a new era in their lives. Their hopes for a revolution, born in Italy and nurtured over almost two decades in the United States, did not disappear. But the specter of fascism became their daily fare. The Italian chamber of labor never became the powerful agent of revolutionary education and assimilation that they had hoped it would be. Nor were they able to prevent fascism from gaining a foothold among Italian immigrants in the United States. The forces against them were too great, and their own coalition too fragile. But as disappointing as this must have been for them, few failed to realize the implications of their efforts. If the chamber had not existed and had not been ready to channel its resources into the antifascist movement, the voice of Mussolini's followers would have gone uncontested in the Italian American community in the crucial first years of his reign. Equally important, the American public would have been alerted to the fascist menace far later than it was.

CONCLUSION

"That Agony Is Our Triumph": Sacco and Vanzetti and the End of an Era of Italian American Radicalism

The rise of fascism in Italy in 1922 changed the lives of Italian American syndicalists and other radicals irrevocably. From that moment, this generation of Italian American Leftists devoted themselves to battling fascism rather than working toward a more just society. But nothing symbolized the end of this era of Italian American radicalism more clearly than the trial and executions of Nicola Sacco and Bartolomeo Vanzetti in 1927. Their executions were the culmination of the postwar Red Scare and nativism; they showed how dangerous—and how life-threatening—it had become to be an immigrant radical in the United States. In 1912, a national and international liberal and Left coalition had saved Ettor and Giovannitti when they were on trial during the Lawrence strike. After the war, an even broader coalition could not save Sacco and Vanzetti.

Sacco and Vanzetti's plight personified the history of this generation of Italian American radicalism.[1] Sacco and Vanzetti were anarchists, followers of Luigi Galleani. Like the Italian American syndicalists who fought to make their trial a national and international issue, they were members of a movement that usually operated clandestinely or on the fringes of the American Left and labor movement. Their most significant contributions came at moments when their own lives were in immediate danger. The syndicalists spent their lives balancing and reformulating their ethnic and class identities in response to events in their adopted and native countries. Like them, Sacco and Vanzetti's relationship to American society was ultimately—and tragically—determined by both their ethnic identity and their class politics. Once again, the ex-

periences of Italian American radicals belie recent claims by scholars
such as Todd Gitlin and Michael Kazin about the central, even sole, importance of social class in social movements before the 1960s.[2] Sacco
and Vanzetti, and the Italian American radicals who fought for them,
did not—could not—focus exclusively on class issues. For many American intellectuals, the Sacco and Vanzetti case was a radicalizing moment that redefined their political mindset for at least the next decade.
For the prisoners themselves, and for this generation of Italian American radicals, it was the culmination of a series of challenges they faced
throughout their lives on the basis of both their ethnic identity and
class beliefs. It was also the culmination of Italian American radicals'
distinctive contribution to American working-class culture in these
years—as martyrs ever willing to sacrifice themselves for social progress.

Even before Sacco and Vanzetti were arrested in Brockton, Massachusetts, on May 5, 1920, they and their fellow anarchists were in the throes
of the Red Scare. Luigi Galleani and several *Galleanisti* had been deported less than a year earlier.[3] Though frequently depicted as pastoral
immigrants by American liberals outraged at their treatment, Sacco and
Vanzetti, like their fellow anarchists, were deeply committed revolutionaries. The *Galleanisti* were the most extreme radicals on the Italian
American Left. Unlike the syndicalists, whose attitudes toward violence
were more complex, Galleani firmly believed that the only way to recreate society was first to destroy the existing structures. He also believed,
in the face of the enormous violence against workers he had witnessed
in the United States, that violent retribution was completely justified
and necessary. He had published an instruction manual on constructing explosives; at his deportation hearing, he hinted strongly at his followers' involvement in bombing incidents in the United States.[4] Galleani, moreover, refused to accept his deportation quietly. He called for
fellow anarchists to punish their persecutors. As Paul Avrich and Nunzio
Pernicone have argued, it is highly likely that *Galleanisti* were responsible for bombs mailed and hand delivered to prominent capitalists and
politicians in May and June of 1919. Available evidence suggests that
Sacco and Vanzetti were, if not involved in the bombings, certainly
aware that they were being carried out.[5]

   Federal authorities were determined to identify the bombers, especially
since one of the targets had been Attorney General Palmer. They began

to round up *Galleanisti;* one of the first they arrested in March 1920 was Andrea Salsedo. Just two days prior to their arrest, Sacco and Vanzetti learned that the body of Salsedo, by then detained in isolation for weeks, had been found shattered on the sidewalk underneath the windows of the Department of Justice. Vanzetti was deeply alarmed by his comrade's mysterious death. He, like many others, was convinced at the time that Salsedo had been pushed out the window. (Evidence now suggests he committed suicide, remorseful about informing on his comrades and unhinged by beatings and his lengthy and illegal incarceration.)[6]

Italian American syndicalists, keenly aware of the dangers facing the *Galleanisti,* tried unsuccessfully to help Vanzetti avoid arrest. He visited Tresca's office in New York soon after Salsedo died. A contributor to Tresca's paper told Vanzetti that more arrests were inevitable, and that he should collect any anarchist literature and evidence of involvement in the bombings in his and other *Galleanisti*'s possession and hide it until the newest wave of arrests ended.[7] Sacco and Vanzetti were attempting to pick up a car for this purpose when arrested for the robbery and murder of a paymaster and guard of a South Braintree factory. Fearing they had been implicated in the bombing campaign—they had likely been hiding dynamite the night they were arrested—they lied to the police when questioned about their political beliefs and their activities that night.[8]

Thus began their seven-year ordeal in the courts, throughout which their anarchism and their status as immigrants denied them any opportunity for a fair trial. It is important to realize that their involvement in any bombings is still unproven. Nor were they on trial for charges related to the bombing campaign—though these were the only charges Sacco would have considered respectable. He was apparently insulted by the crime with which he and Vanzetti were charged. He objected by saying, "If I was arrested because of the Idea I am glad to suffer. . . . If I must I will die for it. But they have arrested me for a gunman job."[9] Vanzetti was first tried for attempted robbery. Though dozens of people had bought eels, the Italians' traditional fare on Christmas Eve, from Vanzetti the day of the robbery, the jury dismissed the testimony of fellow Italian immigrants. Vanzetti's ethnicity was central throughout this trial. He was convicted because of testimony of eyewitnesses such as the fourteen-year-old boy who told the court, "I could tell he was a foreigner, I could tell by the way he ran."[10] During Sacco and Vanzetti's trial, the judge was openly disdainful of the defendants and of anarchists in general. After the two men were found guilty, the judge rejected every motion for a new trial, despite the discovery of new evidence. After rejecting five motions for a new trial in one day, he boasted to a friend, "Did you see what I did with those anarchist bastards the other day?"[11] From the day Sacco and Vanzetti were arrested until their execution seven years later, theirs was never a criminal case; it was a political trial.

Though few outside of their radical circle had heard of the two anarchists in 1920, fellow Italian American leftists realized the implications of their arrest. Tresca, ever vigilant, was the first to call attention to the arrests in the immigrant radical community. He undoubtedly knew that they were capable of violence in the name of anarchism—"the Idea"— but he was just as certain they would not have been involved in crimes such as robbery and murder. In mid-June, he announced in *Il Martello*, "The innocence of these two men must be brought out. Sacco as well as Vanzetti are well known veterans of the movement for freedom . . . who may be guilty of political heresy, but not of a common crime."[12] Tresca contacted Giovannitti and members of the Italian chamber of labor to help him alert the Italian American community, and they responded quickly. In late August 1920, days after Vanzetti's conviction for robbery, Tresca, Giovannitti, Frank Bellanca, and Luigi Antonini of the ILGWU spoke at the first of many meetings for the two prisoners.[13]

Their appeal to Italian American workers was couched in ethnic as well as class terms. Sacco and Vanzetti were victims of "race hatred" as well as of antiradicalism. The two anarchists were arrested just as the combined force of the Red Scare and nativism peaked in the United States. The fear of radicals had become inseparable from a broader fear of immigrants, which would result in the harshly restrictive Immigration Acts of 1921 and 1924. Public hysteria and fear of Italian immigrants reached their height in West Frankfort, Illinois, just two weeks before the anarchists were arrested. Several Italians were lynched and hundreds more were stoned, clubbed, and driven from their homes by townspeople convinced an Italian had kidnapped and murdered two young boys.[14]

Italian American leftists leapt to defend Sacco and Vanzetti not only because of their shared ethnicity, but also because they were fellow radicals. Though the Italian American Left had a long history of factionalism—in which the *Galleanisti* often played a prominent role—it had an equally long history of mutual support in times of crisis. Sacco and Vanzetti, like Galleani, were antiorganizational anarchists and were outspoken opponents of syndicalism. Vanzetti wrote from jail in 1923, knowing that the syndicalists were fighting for his life, "I am a bitter polemicist, a merciless theorist. . . . With my letters upon 'Syndicalism,' I am actually causing sorrow to many."[15] Though their ideological squabbling rarely ceased, it never prevented them from defending each other when their lives were at stake. Both Sacco and Vanzetti had contributed to Ettor and Giovannitti's defense fund in 1912. The only time either man had been arrested previous to their trial was when Sacco was jailed briefly for protesting Tresca's arrest during the Mesabi Range strike in 1916.[16] Mutual defense, like ideological infighting, was an obligation in the Italian American Left.

By the time of the trial, the Italian American Left's support for Sacco and Vanzetti was based not only on the shared dream of a revolution, but also on a sense of shared—and often covert—history in the United States. Sacco and Vanzetti both arrived in the United States in 1908. By 1913, each had joined a small anarchist group in Massachusetts—Vanzetti in Plymouth, and Sacco in Milford.[17] They subscribed to *Cronaca Sovversiva*, attended (and, in Vanzetti's case, spoke at) anarchist meetings, and participated in strikes with other Italian immigrants. Despite the intensity of their commitment to anarchism, they lived lives of relative obscurity. Vanzetti told an interviewer during his trial, "If it had not been for these thing, I might have live out my life talking at street corners to scorning men. I might have die, unmarked, unknown, a failure."[18] Their isolation resulted not only from the extremity of their radicalism, but also the constant danger they faced if they made their beliefs and activities too widely known. For example, their opposition to American participation in World War I, and the wave of deportations of immigrant radicals that accompanied it, convinced Sacco and Vanzetti to flee to Mexico in May 1917. Though they returned to the United States only a few months later, both men assumed aliases they would not abandon for another year.[19]

The lives Sacco and Vanzetti led, filled with painstaking work for a radical ideal and with the constant need to hide their movements or risk persecution, were shared by Italian American syndicalists during and after their involvement in the FSI. They established a larger presence in the American labor movement than the *Galleanisti* did, but Federation syndicalists, too, battled isolation and the ever-present danger of deportation and even execution. FSI syndicalists emerged from obscurity in Lawrence in 1912, but here, too, they drew attention to their cause by putting their own lives in danger. Their prominence had as much to do with the campaign to save Giovannitti's life as it did with their leadership of the strike. During the war, the FSI shut itself off from its American allies while immersed in the devastating intervention debate. After the debate ended, FSI members changed the name of their newspaper twice and hid its mailing lists to avoid deportation. These efforts were ultimately unsuccessful—the editor of *Il Proletario* and several other FSI members were arrested and deported.

Even those who moved toward the mainstream of the American labor movement, including Giovannitti and Tresca, continued to live a precarious existence. Tresca had been arrested and tried for murder in Mesabi in 1916. Both he and Giovannitti had been arrested and threatened with deportation in 1917. Though they were released, in later years they were often still compelled to move cautiously, and at times clandestinely. When Tresca spoke in Lawrence in 1919, he had to sneak into the city, hide under the stage until it was time for him to speak, and then sneak back out of the city. After he spoke, Anthony Capraro, who arranged his visit, was nearly killed by a vigilante mob.

Tresca's ties to the mainstream labor movement aroused the ire of the fiercely antiorganizational *Galleanisti*, but it was because of these connections that Sacco and Vanzetti turned to him for help when they were arrested. As Nunzio Pernicone has noted, Tresca was the "great fixer" of the Italian radical movement. He was the one to whom all of them— even Galleani's followers—turned when facing prosecution or other trouble with the authorities.[20] It was the Italian Committee for Political Victims, which Tresca had helped organize, that Vanzetti visited after Salsedo's death in April 1920. Tresca communicated with a wide range of radicals and unionists, albeit not always easily. Because of his past involvement with the IWW, his life in Greenwich Village, and his work with the ACWA, he also had easy access to American leftists and labor organizers.

Not surprisingly, it was Tresca who alerted the American Left and labor community about what would become one of the most notorious trials of the century. After Vanzetti's conviction on the robbery charge, Tresca told Elizabeth Gurley Flynn, "Elizabetta, there are two Italian comrades in big trouble in Massachusetts. . . . You investigate . . . and maybe get the Americans to help."[21] At Vanzetti's request, Tresca and Flynn hired labor lawyer Fred Moore to defend the two anarchists. Moore, a hard-working though erratic lawyer, had defended Ettor and Giovannitti in 1912.[22]

By 1924, Sacco became so angry about Moore's conduct that he would demand a new lawyer; Moore's dismissal would further alienate the *Galleanisti* from Tresca. As the trial concluded, they became outspokenly distrustful of Tresca, and in the late 1920s they launched a smear campaign against him, accusing him of being a paid government spy.[23] An old friend of Tresca's reflected years later on his relations with the *Galleanisti*: "They hated Carlo because he was their link with reality. In reality, their ideas were not effective. Carlo was effective."[24]

Tresca may or may not have been their "link with reality," but he was indisputably Sacco and Vanzetti's first link to American society when their trial began. Because of Tresca's efforts, and those of Flynn and Moore, by the end of 1921 there was virtually no one in the American Left or liberal communities who was unaware of the trial. At the end of the Red Scare, it was not difficult to convince labor leaders and fellow radicals that a fair verdict was unlikely. Tresca, Flynn, and Moore secured the support of the American Civil Liberties Union, the ACWA, the ILGWU, and the Socialist Party. After Eugene Debs's release from prison in December 1921 he sent five dollars—his prison pay—to the Sacco-Vanzetti Defense Committee.[25] Even AFL leaders and numerous Boston Brahmin women were convinced that Sacco and Vanzetti had been unjustly convicted. Tresca worked on the anarchists' behalf throughout their trial, despite growing tension with the *Galleanisti*. He opened the pages of *Il Martello* to the anarchists' Sacco-Vanzetti Defense Committee, raised funds in the Italian American and larger American communities, and was the main Italian speaker at every mass rally held at Union Square in New York as the execution date approached.[26]

The Sacco and Vanzetti trial marked the apex of the Italian American Left's impact, not only on American culture, but on Left and labor communities internationally. For a final time this generation of Italian immigrant leftists would risk their lives—this time fatally—for social justice. Support for Sacco and Vanzetti grew, until by the eve of their execution they had become, as a *New Republic* writer asserted, the "two most famous prisoners in all the world."[27] This was no idle claim; never has a trial provoked such worldwide indignation. Italian Americans were as divided as they had ever been; fascists and antifascists were battling each other in the streets. Nonetheless, the trial produced unprecedented unity across class and ideological lines in this immigrant community. The fascist-led Sons of Italy joined the Italian American Left in calling for Sacco and Vanzetti's release. Even Mussolini protested the unfairness of the verdict.[28] American intellectuals, poets and artists such as Jane Addams, John Dewey, Dorothy Parker, and Edna St. Vincent Millay, were arrested at mass meetings.[29] John Dos Passos put together a pamphlet titled "Facing the Chair" in 1927, a detailed analysis of the flawed trial, including appeals for Sacco and Vanzetti from Debs, the AFL, and French intellectual Anatole France. Rallies were held for the prisoners in cities across the globe; workers demonstrated in London, Paris, Belfast, Moscow, Berlin, Vienna, Budapest, Bucharest, Rome, and Madrid. There were protests in Norway, Sweden, Denmark, Switzerland, Holland, Japan, and China, as well as in North and South Africa, and Central and South America.[30] Oswald Garrison Villard, editor of *The Nation,* declared, "Talk about the solidarity of the human race! When has there been a more striking example of the solidarity of great masses of people than this?"[31]

The execution of Sacco and Vanzetti in 1927 exposed the lengths to which the American justice system would go to eliminate the perceived dangers posed by working-class radicals—especially if they were immigrants. It also exposed, in the aftermath the postwar campaign against radicals and labor unions, a nation still deeply divided. Villard warned, "Let those who would uphold the present system by force...beware lest August 10, 1927, be forever recorded as the day of a great American change."[32] A deeply disillusioned John Dos Passos solemnly declared, "[A]ll right we are two nations."[33] For these men, and for many others who had protested, their inability to save Sacco and Vanzetti ended their faith in American justice, and even in American society as it was governed.

Shortly before his execution, Vanzetti defiantly declared that the "last moment belongs to us—that agony is our triumph."[34] He realized that his and Sacco's deaths brought greater attention, and even sympathy, to their cause than any proselytizing they could have done while they lived. Vanzetti's words were equally applicable to a generation of Italian American syndicalists and radicals as a whole.

The deaths of Sacco and Vanzetti did not mark the death of the Italian American Left as a whole. A new and vital generation of radicals, often affiliated with the Communist Party, emerged in the 1920s. Labor leaders and radical intellectuals such as Vito Marcantonio, Luigi Antonini, Louis Fraina, and numerous others fought for social justice into the 1930s and 1940s. Although never large numerically, the Italian American presence in the Communist Party, and the Communist Party's presence in Italian American communities, remained significant in these decades.[35]

But for Italian American syndicalists and other leftists who had come of age before World War I, Sacco and Vanzetti's execution was a signal event. From the FSI to the ACWA to the Italian chamber of labor to the antifascist movement, syndicalists and other radicals with whom they merged their energies had risked their lives fighting for better lives for fellow immigrants. After the war, in their battles against the Red Scare and fascism, they measured success by their ability to make American society see the dangers inherent in the lives of Italian Americans—particularly those who professed unpopular beliefs. In this sense, it was fitting that their defense of Sacco and Vanzetti, their moment of greatest visibility, was the last unified action of this generation of Italian American leftists.

Epilogue

In the years following Sacco and Vanzetti's executions, former FSI syndicalists, long since splintered from the organization they had joined with such optimism before the war, took a number of different paths. Several had returned to Italy during or just after the war, either by choice or by force. The deportees and return migrants counted both faithful fascists and adamant antifascists. Among those who remained in the United States, some faded out of the movement, weary of fighting or felled by health problems. Most remained committed to the fight against fascism, although they continued to struggle with factionalism in their own ranks.

The most infamous of those who returned to Italy was Edmondo Rossoni. Rossoni had been appointed head of the CNCS, the Fascist labor federation, in January 1922. Throughout his leadership of the CNCS, he continued to consider himself an advocate for the working class.[1] To his credit, by 1925 he had alienated *confindustria* (the association of Italian industrialists), the leadership of the Fascist Party, and most fascists who sought better relations with leading Italian industrialists.[2] Rossoni remained so vocal that by late 1927, Mussolini warned him about his "subversive" behavior and told him to stop holding congresses and making speeches. In 1928, Mussolini stripped Rossoni of his power. Rossoni remained with the Fascist Party, even gaining a cabinet position as minister of agriculture and forests by 1935. He voted, without comment, to remove Mussolini as prime minister in July 1943. In the next two years he was sentenced to death both by a Fascist tribunal and by the provisional Italian government established in 1945. The latter sentence was rescinded in 1952; Rossoni returned from Canada, to which he had fled, and lived in Italy until his death in 1965.[3]

In the early days of fascist rule, Rossoni found a sympathizer in Giovanni Baldazzi, editor of *Il Proletario,* before his deportation in 1917. Baldazzi had returned to Italy in the early 1920s, and by 1924 he was working with Rossoni, editing the fascist magazine *Stirpe.* Despite his syndicalist background, he remained above suspicion until 1935, when Fascist authorities intercepted a letter to Baldazzi from Count Sforza, one of the leading *fuorusciti* antifascists in the United States.[4] In 1937 the interior minister identified Baldazzi as an opponent of fascism. After three years under surveillance, Baldazzi wrote a letter to Mussolini asking him to intervene. He protested that, despite the indiscretions of his youth, he was a faithful follower. He had worked as a translator for the Italian National Olympic Committee between 1931 and 1936, and had received favorable reports from all of the managers for whom he had worked. The appeal seems to have worked. By the end of the year, Fascist authorities were considering ending their surveillance of him.[5]

Not all of the syndicalists who returned to Italy ended up in the Fascist Party. Angelo Faggi, for example, remained a vehement opponent of Mussolini. Faggi, the editor of *Il Nuovo Proletario* who had dismissed Alceste de Ambris's protests against his treatment as head of the Italian Workers Mission, had been deported from the United States in 1919. Back in Italy, Faggi joined the executive committee of the Piacenza chamber of labor and used his position to push for both a syndicalist revolution and support for the Russian revolution. He fought back violently against the fascists in the early 1920s. He was a member of one of the *arditi del popolo,* armed squads organized to combat the fascist *squadristi.* Faggi also apparently took part in an action at the Diana Theater in Milan in 1921. As a protest against bourgeois indifference to the attacks of the fascist *squadristi,* he and several other leftists planted an explosive device at the theater which killed several people. The explosion shocked Italian authorities, and Faggi fled the country.

Faggi's transnational existence did not end with his deportation and his return to Italy. With the help of anarchist Errico Malatesta, in the aftermath of the bombing he made his way to Nice, France. Given his experience living and organizing in the United States years before and his abhorrence of fascism, Faggi had little trouble finding a sense of purpose in his new home. After Mussolini's victory in Italy, Faggi, now in France, dedicated himself to fighting fascism. By 1936, he was a member of the French Popular Front, working towards the collapse of Mussolini's government.[6]

In the United States, though most former FSI members continued to battle fascism, some curtailed or even ceased their radical activity. Giovanni di Gregorio was forced by faltering health to limit his activities. In 1925 he developed a serious stomach malady. He remained an opponent of Mussolini, but his ill health prevented his active involvement in the antifascist movement. By the end of the 1930s, he was living a withdrawn life in East Harlem, New York.[7] Leonardo Frisina also faded from the antifascist movement, but for much different reasons. He continued to work against fascism and as a labor organizer through the 1920s. In 1930 he took over Giovannitti's position as secretary of the Italian chamber of labor in New York City when Giovannitti worked, briefly, as a screenwriter in Hollywood. But Frisina's long-troubled relationship with fellow leftists—he had been expelled from the FSI in 1913 for unspecified "acts of bad faith"—caught up with him again in the 1930s. In 1932, antifascist comrades caught him writing an approving letter to a member of Mussolini's cabinet, and accused him of being a spy. By 1936 Frisina was completely cut off from his former allies and from the antifascist movement.[8]

Ex–Federation members who remained in the antifascist movement were compelled to weather factionalism that had started when the AFANA broke apart. The paths taken by Giovannitti and Tresca characterize the choices they made. Giovannitti allied himself with the socialists, most prominent among them Girolamo Valenti and Luigi Antonini, who had left the AFANA. Valenti was one of the first editors of *La Stampa Libera*, the most important antifascist newspaper in the United States after *Il Nuovo Mondo* ceased publication in 1930. By the middle of the 1930s, Valenti was producing and narrating radio shows exposing the evils of fascist Italy.[9] Antonini too was invaluable to the antifascist movement. Head of the largest Italian local in the United States, local 89 of the ILGWU in New York City, he was one of the movement's most important sources of support and money. Antonini and Valenti remained influential leaders of the antifascist movement even as *fuorusciti* led by Gaetano Salvemini and Count Sforza assumed increasing importance.[10]

Giovannitti lent the considerable weight of his fame to this group of antifascists. He became director of the Italian Labor Education Bureau, founded in 1934 by the ILGWU and the ACWA, after his brief stint in California. He appeared regularly at their antifascist demonstrations and commemorations throughout the 1930s, and even spoke in place of Antonini at a 1938 meeting of the Anti-Fascist Action Committee. Giovannitti aligned himself not only with socialist antifascists and with the *fuorusciti*—he was a member, with Salvemini and Sforza, of the Mazzini Society from its founding in 1939—but also with the emerging generation of Italian-American labor leaders. At the 1938 meeting, when he spoke for Antonini, and at an ILGWU convention in 1934, for example, he shared the speakers' platform with Italian-American Communist congressman Vito Marcantonio.[11] At the ILGWU convention, Fiorello La Guardia had been on the platform, as well. Ultimately, though, Giovannitti's impact on the antifascist movement was more symbolic than substantive. He battled depression and alcoholism throughout the 1930s, convinced that his best years had ended before World War I. He lived until the last day of 1959, but was bedridden for the final ten years of his life. He complained of a paralysis of the legs that left doctors baffled and even his own family unconvinced.[12]

While Giovannitti offered his waning energies to the most powerful antifascist faction, Tresca remained an unabashedly radical, brash, and often alienating opponent of fascism and any other form of oppression or injustice he perceived. He worked briefly with the Communist-led AFANA, participating in meetings and demonstrations with Pietro Allegra and other Italian American Communists in the early 1930s. Over time, however, Tresca grew increasingly dismayed by the Communists. He blamed them for breaking up a hotel workers' strike in New York City in 1934 and condemned them for their actions against anarchists and syndicalists during the Spanish Civil War.[13] In 1938, in an uncharacteristic act that indicated the depth of his anger, Tresca went before a grand jury and implicated a Communist Party member in the disappearance of Juliet Poyntz, a disillusioned Communist Tresca had known since 1913. This turned the Communists firmly against him. Allegra angrily labeled him "politically dead" in a pamphlet titled "The Moral Suicide of Carlo Tresca."[14] Undeterred, Tresca continued to battle against fascism both in Italy and in the United States.

In the last years of his life, he dedicated himself to preventing Generoso Pope from whitewashing his past as a fascist sympathizer. Pope owned *Il Progresso Italo-Americano,* the Italian-language daily with the largest circulation in the United States. Though his support for Mussolini throughout the 1920s and 1930s was well documented, he was so powerful in the Italian American community that Franklin Delano Roosevelt appointed him as chairman of the Italian division of the Democratic National Committee in 1936. When the United States entered World War II, and especially after Allied victory became a certainty, Pope began to try to distance himself from his earlier endorsement of fascism. Tresca was determined that Pope would be unsuccessful in this effort. In *Il Martello* and at public meetings, he presented evidence not only of Pope's support for Mussolini, but also of his connections to gangsters in the New York area. He published accusations detailing how Pope used Mafia connections to silence his adversaries. Pope's henchmen, Tresca insisted, had threatened the staff at *La Stampa Libera* and at *Il Martello* with violence if they published attacks against him.[15]

Generoso Pope caused one of the final rifts in the antifascist movement by forging an alliance with antifascist leader Luigi Antonini. Though Antonini had been a vocal opponent of Pope's in the early 1930s, they declared a truce in 1935. By the early 1940s, both men recognized that their mutual support could ensure each a leading role in the postwar Italian American community. This alliance infuriated many antifascists.[16]

It made Tresca a sworn enemy of Antonini's, and even complicated Tresca's relationship with Giovannitti. Giovannitti, who maintained ties to Antonini into the early 1940s, reflected on his relationship with Tresca at a dinner given in his friend's honor on January 9, 1943. He recounted an incident: "One day I met Carlo. I asked Carlo, 'Let me see the new issue of *Il Martello*?' 'No,' replied Tresca, 'We'll eat together tonight and be friends. You can read the paper tomorrow. Today it is all against you.'"[17] Despite his obvious affection for Giovannitti, Tresca was an unceasing critic of anyone—even when it was an old friend—who corrupted the antifascist movement.

Tresca planned a return to Italy after Mussolini's demise; though the Fascist regime collapsed just months later, he never got the chance. On January 11, Tresca was shot and killed outside his office in Greenwich Village. The Communist Party's *Daily Worker* ran a cartoon on its editorial page, bemoaning the effect Tresca's death would have. It showed a bomb being thrown through a window and landing amidst a group meeting at a table bearing a placard reading "Italian-American Anti-Fascist Unity."[18] The cartoon reflected wishful thinking, at best. By 1943,

Tresca had an impressive list of enemies, many of them in the antifascist movement. The *L'Adunata dei Refrattari* group, remnants of the *Galleanisti,* had been accosting him since Sacco and Vanzetti's trial, and communist sympathizers had threatened to kill him. Both groups were suspected, at least for a time, of complicity in his murder. The evidence amassed by the Carlo Tresca Memorial Committee and by later investigators, however, suggests that Carmine Galante killed him because of his antifascist activity. Galante was then a minor mafioso, probably acting on orders from Frank Garofalo, an underworld leader and Generoso Pope's close companion. It was Pope's relationship to Garofalo that Tresca had helped expose.[19]

Tresca's death revealed the myriad challenges he had been battling and that the next generation of Italian Americans would face as well. Galante was never indicted for Tresca's murder, which remains unsolved. There was enormous circumstantial evidence collected by the authorities and Tresca's friends who were investigating the crime. It not only pointed to Galante, but also offered a glimpse at the extent to which organized crime had infiltrated Italian American institutions.[20] The fight against organized crime was one of many Tresca had fought until his death; it was a fight that a new generation of Italian American activists would now have to take up.

Notes

Introduction

1. See, for example, "Newark, N.J.: Conferenza Rossoni" *Il Proletario*, November 10, 1911, 3; "Morgan, Pa.: Conferenza Rossoni" *Il Proletario*, November 10, 1911, 3; "Youngstown, Pa.: Conferenza Rossoni" *Il Proletario*, November 10, 1911, 3; "Cincinnati, Ohio: Conferenza Rossoni" *Il Proletario*, December 5, 1911, 3; "San Francisco" *Il Proletario*, December 5, 1911, 3; "La Sarabanda Patriottica" *Il Proletario*, November 17, 1911, 2; "New Kensington, Pa.: Un trionfo proletario" *Il Proletario*, December 15, 1911, 3; "Rochester, Pa." *Il Proletario*, December 15, 1911, 3; "Franklin, Ma: Nuovi Ribelli" *Il Proletario*, January 26, 1912, 2; Albino Braida, "L'Italia di Carta: San Francisco, Ca." *Il Proletario*, February 2, 1912, 4.

2. Nicola Vecchi, "Lettera Aperta a Sua Maestà le Regina d'Italia," *Il Proletario*, December 7, 1912.

3. There is a considerable body of scholarship on the Lawrence strike, and especially on the IWW's contribution to the strike. See Philip Foner, *The Industrial Workers of the World, 1905–1917* (New York: International Publishers, 1965), 306–50; Melvyn Dubofsky, *We Shall Be All: A History of the IWW* (Chicago: Quadrangle Books, 1969), 228–58. For a collection of primary documents from the strike, see Joyce Kornbluh, ed., *Rebel Voices: An IWW Anthology* (Ann Arbor: University of Michigan Press, 1964). For analyses of women's contributions to the strike, see Meredith Tax, "The Lawrence Strike" in *The Rising of the Women: Feminist Solidarity and Class Conflict, 1880–1917* (New York: Monthly Review Press, 1980), 241–75; and Ardis Cameron. *Radicals of the Worst Sort: Laboring Women in Lawrence, Massachusetts, 1860–1912* (Urbana: University of Illinois Press, 1993). For treatment of the FSI's participation in the strike, see Edwin Fenton, "The Piano, Shoe, and Textile Workers," in *Immigrants and Unions, A Case Study: Italians and American Labor, 1870–1920* (New York: Arno Press, 1975). See especially 320–66; Elisabetta Vezzosi, "La Federazione Socialista Italiana del Nord America (1911–1921)," Ph.D. diss., Università degli Studi Firenze, 1980, 74–94.

4. Todd Gitlin, *The Twilight of Common Dreams: Why America Is Wracked by Culture Wars* (New York: Metropolitan Books, 1995); Michael Kazin, "The Agony

and Romance of the American Left" *American Historical Review* 100, 5 (December 1995): 1488–1512; Michael Tomasky, *Left for Dead: The Life, Death, and Possible Resurrection of Progressive Politics in America* (New York: The Free Press, 1996); Marcy Darnovsky, Barbara Epstein, and Richard Flacks, eds., *Cultural Politics and Social Movements* (Philadelphia: Temple University Press, 1995).

5. Robin D. G. Kelley, *Yo' Mama's DisFUNKtional!: Fighting the Culture Wars in Urban America* (Boston: Beacon Press, 1997), 123.

6. Ibid., 123.

7. Nina Glick Schiller, Linda Basch, and Cristina Blanc-Szanton, eds., *Towards a Transnational Perspective on Migration: Race, Class, Ethnicity, and Nationalism Reconsidered* (New York: The New York Academy of Sciences, 1992), 1–2.

8. Fortunato Vezzoli, "I Senza Patria!" *Il Proletario*, May 11, 1912.

9. The concepts of multiple and contradictory positions and cultural fluidity I employ here come from the works of cultural studies scholars and especially from Chicano scholars who are incorporating cultural studies theories into their work. See, for example, James Clifford and George E. Marcus, eds., *Writing Culture: The Poetics and Politics of Ethnography* (Berkeley: University of California Press, 1986); Stuart Hall, "Cultural Identity and Diaspora," in Jonathan Rutherford, ed., *Identity: Community, Culture, Difference* (London: Lawrence and Wishart, 1990). See also George Lipsitz, *Dangerous Crossroads: Popular Music, Postmodernism and the Poetics of Place* (New York: Verso, 1994); George J. Sánchez, *Becoming Mexican American: Ethnicity, Culture and Identity in Chicano Los Angeles, 1900–1945* (New York: Oxford University Press, 1993); David Gutiérrez, *Walls and Mirrors: Mexican Americans, Mexican Immigrants, and the Politics of Ethnicity* (Berkeley: University of California Press, 1995); Ernesto Chávez, "Culture, Identity, and Community: Musings on Chicano Historiography at the End of the Millennium," *Mexican Studies/Estudios Mexicanos* 14, 1 (Winter 1998), 213–35.

10. The phrase is borrowed from the title of Arthur M. Schlesinger Jr.'s book, *The Disuniting of America: Reflections on a Multicultural Society* (New York: Norton, 1991).

11. Sean Wilentz, "Ungolden Age" *New Republic* 214, 14: 20–21.

12. Gitlin, 35–36.

13. Ibid., 91.

14. Ibid., 135.

15. Kazin, 1511.

16. Ibid., 1500.

17. Alice Kessler-Harris, "Treating the Male as 'Other': Re-Defining the Parameters of Labor History" *Labor History* 34, 2–3 (Spring–Summer 1993), 192.

18. Schiller, Basch, and Blanc-Szanton, eds., 1–24.

19. See, for example, Gilbert Osofsky, "The Enduring Ghetto," *Journal of American History* LV, 2 (September 1968): 243–55; Michael Omi and Howard Winant, *Racial Formation in the United States: From the 1960s to the 1980s* (New York: Routledge and Kegan Paul, 1986). For an overview of African American historiography, see Joe William Trotter Jr., ed., *The Great Migration in Historical Perspective* (Bloomington: Indiana University Press, 1991), esp. 1–17. See also Eric Arnesen, "Following the Color Line of Labor: Black Workers and the Labor Movement Before 1930," *Radical History Review* 55 (1993): 53–87.

20. Omi and Winant, 12.

21. Ibid., 21.

22. For discussions of Asian American historiography see Ronald Takaki, *Strangers from a Different Shore: A History of Asian Americans* (New York: Penguin Books, 1989), esp. 6–18; Sucheng Chan, *Asian Americans: An Interpretive History* (Boston: Twayne Publishers, 1991), esp. xiii–xv. For discussions of Chicano/a historiography, see Sánchez, 3–14; Gutiérrez, 1–11; Alex Saragoza, "Recent Chicano Historiography: An Interpretive Essay," *Aztlan* 19, 1 (1990), 1–77; David Gutiérrez, "The Third Generation: Reflections on Recent Chicano Historiography," *Mexican Studies/Estudios Mexicanos* 5, 2 (Summer 1989), 281–96; Antonia I. Castañeda, "Women of Color and the Rewriting of Western History: The Discourse, Politics, and Decolonization of History," *Pacific Historical Review* (1992): 501–33; Chela Sandoval, "U.S. Third World Feminism: The Theory and Method of Oppositional Consciousness in the Postmodern World," *Genders* 10 (Spring 1991): 1–23.

23. This was a central assertion of many of the pioneering social mobility studies. See Stephen Thernstrom, *The Other Bostonians: Poverty and Progress in the American Metropolis, 1880–1970* (Cambridge: Harvard University Press, 1973).

24. On the concept of "citizenship," see Chantal Mouffe, *The Return of the Political* (New York: Verso, 1993), especially "Democratic Citizenship and the Political Community," 60–73; Rogers Smith, "The 'American Creed' and American Identity: The Limits of Liberal Citizenship in the United States," *Western Political Quarterly* 41, 2 (June 1988), 225–51; Virginia Sapiro, "Women, Citizenship, and Nationality: Immigration and Naturalization Policies in the United States," *Politics & Society* 13, 1 (1984), 1–26; Charles Tilly, ed., *Citizenship, Identity and Social History* (Cambridge: Cambridge University Press, 1996).

25. Rudolph Vecoli, "*Contadini* in Chicago: A Critique of *The Uprooted*," *The Journal of American History* 51 (1964): 404–17.

26. Certain European immigrant historians have also begun to make efforts to deal with racial difference in the United States in more complex ways, as well. See, for example, Donna Gabaccia, *From the Other Side: Women, Gender, and Immigrant Life in the U.S., 1820–1990* (Bloomington: Indiana University Press, 1994).

27. John Bodnar, *The Transplanted: A History of Immigration in Urban America* (Bloomington: Indiana University Press, 1985).

28. Ibid., 206–16.

29. See James Clifford, "Diasporas," *Cultural Anthropology* IX, 3 (August 1994), 304–5.

30. See Russell A. Kazal, "Revisiting Assimilation: The Rise, Fall, and Reappraisal of a Concept in American Ethnic History," *American Historical Review* 100, 2 (April 1995), 437–71.

31. As Matthew Jacobson's fine work shows, an emphasis on immigrants' diasporic tendencies does not preclude an understanding of their will and capacity to gain acceptance in the United States. See Matthew Frye Jacobson, *Special Sorrows: The Diasporic Imagination of Irish, Polish, and Jewish Immigrants in the United States* (Cambridge: Harvard University Press, 1995). See also Donna Gabaccia and Fraser Ottanelli, "Diaspora or International Proletariat? Italian Labor Migration and the Making of Multi-Ethnic States, 1815–1939," unpublished paper delivered at the 18th International Congress of the International Commission of Historical Sciences, Montréal, Canada, August/September 1995.

32. Ewa Morawska, "The Sociology and Historiography of Immigration," in Vir-

ginia Yans-McLaughlin, ed., *Immigration Reconsidered: History, Sociology, and Politics* (New York: Oxford University Press, 1990), 194–6; Bodnar, 53–54.

33. For the earliest call for research on return migration, see Frank Thistlethwaite, who first called for increased attention to the significance of return migration almost forty years ago in his seminal essay "Migration from Europe Overseas in the Nineteenth and Twentieth Century," in Vecoli and Sinke, 50–57. For more recent studies, see Ewa Morawska, "Return Migrations: Theoretical and Research Agenda," in Vecoli and Sinke, 277–92; Mark Wyman, *Round-Trip to America: The Immigrants Return to Europe, 1880–1930* (Ithaca: Cornell University Press, 1993); Dino Cinel, *The National Integration of Italian Return Migration, 1870–1929* (Cambridge: Cambridge University Press, 1991). For a critical assessment of return migration figures, see Walter D. Kamphoefner, "The Volume and Composition of German-American Return Migration," in Vecoli and Sinke, 293–311.

34. Carl Reeve and Ann Barton Reeve, *James Connolly and the United States: The Road to the 1916 Irish Rebellion* (Atlantic Highlands, N.J.: Humanities Press, Inc., 1978); Austen Morgan, *James Connolly: A Political Biography* (Essex: Manchester University Press, 1988).

35. Gary R. Mormino and George Pozzetta, *The Immigrant World of Ybor City: Italians and Their Latin Neighbors in Tampa, 1885–1985* (Urbana: University of Illinois Press, 1990), 144–45, 149–51.

36. Christopher Abel and Nissa Torrents, eds., *José Martí: Revolutionary Democrat* (Durham: Duke University Press, 1986).

37. Even Ho Chi Minh stopped briefly in New York and Boston as a youth while working as a ship's mate aboard a French ship in 1915 and 1916. Ho Chi Minh wrote a number of articles on race relations in the United States for two French newspapers. Jean Lacouture, *Ho Chi Minh: A Political Biography* (New York: Random House, 1968), 263–64.

38. Donna Rae Gabaccia, *Militants and Migrants: Rural Sicilians Become American Workers* (New Brunswick: Rutgers University Press, 1988); Bruno Cartosio, "Sicilian Radicals in Two Worlds," in Marianne Debouzy, ed., *In the Shadow of the Statue of Liberty: Immigrants, Workers, and Citizens in the American Republic, 1880–1920* (Urbana: University of Illinois Press, 1992), 117–28. See Ernesto Ragionieri, "Italiani all'estero ed emigrazione di lavoratori italiani: un tema di storia del movimento operaio," *Belfagor, Rassegna di Varia Umanità* 17 (6), 640–69; Samuel Bailey and Franco Ramella, eds., *One Family, Two Worlds: An Italian Family's Correspondence Across the Atlantic, 1901–1922* (New Brunswick: Rutgers University Press, 1988).

39. Hartmut Keil, "Socialist Immigrants from Germany and the Transfer of Socialist Ideology and Workers' Culture," in Vecoli and Sinke, 315–38; Ferdinando Fasce, *Tra due sponde: Lavoro, affari e cultura tra Italia e Stati Uniti nell'età della grande emigrazione* (Genoa: Graphos, 1993).

40. Douglas Monroy, "Fence Cutters, *Sedicioso,* and First-Class Citizens: Mexican Radicalism in America," in Buhle and Georgakas, eds., 11–44; Colin M. MacLachlan, *Anarchism and the Mexican Revolution: The Political Trials of Ricardo Flores Magón in the United States* (Berkeley: University of California Press, 1991); Emilio Zamora, *The World of the Mexican Worker in Texas* (College Station: Texas A&M University Press, 1993), especially 133–54.

41. Judy Yung, *Unbound Feet: A Social History of Chinese Women in San Francisco* (Berkeley: University of California Press, 1995), 5–6.

42. Ibid., 55, 100.

43. Paul Buhle and Dan Georgakas, eds., *The Immigrant Left in the United States* (New York: State University of New York Press, 1996); Paul Buhle, *Marxism in the USA from 1870 to the Present: Remapping the History of the American Left* (London: Verso, 1987); Gabaccia, *Militants and Migrants;* Dirk Hoerder, ed., *Struggle a Hard Battle: Essays on Working-Class Immigrants* (DeKalb, Ill.: Northern Illinois University Press, 1986), especially David Montgomery, "Nationalism, American Patriotism and Class Consciousness in the Epoch of World War I," 327–52.

44. Robin D. G. Kelley, *Hammer and Hoe: Alabama Communists During the Great Depression* (Chapel Hill: The University of North Carolina Press, 1990); Vicki Ruiz, *Cannery Women, Cannery Lives: Mexican Women, Unionization, and the California Food Processing Industry, 1930–1950* (Albuquerque: University of New Mexico Press, 1987); Michael Denning, *The Cultural Front: The Laboring of American Culture in the Twentieth Century* (New York: Verso, 1996).

45. See Paul Brissenden. *The IWW: A Study of American Syndicalism* (New York: Russell and Russell, Inc. 1957), 274.

46. David Montgomery, "The 'New Unionism' and the Transformation of Workers' Consciousness in America, 1909–1922," in *Workers' Control in America: Studies in the History of Work, Technology, and Labor Struggles* (Cambridge: Cambridge University Press, 1979), 91–112. For other scholars of the IWW who analyze the Wobblies as American syndicalists, see, for example, Melvyn Dubofsky, *We Shall Be All: A History of the Industrial Workers of the World* (Chicago: Quadrangle Books, 1969); Patrick Renshaw, *The Wobblies: The Story of Syndicalism in the United States* (Garden City, New York: Doubleday and Co., 1967); Brissenden. Though Joseph Conlin originally argued that the IWW was not a syndicalist organization, he, too, eventually amended his argument. See Joseph Conlin, ed., *At the Point of Production: The Local History of the IWW* (Westport: Greenwood Press, 1981), 19.

47. Salvatore Salerno, *Red November, Black November: Culture and Community in the Industrial Workers of the World* (Albany: State University of New York Press, 1989), 94, 109–10, 120.

48. Ibid., 120.

49. Larry Peterson, "The One Big Union in International Perspective: Revolutionary Industrial Unionism 1900–1925," *Le Travailleur: Journal of Canadian Labour Studies* 7 (Spring 1981), 41–66.

50. Pierrette Hondagneu-Sotelo, *Gendered Transitions: Mexican Experiences of Immigration* (Berkeley: University of California Press, 1994), 83.

51. On the construction of masculinity, specifically, in working-class communities, see Elizabeth Faue, *Community of Suffering and Struggle: Women, Men and the Labor Movement in Minneapolis, 1915–1945* (Chapel Hill: University of North Carolina Press, 1991); Ava Baron, ed., *Work Engendered: Toward a New History of American Labor* (Ithaca: Cornell University Press, 1991); *Labor History,* 34, 2–3 (Spring–Summer 1993), ed. Elizabeth Faue. For an excellent work on the implications of racial identity and masculinity for the American middle class, see Gail Bederman, *Manliness and Civilization: A Cultural History of Gender and Race in the United States, 1880–1917* (Chicago: University of Chicago Press, 1995). On masculinity in the American middle class, see Mark Carnes and Clyde Griffen, eds., *Meanings for Manhood: Constructions of Masculinity in Victorian America* (Chicago: University of Chicago Press, 1990); and J.A. Mangan and James Walvin, eds., *Manliness and*

Morality: Middle-Class Masculinity in Britain and America, 1800–1940 (New York: St. Martin's Press, 1987).

52. Ava Baron, "On Looking at Men: Masculinity and the Making of a Gendered Working-Class History" in Ann-Louise Shapiro, ed., *Feminists Revision History* (New Brunswick: Rutgers University Press, 1994), 149.

53. Ibid., 150.

54. Elizabeth Faue, "Gender and the Reconstruction of Labor History: An Introduction," *Labor History* 34, 2–3 (Spring–Summer 1993), 169.

55. Montogmery, *Workers Control in America*, 13.

56. Nick Salvatore, *Eugene V. Debs: Citizen and Socialist* (Urbana: University of Illinois Press, 1982), 228.

57. Hewitt in Baron, ed., 142–67.

58. Faue, *Community of Suffering and Struggle*, especially 69–99.

59. Hondagneu-Sotelo, 193–94. See also Pierrette Hondagneu-Sotelo and Michael Messner, "Gender Displays and Men's Power: The 'New Man' and the Mexican Immigrant Man," in Harry Brod and Michael Kaufman, eds., *Theorizing Masculinities* (Thousand Oaks, Calif.: Sage Publications, 1994), 200–218.

60. Hondagneu-Sotelo and Messner, 208.

61. Michael Kazin, *The Populist Persuasion: An American History* (New York: Basic Books, 1995), 66.

62. Dorothy Gallagher, *All the Right Enemies: The Life and Murder of Carlo Tresca* (New Brunswick: Rutgers University Press, 1988).

1. An International Organization of Nationalists

1. For a history of the Federazione Socialista Italiana, see Mario de Ciampis, "Storia del movimento socialista rivoluzionario italiano," *La Parola del Popolo, Cinquantesimo Anniversario, 1908–1958*, 9(December 1958–January 1959), 136–63; Elisabetta Vezzosi, "La Federazione Socialista Italiana del Nord America (1911–1921)," Ph.D. diss., Università degli Studi di Firenze, 1980; Elisabetta Vezzosi, "La Federazione Socialista Italiana del Nord America tra autonomia e scioglimento nel sindacato industriale, 1911–1921," *Studi Emigrazione*, XXI, 73 (March 1984), 81–110. Studies of the Italian American Left generally include Rudolph Vecoli, "The Italian Immigrants in the United States Labor Movement from 1880 to 1929," in Bruno Bezza, ed., *Gli Italiani fuori d'Italia* (Milan: Franco Angeli, 1983), 257–306; Bruno Ramirez, "Immigration, Ethnicity, and Political Militance: Patterns of Radicalism in the Italian American Left, 1880–1930," in Valeria Gennaro Lerna, ed., *From 'Melting Pot' to Multiculturalism: The Evolution of Ethnic Relations in the United States and Canada* (Rome: Bulzoni Editore, 1990), 115–41; on the early years of Italian American radicalism, see Anna Maria Martellone, "Per Una Storia della Sinistra Italiana negli Stati Uniti: Riformismo e Sindacalismo, 1880–1911" in Franca Assante, ed., *Il Movimento Migratorio Italiano dall'Unità Nazionale ai Giorni Nostri* (Naples: Istituto Italiano per la Storia del Movimento Sociali e delle Strutture Sociali, 1976), 181–95.

2. Vecoli in Bezza, especially 272–74; Bruno Cartosio, "Italian Workers and Their Press in the United States, 1900–1920" in Christine Harzig and Dirk Hoerder, eds., *The Press of Labor Migrants in Europe and North America 1880s to 1930s* (Bremen: Labor Newspaper Preservation Project, 1985), 423–41. See also Bruno Cartosio,

"Sicilian Radicals in Two Worlds," in Marianne Debouzy, ed., *In the Shadow of the Statue of Liberty: Immigrants, Workers, and Citizens in the American Republic, 1880–1920* (Urbana: University of Illinois Press, 1992), 117–128.

3. Donna Gabaccia, *Militants and Migrants: Rural Sicilians Become American Workers* (New Brunswick: Rutgers University Press, 1988), 55–66; Vecoli in Bezza, 271–72.

4. Nunzio Pernicone, "The Italian Labor Movement," in Edward Tannenbaum and Emiliana Noether, eds., *Modern Italy: A Topical History Since 1861* (New York: New York University Press, 1974), 201–2; Maurice F. Neufeld, *Italy: School for Awakening Countries: The Italian Labor Movement in Its Political, Social, and Economic Setting from 1800 to 1960* (Ithaca, New York: Cayuga Press, 1961), 220–21.

5. The best study of Italian anarchism is Nunzio Pernicone, *Italian Anarchism, 1864–1892* (Princeton: Princeton University Press, 1993).

6. Paul Avrich, *Sacco and Vanzetti: The Anarchist Background* (Princeton: Princeton University Press, 1991), 45.

7. For a brief introduction to Bakunin, see Paul Avrich, *Anarchist Portraits* (Princeton: Princeton University Press, 1988), especially 5–52.

8. Nunzio Pernicone, "Luigi Galleani and Italian Anarchist Terrorism in the United States," *Studi Emigrazione*, XXX, 111 (September 1993), 469–88; Pernicone, *Italian Anarchism*, 82–128. For more on Galleani, see Ugo Fedeli, *Luigi Galleani: Quarant'anni di lotte rivoluzionarie 1891–1931* (Edizioni "L'Antistato": Cesena, 1956); Rudolph Vecoli, "Luigi Galleani," in Mari Jo Buhle, Paul Buhle, and Dan Georgakas, eds., *Encyclopedia of the American Left* (New York: Garland Publishing Co., 1990), 251–53.

9. See Vecoli, "Luigi Galleani," 251–53; Avrich, *Anarchist Portraits*, 48–52; Pernicone, "Luigi Galleani and Italian Anarchist Terrorism in the United States," 482–83.

10. Vezzosi, "La Federazione Socialista Italiana del Nord America (1911–1921)," 3–4; de Ciampis, 138; Martellone, 185.

11. Cartosio, 432.

12. Ibid., 432–33.

13. Nunzio Pernicone, "The Italian Labor Movement," 201–2; Neufeld, 220–21.

14. Pernicone, "The Italian Labor Movement," 201–2.

15. Alexander De Grand, *The Italian Left in the Twentieth Century: A History of the Socialist and Communist Parties* (Bloomington: Indiana University Press, 1989), 13–18; Neufeld, 222–30; Pernicone, "The Italian Labor Movement," 202–4.

16. De Ciampis, 138.

17. Giacinto Menotti Serrati Casellario Politico Centrale [CPC], busta 4769; de Ciampis, 140–41. CPC files were kept by the police on all Italian radicals in Italy and abroad.

18. De Ciampis, 141.

19. Most of these had already existed as SLP sections. Vezzosi, "La Federazione Socialista Italiana del Nord America (1911–1921)," 8.

20. Carlo Tresca, unpublished autobiography (available at the Immigration History Research Center, Minneapolis, Minn.), 31–32, 45–57, 75–85; Carlo Tresca CPC, busta 5208.

21. Bruno Ramirez, "Immigration, Ethnicity, and Political Militance: Patterns of Radicalism in the Italian-American Left, 1880–1930," 127–28; Pernicone, "The Italian Labor Movement," 201.

22. Tresca wasn't the first Italian immigrant radical to declare himself a syndicalist; however, he did popularize the ideology within the FSI. The first syndicalists among the Italian Americans were the members of the Unione Socialista Italiana, a socialist section in New York City that had moved to distinguish itself from the still largely intransigent FSI during the crisis wrought by Serrati's departure. Its members included Raimondo Fazio and Alberto Argentieri. (Raimondo Fazio CPC, busta 1982; Vezzosi, *Il Socialismo Indifferente: Immigrati italiani e Socialist Party negli Stati Uniti del primo Novecento* [Rome: Edizioni Lavoro, 1991], 42).

23. Franco Ramella, "Immigration from an Area of Intense Industrial Development: The Case of Northwestern Italy," in Rudolph J. Vecoli and Suzanne M. Sinke, *A Century of European Migrations, 1830–1930* (Urbana: University of Illinois Press, 1991), 261–74.

24. For studies of Italian syndicalism, see Zeev Sternhell with Mario Sznajder and Maia Asheri, *The Birth of Fascist Ideology: From Cultural Rebellion to Political Revolution* (Princeton: Princeton University Press, 1994); David D. Roberts, *The Syndicalist Tradition and Italian Fascism* (Chapel Hill: University of North Carolina Press, 1979).

25. Pernicone, 203–5; Sternhell, 134–37.

26. The FSI had by this point voted to move *Il Proletario* to Philadelphia.

27. Tresca, unpublished autobiography, 71–74.

28. Mario de Ciampis, "History of *Il Proletario*" (unpublished), Immigration History Research Center, Minneapolis, Minn., 21.

29. Ibid., 8.

30. Ibid., 215–22.

31. Nunzio Pernicone, "Carlo Tresca," in *Encyclopedia of the American Left*, 780–82; Carlo Tresca CPC, busta 5208.

32. Giuseppe Bertelli CPC, busta 554; de Ciampis, "History of *Il Proletario*," 570. See also Giuseppe Bertelli, *Chi siamo e che cosa vogliamo* (Firenze: Nerbini, 1902).

33. De Grand, 22.

34. Sternhell, 135–37; Pernicone, "The Italian Labor Movement," 204; Neufeld, 347–48.

35. De Ciampis, "History of *Il Proletario*," 570, 664.

36. Eugene Miller and Gianna Sommi Panofsky, "The Beginnings of the Italian Socialist Movement in Chicago," in Joseph L. Tropea, James E. Miller, and Cheryl Beattie-Repetti, eds., *Support and Struggle: Italians and Italian Americans in a Comparative Perspective* (Staten Island: The American Italian Historical Association, 1986), 58.

37. Giacinto Menotti Serrati CPC, busta 4769; de Ciampis, 140–41.

38. Giovanni Di Palma-Castiglione CPC, busta 1812; for more on the Italian Legion in Greece, see Pernicone, *Italian Anarchism*, 184.

39. Virgilio Tedeschi CPC, busta 5057.

40. Arturo Giovannitti CPC, busta 2439.

41. Samuel L. Bailey, "Cross-Cultural Comparison and the Writing of Migration History: Some Thoughts on How to Study Italians in the New World," in Virginia Yans-Mclaughlin, ed., *Immigration Reconsidered: History, Sociology, and Politics* (New York: Oxford University Press, 1990), 248.

42. Dorothy Gallagher, *All the Right Enemies: The Life and Murder of Carlo Tresca* (New Brunswick: Rutgers University Press, 1988), 22.

43. "Per Nostre Idee," *La Parola dei Socialisti,* May 16, 1908.

44. De Ciampis, "Storia del movimento socialista rivoluzionario italiano," 140–41; for a brief overview of the SLP, see Paul Buhle, "Socialist Labor Party," in *Encyclopedia of the American Left,* 711–16; see also L. Glen Seratan, *Daniel De Leon: The Odyssey of an American Marxist* (Cambridge: Harvard University Press, 1979).

45. De Ciampis, "History of *Il Proletario,*" 15.

46. Vezzosi, "La Federazione Socialista Italiana del Nord America (1911–1921)," 87–88; Ramirez, 11–14.

47. De Ciampis, "History of *Il Proletario,*" 622.

48. Ibid., 592; Elisabetta Vezzosi, *Il Socialismo Indifferente,* 40–43.

49. Miller and Panofsky, 60–63.

50. De Ciampis, "History of *Il Proletario,*" 1017.

51. De Ciampis, "Storia del movimento socialista rivoluzionario italiano," 141–42; Vezzosi, *Il Socialismo Indifferente,* 30–33.

52. De Ciampis, "Storia del movimento socialista rivoluzionario italiano," 142; Cartosio, 426–27.

53. De Ciampis, "History of *Il Proletario,*" 1076, 1347, 1353.

54. For example, Giacinto Menotti Serrati, "A Signor Galleani," *Il Proletario,* July 15, 1902; G. M. Serrati, "A *La Questione Sociale,*" *Il Proletario,* October 4, 1902.

55. Paolo Valera, *Giacinto Menotti Serrati, direttore dell' Avanti!.* (Casa Editrice La Folla, Milan, 1920), 37–38; Luigi Galleani, CPC, busta 2241; Giacinto Menotti Serrati CPC, busta 4769.

56. For example, El Vecchio, "L'Assassinio di Elia Corti al Socialist Block la sera di sabato," *La Cronaca Sovversiva,* October 10, 1903; *La Cronaca Sovversiva:* "L'Assassinio di Elia Corti," *La Cronaca Sovversiva,* November 21, 1903; The Anarchists of the United States, "Giacinto Menotti Serrati: spia ed assassino," *La Cronaca Sovversiva,* January 2, 1904 (two-page supplement). "El Vecchio" (the old one) was one of Galleani's pen names.

57. De Ciampis, "Storia del movimento socialista rivoluzionario italiano," 142–43. See also Valera, 37–38.

58. Vezzosi, *Il Socialismo Indifferente,* 40–41.

59. Fenton, 481.

60. Vecoli in Bezza, 274.

61. Gary Mormino and George Pozzetta. *The Immigrant World of Ybor City: Italians and Their Latin Neighbors in Tampa, 1885–1985* (Urbana: University of Illinois Press, 1990 [1987]), 145–53; Virginia Yans-McLaughlin, *Family and Community: Italian Immigrants in Buffalo, 1880–1930* (Urbana: University of Illinois Press, 1982 [1977]), 123–30; 225–38.

62. Vezzosi, *Il Socialismo Indifferente,* 141–60.

63. Edwin Fenton, *Immigrants and Unions, A Case Study: Italians and American Labor, 1870–1920* (New York: Arno Press, 1975), especially 458–558; Vezzosi, *Il Socialismo Indifferente,* especially 110–24; Vecoli in Bezza, 293–98.

64. Vecoli in Bezza, 274.

65. Pierrette Hondagneu-Sotelo and Michael Messner, "Gender Displays and Men's Power: The 'New Man' and the Mexican Immigrant Man," in Harry Brod and Michael Kaufman, eds., *Theorizing Masculinities* (Thousand Oaks, Calif.: Sage Publications, 1994), 200–218.

66. Giuseppe Bertelli, n.t., *La Parola dei Socialisti,* July 25, 1909.

67. Ibid.

68. De Ciampis, "History of *Il Proletario,*" 276.

69. Ibid., 724, 800.

70. Georges Sorel, *Reflections on Violence* (New York: B. W. Huebsch, 1914).

71. Pernicone, "Luigi Galleani and Italian Anarchist Terrorism in the United States," 476–77. For more on the divisiveness of Italian anarchists in the United States, see Paul Avrich, *Sacco and Vanzetti,* 52–53. For more on the Italian American anarchist movement generally, see Gino Cerrito, "Sull'Emigrazione Anarchia Italiana negli Stati Uniti d'America" *Volontà* 22 (July/August 1969), 269–76; Augusta Molinari, "I Giornali delle Comunità Anarchiche Italo-Americane" *Movimento operaio e socialista* 4, 1–2 (January/June 1981), 117–30.

72. Rudolph Vecoli, "'Primo Maggio' in the United States: An Invented Tradition of the Italian Anarchists," in Andrea Panaccione, ed., *May Day Celebration, Quaderni della Fondazione G. Brodolini* (Venice: Marsilio Editori, 1988), 59–62; Avrich, 46–48; Pernicone, "Luigi Galleani and Italian Anarchist Terrorism in the United States," 477.

73. Fenton, 490–91.

74. Carlo Tresca, unpublished autobiography, 89–90.

75. Avrich, *Sacco and Vanzetti,* 45–57; see also Mormino and Pozzetta, especially 148–74.

76. See, for example, Donna Gabaccia, *Militants and Migrants;* Mormino and Pozzetta, *The Immigrant World of Ybor City;* Yans-McLaughlin, *Family and Community;* Miller and Panofsky, 55–70.

77. See David Montgomery, *Workers' Control in America: Studies in the History of Work, Technology, and Labor Struggles* (Cambridge: Cambridge University Press, 1979), 91–112.

78. John Bodnar, *The Transplanted: A History of Immigrants in Urban America* (Bloomington: Indiana University Press, 1985), 53; Edwin Fenton, *Immigrants and Unions.*

79. Vecoli, "'Primo Maggio' in the United States: An Invented Tradition of the Italian Anarchists," especially 70–74; Avrich, *Sacco and Vanzetti,* 54–56.

80. Gallagher, 30–31.

81. Sternhell, 135.

82. Fortunato Vezzoli CPC, busta 5393.

83. Flavio Venanzi CPC, busta 5346.

84. Edmondo Rossoni CPC, busta 4466; see also John J. Tinghino, *Edmondo Rossoni: From Revolutionary Syndicalism to Fascism* (New York: Peter Lang, 1991); Ferdinando Cordova, ed., *Uomini e volti del Fascismo* (Roma: Bulzoni, 1980), 352–60.

85. Arturo Giovannitti CPC, busta 2439; Robert D'Attilio, "Arturo Giovannitti," in Mari Jo Buhle, Paul Buhle, and Harvey J. Kaye, eds., *The American Radical* (New York: Routledge, 1994), 135–42; Nunzio Pernicone, "Arturo Massimo Giovannitti," in John A. Garraty and Mark C. Carnes, eds., *American National Biography* (New York: Oxford 1999), 80–82.

86. De Ciampis, "The History of *Il Proletario,*" 627.

87. The experiences in the United States that Italian leftists took home with them could create problems as easily as opportunities. The battle Luigi Galleani and Giacinto Serrati had waged in 1902 and 1903 had a ripple effect in Italy years later

when Benito Mussolini, who had met Serrati just after the incident in Barre, sought to discredit him in 1914 by resurrecting the story (Fedeli, 130).

2. A Transnational Syndicalist Identity

1. Crispi quoted in Claudio Segrì, *The Fourth Shore: The Italian Colonization of Libya* (University of Chicago Press: Chicago, 1974), 12.

2. Maurice Neufeld, *Italy: School for Awakening Countries. The Italian Labor Movement in Its Political, Social, and Economic Setting from 1800–1960* (Ithaca: Cayuga Press, 1961), 216–17.

3. Mario de Ciampis, "Storia del movimento socialista rivoluzionario italiano," *La Parola del Popolo, Cinquantesimo Anniversario, 1908–1958,* 9 (December 1958–January 1959), 154.

4. Carlo Tresca, unpublished autobiography, 134. Historians who have made this argument include Rudolph Vecoli, "The Italian Immigrants in the United States Labor Movement from 1880 to 1929," in Bruno Bezza, ed., *Gli Italiani fuori d'Italia* (Milan: Franco Angeli, 1983), 257–306; Bruno Cartosio, "Italian Workers and Their Press in the United States, 1900–1920," in Christine Harzig and Dirk Hoerder, eds., *The Press of Labor: Migrants in Europe and North America, 1880s to 1930s* (Bremen: Labor Newspaper Preservation Project, 1985), 423–41.

5. Todd Gitlin, *The Twilight of Common Dreams: Why America is Wracked by Culture Wars* (New York: Metropolitan Books, 1995); Michael Kazin, "The Agony and Romance of the American Left," *American Historical Review* 100, 5 (December 1995): 1488–1512; Marcy Darnovsky, Barbara Epstein, and Richard Flacks, eds., *Cultural Politics and Social Movements* (Philadelphia: Temple University Press, 1995).

6. John Diggins, *Mussolini and Fascism: The View from America* (Princeton: Princeton University Press, 1972), esp. 116–17. See also Bruno Ramirez, "Immigration, Ethnicity, and Political Militance: Patterns of Radicalism in the Italian American Left, 1880–1930," in Valeria Gennaro Lerda, ed., *From 'Melting Pot' to Multiculturalism: The Evolution of Ethnic Relations in the United States and Canada* (Rome: Bulzoni Editore, 1990), 115–41. Ramirez's excellent essay analyzes the Italian American Left both as a product of the Italian Left and as an actor in the American Left. He, too, however, concludes that except in a few exceptional instances, the Italian American Left "either neglected or outrightly dismissed" the issue of ethnicity (140).

7. See Stanford and Ezel Shaw, *History of the Ottoman Empire and Modern Turkey* Vol. 2 (Cambridge University Press: Cambridge, 1977), 289; William Miller, *The Ottoman Empire and Its Successors, 1801–1927* (Cambridge University Press: Cambridge, 1934), 496–97.

8. The *Risorgimento,* which culminated in 1861, was the political struggle to reunify Italy and to free it from foreign domination—Italy (or, rather, the various Italian states before reunification) had been ruled by both the Hapsburgs and the Austrian empire. For a voluminous narrative history of the *Risorgimento,* see George Martin, *The Red Shirt and the Cross of Savoy: The Story of Italy's Risorgimento (1748–1871)* (Dodd, Mead and Co.: New York. 1969).

9. Charles Lapworth, *Tripoli and Young Italy* (Stephen Swift and Co. Ltd.: London, 1912), 37.

10. This introductory section outlining the course of the war and Italy's various reasons for choosing to attack Libya is drawn from Richard Bosworth, *Italy and the Approach of the First World War* (St. Martin's Press: New York. 1983), especially 77–120; Richard Bosworth, "Italy and the End of the Ottoman Empire," in Marian Kent, ed., *The Great Powers and the End of the Ottoman Empire* (George Allen and Unwin: London, 1984), 52–75; Segrì's *Fourth Shore,* especially 3–32. See also Timothy Childs, *Italo-Turkish Diplomacy and the War Over Libya, 1911–1912* (E. J. Brill: Leiden, The Netherlands, 1990), especially 3–28. For contemporary reflections on Italy's entry into the ranks of imperial powers, see W. K. McClure, *Italy in North Africa: An Account of the Tripoli Enterprise* (Constable and Co.: London, 1913); and Charles Lapworth, *Tripoli and Young Italy* (Stephen Swift and Co.: London, 1912). A much more recent treatment sympathetic to Italy's war is John Gooch, *Army, State, and Society in Italy, 1870–1915* (St. Martin's Press: New York, 1989). For studies of the Italo-Turkish war that analyze Italian radicals' perspectives, see John Thayer, *Italy and the Great War: Politics and Culture, 1870–1915* (University of Wisconsin Press: Madison, 1964), especially 237–69; and David Roberts, *The Syndicalist Tradition and Italian Fascism* (Chapel Hill: University of North Carolina Press, 1979), esp. 16, 53, 101–4.

11. Ewa Morawska, "The Sociology and Historiography of Immigration," in Virginia Yans-McLaughlin, *Immigration Reconsidered: History, Sociology, and Politics* (New York: Oxford University Press, 1990), 187–238; John Bodnar, *The Transplanted: The History of Immigrants in Urban America* (Bloomington: Indiana University Press, 1985), 45, 60.

12. Segrì, 3–4, 8. For a brief analysis of the "southern problem" produced by the *Risorgimento* and how it was handled in early twentieth century Italy, see Antonio Gramsci, *Selections from the Prison Notebooks of Antonio Gramsci* (International Publishers: New York, 1987), 92–99.

13. Bosworth, in Kent, 81–82.

14. Bosworth, *Italy and the End of the Ottoman Empire,* 55.

15. See Bifolco, "Un barile di menzogne" *Il Proletario,* November 24, 1911; and Lapworth, 18.

16. Bosworth, "Italy and the End of the Ottoman Empire," in Kent, 60; Stanford and Ezel Shaw, v. 2, 290.

17. For a summary of the course of the war, see Thayer, 250–51; Gooch, 140–43.

18. This quote was recorded by a correspondent from Trenton, New Jersey; see "Trenton, NJ: Comizio Protesta" *Il Proletario,* November 10, 1911, 3. For accounts of Rossoni's lecture tour, see "Newark, N.J.: Conferenza Rossoni," *Il Proletario,* November 10, 1911, 3; "Morgan, Pa.: Conferenza Rossoni," *Il Proletario,* November 10, 1911, 3; "Cleveland, Ohio: Conferenza Rossoni," *Il Proletario,* November 10, 1911, 3; "Cincinnati, Ohio: Conferenza Rossoni," *Il Proletario,* December 5, 1911, 3; "San Francisco," *Il Proletario,* December 5, 1911, 3. For accounts of run-ins between FSI section members and prowar Italian Americans, see "La Sarabanda Patriottica," *Il Proletario,* November 17, 1911, 2; "New Kensington, Pa.: Un trionfo proletario," *Il Proletario,* December 15, 1911, 3; "Franklin, Mass.: Nuovi Ribelli" *Il Proletario,* January 26, 1912, 2; Albino Braida, "L'Italia di Carta: San Francisco, Calif.," *Il Proletario,* February 2, 1912, 4.

19. "I Patriottardi alla Riscossa," *Il Proletario,* December 8, 1911, 1–2.

20. Roberts, 104.

21. Giovanni di Gregorio Casellario Politico Centrale (CPC) file, busta 1792, Archivio Centrale dello Stato, Rome, Italy.

22. Giovanni di Gregorio, "War, Its Causes, and How to End It," *Il Proletario,* January 12, 1912, 2–3.

23. Ibid. The war "between this country and Spain" to which di Gregorio refers to is the Spanish-American war.

24. Arturo Giovannitti, "The Brigandage of Tripoli," *International Socialist Review,* 12 (March 1912), 574. The *International Socialist Review* was the theoretical journal of the American Socialist Party.

25. Bifolco, "Le Barbarie della Civiltà" *Il Proletario,* January 5, 1912, 4.

26. Ibid. For Italian syndicalists' arguments against—and in favor of—the war, see Giulio Barni, et al., *Pro e contro la guerra di Tripoli: Discussioni nel campo rivoluzionario* (Naples: Società Editrice Partenopea, 1912).

27. Arturo Giovannitti, "The Brigandage of Tripoli," 574.

28. Ibid.

29. Bifolco, "Le Glorie dell'Italia," *Il Proletario,* December 15, 1911, 2.

30. Leonardo Frisina, "La Guerra e il Meridionale: La Tripolitania e la Calabria," *Il Proletario,* January 5, 1912, 2.

31. Ibid. Frisina is undoubtedly referring to the earthquake and tidal wave that hit the Strait of Messina between Sicily and mainland Italy in 1908. Over 100,000 people in the town of Messina were killed, another 20,000 died in the city of Reggio-Calabria, and over 300 smaller towns were completely destroyed.

32. Giovanni Gianchino, "Tripoli e la Sicilia," *Il Proletario,* January 5, 1912, 2.

33. Ibid.

34. Il Corsaro, "La Civiltà Italiana a Tripoli," *Il Proletario,* January 5, 1912.

35. Giovanni Gianchino, "Tripoli e la Sicilia," *Il Proletario,* January 5, 1912, 2.

36. Leonardo Frisina, "La Civiltà d'Italia" *Il Proletario,* April 19, 1912.

37. Ibid.

38. See Frank M. Snowden, *Violence and Great Estates in the South of Italy: Apulia, 1900–1922* (Cambridge: Cambridge University Press, 1986), 65–67.

39. Roberts, 54; for a discussion of Italian syndicalists' perspective on southern Italians, see 53–57.

40. Ibid., 90.

41. Arturo Giovannitti, "The Brigandage of Tripoli," 574.

42. Roberts, 90.

43. Quoted in Roberts, 103–4.

44. Ibid.

45. Libero Tancredi CPC, busta 4362.

46. Zeev Sternhell with Mario Sznajder and Maia Asheri. *The Birth of Fascist Ideology: From Cultural Rebellion to Political Revolution* (Princeton: Princeton University Press, 1994), 170.

47. Giuliano Procacci, *History of the Italian People* (London: Penguin Books, 1991 [1970]), 397.

48. "Correspondence," *Il Proletario,* February 2, 1912.

49. Oscar Mazzitelli, "Il Problema Meridionale e la Guerra," *Il Proletario,* January 12, 1912; Oscar Mazzitelli CPC file, busta 3181.

50. Bifolco, "Un barile di menzogne," *Il Proletario,* November 24, 1911. New York and Buenos Aires were two of the major areas of settlement for Italian immigrants.

51. Segrì, *The Fourth Shore,* 4.

52. This quote was taken from Fortunato Vezzoli, "Il racconto d'un condannàto a morte," *Il Proletario*, November 17, 1911. This was the second installment of the article; the first one was printed in *Il Proletario* on November 10, 1911.

53. Fortunato Vezzoli, "Il racconto d'un condannàto a morte," *Il Proletario*, November 10, 1911.

54. Fortunato Vezzoli, "Il racconto d'un condannàto a morte," *Il Proletario*, November 17, 1911.

55. Fortunato Vezzoli, "I Senza Patria!", *Il Proletario*, May 11, 1912; Giovanni di Gregorio, "Patriottismo," *Il Proletario*, May 3, 1913, 5.

56. Di Gregorio, "Patriottismo," *Il Proletario*, May 3, 1913, 5.

57. Ibid.

58. Fortunato Vezzoli, "I Senza Patria!", *Il Proletario*, May 11, 1912.

59. Ibid.

60. Di Gregorio, "Patriottismo," *Il Proletario*, May 3, 1913, 5.

61. E. J. Hobsbawm, *Nations and Nationalism Since 1870: Programme, Myth and Reality* (Cambridge: Cambridge University Press, 1992), esp. 101–30.

62. See Ronald S. Cunsolo, "Enrico Corradini and the Italian Version of Proletarian Nationalism," *Canadian Review of Studies in Nationalism*, XII 1 (1985), 47–63.

63. Quoted in Sternhell, 164.

64. Procacci, 393.

65. Quoted in Cunsolo, 52.

66. Roberts, 118–19.

67. Sternhell, 166.

68. Quoted in Sternhell, 164–65.

69. Roberts, 119.

70. Alberto Argentieri, "Lettere d'Italia," *Il Proletario*, December 29, 1911.

71. Alberto Argentieri, "L'Oscena Gazzarra di Tripoli," *Il Proletario*, November 3, 1911.

72. "Nicola Vecchi," in Franco Andreucci and Tommaso Detti, eds., *Il Movimento operaio italiano: Dizionario biografico, 1853–1943* (Rome: Editori Riuniti, 1978), 191–95.

73. Nicola Vecchi, "Per un Ritorno in Massa," *Il Proletario*, December 14, 1912.

74. Ibid.

75. Benedict Anderson, *Imagined Communities: Reflections on the Origin and Spread of Nationalism*, rev. ed. (New York: Verso Press, 1991).

76. For an insightful analysis of the ways in which Italian migrant antifascists in Latin America used the "Garibaldian tradition," see Pietro Rinaldo Fanesi, "L'antifascismo italiano in America latina e la tradizione garibaldina," unpublished paper presented at the "For Us there Are No Frontiers" conference, Tampa, Fla., April 1996.

77. "Come fu trattato Hervé in Italia" *Il Proletario*, December 7, 1912. On Hervé's conversion, see Paul Mazgaj, *The Action Française and Revolutionary Syndicalism* (Chapel Hill: The University of North Carolina Press, 1979), 200–2; Sternhell, 243–45.

78. "Come fu trattato Hervé in Italia," *Il Proletario*, December 7, 1912.

79. Alceste de Ambris, "Un'intervista con Cipriani," *Il Proletario*, December 8, 1911.

80. De Ciampis, 1407–10.

81. "New York, N.Y.: Commemorazione di Rapisardi," *Il Proletario*, January 26, 1912, 3.

82. Hobsbawm, 123.

83. "New Kensington, Pa.," *Il Proletario*, December 15, 1911, 3.

84. John L. Stanley, ed., *From Georges Sorel: Essays in Socialism and Philosophy* (New Brunswick: Transaction Books, 1987), 42, 99ff.; Sternhell, 66.

85. Roberts, 78.

86. Quoted in Nunzio Pernicone, "Luigi Galleani and Italian Anarchist Terrorism in the United States," *Studi Emigrazione*, XXX, 111 (September 1993), 470.

87. Andreucci and Detti, 191–95.

88. Nicola Vecchi, "La Guerra," *Il Proletario*, November 9, 1912.

89. "Il Cittadino Browning," *Il Proletario*, December 22, 1911, 1.

90. Fortunato Vezzoli, "Anti-militarismo e Primo Maggio," *Il Proletario*, March 5, 1913.

91. Arturo M. Giovannitti, "Syndicalism—The Creed of Force," *The Independent* 76, 3387 (October 30, 1913), 209.

92. For more on the IWW's position on violence, see, for example, Philip S. Foner, *History of the Labor Movement in the United States. Volume IV: The Industrial Workers of the World* (New York: International Publishers, 1965), 164–66; Melvyn Dubofsky, *We Shall Be All: A History of the Industrial Workers of the World* (Chicago: Quadrangle Books, 1969), 160–64; Paul Brissenden, *The IWW: A Study of American Syndicalism* (New York: Russell and Russell Inc., 1957 [1919]), 278–81.

3. The Lawrence Strike of 1912

1. Carlo Tresca, unpublished autobiography, n.d., 140. The autobiography is at the Immigration History Research Center, Minneapolis, Minn.

2. There is a considerable body of scholarship on the Lawrence strike and the IWW's contribution to the strike. See Philip Foner, *The Industrial Workers of the World, 1905–1917* (New York: International Publishers, 1965), 306–50; Melvyn Dubofsky, *We Shall Be All: A History of the IWW* (Chicago: Quadrangle Books, 1969), 228–58. For primary documents from the strike, see Joyce Kornbluh, ed., *Rebel Voices: An IWW Anthology* (Ann Arbor: University of Michigan Press, 1964). For analyses of women's contributions to the strike, see Meredith Tax, "The Lawrence Strike," in *The Rising of the Women: Feminist Solidarity and Class Conflict, 1880–1917* (New York: Monthly Review Press, 1980), 241–75; and Ardis Cameron, *Radicals of the Worst Sort: Laboring Women in Lawrence, Massachusetts, 1860–1912* (Urbana: University of Illinois Press, 1993).

3. On the FSI's participation in the strike, see Edwin Fenton, "The Piano, Shoe, and Textile Workers," in *Immigrants and Unions, A Case Study: Italians and American Labor, 1870–1920* (New York: Arno Press, 1975), 320–66; Elisabetta Vezzosi, "La Federazione Socialista Italiana del Nord America (1911–1921)," Ph.D. diss., Università degli Studi Firenze, 1980, 74–94.

4. David Goldberg, *A Tale of Three Cities: Labor Organization and Protest in Paterson, Passaic and Lawrence, 1916–1921* (New Brunswick: Rutgers University Press, 1989), 86–89.

5. Ibid., 90–91.

6. Foner, 311.

7. Tax, 248.

8. John Higham, *Strangers in the Land: Patterns of American Nativism 1860–1925* (New Brunswick: Rutgers University Press, 1955), especially 131–58.

9. James R. Barrett and David Roediger, "Inbetween Peoples: Nationality and the 'New Immigrant' Working Class," *Journal of American Ethnic History* 16, 3 (Spring 1997), 3–44.

10. See, for example, Edward Ross, *The Old World in the New: The Significance of Past and Present Immigration to the American People* (New York: Century Co., 1914).

11. See especially Matthew Frye Jacobson, *Whiteness of a Different Color: European Immigrants and the Alchemy of Race* (Cambridge: Harvard University Press, 1998); David Roediger, *The Wages of Whiteness: Race and the Making of the American Working Class* (New York: Verso, 1991); Eric Lott, *Love and Theft: Blackface Minstrelsy and the American Working Class* (New York: Oxford University Press, 1993); David Roediger, *Towards the Abolition of Whiteness: Essays on Race, Politics, and Working Class History* (New York: Verso, 1994).

12. See, for example, Henry Pratt Fairchild, *The Melting Pot Mistake* (Boston: Little, Brown and Co., 1926); H. B. Woolsten, "Rating the Nations," *American Journal of Sociology* (July–May 1916–1917), 281–390.

13. Donna Rae Gabaccia, *Militants and Migrants: Rural Sicilians Become American Workers* (New Brunswick: Rutgers University Press, 1988), 103–4, 109–110; Gary R. Mormino and George E. Pozzetta, *The Immigrant World of Ybor City: Italians and Their Latin Neighbors in Tampa, 1885–1985* (Urbana: University of Illinois Press, 1990), 57, 82–83, 120.

14. Even here there are historical parallels between the experiences of southern Italians and the current assault on people of Mexican heritage who are accused of being unwilling to surrender their language and heritage and of having low naturalization rates.

15. See Peppino Ortoleva, "Una Voce del Coro: Angelo Rocco e lo Sciopero di Lawrence del 1912," *Movimento operaio e socialista*, IV, 1–2 (1981), 5–32; Kornbluh, 178; Foner, 317.

16. Ortoleva, 6.

17. Kornbluh, 190.

18. Ibid., 147; Dubofsky, 236.

19. "Joseph J. Ettor and Arturo Giovannitti," *Industrial Worker*, July 25, 1912, 3.

20. For an excellent comparative analysis of syndicalism in Europe and the United States, see Larry Peterson, "The One Big Union in International Perspective: Revolutionary Industrial Unionism 1900–1925," *Le Travailleur: Journal of Canadian Labour Studies* 7 (Spring 1981), 41–66.

21. See, for example, Philip Foner, *The Policies and Practices of the American Federation of Labor, 1900–1909* (New York: International Publishers, 1964), 219–307. For a less critical analysis of the AFL, see Bruce Laurie, *Artisans into Workers: Labor in Nineteenth-Century America* (New York: Noonday Press, 1989), 176–210.

22. Edmondo Rossoni, "Senza Titolo," *Il Proletario*, November 7, 1911, 3.

23. Vezzosi, 78.

24. Tax, 262.

25. Foner, 329.

26. Mary Marcy, "The Battle for Bread at Lawrence," *International Socialist Review* 9 (March, 1912), 536.

27. Foner, 317–25.

28. Kornbluh, 179–80, 158.

29. Elizabeth Gurley Flynn, *Rebel Girl: An Autobiography of My First Life (1906–1926)* (New York: International Publishers, 1955), 135.

30. Cameron, 135–55.

31. Cameron, 117–69; for the Haywood comment, see 126.

32. See Vezzosi, 80–81; Adriana Dadà, "I radicali italo-americani e la società italiana," *Italia contemporanea* 146–7 (June 1982), 132; Ortoleva, 13, 23.

33. Cameron, 50; Foner, 324–26.

34. Quoted in Vezzosi, 81. See "Il secondo gruppo di esuli a New York," *Il Proletario*, March 1, 1912.

35. Quoted in Foner, 326.

36. Ibid.

37. See Joan Jensen and Sue Davidson, eds., *A Needle, a Bobbin, a Strike: Women Needleworkers in America* (Philadelphia: Temple University Press, 1984), especially 81–182.

38. "Il Nemico Peggiore," *Il Proletario*, March 1, 1912, 2. The "worst enemy" referred to here is, of course, John Golden.

39. This is how writers for *Il Proletario* frequently referred to the AFL. See Nemo, "Dal Campo della Lotta," *Il Proletario*, February 16, 1912, 1.

40. See Foner, 338–40.

41. Ibid., 343.

42. Edmondo Rossoni, "La Vittoria Conquistata!: Catene Spezzate," *Il Proletario*, March 15, 1912, 1.

43. Edmondo Rossoni, "Vittoria!", *Il Proletario*, September 14, 1912, 1–2.

44. Edmondo Rossoni, "E' L'Ora del Sindacalismo Rivoluzionario," *Il Proletario*, June 29, 1912.

45. Albino Braida, "Unionismo Industriale e Parliamentarismo," *Il Proletario*, July 6, 1912; Elisabetta Vezzosi, "La Federazione Socialista Italiana del Nord America tra autonomia e scioglimento nel sindacato industriale, 1911–1921" *Studi Emigrazione*, XXI, 73 (March 1984), 97.

46. Foner, 336.

47. Carlo Tresca, "La Logica della Rivoluzione," *Il Proletario*, May 18, 1912, 1.

48. Tresca autobiography, 112–26; Dorothy Gallagher, *All the Right Enemies: The Life and Murder of Carlo Tresca* (New Brunswick, New Jersey: Rutgers University Press, 1988), 31, 278.

49. Vezzosi, "La Federazione Socialista Italian del Nord America," 91.

50. For more, see Tresca's autobiography, 154–72.

51. Kornbluh, 173.

52. Ferdinando Fasce, *Tra due sponde: Lavoro, affari e cultura tra Italia e Stati Uniti nell'età della grande emigrazione* (Genoa: Graphos, 1993), 22–27.

53. Vezzosi, "La Federazione Socialista Italiana del Nord America," 97; Edmondo Rossoni Casellario Politico Centrale (CPC), busta 4466, Archivio Centrale dello Stato, Rome, Italy; Tinghino, 44–46; Arturo Giovannitti CPC, busta 2439; "Arturo Giovannitti, poeta dei diseredati, dei ribelli e del divenire sociale, non e' più," *Giustizia*, January 1960, 8; Fasce, 26; Foner, 343.

54. Fasce, 25–27; Dadà, 132.

55. Leda Rafanelli, "Per la Vittime Nostre," *Il Proletario*, September 14, 1912.

56. Ibid. Maria Rygier was an outspoken activist in Apulia, well known for her anticlericalism and her advocacy of women's leagues. Frank M. Snowden, *Violence and Great Estates in the South of Italy: Apulia, 1900–1922* (Cambridge: Cambridge University Press, 1986), esp. 114–15.

57. Fenton, 514.

58. Kornbluh, 164.

59. This story was related to me by Paul Buhle, Director of the Oral History of the Left at Tamiment Library, New York University.

60. Tresca, 157–58.

61. Ibid., 186–88.

62. Fortunato Vezzoli, "Per Ettor e Giovannitti," *Il Proletario*, May 18, 1912; see also Flavio Venanzi, "Senza tregua!", *Il Proletario*, May 18, 1912.

63. Edmondo Rossoni, "I Veri Cospiratori," *Il Proletario*, July 6, 1912, 1.

64. Theresa Bonacorsi, quoted in June Namias, ed., *First Generation: In the Words of Twentieth-Century American Immigrants* (Boston: Beacon Press, 1978), 33.

65. Edmondo Rossoni, "La Vittoria Conquistata!: Catene Spezzate," *Il Proletario*, March 15, 1912, 1. Rossoni's reference was to southern Italian peasants who, especially in Sicily, staged revolts regularly throughout the nineteenth and early twentieth centuries, usually protesting against taxes or food shortages. See Gabaccia, *Militants and Migrants*, 27.

66. Libero Tancredi, "La Gloria d'un Infamia," *Il Proletario*, September 14, 1912, 2.

67. Ibid.

68. Ibid.

69. Edmondo Rossoni, "Vittoria!", *Il Proletario*, September 14, 1912, 1–2.

70. Bill Haywood, n.t., *Il Proletario*, September 14, 1912.

71. Vezzosi, "La Federazione Italiana del Nord America," 92.

72. Flynn, 148.

73. Ibid.

74. Ibid., 147; Ortoleva, 13–14.

75. Flynn, 149.

76. Edmondo Rossoni, "Primo Maggio di Guerra," *Il Proletario*, May 1, 1912.

77. Arturo Massimo Giovannitti. *The Collected Poems of Arturo Giovannitti* (Chicago: Egidio Clemente and Sons, 1962).

78. Tresca, 191. Tresca's use of the term "manly" rather than "masculine" merits comment here. Gail Bederman offers an insightful distinction between "manliness" and "masculinity." See Gail Bederman, *Manliness and Civilization: A Cultural History of Gender and Race in the United States, 1880–1917* (Chicago: University of Chicago Press, 1995). The former stood for the loftiest ideals of (Victorian) manhood—sexual self-restraint, powerful will, strength of character. It was, in Bederman's words, "precisely the sort of middle-class Victorian cultural formulation which grew shaky in the late nineteenth century" (Bederman, 18). Masculinity, by contrast, was used increasingly in the first decades of the twentieth century to signify more virile characteristics—aggressiveness, physical force, and male sexuality. Though Tresca used the term "manly," the context in which he used it suggests that he meant to convey that Giovannitti was the embodiment of masculinity.

79. Edmondo Rossoni, "Primo Maggio di Guerra," *Il Proletario*, May 1, 1912.

80. Ibid.

81. Fortunato Vezzoli, "Per Ettor e Giovannitti," *Il Proletario*, May 18, 1912.

82. Bellalma Forzata Spezia, "Chi sono i colpevoli," *Il Proletario*, May 25, 1912; quoted in Vezzosi, "La Federazione Socialista Italiana del Nord America," 88–89.

83. Alceste De Ambris, "La Nostra Debalezza," *Il Proletario*, September 14, 1912, 2.

84. Leda Rafanelli, "Per le Vittime Nostre," *Il Proletario*, September 14, 1912, 3. Rafanelli was one of the few women who appeared regularly in the Italian American radical press, but there is no indication that she ever lived in the United States. See Leda Rafanelli CPC, busta 4193.

85. Tresca, 179.

86. Ibid., 179–80.

87. For a full account, ibid., 177–91.

88. Ortoleva, 7; Flynn, 129–30; Foner, 334.

89. Dubofsky, 248.

90. Ibid., 253.

91. Kornbluh, 170. Wood and Turner were both mill owners.

92. Giacomo Li Causi CPC, busta 2783. Li Causi was not a regular contributor to the newspaper.

93. Giacomo Li Causi, "Lo Stato Sostenitore del Capitalismo: A Proposito dello Sciopero di Lawrence," *Il Proletario*, April 12, 1912, 2.

94. Ibid.

95. Carlo Tresca, "La Logica della Rivoluzione," *Il Proletario*, May 18, 1912.

96. Albino Braida, "Unionismo Industriale e Parliamentarismo," *Il Proletario*, July 6, 1912.

97. Libero Tancredi, "La Gloria d'un Infamia," *Il Proletario*, September 14, 1912, 2.

98. Alceste de Ambris, "La nostra debolezza," *Il Proletario*, September 14, 1912.

99. Marcy, 536.

100. Nicola Vecchi, "Lettera Aperta a Sua Maestà la Regina d'Italia," *Il Proletario*, December 7, 1912.

101. Virginia Yans-McLaughlin, *Family and Community: Italian Immigrants in Buffalo, 1880–1930* (Urbana: University of Illinois Press, 1982 [1977]), 235.

102. Arturo Giovannitti, "La Donna e la Forca," *Il Proletario*, June 30, 1911.

103. Raimondo Fazio, "La Donna, il Suffragismo e L'organizzazione industriale," *Il Proletario*, April 5, 1912.

104. "Testimony of William D. Haywood," 46.

105. See Gallagher, especially 110–26; Helen C. Camp, *Iron in Her Soul: Elizabeth Gurley Flynn and the American Left* (Pullman, Wash.: Washington State University Press, 1995), 40–43, 112–13.

106. G. A. Andaloro, "Le Tragedie Proletarie," *Il Proletario*, December 22, 1911.

107. See Francis Shor, "The IWW and Oppositional Politics in World War I: Pushing the System Beyond the Limits," *Radical History Review* 64 (Winter 1996), 74–94. See also Ann Schofield, "Rebel Girls and Union Maids: The Woman Question in the Journals of the AFL and IWW, 1905–1920," *Feminist Studies* 9, 2 (Summer 1983), 335–58.

108. N.a., "Altre Notizie da Lawrence: Le Donne Pregano," *Il Proletario*, March 1, 1912.

109. "Le Crisi nel Socialist Party," *Il Proletario*, December 29, 1911.

110. Ibid.

111. Ibid.

112. Raimondo Fazio, "Da Campo della Lotta alla Capitale della Repubblica," *Il Proletario,* March 8, 1912, 1–2.

113. Ibid.

114. Ibid.

115. There were, in fact, many in the so-called right-wing of the Socialist Party, Victor Berger among them, who favored the AFL over the IWW. See James Weinstein, *The Decline of Socialism in America 1912–1925* (New York: Random House, 1967), especially 29–53.

116. For a brief discussion of sabotage and the IWW, see Salvatore Salerno, *Red November, Black November: Culture and Community in the Industrial Workers of the World* (Albany: State University of New York Press, 1989), 107, 109–10, 112–15.

117. Peter Carlson, *Roughneck: The Life and Times of Big Bill Haywood* (New York: W. W. Norton and Co., 1983), 183.

118. Ibid., 198.

119. "Verso la Luce," *Il Proletario,* March 15, 1912, 4.

120. Ibid.

121. Foner, 405.

122. Fenton, 545.

123. Ortoleva, 24–25. Philip Foner, for example, argues that the parade was a turning point. See Foner, 348–49.

124. Edmondo Rossoni CPC file, busta 4466.

125. Edmondo Rossoni, "Da Lawrence," *Il Proletario,* November 16, 1912, 1–2.

126. Edmondo Rossoni, "Vittoria!", *Il Proletario,* September 14, 1912, 1–2.

127. Ibid.

128. Libero Tancredi, "La Gloria d'un Infamia," *Il Proletario,* September 14, 1912, 2.

129. Ibid.

130. Quoted in David D. Roberts, *The Syndicalist Tradition and Italian Fascism* (Chapel Hill: University of North Carolina, 1978), 108.

131. Tresca, 134.

132. Ibid., 140.

133. Kornbluh, 193.

134. Ibid., 193–94.

135. Di Gregorio sent at least one of these articles, "The American Federation of Labor's Action and Inaction Against the Children of Lawrence," *Il Proletario,* February 16, 1912, to the Socialist *New York Call,* whose editors declined to publish it.

136. John di Gregorio, "Fits of Sympathy for the Lawrence Children," *Il Proletario,* March 1, 1912.

137. John di Gregorio, "Fakomania: A Propos of the Union Square Incident," *Il Proletario,* May 11, 1912.

4. Nationalism and Masculinity Splinter the FSI

1. Edmondo Rossoni, "Discussione . . . inutile sulla guerra: perditempo," *Il Proletario,* April 3, 1915, 2.

2. See George Mosse, *Nationalism and Sexuality: Respectability and Abnormal Sexuality in Modern Europe* (New York: Howard Fertig, 1985), 115–16. See also An-

drew Parker, Maru Russo, Doris Sommer, and Patricia Yaeger, eds., *Nationalisms and Sexualities* (New York: Routledge, 1992).

3. Benedict Anderson, "The New World Disorder," *New Left Review,* May–June 1992, 1–13. See also Benedict Anderson. *Imagined Communities: Reflections on the Origin and Spread of Nationalism* (New York: Verso, 1983).

4. Mario de Ciampis, "History of *Il Proletario*" (unpublished), 2029, 2033–34, 2050, 2065, 2070, 2170; Carlo Tresca autobiography (unpublished), 212–14. (Both manuscripts available at the Immigration History Research Center, Minneapolis, Minn.)

5. See Steve Golin, *The Fragile Bridge: Paterson Silk Strike, 1913* (Philadelphia: Temple University Press, 1988), which examines the relationship between the IWW and Greenwich Village intellectuals during the strike; and Anne Huber Tripp, *The I.W.W. and the Paterson Silk Strike of 1913* (Urbana: University of Illinois Press, 1987). See also Melvyn Dubofsky, *We Shall Be All: A History of the Industrial Workers of the World* (Urbana: University of Illinois Press, 1969 [1988]), especially 263–90; Philip S. Foner, *The Industrial Workers of the World, 1905–1917* (New York: International Publishers Co., 1965), especially 351–72; Elizabeth Gurley Flynn, *The Rebel Girl, An Autobiography: My First Life (1906–1926)* (New York: International Publishers Co., 1955), especially "The Paterson Silk Strike," 152–73.

6. Quoted in Golin, 57.

7. Ibid., 132.

8. Tripp, 236.

9. See Adele Heller and Lois Rudnick, eds., *1915, The Cultural Moment: The New Politics, the New Woman, the New Psychology, the New Art and the New Theatre in America* (New Brunswick: Rutgers University Press, 1991).

10. Tripp, 138–39.

11. "I.W.W. Pageant at Madison Square Garden," *Solidarity,* June 7, 1913, 4. The advertisement for the pageant appeared in *Il Proletario* on the same day.

12. Tripp, 142–46.

13. Flynn, 169–70.

14. Golin, 187–92.

15. Quoted in Golin, 205.

16. Giovanni di Gregorio, "Reflections Upon Paterson Strike," *Solidarity,* August 30, 1913, 2.

17. Quoted in Golin, 206.

18. Giovanni di Gregorio, "Reflections Upon Paterson Strike," *Solidarity,* August 30, 1913, 2.

19. David Roberts, *The Syndicalist Tradition and Italian Fascism* (Chapel Hill: University of North Carolina Press, 1979), 87; Zeev Sternhell with Mario Sznajder and Maia Asheri, *The Birth of Fascist Ideology: From Cultural Rebellion to Political Revolution* (Princeton: Princeton University Press, 1994), 139.

20. Roberts, 87–88; Sternhell, 203; Ferdinando Cordova, *Uomini e Volti del Fascismo* (Rome: Bulzoni editore, 1971), 370–71.

21. See Spencer Di Scala, "'Red Week' 1914: Prelude to War and Revolution," in Frank Coppa, ed., *Studies in Modern Italian History: From the Risorgimento to the Republic* (Peter Lang: New York, 1986), 123–33.

22. Ibid.

23. Roberts, 74.

24. Alceste de Ambris, "Dopo la Bufera: Il Fatto Nuovo," *Il Proletario,* July 4, 1914, 1.

25. David Roberts argues that Red Week did not constitute a turning point for Italian syndicalists. See Roberts, 74–75, 101–2.

26. Wayne Westergard-Thorpe, "Towards a Syndicalist International: The 1913 London Congress," *International Review of Social History,* XXIII, 1, 1978, 58n.

27. Ibid., 67.

28. De Ciampis, "History of *Il Proletario,*" 2165.

29. See David Montgomery, *Workers' Control in America: Studies in the History of Work, Technology, and Labor Struggles* (Cambridge: Cambridge University Press, 1979), especially 91–112.

30. Albert Lindemann, *A History of European Socialism* (New Haven: Yale University Press, 1983), 186–89.

31. See Montgomery, "Nationalism, American Patriotism, and Class Consciousness in the Epoch of World War I," in Dick Hoerder, *Struggle a Hard Battle: Essays on Working-Class Immigrants* (DeKalb, Ill.: Northern Illinois University Press, 1986), 340–41. See also Joseph Stipanovich, "Immigrant Workers and Immigrant Intellectuals in Progressive America: A History of the Yugoslav Socialist Federation, 1900–1918," (Unpublished Ph.D. diss., University of Minnesota, 1977), 213–17.

32. Mary Cygan, "Polish Americans," in Mari Jo Buhle, Paul Buhle, and Dan Georgakas, eds., *Encyclopedia of the American Left* (New York: Garland Publishing, Inc., 1990), 584–85; Norman Davies, *God's Playground: A History of Poland,* Vol. 2 (New York: Columbia University Press, 1982), 53–56; Jacobson, 223–24.

33. Lindemann, 190–91; Alexander De Grand, *The Italian Left in the Twentieth Century: A History of the Socialist and Communist Parties* (Bloomington: Indiana University Press, 1989), 27.

34. Roberts, 106.

35. Alceste de Ambris, "I Sindacalisti e la Guerra," *Il Proletario,* September 12, 1914.

36. Flavio Venanzi, *Scritti Politici e Letterarii* (New York: Venanzi Memorial Committee ed., 1921).

37. Mario de Ciampis, "Storia del movimento socialista rivoluzionario italiano," *La Parola del Popolo, Cinquantesimo Anniversario, 1908–1958,* 9 (December 1958–January 1959), 160.

38. See Rudolph Vecoli, "The War and Italian American Syndicalists," unpublished essay, 1978; and Elisabetta Vezzosi, "Class, Ethnicity, and Acculturation in *Il Proletario:* The World War One Years," in Christiane Harzig and Dirk Hoerder, eds., *The Press of Labor Migrants in Europe and North America 1880s to 1930s* (Bremen: Labor Newspaper Preservation Project, 1985), 443–58. For more on the participants in the debate, see Vecoli, 6, 8–9; de Ciampis, 160–61; Arturo Giovannitti, "Flavio Venanzi: Letterato, Conferenziere Agitatore Sindicalista," *La Parola del Popolo,* November–December 1978, 101. For more on Baldazzi, see de Ciampis, "History of *Il Proletario,*" 2240. See also Flavio Venanzi Casellario Politico Central, busta 5346; Archivio Centrale dello Stato, Rome, Italy, Giovanni Baldazzi CPC, busta 268; Giuseppe Cannata CPC, busta 1006.

39. Alceste de Ambris, "I Sindacalisti e la Guerra," *Il Proletario,* September 12, 1914.

40. Westergard-Thorpe, 48–49.

41. Edmondo Rossoni, "Dall'Utopia alla Realtà," *Il Proletario*, September 26, 1914.

42. Ibid.

43. Edmondo Rossoni, "Internazionalismo e conflagraziona Europea: La vita non è sacra!", *Il Proletario*, August 15, 1914.

44. Ibid.

45. John J. Tinghino, *Edmondo Rossoni: From Revolutionary Syndicalism to Fascism* (New York: Peter Lang, 1991), 42–43.

46. Alceste de Ambris, "I Sindacalisti e la Guerra," *Il Proletario*, September 12, 1914.

47. Lindemann, 185.

48. Alceste de Ambris, "I Sindacalisti e la Guerra," *Il Proletario*, January 23, 1915.

49. Ibid.

50. Postscript to Albino Braida, "Sindacalismo e nazionalità," *Il Proletario*, January 23, 1915.

51. See Paul Avrich, *Anarchist Portraits* (Princeton: Princeton University Press, 1988), esp. 53–78, and 79–106.

52. Libero Tancredi, "Polemiche rivoluzionarie," *Il Proletario*, October 10, 1914.

53. Edmondo Rossoni, "Per Afferrar l'Anguilla," *Il Proletario*, October 3, 1914.

54. Vecoli, 8.

55. Giuseppe Cannata, "Dietro le quinte del conflitto," *Il Proletario*, August 15, 1914.

56. Ibid.

57. Ibid.

58. Flavio Venanzi, "Contro Tutte le Patrie e per l'Internazionale Operaia: Dalla Realtà all'Utopia," *Il Proletario*, September 9, 1914; de Ciampis, "History of *Il Proletario*," 2241.

59. Vecoli, 9.

60. Giovanni Baldazzi, "Psicologia sovversiva," *Il Proletario*, January 23, 1915.

61. Flavio Venanzi, "Discussione sulla guerra: per intenderci chiaramente," *Il Proletario*, April 10, 1915, 3.

62. Flavio Venanzi, "Contro Tutte la Patrie a per l'Internazionale Operaia: Dalla Realtà all'Utopia," *Il Proletario*, September 9, 1914.

63. Ibid.

64. Vecoli, 10; de Ciampis, "History of *Il Proletario*," 2253.

65. Vecoli, 10.

66. For more on Galleani, see Rudolph Vecoli, "Luigi Galleani," 251–53 in the *Encyclopedia of the American Left*. See also Paul Avrich, *Sacco and Vanzetti: The Anarchist Background* (Princeton: Princeton University Press, 1991).

67. Mentana, "Per la Guerra, per la neutralita, o per la pace?", *La Cronaca Sovversiva*, November 7, 1914, 1. "Mentana" was one of Galleani's pen names.

68. Vecoli, 12–13.

69. La Commissione Esecutiva della F.S.I. "Per la Serenità di Giudizio e contro il Settarismo," *Il Proletario*, October 31, 1914.

70. Odilla Bioletto, "Le Donne e la Guerra," *Il Proletario*, December 26, 1914.

71. Odilla Bioletto CPC, busta 657.

72. Helen C. Camp, *Iron in Her Soul: Elizabeth Gurley Flynn and the American Left* (Pullman, Wash.: Washington State University Press, 1995), 42.

73. Flynn, 333.

74. Michael Gold to Miss Albert, February 6, 1926, Elizabeth Gurley Flynn papers, microfilm reel 4202, Tamiment Library, New York University, New York.

75. Frank Snowden, *Violence and Great Estates in the South of Italy: Apulia, 1900–1922* (Cambridge: Cambridge University Press, 1986), 114–15.

76. Leda Rafanelli CPC, busta 4193.

77. Angiolina Algeri CPC, busta 65.

78. Bellalma Forzata Spezia CPC, busta 4908.

79. De Ciampis, "History of *Il Proletario*," 954.

80. Libero Tancredi, "Polemiche rivoluzionarie," *Il Proletario*, October 10, 1914.

81. Maurice Agulhon, "On Political Allegory: A Reply to Eric Hobsbawm," *History Workshop Journal* 8 (Spring 1979), 169.

82. Libero Tancredi, "Polemiche rivoluzionarie," *Il Proletario*, October 10, 1914.

83. Ibid.

84. For a discussion of the metaphorical uses of gendered language in political debate, see Joan Scott, "Rewriting History," in Margaret Randolph Higonnet, Jane Jensen, Sonya Michel, and Margaret Collins Weitz, eds., *Behind the Lines: Gender and the Two World Wars* (New Haven: Yale University Press, 1987), 19–30.

85. Gail Bederman, *Manliness and Civilization: A Cultural History of Gender and Race in the United States, 1880–1917* (Chicago: University of Chicago Press, 1995), 10–15. For other studies on masculinity in the American middle class, see Mark Carnes and Clyde Griffen, eds., *Meanings for Manhood: Constructions of Masculinity in Victorian America* (Chicago: University of Chicago Press, 1990); and J. A. Mangan and James Walvin, eds., *Manliness and Morality: Middle-Class Masculinity in Britain and America, 1800–1940* (New York: St. Martin's Press, 1987).

86. Arturo M. Giovannitti, "Syndicalism—The Creed of Force," *The Independent*, October 30, 1913, 211.

87. Edmondo Rossoni, "Internazionalismo e conflagraziona Europea: la vita non è sacra!", *Il Proletario*, August 15, 1914.

88. Flavio Venanzi, "La Decadenza del Pacifismo," *Scritti Politici e Letterarii*, 26.

89. Higgonet et al., 5.

90. Edmondo Rossoni, "Per Afferrar l'Anguilla," *Il Proletario*, October 3, 1914.

91. Edmondo Rossoni, "Internazionalismo e conflagraziona Europea: la vita non è sacra!", *Il Proletario*, August 15, 1914.

92. Ibid.

93. Edmondo Rossoni, "Liberta' e Sangue!", *Il Proletario*, January 30, 1915.

94. Auguste Barbier, *Satires et Poèmes* (Paris: Félix Bonnaire, éditeur, 1837), 9–10. See also Eric Hobsbawm, "Man and Woman in Socialist Iconography," *History Workshop Journal* 6 (Autumn 1978), 122–23.

95. See Mosse, 90–113.

96. Hobsbawm, 122–23.

97. Mosse, 176.

98. My thanks to Terance Kissack for providing me with this insight during a discussion of another version of this chapter.

99. George Chauncey, *Gay New York: Gender, Urban Culture, and the Making of the Gay Male World, 1890–1940* (New York: Basic Books, 1994), 80–86.

100. Ibid., 80. Italics are his.

101. Ibid.

102. J. L. Talmon, *The Myth of the Nation and the Vision of Revolution: The Origins of Ideological Polarisation in the Twentieth Century* (Berkeley: University of California Press, 1981), 458–59, 466–67.

103. De Ciampis, "History of *Il Proletario*," 997.

104. Ibid., 2012.

105. Edmondo Rossoni, "Per L'Afferrar l'Anguilla," *Il Proletario*, October 3, 1914.

106. Edmondo Rossoni, "Liberta' e Sangue!", *Il Proletario*, January 30, 1915.

107. Edmondo Rossoni, "Il Sindacalismo nei suoi Capisaldi a nelle sue Linee d'Azione," *Il Proletario*, May 1, 1915.

108. Ibid.

109. Vezzosi, 446.

110. Quoted in Vecoli, 17.

111. Flavio Venanzi, "Per la serenità di giudizio," *Il Proletario*, April 3, 1915, 2.

112. Fortunato Vezzoli, "Contro la guerra d'oggi, per quella del domani," *Il Proletario*, March 13, 1915.

113. Ibid.

114. Ibid.

115. Harry Uswald, "Militarism and Socialism: An Analysis of the Factors that Led European Socialists to Support the War," *International Socialist Review* V.XV, 5 (November 1914), 297.

116. W. H. Leffington, "Are We Ready?" *International Socialist Review* V.XV, 7 (January 1915), 405.

117. See Francis Shor, "The IWW and Oppositional Politics in World War I: Pushing the System Beyond its Limits," *Radical History Review* 64 (Winter 1996), 74–94; Frederick C. Giffin, *Six Who Protested: Radical Opposition to the First World War* (Port Washington, N.Y.: Kennikat Press, 1977), 121.

118. William Bohn, "International Notes," *International Socialist Review* 15 (February 1915), 497–98.

119. Tinghino, 71–72; de Ciampis, "History of *Il Proletario*," 2253.

120. De Ciampis, "Storia del movimento socialista rivoluzionario italiano," 161.

121. Bellalma Forzata Spezia, "E' Tornata!" *L'Italia Nostra*, September 4, 1915.

122. Sternhell, 140; Roberts, 132.

123. Sternhell, 28.

124. See Charles Bertrand, "The Biennio Rosso: Anarchists and Revolutionary Syndicalists in Italy, 1919–1920," *Réflexions Historiques* 9, 3 (1982), 383–402.

125. Ibid., 388.

126. Roberts, 199.

127. Ibid., 179–81, 227–30.

128. Sternhell, 33.

129. Tinghino, 3–4, 213–14.

130. A. James Gregor, *Young Mussolini and the Intellectual Origins of Fascism* (Berkeley: University of California Press, 1979), 170–71.

131. Bellalma Forzata Spezia CPC, busta 4908.

132. Victoria De Grazia, *How Fascism Ruled Women, 1922–1945* (Berkeley: University of California Press, 1992), 25.

133. Barbara Spackman, "The Fascist Rhetoric of Virility" *Stanford Italian Review*, 8: 1–2 (1990), 84.

134. Duilio Mari CPC, busta 3054.

135. Angelo Faggi CPC, busta 1925.

136. Giovanni Baldazzi CPC, busta 268.

137. Giovanni Baldazzi CPC, busta 268.

138. Giuseppe Cannata, "Problemi Nostri," *Il Proletario,* November 14, 1914.

139. Fortunato Vezzoli, "Contro la guerra d'oggi, per quella del domani," *Il Proletario,* March 13, 1915.

140. Although Vezzosi states that Giovannitti was made a manager of *Il Proletario* along with Venanzi and Rossoni in May 1914, I found nothing to suggest that he contributed to the paper at all during the debate. See Vezzosi, 444.

5. The Mainstreaming of Italian American Syndicalism

1. Onorio Mirabello, "In Tema di Rivoluzione," *Il Proletario,* July 29, 1916, 2.

2. See David Montgomery, *The Fall of the House of Labor: The Workplace, the State, and American Labor Activism, 1865–1925* (Cambridge: Cambridge University Press, 1987), 6, 332.

3. See Elisabetta Vezzosi, "La Federazione Socialista Italiana del Nord America (1911–1921)," (Ph.D. diss., Università degli Studi di Firenze, 1980), 250.

4. Giuseppe Cannata, "Contro il Regno del terrore," *Il Proletario,* December 2, 1916, 1.

5. Steven Fraser, "Landslayt and Paesani: Ethnic Conflict and Cooperation in the Amalgamated Clothing Workers of America," in Dirk Hoerder, ed., *Struggle a Hard Battle: Essays on Working-Class Immigrants* (DeKalb, Ill.: Northern Illinois University Press, 1986), 280–303; see also Steven Fraser, *Labor Will Rule: Sidney Hillman and the Rise of American Labor* (New York: The Free Press, 1991). See also Matthew Josephson, *Sidney Hillman: Statesman of American Labor* (Garden City, New York: Doubleday and Co., 1952); Edwin Fenton, *Immigrants and Unions, A Case Study: Italians and American Labor, 1870–1920* (New York: Arno Press, 1975), esp. 547–58; Philip Foner, *On the Eve of America's Entrance into World War I: 1915–1916* (New York: International Publishers, 1982), esp. 106–15; David J. Goldberg, *A Tale of Three Cities: Labor Organization and Protest in Paterson, Passaic, and Lawrence, 1916–1921* (New Brunswick: Rutgers University Press, 1989), esp. 83–164.

6. On women in the ACWA, see Nina Asher, "Dorothy Jacobs Bellanca: Women Clothing Workers and the Runaway Shops," in Joan Jensen and Sue Davidson, eds., *A Needle, A Bobbin, A Strike: Women Needleworkers in America* (Philadelphia: Temple University Press, 1984), 195–226; N. Sue Weiler, "Uprising in Chicago: The Men's Garment Workers Strike, 1910–1911," in Jensen and Davidson, 114–39; and Carolyn Daniel McCreesh, *Women in the Campaign to Organize Garment Workers, 1880–1917* (New York: Garland Publishing, 1985), esp. 117–23.

7. Philip Foner, *The Industrial Workers of the World 1905–1917* (New York: International Publishers, 1965), 512–13; Melvyn Dubofsky, *We Shall Be All: A History of the Industrial Workers of the World,* 2d ed. (Urbana: University of Illinois Press, 1969 [1988]), 330.

8. Quoted in Dubofsky, 343.

9. Ibid., 314–15.

10. Mario de Ciampis, "History of *Il Proletario*" (unpublished, Immigration History Research Center, Minneapolis, Minn.), 2265–66; Elisabetta Vezzosi, "La Federazione Socialista Italiana del Nord America (1911–1921)," 281–83.

11. Giovanni Baldazzi Casellario Politico Centrale (CPC), busta 268, Archivio dello Stato Centrale, Rome, Italy.

12. Mario de Ciampis, "History of *Il Proletario*," 2268–70. See also Angelo Faggi CPC, busta 1925.

13. Angelo Faggi, "I sindacalisti e la guerra," *Il Proletario,* July 8, 1916, 1.

14. Efrom Bartoletti, "I ribelli del Minnesota," *Il Proletario,* August 19, 1916, 1; Efrom Bartoletti, *Evocazioni e Ricordi* (Bergamo: La Nuova Italiana Letteraria, 1959).

15. Dubofsky, 325; Foner, 499.

16. Il Proletario, "Eviva l'IWW," *Il Proletario,* July 29, 1916. See also Il Proletario, "Che fare?", *Il Proletario,* August 12, 1916.

17. N.a., "Eviva lo Sciopero Generale," *Il Proletario,* September 9, 1916. See also, for example, Onorio Massimo, "Per lo Sciopero Generale," *Il Proletario,* September 2, 1916.

18. Carlo Tresca, "Appello ai Minatori per lo Sciopero Generale," *Il Proletario,* August 26, 1916.

19. Saverio Piesco, "Lo sciopero e l'organizzazione," *Il Proletario,* July 29, 1916.

20. Saverio Piesco CPC, busta 3965. Piesco was born in Casalvecchio in the province of Foggia on October 31, 1888.

21. Onorio Mirabello, "Il Sindacato primo e dopo la Rivoluzione," *Il Proletario,* August 12, 1916, 3.

22. See, for example, Salvatore Piesco, "Lo sciopero e l'organizzazione," *Il Proletario,* July 29, 1916; Giuseppe Cannata, "Guerra per la vita e la libertà," *Il Proletario,* August 12, 1916,1; Onorio Massimo, "Per lo Sciopero Generale," *Il Proletario,* September 2, 1916, 2; Angelo Faggi, "La vera accusata," *Il Proletario,* December 2, 1916, 3.

23. Elizabeth Gurley Flynn, *The Rebel Girl: An Autobiography: My First Life (1906–1926)* (New York: International Publishers, 1955), 207; Foner, 501; Dubofsky, 326–27.

24. Noi, "Ottimismo pericoloso," *Il Proletario,* October 14, 1916, 1.

25. Tresca published *La Plebe* from 1906 to 1909, *L'Avvenire* from 1909 to 1917, and *Il Martello* from 1917 until his assassination in 1943. *La Plebe* and *L'Avvenire* were published in Philadelphia and New Kensington, respectively.

26. "Come si svolge l'agitazione," *Il Proletario,* August 26, 1916.

27. "Intensifichiamo l'agitazione," *Il Proletario,* August 19, 1916, 1.

28. Ibid.

29. A. T. Berna, "Solidarietà internazionale: L'agitazione pro Carlo Tresca e compagni in Isvizzera," *Il Proletario,* October 21, 1916, 2.

30. "Solidarietà internazionale: una importante assemblea dei ferrovieri di Milano," *Il Proletario,* October 21, 1916, 1–2; reports to the Police Headquarters in Milan, August 26, 1916; August 30, 1916; October 17, 1917; December 2, 1916; and the Prefect of Florence, September 25, 1916 in categoria 31 [guerre], cart. 576, Archivio dello Stato, Milan, Italy.

31. Arturo Caroti, "Per Carlo Tresca," Libreria Editrice *Avanti!,* Milan, 1916; Report to the Questura di Milano, August 30, 1916; Arturo Caroti CPC, busta 1105; Elisabetta Vezzosi, *Il Socialismo Indifferente: Immigrati italiani e Socialist Party*

negli Stati Uniti del primo Novecento (Rome: Edizioni lavoro, 1991), 41–43; Fenton, 534–35.

32. Report of the Questura di Milano, August 30, 1916, Archivio dello Stato, Milano.

33. Commissioner Monforte, Questura di Milano, October 7, 1916, Archivio dello Stato, Milan, Italy.

34. See, for example, Circolare Telefonica, Questura di Milano, December 2, 1916, Archivio dello Stato, Milan, Italy.

35. Angelo Faggi, "Il Contegno equivoco del Governo Italiano," *Il Proletario*, November 18, 1916, 1.

36. "Solidarietà internazionale: una importante assemblea dei ferrovieri di Milano," *Il Proletario*, October 21, 1916, 1–2.

37. Carlo Tresca CPC, busta 5208; Macchi di Cellere, Regia Ambasciata d'Italia in Washington, to R. Ministero degli Affari Esteri, Roma, September 12, 1916.

38. Macchi di Cellere, Regia Ambasciata d'Italia in Washington, to R. Ministero degli Affari Esteri, Roma, October 1, 1916.

39. Angelo Faggi, "Il Contegno equivoco del Governo Italiano," *Il Proletario*, November 18, 1916, 1.

40. "Come si svolge l'agitazione," *Il Proletario*, August 5, 1916; "Come si svolge l'agitazione," *Il Proletario*, August 26, 1916. Giovannitti appeared with FSI members, for example, in Philadelphia and in Boston, Roxbury, and Milford, Massachusetts.

41. Arturo Giovannitti, "Carlo Tresca," *La Lotte di Classe*, September 1, 1916, 1–2.

42. See Mario de Ciampis, "Storia del movimento socialista rivoluzionario italiano," *La Parola del Popolo, Cinquantesimo Anniversario, 1908–1958* 9 (December 1958–January 1959), 150–51, 152.

43. See, for example, Raimondo Fazio, "Proletari impiedi!", *L'Avvenire*, December 1, 1916, 1; Raimondo Fazio, "Una frase troncata," *L'Avvenire*, December 15, 1916; Giovanni di Gregorio, "Comizio Pro-Tresca," *La Lotte di Classe*, August 4, 1916.

44. Il Proletario, "La Grande Vittoria," *Il Proletario*, December 23, 1916, 1.

45. See, for example, Dubofsky, 425, 428. See also Flynn, 236–37.

46. Carlo Tresca, "Un'ultima, esauriente doverosa risposta ai miei accusatori," *Il Martello*, December 1, 1920, 3–8.

47. Ibid., 6–8.

48. N. Sue Weiler, "The Uprising in Chicago," 117.

49. Ibid., 122.

50. *Documentary History of the Amalgamated Clothing Workers of America, 1914–1916.* "Nashville Convention," esp. 26–40. The volumes of this documentary history consist of the reports from the various ACWA conventions. Henceforth, citations from these volumes will be noted only with the convention site and the year of the convention. See also N.a., "Memento: L'avvento dell'Amalgamated nel movimento operaio," *Il Lavoro*, March 17, 1917, 1–2.

51. New York Convention, 1914, 74.

52. Ibid., 74–5.

53. See Fraser, *Labor Will Rule*, 105.

54. See Fenton, 532–36, 545–46.

55. Anthony Capraro, "La questione dei contratti," *Il Lavoro*, January 17, 1920, 4.

56. Luigi Seroti, "É l'ACWA una Organizzazione rivoluzionaria?", *Il Nuovo Proletario*, December 20, 1919, 4.

57. Baltimore Convention, 1918, 132–52.

58. Ibid., 163.
59. Ibid., 165.
60. David Montgomery, *Workers' Control in America: Studies in the History of Work, Technology, and Labor Struggles* (Cambridge: Cambridge University Press, 1979), especially 91–112; Paul Buhle, "Workers' Control," in Mari Jo Buhle, Paul Buhle, and Dan Georgakas, eds., *Encyclopedia of the American Left* (New York: Garland Publishing, Inc., 1990), 846–48; Steven Fraser, "Dress Rehearsal for the New Deal: Shop-Floor Insurgents, Political Elites, and Industrial Democracy in the Amalgamated Clothing Workers," 212–55.
61. Alice Kessler-Harris, *Out to Work: A History of Wage-Earning Women in the United States* (New York: Oxford University Press, 1982), 138. See also Miriam Cohen, *Workshop to Office: Two Generations of Italian Women in New York City, 1900–1950* (Ithaca: Cornell University Press, 1992), 56–86, esp. 52–53; Elizabeth Ewen, *Immigrant Women in the Land of Dollars: Life and Culture on the Lower East Side, 1890–1925* (New York: Monthly Review Press, 1985).
62. Kessler-Harris, 151.
63. Quoted in McCreesh, 220.
64. See New York convention, 1914, 100; Rochester convention, 1916, 193–95; Baltimore convention, 1918, 57, 214.
65. McCreesh, 121–22.
66. Chicago convention, 1922, 353, 382.
67. Ann Schofield, "Rebel Girls and Union Maids: The Woman Question in the Journals of the AFL and IWW, 1905–1920," *Feminist Studies* 9, 2 (Summer 1983), 335–58.
68. Nashville Convention, 33–34.
69. N.a. "Memento: L'avvento dell'Amalgamated nel movimento operaio," *Il Lavoro*, March 17, 1917, 1.
70. See "Report of Credential Committee," Rochester Convention, 1916, 119–21.
71. Mary Streiber, "The Amalgamated Hoax," *Il Proletario*, February 17, 1917. Reprinted from *Solidarity.*
72. Ibid.
73. Nina Lynn Asher, "Dorothy Jacobs Bellanca: Feminist Trade Unionist, 1894–1946" (Ph.D. diss., SUNY Binghamton, 1982), 86; Josephson, 143–44.
74. Rochester, 1916, 162.
75. Josephson, 144–45.
76. See Fenton, 545–48.
77. Rochester Convention, 1916, 165.
78. Frank Bellanca, "Scabs and Scab-Agencies: Proven Facts of the Scandalous Scabbism of the I.W.W.," Società Tipografica Italiana, New York, n.d.
79. Baltimore Convention, 1918, 80.
80. Fraser, *Labor Will Rule*, 103.
81. Ibid.
82. Ibid.
83. Josephson, 147–48.
84. Ibid.
85. Nina Lynn Asher, 90.
86. Philip De Luca, "La fine ed il ... principio delle lotte di Baltimore," *Il Lavoro*, March 3, 1917; Girolamo Valenti, "Ancora delle Lotte di Baltimore: Dal Sindacalismo

bagalone al Sindacalismo perfidioso," *Il Lavoro,* March 10, 1917; Giovanni Baldazzi CPC, busta 268.

87. Philip De Luca, "La fine ed il ... principio delle lotte di Baltimore," *Il Lavoro,* February 24, 1917, 1.

88. Tommaso De Angelis, "Per la verità dei fatti di Baltimore," *Il Lavoro,* April 17, 1917, 3–4.

89. Ibid.

90. Fenton, 545.

91. Bruno Ramirez, "Immigration, Ethnicity, and Political Militance: Patterns of Radicalism in the Italian American Left, 1880–1930," in Valeria Gennaro Lerna, ed., *From 'Melting Pot' to Multiculturalism: The Evolution of Ethnic Relations in the United States and Canada* (Rome: Bulzoni Editore, 1990), 1.

92. Vezzosi, *Il Socialismo Indifferente,* 151–52; Girolamo Valenti CPC, busta 5291.

93. Girolamo Valenti, "Ancora delle Lotte di Baltimore: Dal Sindacalismo bagalone al Sindacalismo perfidioso," *Il Lavoro,* March 10, 1917, 1.

94. Ibid.; see also Frank Bellanca, "Scabs and Scab-Agencies," esp. 15–18.

95. Montgomery, 91–112; Larry Peterson, "The One Big Union in International Perspective: Revolutionary Industrial Unionism 1900–1925," *Le Travailleur: Journal of Canadian Labour Studies* 7 (Spring 1981), 41–66.

96. Fraser, *Labor Will Rule,* 134–38.

97. Nick Salvatore, *Eugene V. Debs: Citizen and Socialist* (Urbana: University of Illinois Press, 1982), 314; William Preston, *Aliens and Dissenters* (Cambridge: Harvard University Press, 1963), 144–49.

98. See Robert K. Murray, *Red Scare: A Study in National Hysteria, 1919–1920* (New York: McGraw-Hill Book Company, 1955), 231–35.

99. Dubofsky, 406–7.

100. Murray, 14, 207.

101. Giovanni Baldazzi CPC, busta 268; Angelo Faggi CPC, busta 1925.

102. Luigi Galleani CPC, busta 2241; see Paul Avrich, *Sacco and Vanzetti: The Anarchist Background* (Princeton: Princeton University Press, 1991), especially "Deportations Delirium," 122–36.

103. Vincenzo Vacirca, "'Tenebre Rosse' di A. Giovannitti," *Il Lavoro,* July 27, 1918.

104. Arturo Giovannitti, "L'operaia e l'agonia di Lawrence, Mass.," *Il Martello,* May 20, 1919, 5; *Il Lavoro,* May 10, 1919, 1.

105. Teseo Tomassini, "Conferenza Tresca," *Il Lavoro,* March 24, 1917, 2.

106. Rudolph J. Vecoli, "Anthony Capraro and the Lawrence Strike of 1919," in George E. Pozzetta, ed., *Pane e Lavoro* (Ontario: Multicultural History Society of Ontario, 1980), 3–4.

107. Goldberg, 98–99; Vecoli, 5.

108. Boston Convention, 1920, 215.

109. Goldberg, 158–63.

110. Vecoli, 6.

111. Ibid., 11–12.

112. Goldberg, 101–2.

113. Gioacchino Artoni CPC, busta 203; Vittorio Buttis CPC, busta 915; Vittorio Buttis, *Memorie di vita di tempeste sociali* (New York, 1940) 104–12; Vecoli, 13; Vezzosi, *Il Socialismo Indifferente,* 175, 185.

114. Goldberg, 102; Vecoli, 15.

115. Flavio Venanzi, *Scritti Politici e Letterarii* (New York: Venanzi Memorial Committee Editore, 1921), 33–36; see also Arturo Giovannitti, *The Collected Poems of Arturo Giovannitti* (Chicago: E. Clemente and Sons, 1962), especially "On Lenin's Fiftieth Birthday," 59–60, and "Moscow 1921," 127.

116. Goldberg, 104–5.

117. Vecoli, 10; Goldberg, 128.

118. Strike Committee, "Perchè i Tessitori di Lawrence sono in isciopero," *Il Nuovo Proletario*, March 1, 1919. FSI leaders named their newspaper *Il Nuovo Proletario* after the brief period in 1918 when it was called *La Difesa*.

119. Gino, "Ad un giornale 'Bolsheviko'," *Il Nuovo Proletario*, August 16, 1919, 3.

120. Ibid.

121. Goldberg, 112.

122. Arturo Giovannitti and Carlo Tresca, letter to Lawrence strikers, New York City, n.d., Anthony Capraro papers, Box 8, Immigration History Research Center, Minneapolis, Minn.

123. Ibid.

124. Fenton, 552.

125. Arturo Giovannitti, "Ai margini del grande sciopero," *Il Lavoro*, March 15, 1919, 4.

126. Ibid.

127. Cohen, 6–10; Kessler-Harris, 123–24; McCreesh, 104; Fenton, 490–91. See also Elizabeth H. Pleck, "A Mother's Wages: Income Earning among Married Italian and Black Women, 1896–1911," in Nancy F. Cott and Elizabeth H. Pleck, eds., *A Heritage of Her Own: Toward a New Social History of American Women* (New York: Simon and Schuster, 1979), 376–92; Donna Gabaccia, *From the Other Side: Women, Gender, and Immigrant Life in the U.S., 1820–1990* (Bloomington: Indiana University Press, 1994), 68–70.

128. Arturo Giovannitti, "La Donna e la Forca," *Il Proletario*, June 30, 1911. For an account of the perspectives of male Italian organizers in the ACWA, see Fraser, *Labor Will Rule*, 107–9; Fenton, 500.

129. Arturo Giovannitti, "Ai margini del grande sciopero," *Il Lavoro*, March 15, 1919, 4.

130. Anthony Capraro to A. J. Muste, January 14, 1920, Anthony Capraro papers, Box 2.

131. Arturo Giovannitti, "A Meeting at Astoria Hall," n.d., Onorio Ruotolo papers, folder 35, Immigration History Research Center, Minneapolis, Minn.

132. Anthony Capraro to Augusto Bellanca, April 3, 1919, Anthony Capraro papers, Box 5.

133. Goldberg, 119.

134. Goldberg, 120; Vecoli, 15.

135. Quoted in Vecoli, 6.

136. Ibid.

137. Tresca, unpublished autobiography, 186–88.

138. "Carlo Tresca parla agli scioperanti di Lawrence," *Il Martello*, May 20, 1919, 7; and Il Corrispondente, "Carlo Tresca parla in Lawrence a dispetto della polizia," *Il Martello*, May 15, 1919, 11; Rudolph Vecoli, "Anthony Capraro and the Lawrence Strike of 1919," 15–16.

139. Vecoli, 16; Goldberg, 121.

140. Goldberg, 122.

141. Frank Bellanca, "The Urgent Needs of the Hour," *Il Lavoro*, March 31, 1917; New York Convention, 1914, 67; Bellanca, "Verso l'Unionismo industriale: uno del maggiori e più sentiti ed urgenti problemi della prossima Convenzione dell'Amalgamated Clothing Workers of America," *Il Lavoro*, May 1, 1920, 3–4.

142. Vecoli, 19–20; Anthony Capraro to A. J. Muste, March 1, 1920, Anthony Capraro papers, Box 2.

143. Goldberg, 120–21.

144. Anthony Capraro to Teseo Tomassini, President of the Rochester ACWA, "Facendo di tutt'erba un Fascio!: Perché non ci chiamiamo 'Sindacalisti'?", n.d., Anthony Capraro papers, Box 8.

145. Steven Fraser, Amalgamated Clothing Workers of America," *Encyclopedia of the American Left*, 16–18.

6. The Italian American Left against the Postwar Reaction

1. "La Camera di lavoro e l'agitazione anti-fascista," *La Giustizia*, April 21, 1923.

2. The only source is Mario de Ciampis, "History of *Il Proletario*," 2337–42, 2346, 2354–55, 2357–58, 2363, unpublished. Available at the Immigration History Research Center, Minneapolis, Minn.

3. De Ciampis, 2338.

4. De Ciampis, 3358–65.

5. Flavio Venanzi, "Il Caràttere degli Uomini," *Ai Socialisti del Re*, December 15, 1918, 2.

6. Anthony Capraro, "Compagni d'Italia, Salve!", *Ai Socialisti del Re*, December 15, 1918, 6.

7. Ibid.

8. Quoted in Charles Bertrand, "The Biennio Rosso: Anarchists and Revolutionary Syndicalists in Italy, 1919–1920," *Réflexions historiques* 9, 3 (1982), 388.

9. Elisabetta Vezzosi, "Le Federazione Socialista Italiana del Nord America (1911–1921)" Ph.D. diss. (Università degli Studi di Firenze, 1980), 392–93.

10. David D. Roberts. *The Syndicalist Tradition and Italian Fascism* (Chapel Hill: University of North Carolina Press, 1979), 177; Zeev Sternhell with Mario Sznajder and Maia Asheri, *The Birth of Fascist Ideology: From Cultural Rebellion to Political Revolution* (Princeton: Princeton University Press, 1994), 141; John J. Tinghino, *Edmondo Rossoni: From Revolutionary Syndicalism to Fascism* (New York: Peter Lang, 1991), 86; Edmondo Rossoni Casellario Politico Centrale, busta 4466, Archivio Centrale dello Stato, Rome, Italy.

11. Quoted in Tinghino, 94.

12. Bertrand, 386.

13. Carlo Tresca, "Dimmi con Chi Vai e Ti Diro' Chi Sei," *Ai Socialisti del Re*, December 15, 1918.

14. Frank Bellanca, "De Ambris finito in bocca a Gompers: Guardando i futuri rapporti tra il proletariato italiano di America e quello di Italia," *Ai Socialisti del Re*, December 15, 1918.

15. "Una lettera di Alceste de Ambris ed una Risposta," *Il Nuovo Proletario*, December 14, 1918, 1.

16. Ibid.

17. Vincenzo Vacirca, "Noterelle Quattropalliste," *Ai Socialisti del Re*, December 15, 1918, 6.

18. Ibid.

19. Ibid.

20. Martin Clark, *Modern Italy: 1871–1982* (New York: Longman Group Limited, 1984), 215. *Fascio* means "group" or "bunch" in Italian, and the term was used by a variety of political organizations before Mussolini claimed it for his own in early 1919.

21. Pietro Allegra of the Fascio Rivoluzionario Italiano, "Il battesimo dell'on. Quattropalle," *Ai Socialisti del Re*, December 15, 1918, 7.

22. Ibid.

23. Edmondo Rossoni CPC, busta 4466.

24. Samuel Gompers, *Seventy Years of Life and Labor: An Autobiography* (Ithaca: ILR Press, 1984), 188.

25. Simeon Larson, *Labor and Foreign Policy: Gompers, the AFL, and the First World War, 1914–1918* (Rutherford: Fairleigh Dickinson University Press, 1975), 41.

26. Ibid.

27. Ibid., 149.

28. Ibid., 148.

29. Gompers, 205.

30. Flavio Venanzi, "Il Caràttere degli Uomini," *Ai Socialisti del Re*, December 15, 1918, 2.

31. Carlo Tresca, "Dimmi con Chi Vai e Ti Diro' Chi Sei," *Ai Socialisti del Re*, December 15, 1918, 16–17.

32. Ibid.

33. Gompers, 161.

34. John Higham, *Strangers in the Land: Patterns of American Nativism 1860–1925* (New Brunswick: Rutgers University Press, 1955), 71.

35. Gompers, 162.

36. Higham, 305.

37. Frank Bellanca, "De Ambris finito in bocca a Gompers: Guardando i futuri rapporti tra il proletariato italiano di America e quello di Italia," *Ai Socialisti del Re*, December 15, 1918, 11.

38. The unity was not complete—neither the FSI nor any Italian American anarchists contributed to *Ai Socialisti del Re*.

39. Edmondo Rossoni CPC, busta 4466; Tinghino, 10, 38–41.

40. Edwin Fenton, *Immigrants and Unions, A Case Study: Italians and American Labor, 1870–1920* (New York: Arno Press, 1975), 513, 548–50.

41. Clark, 206.

42. Roberts, 138; Federico Chabod, *A History of Italian Fascism* (New York: Random House, 1963), cited in Shepard B. Clough and Salvatore Saladino, *A History of Modern Italy: Documents, Readings and Commentary* (New York: Columbia University Press, 1968), 360; Clark, 206–7.

43. Clark, 207.

44. Ibid., 210.

45. Angelo Faggi CPC, *busta* 1925.

46. Bertrand, 394.

47. Ibid.

48. Harry Hearder, *Italy: A Short History* (New York: Cambridge University Press, 1990), 222.

49. Ibid.

50. Chabod, in Clough and Saladino, 364–65.

51. Ibid., 363–64.

52. Bertrand, 395–97.

53. Hearder, 222.

54. Girolamo Valenti, "Il pensiero di Arturo Giovannitti sulla rivoluzione in Italia," *Il Lavoro*, October 26, 1920.

55. Ibid.

56. Elisabetta Vezzosi, "La Federazione Socialista Italiana del Nord America (1911–1921)," 349–50.

57. Raimondo Fazio, "Camera di Lavoro o Fascio Operaio?", *La Giustizia*, August 2, 1919, 5. (*La Giustizia* was the newspaper of Italian Local 89 of the ILGWU.)

58. Ibid.

59. Flavio Venanzi, "La Camera di Lavoro di New York," *Il Lavoro*, August 30, 1919, 6.

60. "Per la Camera del Lavoro Italiana di NewYork: dichiarazione del comitato provvisorio," *Il Lavoro*, July 19, 1919.

61. Flavio Venanzi, "La Camera di Lavoro di New York," *Il Lavoro*, August 30, 1919, 6.

62. "The Italian Chamber of Labor Towards Its Maximum Development," *La Giustizia*, August 7, 1920.

63. Flavio Venanzi, "La Camera di Lavoro di New York," *Il Lavoro*, August 30, 1919, 6.

64. "La Camera del lavoro italiana . . . iniziera' un'energica campagna di reclutamento e di educazione," *Il Lavoro*, May 29, 1920, 3.

65. See, for example, Flavio Venanzi, "Speculazione e Aumento dei Prezzi," *Il Lavoro*, February 21, 1920, 5–6.

66. Ibid.

67. Ibid.

68. Frank Bellanca, "L'ascesa della Camera del Lavoro nel movimento operaio di America," *Il Lavoro*, August 14, 1920, 1–2.

69. Arturo Giovannitti, "Secondo Congresso Annuale: Riassunto Morale dalla Segr. Generale della Camera di Lavoro Italiano," *Il Lavoro*, March 5, 1921.

70. For an account of the 1919 steel strike, see David Brody, *Labor in Crisis: The Steel Strike of 1919* (Philadelphia: J. B. Lipincott, 1965). For accounts of the Seattle General Strike, see Harvey O'Connor, *Revolution in Seattle: A Memoir* (Seattle: Left Bank Books, 1964); David Montgomery, *The Fall of the House of Labor: The Workplace, the State, and American Labor Activism, 1865–1925* (Cambridge: Cambridge University Press, 1987), 389.

71. Montgomery, 407.

72. Quoted in Brody, 129.

73. William Preston, Jr. *Aliens and Dissenters: Federal Suppression of Radicals, 1903–1933* (Cambridge: Harvard University Press, 1963 [1994]), 220–28.

74. Ibid., 208–37.

75. Quoted in Higham, 242.

76. Quoted in Larson, 142.

77. *Revolutionary Radicalism: Its History, Purpose and Tactics,* vols. I–IV (Albany: J. B. Lyon, 1920).

78. From "The Closed Shop Is Opposed to Human Development," *Open Shop Review,* July 1920. Reproduced in Lamar T. Beman, ed., *Selected Articles on The Closed Shop* (New York: H. W. Wilson, 1921), 185–86.

79. Montgomery, 406.

80. Arturo Giovannitti, "In Memoria di Flavio Venanzi," *La Giustizia,* May 6, 1922, 6.

81. Arturo Giovannitti, "Secondo Congresso Annuale: Riassunto Morale dalla Segr. Generale della Camera di Lavoro," *Il Lavoro,* March 5, 1921.

82. Ibid.

83. Ibid.

84. Ibid.

85. Frank Bellanca, "L'ascesa della Camera del Lavoro nel movimento operaio di America," *Il Lavoro,* August 14, 1920, 1–2.

86. Ibid.

87. George Sánchez. *Becoming Mexican American: Ethnicity, Culture and Identity in Chicano Los Angeles, 1900–1945* (New York: Oxford University Press, 1993), especially 227–52; Gary Gerstle. *Working-Class Americanism: The Politics of Labor in a Textile City, 1914–1960* (New York: Cambridge University Press, 1989).

88. John di Gregorio, "Americanization," *Rinascimento,* May 1, 1920. From the Elizabeth Gurley Flynn papers, Taminent Library, New York University, microfilm P1400. (*Rinascimento* was the paper of the ACWA local 176.)

89. Ibid.

90. Ibid.

91. Raimondo Fazio, "Camera di Lavoro o Fascio Operaio?" *La Giustizia,* August 2, 1919.

92. Arturo Giovannitti, "Secondo Congresso Annuale: Riassunto Morale dalla Segr. Generale della Camera di Lavoro Italiano," *Il Lavoro,* March 5, 1921.

93. Ibid.

94. "Giovannitti, Segr. Generale della Camera di Lavoro I Prende posto nell'Internazionale," *La Giustizia,* December 2, 1922, 2.

95. Fenton, 485ff.

96. Arturo Giovannitti, "Secondo Congresso Annuale: Riassunto Morale dalla Segr. Generale della Camera di Lavoro Italiano," *Il Lavoro,* March 5, 1921.

97. Alexander De Grand, *Italian Fascism: Its Origins and Developments* (Lincoln, Neb.: University of Nebraska Press, 1982), 31; Clark, 215–16.

98. Roberts, 178–79; Sternhell, 184–85; Tinghino, 102.

99. Denis Mack Smith, *Italy: A Modern History* (Ann Arbor: The University of Michigan Press, 1969), 351–52; Clark, 213, 216–17, 219.

100. Bertrand, 388–89; Roberts, 178–81, 188; Sternhell, 185.

101. De Ciampis, "History of *Il Proletario,*" 2973.

102. Ego Sum, "Il Fascismo," *Il Martello,* February 12, 1921, 1.

103. Gino Baldesi, "Che cosa è il fascismo?" *Il Lavoro,* February 19, 1921, 7.

104. Ibid.

105. Carlo Tresca, "L'indomabile proletariato d'Italia sfida il fascismo, lotta eroicamente e resta in piedi, sola speranza del domani: questa è la conclusione," *Il Martello*, August 12, 1922, 1.

106. Tinghino, 124.

107. Smith, 345–47.

108. Clark, 221.

109. Carlo Tresca, "Brigantaggio Fascista," *Il Martello*, October 21, 1922, 1.

110. "Il corrispondente del 'Lavoro' visita l'On. Mussolini," *Il Lavoro*, December 9, 1922, 2.

111. See John Diggins, *Mussolini and Fascism: The View from the United States* (Princeton: Princeton University Press, 1972). Madeline Goodman, "The Evolution of Ethnicity: Fascism and Antifascism in the Italian American Community, 1914–1945" (Ph.D. diss., Carnegie-Mellon University, 1993).

112. Diggins, 95, 97–98.

113. Gaetano Salvemini, "Italian Fascism," unpublished study, New York City, n.d., 17, from the Elizabeth Gurley Flynn papers, microfilm P1400.

114. Gaetano Salvemini, *Italian Fascist Activities in the United States* (New York: Center for Migration Studies, 1977), 12.

115. Salvemini, "Italian Fascism," 18.

116. Diggins, 94–95.

117. Ibid., 91–93.

118. Arturo Giovannitti, "La Camera di Lavoro di New York per impedire l'avanzata del fascismo in America," *La Giustizia*, March 31, 1923, 3–5; also published as "Uniamoci tutti contro il fascismo," in *Il Lavoro*, March 31, 1923.

119. Ibid.

120. "La Camera di Lavoro e l'agitazione anti-fascista," *Il Lavoro*, April 21, 1923.

121. *Il Lavoro*, "Il Fascismo in Azione: Primo Sangue Operaio sparso in America," *Il Lavoro*, May 11, 1923, 1–2.

122. Salvemini, 18.

123. See, for example, Giovannitti's account of the chamber's support for a group of striking shoe workers in Brockton, Mass., in "Il Convegno della Camera di Lavoro di New York," *La Giustizia*, June 9, 1923.

124. Leonardo Frisina, "Our Italian Labor Institutions," *Prometeo*, May 1, 1927, 10, Elizabeth Gurley Flynn papers, microfilm P1400.

125. "Il vero significato della condanna di Carlo Tresca," *Il Lavoro*, December 22, 1923.

126. Gallagher, 129.

127. Quoted in Gallagher.

128. Diggins, 123, 128.

129. "La Camera di Lavoro e l'agitazione anti-fascista," *Il Lavoro*, April 21, 1923; "Effemeridi del movimento anti-fascista promosso dalla Camera di Lavoro di New York," *Il Lavoro*, May 19, 1923, 1–2.

130. Giovanni di Gregorio, "Tenetevi i Dollari!" *Il Lavoro*, August 19, 1923, 1–2.

131. Quoted in Gallagher, 134.

132. Giovanni di Gregorio, "E' Passato Il Popolo?" *Il Lavoro*, August 11, 1923.

133. "'Notes on the Anti-Fascist Movement' as promoted by the Italian Chamber of Labor," *Il Lavoro*, May 19, 1923; Arturo Giovannitti et al. to Nicholas Murray But-

ler, reprinted in "La Camera del Lavoro di New York," *La Giustizia,* March 31, 1923; "Uniamoci Tutti Contro il Fascismo," *Il Lavoro,* March 31, 1923.

134. Gallagher, 127.

135. Diggins, 118.

136. Ibid., 174.

137. "Warns of Fascisti as a Menace to the U.S.," *New York Times,* April 7, 1924; Elizabeth Gurley Flynn papers, reels 4201, 4202.

138. Diggins, 121.

139. Ibid., 172–73.

140. Joseph Giganti interview with Paul Buhle, July 26, 1983.

141. Rudolph Vecoli, "The Italian Immigrants in the United States Labor Movement from 1880 to 1929," in Bruno Bezza, ed., *Gli Italiani Fuori d'Italia: Gli emigrati italiani nei movimento operai dei paesi d'adozione 1880–1940* (Milano: Franco Angeli Editore, 1983), 303–5; De Ciampis, 2613, 2818, 2947; "La Camera di Lavoro Italiana e l'agitazione antifascista," *Il Lavoro,* April 21, 1923.

142. Vecoli, 305.

Conclusion

1. There is an extensive body of work on Sacco and Vanzetti and their trial. See, for example, Paul Avrich, *Sacco and Vanzetti: The Anarchist Background* (Princeton: Princeton University Press, 1991); Robert D'Attilio, "Sacco-Vanzetti Case," in Mari Jo Buhle, Paul Buhle, and Dan Georgakas, eds., *Encyclopedia of the American Left* (New York: Garland Publishing, 1990), 667–70; Robert D'Attilio and Jane Manthorn, eds., *Sacco-Vanzetti: Developments and Reconsiderations, 1979* (Boston: Boston Public Library, 1979); Herbert B. Ehrmann, *The Case That Will Not Die* (Boston: Beacon Press, 1969); Roberta Strauss Feuerlicht, *Justice Crucified: The Story of Sacco and Vanzetti* (New York: McGraw-Hill, 1977); Brian Jackson, *The Black Flag: A Look Back at the Strange Case of Nicola Sacco and Bartolomeo Vanzetti* (Boston: Routledge and Kegan Paul, 1981); Nunzio Pernicone, "Carlo Tresca and the Sacco-Vanzetti Case," *The Journal of American History* 66 (December 1979), 535–47; William Young and David E. Kaiser, *Postmortem: New Evidence in the Case of Sacco and Vanzetti* (Amherst: University of Massachusetts Press, 1985). See also John Dos Passos, *Facing the Chair: Story of the Americanization of Two Foreignborn Workingmen* (Boston: Sacco-Vanzetti Defense Committee, 1927); and Marion Denman Frankfurter and Gardner Jackson, eds., *The Letters of Sacco and Vanzetti* (New York: The Viking Press, 1928).

2. Todd Gitlin, *The Twilight of Common Dreams: Why America is Wracked by Culture Wars* (New York: Metropolitan Books, 1995); Michael Kazin, "The Agony and Romance o f the American Left," *American Historical Review* 100, 5 (December 1995): 1488–1512.

3. Avrich, 134–36.

4. Avrich, 99–101; Pernicone, "Luigi Galleani and Italian Anarchist Terrorism in the United States," *Studi Emigrazione,* XXX, 111 (September 1993), 482–83.

5. Avrich, 98–101; 158–62; Nunzio Pernicone, "Luigi Galleani and Italian Anarchist Terrorism in the United States," 483–85.

6. Avrich, 188–95; Pernicone, "Luigi Galleani and Italian Anarchist Terrorism in the United States," 486–87.

7. Dorothy Gallagher, *All the Right Enemies: The Life and Murder of Carlo Tresca* (New Brunswick: Rutgers University Press, 1988), 78.

8. Avrich, 196–204; Pernicone, "Luigi Galleani and Italian Anarchist Terrorism in the United States," 487.

9. Quoted in Avrich, 204.

10. Feuerlicht, 165.

11. Ibid., 349.

12. Gallagher, 79.

13. "Lavoratori Italiani!" *La Giustizia*, August 28, 1920, 5.

14. John Higham, *Strangers in the Land: Patterns of American Nativism* (New Brunswick: Rutgers University Press, 1955), 264–65.

15. Frankfurter and Jackson, *The Letters of Sacco and Vanzetti*, 94.

16. Avrich, 26, 29–30; Elizabeth Gurley Flynn, *The Rebel Girl: An Autobiography: My First Life (1906–1926)* (New York: International Publishers, 1955), 306–7.

17. Avrich, 27, 37–38.

18. Quoted in Feuerlicht, 344. Feuerlicht points out that this quote was the interviewer's loose paraphrase of what Vanzetti told him; Vanzetti, the interviewer noted, "said it somehow more simply, more powerfully and touchingly" (345).

19. Avrich, 66, 70.

20. Pernicone, "Carlo Tresca and the Sacco-Vanzetti Case," 540.

21. Flynn, 299–300.

22. Pernicone, "Carlo Tresca and the Sacco-Vanzetti Case," 540–41.

23. Ibid., 546–47.

24. Quoted in Gallagher, 76.

25. Ibid., 81; *Documentary History of the Amalgamated Clothing Workers of America:* Proceedings of the Fifth Biennial Convention of the ACWA Held in Chicago, Illinois, May 8–13, 1922, 345–47; Nick Salvatore, *Eugene V. Debs: Citizen and Socialist* (Urbana: University of Illinois Press, 1982), 328.

26. Pernicone, "Carlo Tresca and the Sacco-Vanzetti Case," 541.

27. Bruce Bliven, "In Dedham Jail," *New Republic*, June 22, 1927.

28. Jackson, 76.

29. Feuerlicht, 389–90.

30. Ibid., 393.

31. Oswald Garrison Villard, "Justice Underfoot," *The Nation*, August 17, 1927.

32. Ibid.

33. John Dos Passos, *The Big Money* (New York: New American Library, 1969), 469.

34. Quoted in Feuerlicht, 344.

35. Gerald Meyer, "Italian Americans and the American Communist Party: Notes on a History," http://www.libertynet.org/balch/meyer.htm; Gerald Meyer, *Vito Marcantonio: Radical Politician, 1902–1954* (Albany: SUNY Press, 1989); Paul Buhle, *A Dreamer's Paradise Lost: Louis C. Fraina/Lewis Corey (1892–1953) and the Decline of Radicalism in the United States* (Atlantic Highlands, New Jersey: Humanities Press, 1995); Philip Cannistraro, "Luigi Antonini and the Italian Anti-Fascist Movement in the United States, 1940–1943," *Journal of American Ethnic History* V, 1 (Fall 1985), 21–40.

Epilogue

1. For his philosophy as a fascist, see Edmondo Rossoni, *La idee della ricostruzione: discorsi sul sindacalismo fascista* (Florence: Bemporad and Son, 1923).

2. John J. Tinghino, *Edmondo Rossoni: From Revolutionary Syndicalism to Fascism* (New York: Peter Lang, 1991), 184.

3. Ibid., 209, 219–20.

4. The *fuorusciti* were the antifascist political exiles who had been driven from Italy by Mussolini's rise to power.

5. Giovanni Baldazzi Casellario Politico Centrale, busta 268, Archivio Centrale dello Stato, Rome, Italy.

6. Angelo Faggi CPC, busta 1925. See also Ugo Fedeli CPC, busta 1985.

7. Giovanni di Gregorio CPC, busta 1792.

8. Leonardo Frisina CPC, busta 2185.

9. Girolamo Valenti CPC, busta 5291. See Fraser Ottanelli, "Italian-American Antifascism and the Remaking of the US Working Class," unpublished paper, 1996, 11, 14.

10. Luigi Antonini CPC, busta 160; See also Philip Cannistraro, "Luigi Antonini and the Italian Anti-Fascist Movement in the United States, 1940–1943" *Journal of American Ethnic History* V, 1 (Fall 1985), 21–40.

11. The most recent work on Marcantonio is Gerald Meyer, *Vito Marcantonio: Radical Politician, 1902–1954* (Albany: SUNY Press, 1989).

12. Arturo Giovannitti CPC, busta 2439; Girolamo Valenti CPC, busta 5291; Luigi Antonini CPC, busta 160; Nunzio Pernicone, "Arturo Massimo Giovannitti," in John A. Garraty and Mark C. Carnes, eds. *American National Biography* (New York: Oxford, 1999), 80–82.

13. Carlo Tresca CPC, busta 5209; Girolamo Valenti CPC, busta 5291; for more on Tresca's relationship to the Communists, see Dorothy Gallagher, *All the Right Enemies: The Life and Murder of Carlo Tresca* (New Brunswick: Rutgers University Press, 1988), 167–76.

14. Pietro Allegra, "Il suicidio morale di Carlo Tresca"; Gallagher, 172–74.

15. Cannistraro, 22–23; "Who Killed Carlo Tresca?" 21–23; "Memorandum Re: Assassination of Carlo Tresca," 2–3, Carlo Tresca Memorial Papers, box 3, New York Public Library.

16. Cannistraro, 24–34.

17. N.a., "Carlo's Last Supper," *New York Call,* February 5, 1943, 6. Elizabeth Gurley Flynn papers, microfilm roll 4205, Tamiment Library, New York University.

18. "Squash That Threat," *Daily Worker,* January 21, 1943. Elizabeth Gurley Flynn papers, microfilm reel 4205.

19. Gallagher, 215–27; 272–73; "Who Killed Carlo Tresca?" 7 ff.; Ezio Taddei, "The Tresca Case," Elizabeth Gurley Flynn papers. (The Carlo Tresca Memorial Committee was an organization composed of American liberals and leftists dedicated both to pursuing the mysterious circumstances of Tresca's death and to preserving his memory.)

20. Gallagher, 215–73.

Index

Regionalism in Italy, 36, 63–64, 84, 110–11. *See also* FSI
Rende, Raffaele, 235
Risorgimento, 36, 62, 63, 85–86, 88
Roberts, David, 88, 146, 169
Rocco, Angelo, 96, 116
Roediger, David, 95
Rondani, Dino, 31, 32–33, 38, 41–42, 189
Roosevelt, Franklin Delano, 269
Rossoni, Edmondo, 45, 55, 142, 231; and fascism, 244–45, 247, 265–66; and Lawrence strike (1912), 98, 104, 106, 109, 110, 111, 113–14, 128–30, 131, 132; and nationalism, 137, 144, 145, 147, 148–51, 152, 153, 154–55, 156–57, 158–65, 167–73, 182; and opposition to Italy's war in Tripoli, 65–66, 76, 85, 86; and World War I intervention debate, 135, 138, 226
Ruotolo, Onorio, 191
Rygier, Maria, 107, 156

Sacco and Vanzetti, 21, 24, 27, 46, 119, 153, 205, 256–64, 265. *See also* ACWA; AFL; Luigi Galleani; Galleanisti; Arturo Giovannitti; Italian American syndicalists; Carlo Tresca
Sacco-Vanzetti Defense Committee, 262
St. Vincent Millay, Edna, 263
Salerno, Sal, 17–18
Salsedo, Andrea, 258, 261
Salvatore, Nick, 19, 20
Salvemini, Gaetano, 267, 268
Sanchez, George, 241
Sanger, Margaret, 102, 251, 252
Schlossberg, Joseph, 195
Seattle general strike, 237
Second International (international socialism), 145, 148, 150
Sedition act, 204
Serrati, Giacinto Menotti, 31, 33–34, 38, 41–42, 44, 45–46, 50, 56, 136, 189
Sforza, Count Carlo, 266, 267
Shirtwaist strike (1909), 51
SLP (Socialist Labor Party), 14, 41–43, 195
Socialist Labor Party. *See* SLP
Socialist Party of America. *See* SPA
Socialist Trades and Labor Alliance (STLA), 42

Social movements: new, 3, 6, 7, 8, 10; old, 3, 6, 8, 13, 22, 60, 80, 251
Solidarity, 199
Sons of Italy, 24, 249–50, 263
Sorel, Georges, 50, 61, 87–88, 89, 163–64
SPA (Socialist Party of America), 34, 42–43, 94, 102, 103, 146, 166, 208, 234, 262; and IWW, 123–26
Spackman, Barbara, 169–70
Squadristi, 244–45, 246–47, 266
Sternhell, Zeev, 54, 55, 76, 168, 169
Stirpe, 266
STLA (Socialist Trades and Labor Alliance), 42
Syndicalism, 3, 4, 17–18, 35–36, 42, 48, 87–88; French, 85, 98, 151. *See also* CGT; FSI; Italian American syndicalists; IWW

Tancredi, Libero (Massimo Rocca), 45, 75, 86, 110–11, 118, 129–30, 131, 157–58, 161, 168, 169, 247
Transnationalism, 2, 3, 5, 9, 10–16, 22–24, 33–35, 39–40, 75, 219, 220–30, 255, 266. *See also* FSI; Italian American syndicalists; Italian chamber of labor (New York)
Treaty of Lausanne, 65
Tresca, Carlo, 22, 31, 40, 49, 53–54, 56, 60, 136, 156; and ACWA, 179–80, 193, 204, 205–6, 208, 210, 213–16, 217–18; and antifascism, 221, 246, 247, 250–51, 252–53, 254–55, 267, 268–70; vs. the colonial elite, 44–45; editor of *Il Proletario,* 34–37, 38, 52; and Giovannitti, 55, 113, 269; and Italian chamber of labor (New York), 230–31; and Italian Workers Mission, 220, 222, 224, 228–29; and IWW, 42–43, 53, 97; and Lawrence strike (1912), 92, 106–7, 108–9, 111–3, 115–16, 118–19, 121–22, 130–31; and Lawrence strike (1919), 180, 206, 208, 210, 213–16, 217–18; and Mesabi Range strike (1916), 178–79, 183–84, 185–93; and Paterson strike (1913), 139, 141; and Sacco and Vanzetti, 258, 259, 260, 261–62

Michael Miller Topp is associate professor of history at the University of Texas, El Paso. He previously taught at Brown University, the Rhode Island School of Design, the University of Rhode Island, and Tufts University.